Behavioral Sociology

The Experimental Analysis

of Social Process

Behavioral Sociology

The Experimental Analysis of Social Process

ROBERT L. BURGESS   DON BUSHELL, JR.

Columbia University Press New York and London 1969

Contributors

Ronald L. Akers
University of Washington

Marion H. Ault
Southern Illinois University

Donald M. Baer
University of Kansas

Sidney W. Bijou
University of Illinois

John D. Burchard
University of North Carolina

Robert L. Burgess
University of Washington

Don Bushell, Jr.
University of Kansas

Richard M. Emerson
University of Washington

David K. Giles
University of Kansas

R. Vance Hall
University of Kansas

Robert P. Hawkins
Western Michigan University

George C. Homans
Harvard University

John H. Kunkel
Arizona State University

Mary Louise Michaelis
Webster College

Dennis E. Mithaug
University of Washington

Robert F. Peterson
University of Illinois

David R. Schmitt
University of Washington

Edda Schweid
University of Washington

James A. Sherman
University of Kansas

B. F. Skinner
Harvard University

James A. Wiggins
University of North Carolina

Montrose M. Wolf
University of Kansas

Patricia A. Wrobel
University of Pittsburgh

Preface

Customarily, the preface of a book is that before-the-fact episode in which the authors state, after the fact, what the ensuing volume is about. When something has been omitted or forgotten, nobody seems to question the disclaimers which state that the missing item was never intended to be included in the first place. Consequently, the skillful preface writer can disarm most of his critics by carefully stating what the book is not all about. Such being the case, we would like to avoid any future buffeting by insisting that we are not attempting to build any conceptual bridges between disciplines. There is no need for a major effort to span chasms by fostering a sociological-psychological-behavioral science. The simple fact is that the variations within contemporary social science disciplines are far greater than the variations between the disciplines.

Nevertheless, sitting as we all are in the midst of an overwhelming information explosion, the expected practice of simply "keeping in touch" has become virtually a full-time job. Narrower specialization seems to be the best defensive ploy available, but with the intellectual division of labor gone wild, it is easy to lose track of what's going on two doors down the academic corridor. It was over this dilemma that the authors of the present collection worried—at first independently, then together because it was more reinforcing. We were, and remain, concerned over the fact that there is a new and growing field within experimental psychology which has a great deal to say to our discipline, sociology. The strength of this new work, which has its origins in the writing and research of J. R. Kantor, B. F. Skinner, C. B. Ferster, F. S. Keller, and W. N. Schoenfeld, is that it takes an empirical-inductive approach to the analysis of behavior and has come a long way in producing a sophisticated methodology to carry out its analyses. Research in this area has recently built upon its early laboratory study of animal behavior to produce some exciting results with human subjects acting in social situations.

The experimental analysis of behavior is, by any standard, a newcomer in the academic world. When we were first discussing the contents of such a book, only a few universities offered formal training in the field. In the past few years this research orientation has diffused rapidly and widely across the country. The literature relating the analysis of human social behavior now includes hundreds of citations, whereas a handful of studies represented the field a short time ago. In April, 1968, the *Journal of Applied Behavior Analysis* published its first issue. This new journal is devoted to the experimental analysis of socially significant human behavior, and its establishment is both a barometer of and a stimulant for expanded activity in the growing young field.

Behavior analysis is also attracting a growing number of researchers who are sociologists by background and credentials. Twelve of the eighteen contributions to the present collection were written by card-carrying sociologists. These men have found that the orientation and methodologies of the experimental analysis are well suited to the examination of some basic sociological problems. It is their research, together with the seminal experiments of some psychologists working in social situations, that shapes the thesis of the collection.

Because the articles which follow are all based on an integrated set of behavioral principles, the collection is more cohesive than most books of readings. We have provided chapters at the beginning of each of the three major sections which introduce the basic themes of the section and highlight pertinent aspects of the methods and theory underlying the experimental analysis in three contexts. The sequence of Parts recapitulates the history of this burgeoning discipline by moving from the laboratory, to the field, to theoretical frameworks for empirical work yet to come. The consistent use of behavioral principles and techniques at all levels of analysis is clearly illustrated by the assembled articles. From the laboratory analysis of worker supervision to the design of a culture a unity of perspective and procedure is displayed which ought to delight students with applied interests as well as those of a more theoretical bent.

This approach to the study of human social behavior is producing results of importance to sociology, yet only a handful of sociologists has had the opportunity to become aware of the implications of this work for our own discipline. The purpose of this collection, then, is to draw together a number of articles—some already in print, others especially written for it—which describe the experimental analysis of behavior in terms of its sociological applications and implications.

It is customary for an author to accept full responsibility for whatever deficiencies and shortcomings his book may have, simultaneously asserting that the strengths and virtues of the opus, if any, are the direct result of thoughtful colleagues, eager students, industrious secretaries, and a patient wife. Only the experience of attempting to communicate through a book can adequately teach that such acknowledgments are not *pro forma* ritual or ceremonial flagellation. We have learned. The present collection is very different from our original draft, because generous colleagues among students and faculty paid us the high compliment of appraising our efforts. We are particularly grateful to Carl Backman, Tom Brigham, Herbert Costner, Weldon Johnson, Otto Larsen, and George Miller. Our indebtedness to one man, however, is so great that it can only be acknowledged by dedicating this collection to our extraordinary teacher, L. Keith Miller.

R. L. Burgess
D. Bushell, Jr.

Contents

PART II:
The Experimental Analysis of
Social Process in the Field

Prologue

The Sociological Relevance of Behaviorism

George C. Homans

Although I am by academic title a sociologist, and although in this essay I shall be chiefly considering the relevance of behavioral psychology to sociology, I still consider the former fundamental to all the sciences concerned with the social behavior of men. Besides sociology, these sciences include anthropology, political science, economics, and, above all, history. Let us not worry about whether these are sciences at all. Any activity that tries to state relationships between properties of nature, whether or not the statements are exact or general, whether or not they make predictions possible, so long as the test of the truth of the statement lies in the data themselves, is a scientific activity, and by this standard much of the activity of all the social sciences is certainly scientific.

DISCOVERY

Now any science has two related tasks: discovery and explanation. Since discovery is the statement and test of relationships between properties of nature, it is the be-all, though not the end-all, of any science. Let me take a trivial example. In the course of much swimming along the coast of New England I made in my youth a discovery, which of course others had made before me, that, other things equal, the surface water near a coast in summer is warmer when the wind is onshore (blowing toward the coast) than when it it offshore. This discovery stated a relationship between properties of nature, between the direction of the wind and the temperature of the water. To allow a relationship to be stated, the properties must be variables, each of which must be able to take at least two different values (onshore and offshore) but may take many (temperature). The celebrated "other things equal" refers to the fact that, if the temperature of the water is affected, as of course it often is, by other things than the direction of the wind, the stated relationship may be masked.

The relationship between wind direction and water temperature could readily be tested statistically under natural conditions —as in effect I tested it myself. It could also be tested by reproducing the crucial conditions experimentally in a laboratory. But it is well to remind ourselves, in a book so much concerned with experimental science, that our confidence in the truth of a relationship need not depend on its experimental reproduction. If it did, we should have much less science than we have in fact.

EXPLANATION

A discovery, a statement of a relationship between properties of nature, I shall henceforward call a proposition. But although the statement and test of propositions is the condition that must be satisfied if a human activity is to be judged a science, we should be much disappointed if that were all a science did. We do not begin to be satisfied with a science unless it explains as well as discovers, unless it tells us not only *that* relationships hold good but also *why* they hold good.

Let us follow up my example and ask how we explain why the water along a coast in summer is warmer when the wind is onshore than when it is offshore. Warmer water tends to rise toward the surface, and in any event the sun heats the surface layers more than it does the deeper ones. Accordingly, the surface water tends to be warmer than the lower depths. And it is the surface, not the depths, that the wind acts on. Any onshore wind, then, tends to move the warmer water toward the coast. An offshore wind, on the contrary, tends to move the warm surface away; along the coast, by the rule that "water tends to seek its own level," it is replaced by colder water welling up from lower layers. Therefore the surface water along the coast is likely to be warmer with an onshore wind than with an offsure one. *Q.E.D.*

I have not spelled out all the steps in this argument, but the reader can readily do so if he wishes. Let us look rather at its general characteristics. First, each step itself consists of a proposition.

The proposition "Warmer water tends to rise" states a relationship between the temperature and the direction in which water moves. Second, some of the propositions are more general than others. For instance, the statement that warm water tends to rise is more general than the statement that water is warmer toward the surface than lower down, for the former refers to water in all states of motion and not just to water when the motion reaches completion. Third, some of the propositions state the "given" conditions in which the general propositions are to be applied. These conditions are given in the sense that we do not undertake to explain them further, though no doubt we might do so if we chose. Thus we simply take as given the fact that the wind blows onshore on some occasions and offshore on others. Finally, the explicandum, the proposition to be explained, follows as a logical conclusion from the other propositions in a deductive system. When the explicandum thus follows, it is said to have been explained.[1]

Normally we put the more general propositions first in spelling out the deductive system. For when we say that one proposition is more general than another, we are saying that the former cannot be deduced from the latter, just as it is impossible to deduce the fact that all men are mortal from the fact that Socrates is mortal.

In our example, our general propositions have included such things as "Warmer water tends to rise" and "Water seeks its own level;" but these in turn could be explained, that is, deduced from, still more general propositions, from those of thermodynamics and of Newtonian mechanics, for instance, from the proposition stating that the volume of any substance, and not just water, tends to increase with a rise in its temperature. But sooner or later, as we move up the explanatory chain toward the more and more general propositions, we always reach a proposition that cannot itself be explained. That is, it cannot be explained in the existing state of scientific development, but this state is unlikely to remain unchanged forever.

A word about prediction is in order. If we know an empirical proposition, even if we are unable to explain it, we are able to make a limited kind of prediction. If we know the proposition I started with, we can predict that the next time the wind blows

---

[1] See the following: R. B. Braithwaite, *Scientific Explanation,* Cambridge: Cambridge University Press, 1953; E. Nagel, *The Structure of Science,* New York: Harcourt, Brace & World, 1961, esp. Ch. 3; C. G. Hempel, *Aspects of Scientific Explanation,* Glencoe, Ill.: The Free Press, 1965, pp. 331-489.

offshore the water for swimming will get colder. If we know its explanation, including of course the general propositions, we can make a wider range of predictions under a variety of given conditions. Thus, if we know thermodynamics in a rudimentary way, we can predict that hot air as well as hot water rises, and that the air near the ceiling in a room is likely to be warmer than the air near the floor. We have deduced from the general propositions a new empirical conclusion under new given conditions. To test it, we might create the conditions experimentally and determine whether the conclusion follows in fact as it does in logic. This kind of prediction runs parallel to explanation, but *ante* rather than *post factum*.

The explanation of a phenomenon is the theory of the phenomenon: no other meaning can be given to the word "theory." But it is fair to say that when we speak of theory we usually refer not to a single explanation, a single deductive system, like our explanation of the relation between wind direction and water temperature, but to a cluster of explanations, all having some of the same general propositions in common, of a number of different empirical phenomena. Thus someone might write a book called *The Theory of Water Temperatures*, showing the different conditions related to variations in temperature, and the way in which all these relationships follow from a rather small number of general propositions under a wide variety of given conditions. A theory in this sense provides an economic organization of the empirical findings in a scientific field and, in so doing, gives us thorough intellectual satisfaction.

EXPLANATION IN SOCIOLOGY

The reason why I think it necessary to make this brief and obvious statement about the nature of explanation, and therefore of theory, is that the principles of behavioral psychology are the general propositions we use, whether implicitly or explicitly, in explaining all social phenomena. That is their primary relevance to the social sciences. This view is certainly not generally accepted, and the failure to accept it depends, first, on a mistaken view of the nature of theory, and, second, on a trained incapacity to recognize the part played by psychological propositions in social theory. I shall discuss these two problems in order.

The position I have just taken as to the nature of explanation and of theory is now fairly well accepted by the philosophers of science. It ought to be familiar to social scientists, and indeed many of them would accept it if it were put to them in the abstract. But in what they actually say, and in the sort of thing they in fact call theory, they often appear to hold views about the nature of theory that are far different from the one stated above. This is particularly true of sociology. In sociology, no word is mentioned more often than is "theory," and even "general theory." The importance of theory is stressed over and over again. And yet one almost never finds in sociological texts, even in the most "theoretical" ones, any discussion of what a theory *is*. From one point view this is just as well, for any adequate account of theory would immediately show up the hollowness of much that passes under this designation.

One view of the nature of theory, implicit in much theoretical writing, and especially in that of Talcott Parsons, is that a conceptual scheme is a theory. A conceptual scheme is a series of definitions of words. Since the words refer presumably to different classes of data—though in many actual conceptual schemes the distinctions between the classes are not always clear—a conceptual scheme is a scheme of classification or taxonomy. Now a conceptual scheme is vital to any explanation. Explanation consists of propositions relating properties of nature to one another; the properties must be defined, and this is what a conceptual scheme should do. Thus the scheme is part of the "text" that accompanies any scientific explanation. But to say that a conceptual scheme is necessary for explanation is not to say that it is sufficient—far from it. What are necessary are the propositions stating the relationships between the properties defined. Nor is it enough to say that there is *some* relationship, though this is a common feature of the things that are called theories but are in fact only conceptual schemes. Some beginning must be made at stating the nature of the relationship: how one of the properties changes as the other changes. The reason for this necessity is obvious. Unless a proposition is a real proposition in this sense, no definite conclusion can in logic be drawn from it; and since explanation consists in drawing logical conclusions from propositions, it follows that there can be no explanation, and therefore no theory, without propositions. And yet some practitioners of the taxonomic kind of theory claim that they have "derived" other men's theories from their own, more general ones. Upon examination it turns out that what they have done is to try to show that some of their words (concepts) have referents overlapping those of the words used in the other men's theories. But this is

translation, not deduction. People who make such claims should
be required to state their general propositions, and then to show
how the other men's propositions can be deduced from theirs
under specified given conditions. The people who make such claims
will be the last to be able in fact to do this.

If social scientists will once adopt a reasonable view of what
explanation is, the problem of explanation in this field can be
reduced to two questions. First, are there any general propositions
used in the explanation of social phenomena? Second, if so, what
sort of propositions are they? These questions are particularly
likely to come up in sociology in connection with the explanation
of institutions—those relatively persistent patterns of social behavior to whose maintenance the actions of many men contribute.
How, for instance, shall we explain the existence in a particular
society of a ranking of persons, or categories of persons, which
sociologists call a status system?

In a very rough sense, four different kinds of answers have
been given to this question of institutions.[2] First, the particular
institution exists because of its relation to other institutions in a
social system. This I call the structural type of explanation; it is
particularly prevalent in social anthropology. Second, the institution exists because the society could not survive or remain in
equilibrium without it. This is usually called the functional type
of explanation; it is prevalent in sociology. Third, the institution
exists as the end product, however temporary, of a particular historical process. This, the historical type of explanation, is naturally
prevalent in social history. Fourth, the institution exists because
the behavior of men has certain characteristics, which in particular
combinations in particular circumstances create the institution.
This I call psychological explanation, because the study of the
behavioral characteristics of men as such is the province of psychology.

The first, the structural, type of explanation is really not an
explanation at all. Let me take an example from anthropology.
The statement that marriage with father's sister's daughter is preferred in certain societies *because* the societies are organized in
matrilineal descent groups and follow a rule of avunculocal resi-
dence (a grown-up man normally resides where his mother's broth-

[2] G. C. Homans, "Contemporary Theory in Sociology," in R. E. L. Faris
(Ed.), *Handbook of Modern Sociology*, Chicago: Rand McNally, 1964, pp.
951-977.

ers do) is really not an explanation of the marriage preference. It simply says that in these societies the three institutions are correlated; they occur together. This is a very important kind of statement to make, and a great advance has been made in our knowledge of primitive kinship by testing such statements. But the question of why the institutions are associated still remains.

It is also true that structural "explanations," since they always bring in real propositions and correlate at least three institutions, can be cast in a form that looks superficially like a deductive system. Let me take an example from the field of small-group research. Do not worry about how the variables are defined and measured. Look only at the form of the propositional structure.

For any member of a small group:
1. The higher his rank, the greater his centrality.
2. The greater his centrality, the greater his observability.
3. The higher his rank, the greater his observability (derivation) .[3]

All that this system of propositions says is that the three variables are positively correlated. This may well be an important finding in fact, but that is not the question here. The "derivation" does not follow as a matter of logic unless a further condition is stated, and Proposition 3 cannot be said to be explained by the other two. The reason is that one necessary condition for a real explanation is not satisfied. Any one of the three propositions can be derived from the other two—and this is the sign of a structural explanation. The order in which the propositions are written does not, so to speak, make any difference. But in a real explanation at least one of the propositions cannot be derived from the others. The classic syllogism is the simplest form of an explanatory system, and in it the proposition that all men are mortal cannot be logically derived from the propositions that Socrates is a man and that Socrates is mortal. That is, the first proposition is more general than the other two. In so-called structural explanations, the crucial propositions are of the same level of generality.

The problems with the second, the functional, type of explanation are of a different kind. This type of explanation was and is common in the biological sciences; it came to sociology largely by way of Durkheim, particularly in *The Elementary Forms of the Religious Life,* and the social anthropologists under the influence of Durkheim, especially Radcliffe-Brown. The basic structure of

[3] T. K. Hopkins, *The Exercise of Influence in Small Groups,* Totowa, N. J.: Bedminster Press, 1964, p. 51.

this type of explanation, a structure often obscured in actual examples, is the following:

1. If a society is to survive (or remain in equilibrium) it must possess institutions of type x.
2. Bongo is a surviving society (or a society in equilibrium).
3. Therefore, Bongo possesses institutions of type x.

And thus the existence in Bongo society of this type of institution, say methods of resolving conflict, is said to be explained. This sort of explanation is called functional because the part played by the institution in ensuring the survival of the society is said to be its function.

There is nothing wrong in principle with this type of explanation. Unlike so-called structural explanations, it does contain a general proposition (Proposition 1), from which a conclusion can be drawn in logic under the given conditions. True, it has proved difficult in practice to define societal equilibrium, or even survival, or society itself, in such a way that unambiguous conclusions follow from the propositions in which these expressions appear. In explaining the characteristics of organizations of scope smaller than a whole society, the difficulty might be met. For instance, the equilibrium condition for a firm might be defined as making a profit; and the question of whether or not a firm is making a profit may perhaps be answered. Even so, I doubt that anyone has stated the general conditions for making a profit.

It is also true that what we want to explain is usually not the existence of *some* institution of a given class but the existence of a *particular* institution of that class. We do not, so to speak, want to explain why the United States possesses some kind of institution to resolve conflict but why it possesses trial by jury. How functional explanation is to be revised to deal with this problem is not at all clear. It is obviously absurd to set up a new Proposition 1 to read, "If a society is to survive it must possess trial by jury." The actual explanation is inevitably historical, and functional explanation, as practiced up to date, is clearly nonhistorical.

Note that functional explanation is not the same thing as what is called functional analysis. In functional analysis the sociologist points out that an institution, once adopted, has further consequences for a society, and that these consequences may be called "good" or "bad," according to the criterion used. This is a perfectly legitimate activity, but functional explanation goes much further, saying that the institution exists *because* it has consequences for the society and *because* the consequences are "good." Note: good for the society, not for some of its members.

Still, there is nothing wrong in principle with this kind of explanation. It is often used in other sciences, particularly biology. To explain why wild geese fly south in the winter, it is legitimate to point out that they would not survive in the north—a perfectly testable proposition. Yet they do survive, and so many of them must get south somehow. It is true that we are likely to find this kind of explanation unsatisfying to the intellect: we should prefer to know the actual mechanisms that get the geese flying south. And the same is true of functional explanations in sociology. Even if it could be shown that without a particular institution, a society would not survive, we should still like to know how the society managed to acquire and keep something so indispensable. To use the language of Aristotle, we should like to know the efficient as well as the final causes of the institution.

The trouble with functional explanations in sociology is not a matter of principle but of practice. From the characteristic general proposition of functionalism we can draw the conclusion in logic that a society failing to survive did *not* possess institutions of type x—whatever x may be. Now there are societies—a very few —that have not survived in any sense of the word. For some of these societies we have accounts of the social organization before their disappearance, and it turns out that they did possess institutions of type x. If these societies failed to survive, it was not for lack of social institutions, unless resistance to measles and alcohol be a social institution. That is, there is inadequate evidence so far for the truth of the general propositions of functionalism—and after all truth does make a difference. It is conceivable that the difficulties will be overcome, that better statements of the conditions for the survival or equilibrium of any society may be devised, from which nothing but true conclusions will be drawn. But in spite of endless efforts nothing of the sort is in sight. Whatever its status in principle, functional explanation in sociology is in practice a failure.

PSYCHOLOGICAL EXPLANATION IN SOCIOLOGY

Structural explanation is really not explanation at all. Functional explanation leads to false conclusions as well as true ones, and it is intellectually unsatisfying at best. There remain the historical and the psychological types of explanation. We shall see that these two types are really the same, in the sense that they employ the same kind of general proposition. And what is this kind?

Let me take an example. Suppose that we wish to explain why, in England in the eighteenth century, the first steps were taken to introduce power-driven machinery into the textile industry. Note that this is a problem of great importance not only to economic historians but also to sociologists, since these first steps led to the Industrial Revolution, and many of the institutions of modern society are products of industrialization. We point to the expansion of the English export trade in cotton cloth during the eighteenth century. (Of course other developments lie behind this one, but I want to keep the argument as simple as possible.) This expansion led to an increased demand on the part of the industrial entrepreneurs for supplies of cotton thread, a demand that was not fully met by the existing labor force, spinning thread by hand on spinning wheels, so that the wages of spinners began to rise, threatening to raise the price of cloth and thus check the expansion of trade. Under these circumstances it occurred to many persons connected with the textile industry that the problem could be solved by devising and using machinery that could spin several threads at a time if driven by water power or steam. They were familiar with power-driven machinery in other fields, notably grist mills, and so they had little reason to believe that the effort would fail. And if they were successful in solving the problems involved, they could expect, on the basis of past experience and present trends, to increase their profits. Many efforts were in fact made, and some were successful.

This is the way the ordinary explanation would run, but note that it does not take the form of a deductive system. Instead it is what the philosophers would call enthymemic: it does not state the major premises and other propositions needed to turn the argument into a deductive system. Rather, it leaves them unstated at many stages in the argument. For purposes of illustration I shall consider only the last. To point out that entrepreneurs perceived that certain actions would be successful and hence would be richly rewarded does not in logic explain why they actually took the actions in question. The explanation is completed as a deductive system only if we add something like this:

1. Men are likely to take actions that they perceive are, in the circumstances, likely to achieve rewarding results.

2. The entrepreneurs were men.
3. As entrepreneurs, they were likely to find results in the form of increased profits rewarding.

And so forth.

What we have seen, however crudely, in this example is, I believe, completely general. All human institutions are products of processes of historical change. In fact most institutions are continually changing. When we have enough factual information, which we often do not, even to begin explaining historical change, and when we try to supply the major premises of our unstated deductive systems, we find that there are certain premises we absolutely cannot avoid using, and that these premises are not propositions about the interrelations of institutions, as in structural explanation, or propositions about the conditions for the survival of societies, as in functional explanation, but propositions about the behavior of men as men, like Proposition 1 above. That is, they are psychological propositions: in their major premises history and psychology are one.

As we shall see, these propositions are specifically the propositions of behavioral psychology. True, they are often stated in some vulgar form and not as psychologists would state them. Proposition 1 above is a vulgarized form of three major propositions of behavioral psychology. Since in their vulgar form they are familiar to us all, they are often said to be truisms, and their use in completing our deductive systems is said to be trivial. Of course we can construct many intelligible arguments without ever mentioning them. But from the fact that we do not mention them we should not conclude that they are unimportant—quite the contrary. These trivial truisms are nevertheless true; and since, when we drive our search for explanatory generalizations back far enough, we always find ourselves using them and no others, they stand in fact as the most general propositions of social science. This is the ultimate importance of the propositions of behavioral psychology.

But what do I mean by behavioral psychology in its nonvulgar form? Perhaps its propositions are best illustrated by the work reported elsewhere in this book, but let me try to mention a few here. If an action has been rewarded (reinforced), the probability that it will be repeated increases. This I call the *success* proposition. The greater the value of the reward, relative to some alternative, the greater is the probability that the action will be performed.

This I call the *value* proposition. If in the past the occurrence of particular stimuli has been the occasion on which a person's action has been rewarded, then the more similar the present stimuli are to those of the past, the more likely the person is to perform the action now. This I call the *stimulus* proposition. A person whose action has often been rewarded, under particular stimuli, in the past, but is not rewarded, under similar stimuli, in the present, is likely to perform acts of aggression. This I call the *frustration-aggression* proposition. Other examples could be enumerated.[4] In the various behavioral psychologies the propositions are stated in somewhat different words, but I believe the words can be translated into one another. There might also be disagreement among behavioral psychologists as to which were the really fundamental propositions in the field, but even here I think there is a hard core that all would accept.

To support the propositions of behavioral psychology there is a vast body of evidence, both clinical and experimental, for man and for other animals. Indeed there is some question whether there is any other general psychology. Those who claim to be dissatisfied with behavioral psychology are hard put to state what other general propositions they would propose to replace those of behaviorism. Or their own propositions can be shown to follow as conclusions under special circumstances from behaviorism. Even Freudian psychology, so far as it is subject to test, is behavioristic. Behavioral psychology certainly accounts for much unconscious behavior and for the fact that events in a man's childhood may be having an effect on his behavior as an adult. This does not mean that behaviorism can explain all human behavior. I myself am not sure that I could produce a behavioral explanation of, for instance, identification. An immense amount of work remains to be done, and there is much behavior we shall never be able to explain for lack of the requisite information. It is not enough to have general propositions; also required is information about the specific conditions within which the propositions are to be applied. But what behavioral psychology cannot explain no other psychology can explain either. Finally, as I have already suggested, behavioral psychology is not new. It is a psychology many men who are not psychologists have used to explain and predict their own behavior and that of others. They have not stated its propositions in the lan-

---

4 See G. C. Homans, *Social Behavior: Its Elementary Forms,* New York: Harcourt, Brace & World, 1961, Ch. 4.

guage of psychology or tested it experimentally or seen all its implications—some of which, indeed, they would have been reluctant
to accept. But its main propositions certainly do not come to them
altogether as a surprise.

Behavioral psychology seems to me to include within itself the
so-called theory of rational behavior. The rational theory has as
its fundamental proposition something like this: Between the alternative actions open to a man in particular circumstances, he is
likely to choose the one for which the (mathematical) value of p
times v is the larger, where p is the probability, as perceived by
him, of his action being successful in attaining a particular result,
and v is the perceived reward-value to him of that result. His
values may be "bad" values in the eyes of an outsider, and his perceptions may be inadequate or incorrect, but given these specific
perceptions and values, the man acts rationally.

The truths expressed in the rational theory seem to me also
to be expressed in the behavioral theory. The effect of the variable
p is incorporated in the success proposition, that of v in the value
proposition. The element of perception is incorporated in these
two and in the stimulus proposition: it is the past experience of
success and reward under particular stimuli that leads a man to
perceive present success and reward as probable under similar stimuli. Of course we must, for many men, include under stimuli such
things as, for instance, what they have read in books.

But the behavioral theory seems to me broader in scope. The
rational theory has to take a man's perceptions and values at the
time of action as simply given; whereas behavioral psychology, if
there were adequate information about the man's past experience,
might hope to explain why he perceives things as he does and how
he acquired his particular values. It is also difficult to see just how,
for instance, the frustration-aggression proposition could be fitted
into the rational theory. Still, in many cases the predictions and
explanations of behavior made under the rational theory would be
identical with those made under the behavioral one.

OBJECTIONS TO PSYCHOLOGICAL EXPLANATION

My contention is that the propositions of behavioral psychology
are the general explanatory propositions not only of sociology but
also of all the social sciences. This is a sweeping contention, and
certain obvious objections to it must be met right away. It does

not imply that "human nature is the same the world over," if that means that human behavior is concretely the same. We know very well that it is not, and modern anthropology teaches us many new ways in which it is not. All that the contention implies is that certain general principles hold good of all men, but that in different conditions different forms of actual behavior follow. The conditions include different past histories of persons and of groups. Indeed the psychological propositions, with their emphasis on the effects of past experience on present behavior, help to explain why this kind of condition does make a difference.

The propositions of behavioral psychology are stated as if it made no difference whether a person interacted with the physical environment or with another person. Thus an activity that is rewarded is likely to be repeated, no matter where the reward comes from. Accordingly the claim has been made that behavioral psychology is a psychology of the "isolated individual," and that it cannot account for the new phenomena that "emerge" when behavior is social, when at least two human beings are interacting. There is nothing in my present contention to imply that new phenomena do not emerge from social interaction. They are emerging all the time. The question is not whether they emerge but how what emerges is to be explained. My contention is that no new general propositions are required to explain what happens when behavior is social, though of course an important new given condition must be brought in, the fact that at least two persons are interacting. Therefore the behavior of both exemplifies psychological propositions, and not just the behavior of one of them, as in the case of a person interacting with the nonhuman environment. Naturally this may make the behavior of an individual different from what it would have been if he had been alone. But no new general proposition is needed to explain the difference. Let those who contend that behavioral psychology cannot explain the emergent characteristics of social behavior come forward and state the alternative general propositions that they think are necessary for this explanation. Let them show us their deductive systems with their general propositions in place. The fact is that they do not do so. All the usual examples of emergent social phenomena can readily be shown to follow from psychological propositions.

Nor is there anything in my contention to imply that, in order to explain social phenomena, we have to take account of the behavior of every individual concerned—in all but very small groups a manifestly impossible task. But the propositions of behavioral psychology themselves imply that many persons, if their backgrounds and present circumstances are similar, are likely to behave in similar ways. Accordingly we can often, in explanation, deal satisfactorily, though only statistically, with social aggregates, such as members of a middle class in a period of inflation. Sociologists have always done this, and they may go right on doing so. The explanatory propositions do not change: they are still psychological, but they are applied to aggregates. Still, it is well to remember that certain unique individuals, often in special social positions—politicians, writers, scientists—have made more difference to social developments, even those of large scope and long-continued influence, than many sociologists will readily admit.

A related objection is that a psychological theory is necessarily a theory of personality, and therefore obviously inappropriate in explaining social structure. The fallacy here lies in the assumption that, if there are two different things to be explained, two different sets of general propositions are required to explain them. When we try to explain social trends, we consider a number of persons and neglect many sides of their behavior. In explaining the response of a middle class to inflation, it really does not matter if one man is schizoid and another paranoid if they will respond in much the same way to an increase in the price of steak. And they will do so, or at least enough members of the class will do so to allow us to establish and explain a statistical tendency. When, on the other hand, we try to explain the characteristics of a personality, we consider only one person and concentrate on relating many aspects of his behavior to one another and to his past history. What is to be explained differs in the two cases as do the relevant given conditions, but this does not mean that the general propositions used in the explanations are necessarily different too. Far from it—it is my belief that the general propositions used in the two kinds of case will turn out to be the same. After all, it is not as if the actions that constitute a man's personality were different from those that, together with the actions of many others, constitute a society. They are the same identical actions.

PSYCHOLOGICAL REDUCTIONISM
The position taken here is often called reductionist, but we must be careful about what we mean by "reduction." The example that

I always use is thermodynamics. In a very rough sense, thermodynamics consists of statements about the relations between the pressure, temperature, and volume of substances: gases, liquids, solids. These are all physical aggregates: they are made up of enormously large numbers of molecules. The propositions of thermodynamics hold good with wide generality for such physical aggregates. Willard Gibbs showed in his *Statistical Mechanics* that these propositions about aggregates followed from propositions about the mechanics of individual molecules, each possessed of mass, velocity, and direction, under certain kinds of given conditions, such as many molecules of gas colliding with one another at random in an enclosed space. Gibbs showed that the propositions about aggregates (thermodynamics) could be deduced from the propositions about individuals (mechanics) under the given conditions. The former could be reduced to the latter.

If one speaks of psychological reductionism in the social sciences, one may imply that the situation is similar there, and that there are laws applying to social aggregates, which I shall call sociological laws, which can then be derived from propositions about individuals, presumably psychological laws. But there may be few if any propositions that apply with wide generality to social aggregates, such as groups, societies, and classes, and to this extent the analogy with thermodynamics may fail. One such proposition might be that the number of followers in any group is larger than the number of leaders. But this proposition does not have much explanatory power; we can derive from it no proposition that is itself a generalization, but only propositions about individual groups: if A is a group, then in A the number of followers is larger than the number of leaders.

And most propositions about aggregates, propositions that make no direct reference to the behavior of individuals, have no very wide generality; they hold good only within limited conditions. Perhaps some of the laws of economics, such as the so-called laws of supply and demand, come closest to being general. But they explicitly apply only within certain institutional conditions—markets and prices—and only within limits even there. "The higher the price of a commodity, the less a consumer will buy" may not apply when high price gives the commodity great value as a status symbol.

Strangely enough, if there were sociological laws of high generality, we should feel less need for reducing them to psychology.

After all, a person who wants to solve problems in thermodynamics can work directly with its propositions and forget that they can in turn be derived from statistical mechanics. In the same way, if we could explain most of the features of social institutions and their interrelations in societies by constructing deductive systems whose propositions of highest order were sociological, we should go ahead and do so, and we should not, as a practical matter, worry about whether they in turn could be derived from (reduced to) psychological ones. It is just the fact that sociological laws are not very general that creates the need for psychological reduction. Thus the laws of supply and demand follow from psychological propositions under the condition that markets and money prices are institutionalized. But so do the exceptions to the laws: the peculiar demand-curve for perfume follows from the value proposition under the condition that the high price of a perfume is not just a cost to the consumer but a positive value as a status symbol. We need psychology to explain both why social propositions hold good, when they do hold good, and why they do not, when they do not.

THE POSITION OF DURKHEIM

Historically, the chief opponent of the position taken here is the great French sociologist Emile Durkheim. Either directly, or indirectly through his followers in anthropology, such as A. R. Radcliffe-Brown, he has had an enormous and continuing influence on modern social science, and we shall do well to examine his arguments. They are set forth in his little book *The Rules of Sociological Method,* especially in Chapter V, "Rules Relating to the Explanation of Social Facts."

Earlier in the book he defines what he calls a *social fact*: "a social fact is any way of behaving, fixed or not, capable of exercising an external constraint on the individual."[5] And he gives several examples of social facts, one of which is this: "If the population presses into our cities, instead of dispersing itself over the countryside, the reason is that there is a current of opinion, a collective drive, that imposes this concentration on individuals."[6]

[5] E. Durkheim, *Les Règles de la méthode sociologique,* 8th ed., Paris: Alcan, 1927, p. 19.
[6] *Ibid.,* p. 18.

From these and other examples, he later draws the following conclusion about social facts: "Since their essential characteristic consists in the power they possess of exercising from outside a pressure
on individual consciousnesses, it follows that they do not derive
from individual consciousnesses and that, accordingly, sociology is
not a corollary of psychology."[7] He also uses the argument from
emergence:

> In coming together, in penetrating one another, in fusing, individual
> souls give birth to a being, which is psychic if you like, but which con-
> stitutes a psychic individuality of a new order. It is therefore in the nature
> of this individuality, not in that of the units composing it, that one must
> go to look for the proximate and determining causes of the facts that are
> there produced. . . . In consequence, every time a social phenomenon is
> directly explained by a psychic phenomenon, one can rest assured that
> the explanation is false.[8]

But what is the alternative, the true explanation? According to
Durkheim, "The determining cause of a social fact should be
looked for among antecedent social facts, and not among the states
of individual consciousness."[9]

Aside from the issue of emergence, which I dealt with earlier,
Durkheim's argument raises two main questions: What does he
mean by psychology and a psychic phenomenon? Wht does he
mean by explanation? In fairness to him we must remember that
the understanding of neither psychology nor explanation was
nearly as advanced in his day as it is now. What he conceived to
be psychology was a sort of instinctual psychology, and it certainly
assumed that human nature was the same the world over. Durkheim was quite right in speaking of it with scorn: "Thus one currently explains the domestic organization [the family] by the sentiments that parents have for their children and vice-versa. . . ."[10]
He clearly did not conceive of a psychology that, for instance, accounted for the behavior of children toward their parents as a precipitate, over time, of the rewards and punishments the children
had received from their parents. Sociology is surely not a corollary
of the kind of psychology Durkheim had in mind. But this does

7 *Ibid.,* pp. 124-125.
8 *Ibid.,* pp. 127-128.
9 *Ibid.,* p. 135.
10 *Ibid.,* p. 124.

not mean that it is not a corollary of, cannot be derived from, another psychology.

As for explanation, Durkheim believes that one has explained a phenomenon if one has found its cause or causes. He rejects "sentiments" as an explanation of family organization because in his view they are not its causes. And he thinks he can escape from psychological explanation by pointing to social facts that are the causes of other social facts. But this whole notion of explanation is mistaken. On this point I have written elsewhere as follows:

The price rise of the sixteenth century, which I take to be a social fact, was certainly a determining cause of the enclosure movement among English landlords. But were we to construct an explanation why this particular cause had this particular effect, we should have to say that the price rise presented English landlords both with great opportunities for monetary gain and great risks of monetary loss, that enclosure tended to increase the gain and avoid the loss, that the landlords found monetary gain rewarding (which is a state of individual consciousness, if you like), and, finally, that men are likely to take actions whose results they find rewarding—which, as I cannot repeat too often, is a general psychological proposition.[11]

In short, social facts are indeed often the causes of other social facts—that is not in question. But one has not explained phenomena when one has found their causes. Rather it is the relationship between cause and effect that is to be explained. The deductive systems that explain the relationship will always be found to contain not just "psychic phenomena" but psychological propositions as well. It is in this sense that sociology is a corollary of psychology.

From this point of view, it is absurd to say, as Durkheim does in one of his examples of social facts, that the reason for the movement of population into urban areas from the countryside in the latter part of the nineteenth century in France was "a collective urge that imposes this concentration on individuals." Thanks ultimately to the developments we call the Industrial Revolution, the opportunities for employment in urban areas were increasing; and, though this is not so certain, the opportunities for employment in rural areas were apparently decreasing, because of the concurrent developments we call the Agricultural Revolution. Men are likely

[11] G. C. Homans, "Contemporary Theory in Sociology," *op. cit.,* p. 971.

to take actions that will increase their perceived probability of obtaining reward—this is a psychological proposition. Many men in industrial societies are likely to find employment rewarding. Accordingly, in the conditions of France in the nineteenth century, they were likely to move from the country to the city. Of course the persons who moved were likely to hear of the opportunities for employment from other persons or from newspapers. Of course the behavior was social—that is not in question. But there is no more social compulsion, no more social imposition, about the process than is implied by the fundamental proposition about action taken to increase reward as perceived in the given circumstances—and this is a psychological proposition, a proposition about the behavior of men, and not a sociological proposition, a proposition about the behavior of societies. Or, if you prefer, the very compulsion that Durkheim sees as the characteristic of social facts can itself be explained only psychologically.

Aside from his arguments, which carried more weight when he wrote them than they do today, why does Durkheim's position still appeal so strongly to many sociologists? I think one unstated reason is that he appeared to give this new science an identity. If sociology was not a corollary of psychology, it was free to develop theories of its own, and thus give sociologists a reason for existence. I fear Durkheim's position is untenable, but I want to reassure sociologists. There is nothing in what I have said that implies they should give up any of the things they are working on today, except certain kinds of "general theory," which are nontheories anyhow. On the contrary, what is implied, as I shall try to show, is that sociologists have an important new task (actually an old task in a new form), which is theirs if only because the other social sciences have left it to them. And if it hurts to lose one's identity, sociology has many companions in misery, in the sense that all the social sciences, in their general propositions, are one science.

THE TASK OF BEHAVIORAL SOCIOLOGY
I have argued that all existing social behavior is a precipitate of a process of social change, and that the explanation of any social change requires psychological propositions. My method of showing this, as in the case of the beginnings of the Industrial Revolution, was to suggest how the ordinary historical and sociological ex-

planations could be rewritten as deductive systems, and to point out that their hitherto unstated major premises were inescapably psychological propositions. Though it was necessary to carry out this exercise in order to make the point, it must have looked too easy and obvious—obvious just because it was true. The reason why it was obvious must itself have been obvious. In setting up the explanations I disregarded the alternative actions and rewards open to the persons concerned: it was as if they could either take the actions they did or do nothing at all. More important, I took the behavior of all but a single class of persons, such as the entrepreneurs, as given, as unproblematic, and I applied the relevant psychological proposition to explain the behavior of that class. Finally I took the larger social structure and institutions as given, even though the process I was undertaking to explain would eventually bring about a change in this structure. And I asked the explanation to answer only a very simple question: Will the persons in question take a particular action, or won't they? and not, for instance: How many of them will do so, and how much?

In many circumstances this procedure is justified as not too great a simplification of the actual situation. And it is often the best we can do in history, when we try to build up an account of the historical process by first explaining the behavior of one individual or class, then explaining the behavior of another in response to that of the first, and so forth. Although the procedure would always use psychological propositions as its major premises in explanation, even if they were left unstated, it is inherently serial. It has difficulty in coping with simultaneous changes on the part of more than one individual or class, when the behavior of each of them is problematic, and the question is not whether a person will act, but how much he will produce of different kinds of behavior, at what times, in relation to the answers to similar questions about the behavior of other persons and classes.

Though sociologists will make many empirical discoveries, the central intellectual problem of sociology is not analytic—that of discovering new fundamental propositions. I think the principal ones are already discovered and they are psychological. The problem is a rather synthetic one—that of showing how the behavior of many men in accordance with psychological propositions combines to form and maintain relatively enduring social structures. In effect, this has been the central problem for sociology ever since Hobbes. Cannot we do better in dealing with it?

I think that we can, and here is where behavioral sociology finally comes into the picture. Let me take an example. In one sense the caste system of India is unique: in the elaboration of its development there is really nothing like it elsewhere in human societies of the present or, so far as we know, of the past. Its degree of elaboration certainly cannot be explained by reference to geographical or technological conditions alone. Societies at a similar level of technological development, like medieval China and medieval Europe, did not carry their stratification to nearly this extreme. The explanation must be ultimately historical: some unique set of conditions in the past history of India that set a current running strongly in one direction. But we shall probably never know enough about this past history to specify what the conditions were and to explain why they had this effect.

But in another sense the caste system of India is a member of a large class of structures, which we call status systems. Status systems occur in all societies, and indeed in many small groups. At the subsocietal level, in new groups and new organizations, we can see them emerging all the time. The same is true of other aspects of social structure: norms, conformity, power, influence, cooperation. Thus the particular norms that particular groups and societies develop may differ, but the process of norm formation occurs in all. And this is also true of other members of the class that I call fundamental social processes. Just how the fundamental processes combine and recombine to form the particular structures of particular societies we may never be able to explain except within a big margin for doubt. But the fundamental processes themselves we certainly shall be able to explain.

We shall be able to explain them because we shall not have to rely on history. We can observe them now, and in the case of small groups we can observe them in detail. We may well be able to observe them in a number of different societies. We can even manipulate them experimentally. The status system in a small group may be very different from the caste system of India, but in both cases differences in power are associated with differences in status. If, in the small group, we can manipulate the differences in power and then see the corresponding differences in status develop, we cannot doubt that we have reproduced one of the processes that on a much larger scale, over many centuries and with many complications, have produced the Indian caste system. We may even be able experimentally to create different varieties of status system, from the highly differentiated to the relatively undifferentiated.

If we use the principles of behavioral psychology in making our manipulations and in predicting their results, we shall, I feel sure, be able to show that no propositions specifically about groups are needed to explain the emergence and maintenance of social structures. In making the predictions we shall of course have to cope with complicated interactional effects, but the computer has come along just in time to help us solve this kind of problem with a speed of a whole new order of magnitude. The computer was meant for solving synthetic problems.

THE FAILURE OF SOCIAL PSYCHOLOGY

In view of the fact that, after all, psychologists produced the findings of behavioral psychology, it is surprising how little they have done to apply behavioral psychology to the explanation and prediction of social behavior. This failure takes two forms. On the one hand there is a psychologist like B. F. Skinner, a behaviorist if there ever was one, who, when he extends his findings from the actions of pigeons to human social behavior, immediately jumps to a very impressionistic discussion of such things as government and religion, that is, to exceedingly complex subjects with a long history behind them.[12] One would have thought that a better strategy would have been to extend behavioral principles systematically to show their implications in the simpler social situations, such as interaction in small groups. For Skinner the failure might be critical. If he ever tried in fact to create an experimental community such as he describes in fiction in his *Walden Two*, I think he would find that it would not work in quite the way he evidently expects, and the reason would lie in the implications of his own principles as they would apply in such a community. He makes the whole thing look too easy; his own findings imply that differences in status, for instance, would be likely to arise and cause trouble.

On the other hand, there are the psychologists who call themselves social psychologists. They tend to come from the "soft" side of psychology and to find uncongenial such a tough-minded doctrine as behavioral psychology, always implying in private that it

12 B. F. Skinner, *Science and Human Behavior*, New York: The Macmillan Company, 1953.

is somehow inadequate for the explanation of social phenomena but without ever specifying in public what general "social" propositions they would add. Unlike Skinner, they actually study interaction in small groups, but in attempting to account for their findings, they either leave the propositions of behaviorism implicit or deliberately neglect them. For one example, the findings in the active field called "balance theory" are readily explainable by the propositions of behavioral psychology, and the unity of psychology would gain strength if they were so explained.[13] For another example, Thibaut and Kelley attempt to explain certain characteristics of groups while deliberately ignoring what they call "sequential effects."[14] But these effects are nothing less than the effects of past behavior, its success and the value of the rewards it achieves, on present behavior. To leave them out is to leave out the very heart of behavioral psychology and in so doing to forego the possibility of explaining some of the most important features of social behavior.

The problem of explaining and predicting through behavioral principles the operation of fundamental social processes and their combination in particular circumstances is central to all of social science. The failure of psychologists to tackle it gives sociologists their opportunity.

[13] For "balance theory" see F. Heider, *The Psychology of Interpersonal Relations*, New York: John Wiley & Sons, 1958, Ch. 7.

[14] J. W. Thibaut and H. H. Kelley, *The Social Psychology of Groups*, New York: John Wiley & Sons, 1959 p. 19.

PART I

Foundations for the Experimental Analysis of Social Process

In the Prologue Professor Homans has asserted the existence of a debilitating gap between the use of behavioral principles in the explanation of the behavior of individuals and their use in explanations of the formation and maintenance of "relatively enduring social structures." Throughout Part I and the other parts it is intended that the reader have the opportunity to judge what the magnitude of such a gap is and whether it should be widened or narrowed.

There is growing evidence that the principles developed through the experimental analysis of behavior have considerable relevance for the analysis of patterns of socialization, of the development of normative as well as deviant behavior, of personal and group values, and of organizational structure, and for the development, persistence, and change of institutional forms. Even if only a portion of this promise is realized, social research will be a far different enterprise in ten years from what it is today. Whether or not the orientations of the experimental analysis will find widespread use in sociology depends upon how skillfully we can utilize the principles and methodologies which comprise this branch of behavioral science. When sociologists and social psychologists are as comfortable with the tenets of behavioral analysis as they currently are with role theory, structural functionalism, or psychodynamics, the relevance of behavior principles to the analysis of social phenomena may be more accurately assessed. As a beginning, the following collection of articles may be appraised according to how well they satisfy three important criteria. First, are the principles empirically supported? Second, as Professor Homans has suggested, do they have explanatory power? And, third, are they useful in designing effective strategies of action? In short, can behavior theory help us reach better solutions to sociological problems?

Modern behavior theory cannot be presented adequately in a single chapter of a single book. It is hoped, however, that the brief outline of principles in Chapter 1, together with the articles that follow, will stimulate extensive and serious research into the questions raised by Homans. Taken together, the research and theoretical papers which follow paint a more realistic portrait of behavioral analysis than could result from a straight exposition of principles and techniques. The gaps and omissions in contemporary behavior theory must be seen alongside of its strengths, accomplishments, and objectives so that the observed self-assurance of its advocates is not misunderstood. The behaviorist derives his buoyant confidence not from having the answers, but rather from a long history of reinforcement for his problem-solving behavior.

1

Some Basic Principles of Behavior

Don Bushell, Jr., and Robert L. Burgess

> For we must first prepare, as a foundation for the whole, a complete and accurate natural and experimental history. We must not imagine or invent, but discover the acts and properties of nature.　　SIR FRANCIS BACON, 1620

The articles contained in the present collection are concerned primarily with *operant behavior*. Operant behavior is the behavior of individuals that operates on the environment in such a way as to produce some consequence or change in it which, in turn, modifies subsequent performances of that behavior. An executive calling a board meeting is emitting operant behavior; so is a mother scolding a child, a teacher instructing a class, a salesman phoning a client, a foreman complimenting a worker, a man buying a Cadillac, or a scientist conducting research. Each of these complex acts is composed of observable events which produce consequent changes in the actor's environment. The functional relationships existing between such behaviors and their consequences constitute the subject matter of an operant analysis.

This relationship has become the center of attention with the observation that the occurrence of many behaviors is systematically affected by the consequences they have produced. Thus the consequence becomes the independent variable which affects the dependent variable, the future occurrence of the behavior. As Homans has already suggested, a consequence which increases or strengthens the behavior preceding it is by definition a reinforcing consequence. If, in the previous example, the board members summoned by the executive spent the meeting praising his leadership with the result that board meetings were called more often, praise might be identified as a reinforcer for calls to meeting. Similarly, the salesman who made a successful sale to the client he phoned would be expected to increase his rate of phoning clients.

REINFORCEMENT

A reinforcer is consequently similar to what we generally think of as a reward, but there is one very important difference. The reinforcer can only be defined in terms of an observable effect upon its related operant. If the praised executive did not call board meetings more frequently, it might be observed that he was rewarded with praise; but praise could not be classified as a reinforcer. This point needs to be emphasized because it is so frequently misunderstood. As limiting as it may seem, reinforcers simply cannot be identified on *a priori* grounds apart from their effects on behavior.

There are, however, additional factors which make it possible to maximize the probability that a particular event will prove reinforcing under certain circumstances. Obviously, the probability that food will be reinforcing increases as the subject's hunger increases. Whether such factors are called "setting events" (Bijou and Baer, 1961) or "state variables" (Kunkel, Chapter 15 of this book), it is through them that the accurate prediction of reinforcers is possible. The level of *deprivation* of an individual is a crucial determinant of what will prove reinforcing. The fact that experimental subjects deprived of food or water can be reinforced by the presentation of these items, of course, is well understood. More important to the analysis of social behavior, however, is the fact that deprivations are not only physiological; they can be taught. Thus, a knowledge of the learning history of the social individual (even an approximation such as an awareness of the cultural background of the person) provides an immediate basis for making workable predictions about the probability that a given stimulus will be reinforcing. The movie starlet just beginning a career may be deprived of public attention, at least relatively, and thus strongly reinforced by manifestations of it, while the established star may be *satiated* with attention and simply "want to be alone." Again, the effect which attention has upon the individual's behavior must determine whether or not it is a reinforcer.[1]

Up to this point, reinforcement has been illustrated by describing events in which some action of the individual resulted in something being added to his environment. The executive received praise; the salesman obtained his sale; and the starlet got attention. Where environmental changes take the form of presenting or adding stimulus events which thereby increase the probability of be-

[1] In strict usage, only responses are reinforced; people are rewarded. The convention is relaxed in this chapter to avoid stilted phrasing.

havior occurring in the future, the process is termed *positive reinforcement*. There are numerous occasions, however, in which the probability of future occurrence is increased because an act removes or subtracts something from the environment. Turning down the volume on an excessively loud radio removes aversive noise and thus may be *negatively reinforcing*. Leaving a gathering may be negatively reinforcing because it removes a bore or otherwise unpleasant person from one's environment. For most purposes in this book, however, it will make little difference whether a reinforcer is positive or negative. The fact remains that some behaviors produce consequences (the addition or subtraction of stimuli) which increase the future probability of these behaviors. The operation of adding a positive reinforcer (or removing a negative reinforcer) contingent on the occurrence of a response is called reinforcement.

PUNISHMENT

Obviously, not all consequences are reinforcing. Our gregarious executive might call a board meeting only to find himself the target of considerable verbal abuse with the result that fewer board meetings would follow. The salesman might lose his client because he phoned rather than making an appointment for a personal call and, as a result, would cut down considerably on his telephone time. The starlet seeking attention in an injudicious way might get arrested for disturbing the peace and thereafter confine herself to more socially acceptable approaches. A consequence which decreases the frequency of the response that precedes it is a *punisher*. Like reinforcement, punishment may come in many forms, and a particular event may prove reinforcing for one person and punishing for another (Azrin and Holz, 1966; Ayllon and Azrin, 1966). Once again, the ability to predict the effect of a particular consequence depends upon a knowledge of the "setting events" or "state variables" which arise both from physiological properties and from the individual's history. It is highly probable that a severe electric shock will prove punishing to most individuals. Eating white wood grubs, on the other hand, may be punishing or reinforcing, depending upon whether the diner is an Australian aborigine or a midwestern school teacher.

When the consequence of a response is the *addition* of a stimulus to the environment which *reduces* the future occurrence of that response, the process is called *positive punishment*. Sticking one's finger into a live electric socket will add a stimulus which can reasonably be labeled a punisher; a careless step on a steep flight of stairs also may produce consequences which are positively punishing.

In social situations, however, interpersonal control is more often effected by the removal (or threat of removal) of a stimulus than by its presentation. A father may take car privileges away from a disobedient son, or a misguided parent may admonish a child by threatening, "Mommie won't love you if you do that." Responses which *decrease* in strength when they are followed by the loss of reinforcers (response-contingent loss of reinforcement is called *response cost*) are being *negatively punished*. The subject will come up again, but for now it is sufficient to note that response cost is the mainstay of control procedures in social organizations. First, the individual member is socialized to the point that group membership (or other consequences of contrived association) is important (positively reinforcing) to him. Once this is accomplished, undesirable behavior can be minimized by expulsion, incarceration, or the removal of membership privileges. A rapidly growing body of animal research is yielding more and more information about the specific behavioral consequences of punishment. The social phenomenon of the threat, however, lacks comparable empirical investigation. Are the effects of a threat upon the well-socialized individual comparable to those of actual punishment? The immediate suggestion, of course, is that an important aspect of the socialization process is the development of the threat as an effective punisher, just as the promise is developed into an effective reinforcer. How this occurs will be described more fully in the following sections dealing with conditioned reinforcers and discriminative stimuli.

CONTINGENCIES OF REINFORCEMENT

Earlier in this chapter it was stated that the functional relationship between the rate and form of a behavior and its history of past consequences is the subject matter of an operant analysis. These relationships, which constitute basic laws of behavior, are generally expressed in the form of statements of *contingency*. That is, certain changes occur in the environment contingent upon the emission of certain operants in certain patterns. Whether established by nature or by the social environment, these patterns may take on various arrangements, each of which has a characteristic and predictable effect upon its related operant. Responding is a lawful function of these arrangements, which are called *schedules of reinforcement*.

During the early phases of the socialization process, children are typically on high-density schedules of reinforcement when they are being taught a new skill. High density indicates that the ratio between the number of reinforcements and the number of responses is at or very near 1:1. In the extreme case, reinforcement immediately follows each and every response that is emitted. This is called *continuous reinforcement* and will be referred to in some of the subsequent articles simply by the abbreviation CRF. Consider a man playing a broken slot machine which pays back twice what he puts in every time. Under this reinforcement schedule, the lever-pulling response will be emitted at a high, steady rate. So, too, in a primitive illustration of interaction, a father might reinforce his child's utterance, "DADDY," by responding, "HI." As long as the father's "HI" is a reinforcer and follows each response, the word "DADDY" will be emitted at a high, steady rate. So long as each partner in the dyad is reinforced by the other, the "DADDY" . . . "HI" . . . conversation will be a lively one. If the father has to break off the dialogue to answer the telephone, the child's "DADDY" will return to its prereinforcement level (also called the *operant level*). The schedule of reinforcement wherein a previously reinforced response no longer is reinforced is called *extinction*.

There is a reason for mentioning CRF and extinction together since, in a general way, an inverse relationship exists between the density of the reinforcement schedule and the persistence of the behavior under extinction conditions. Thus the CRF schedule, being the most dense, produces response rates which are the least resistant to extinction. If we take another look at the lucky slot-machine player just as the machine stops paying off altogether, we will see him make a few rapid tests, as if to make sure that he's no longer going to reap a steady two-for-one profit, and then stop playing completely and move on to some other activity—perhaps to tell the proprietor that one of his machines is broken. In the same fashion, the child's conversation with his father, having been interrupted by a phone call, will close with a brief burst of "DADDY"s, which then will slow down and shortly be replaced by another activity.

In the development and management of social behavior, it clearly is not practical to rely on continuous reinforcement. It is simply out of the question to expect a salesman to work only so long as every prospect gives him an order. Schedules which have a lower density—that is, where reinforcement is more intermittent— are more frequently encountered in the social world, and they are also more effective in sustaining a relatively high rate of responding during extinction. It is easy to imagine the slot-machine player staying with his marvelous machine considerably longer if it paid off in a changing schedule which let him down gradually from 2 : 1 to 3 : 2 and then 1 : 1, 1 : 2, etc. Indeed, the ratio can be changed quite quickly from one that favors the player to one that favors the house, and the behavior will be sustained even though only an occasional response is reinforced and the majority are unreinforced, or on extinction.

Entire books and hundreds of thousands of experimental hours have been devoted to describing the response patterns established by different reinforcement schedules; thus this topic cannot be considered exhaustively in the present discussion. Appreciation of the research reports which follow, however, will be facilitated by a few additional comments concerning some of the basic aspects of different schedules of *intermittent reinforcement* (Morse, 1966).

Intermittent schedules take two basic forms. In one, the frequency of reinforcement is controlled by the behavior of the individual. These *ratio schedules* apply to much social behavior in which the amount of responding determines the frequency of reinforcement. Ratio schedules produce a very high rate of responding even when the ratio of responses to reinforcement is very lean, say 100 responses per reinforcement. Writing a letter, delivering a speech, traveling to work, and communicating information in a group problem-solving task are examples of behavior on ratio schedules because a number of operants need to be emitted sequentially before they will be followed by reinforcement.

Schedules can be arranged so that reinforcement is independent of the amount of behavior and comes instead from the passage of time. The *interval schedule* is arranged so that the first response after a set amount of time has elapsed will be reinforced. It is hard to find examples of interval schedules in the social world because interaction is more responsive to its own stimuli than to the passage of time. In a sense, however, the seniority systems of large bureaucracies are a form of interval reinforcement since, in some of them, merely coming to work for a given number of years at a given position will be reinforced by an advance in pay grade. Most of our day-to-day social activities, of course, operate on various combinations of ratio and interval schedules. The experimental separation of the various arrangements, as in the following reports, has considerable analytic value, but a single schedule of reinforcement cannot explain a complex interaction process very convincingly.

Not surprisingly, reinforcement sometimes occurs in such a way as to strengthen a behavior, not because there is any causal relationship between the two, but simply because they are accidentally coincident. C. B. Ferster describes the effects of such an accidental coincidence in the following way:

Much of human behavior is necessarily under superstitious, spurious, or adventitious control. The gas explosion occurring at the instant a salesman is about to press the front door buzzer will come to function as a preaversive stimulus, even though pressing the buzzer has no stable relationship in the physical environment to the probability of an explosion. Similarly, the gambler who shouts, "Come seven," just before the throw of the dice brings a seven, will find that his subsequent disposition to say, "Come seven," will be higher, whether or not speaking has any influence on the outcome of the throw. The fact that seven appears on the dice only intermittently does not necessarily nullify the effect of the reinforcement. It simply specifies an intermittent schedule of reinforcement of the response and may, in fact, under appropriate circumstancs, as in the previous discussion of intermittent reinforcement, strengthen the disposition to say, "Come seven." A similar example is the Indian medicine man praying and chanting for rain. The rain, as a reinforcing event for the praying and chanting, occurs on a variable-interval schedule: sooner or later rain will fall, thus reinforcing the praying and dancing. Once the "rainmaker" has a strong disposition to pray for rain, its high frequency will make it likely that the behavior will occur when it finally rains. Superstitious behavior is likely to occur under conditions of strong deprivation or with an extremely powerful reinforcer. It is under these conditions that the initial reinforcement of a response will produce a substantial tendency to respond, and the probability is high that the same response will occur again at the time of the next reinforcement (Nurnberger, Ferster, and Brady, 1963, p. 257).

DISCRIMINATIVE STIMULI

Although the discussion thus far has concentrated on the two-element contingency between response and consequence, the nature of the illustrations already has suggested that the social world cannot be compartmentalized so easily. The much discussed salesman of an earlier illustration probably would not expect to make a sale if he phoned his prospect at 4:00 A.M. Similarly, the probability is greater that the executive previously cited will call his board meeting just after closing a big deal. Very simply, the point is that a variety of conditions (stimuli) in the environment determines the probability of reinforcement for a given response. If we say, "HELLO," when another person comes on the scene, this verbal response is likely to be reinforced by a countergreeting. The same response made when no one else is around, however, will not be reinforced. Through this process of *differential reinforcement*, the arrival of another person will become a *discriminative stimulus*, thereby marking the occasion for the reinforcement of the response, "HELLO." By virtue of the fact that discriminative stimuli (S^Ds) are always present on the occasion of reinforcement, they increase the probability that the previously reinforced response will recur. Parents quickly become discriminative stimuli for a child because in their presence a great variety of responses produces reinforcement. Some stimuli, moreover, are always present when a response is punished, or when it fails to be followed by reinforcement. These stimuli, termed S-deltas (S^Δs), are stimuli in whose presence a response is less likely to occur than in their absence. In short, they decrease the probability that a given act will recur. The schoolroom is discriminative for an entire range of behavior which differs from the behavior that will be reinforced on the playground. Home, office, and church—all are discriminative environments which increase the probability of some behaviors and decrease the probability of others as a result of different reinforcement histories in these settings. It is necessary to deal with a three-element contingency: the discriminative stimulus, the response, and its consequent reinforcement.

The extreme subtlety with which discriminative stimuli (S^Ds and S^Δs) can control social behavior has been analyzed frequently by sociologists, though they may have used other terms. In one instance, the discriminative stimuli consist of the almost hidden signs that are shared by the members of an organization but pass unnoticed by the outsider. Examples include keys worn on the belt which distinguish staff from patient in large hospitals, recognition emblems worn by members of fraternal organizations, characteristic signs of wear in the leather aprons of sawmill workers, quiet differences in dress which distinguish senior from junior executives in large businesses, and, of course, in-group peculiarities in speech. All of these are barely perceptible elements of the environment, yet they function to pattern intricate interactions with great effectiveness. Comparable events have taken place when a sociologist can look at the behavior of a group member and say, "He has been well socialized," and when an experimental psychologist can read his data and assert that the subject is responding "under stimulus control." In both situations, a vast array of discriminative and reinforcing stimuli has come to maintain behavior within predictable limits.

The importance of discriminative stimuli can hardly be overstated. An attentive listener is discriminative for continued talking, while an inattentive listener is discriminative for changing the subject or initiating some other activity. Just as we respond to these discriminative stimuli, we also use them to control the behavior of others. We do this most directly, of course, when issuing commands or instructions. "Bring me that file" is discriminative for the listener, specifying the occasion upon which that response will be reinforced by the approval of the speaker. Some verbal stimuli even go so far as to spell out the response-reinforcement contingency: "Sell a thousand magazines and win a trip to Europe . . ."; "You may have your dessert as soon as you finish your peas."; "We'll give you a 25-cent-an-hour increase if you agree not to strike for the next 3 years."

In the social milieu of the human group, the fact that verbal symbols are discriminative for social behavior makes this form of behavior more complex than any other. It is through symbols that man is able to manufacture the crucial parameters of his own environment—a highly responsive environment capable of determining his social behavior. It is man's ability to develop and use symbols, especially verbal ones, that gives him a decided advantage over other organisms. Consequently, much of the socialization process involves learning to respond to the discriminative stimuli provided by the groups to which one belongs. Important discriminative stimuli include specific individuals as physical stimuli; others' verbal behavior, including statements indicating how we ought to behave in certain circumstances (norms); one's own description of one's physical characteristics and behavior (self-concept); situationally appropriate patterned behavior (roles); style and quality of clothing; and titles. Because the discriminative functions of verbal and other social stimuli have such particular importance for sociology, they will be discussed further in Part III.

Sequences of behavior leading to reinforcement are often long and complicated. Within such sequences, the first response is discriminative for the second, which is discriminative for the third, and so on. An entire sequence of this type is called a *response chain*. The executive calling his board meeting does not do so with a single response, but with a series of actions leading up to the meeting. That is, the completion of each response, or link, sets the occasion for the next response. To appreciate the strength of such chains one need only break a familiar chain and attempt to recite the alphabet backward, or recall the difficulty of executing the getting-to-work chain on the morning that frozen pipes eliminated the usual cup of coffee.

CONDITIONED REINFORCERS

Now that both positive and negative consequences have been discussed, it seems reasonable to consider the zero-point or neutral consequence. The neutral consequence, as its name implies, is one having no effect upon the subsequent occurrence of the behavior which precedes it. In the analysis of social behavior, however, the neutral consequence is an extremely important stimulus because of its uncommitted status. It is, in a manner of speaking, a nonaligned recruit capable of being developed into either a reinforcing or a punishing stimulus.

A mother ministering to her newborn child is frequently in the position of delivering strong primary, or unconditioned, reinforcers by feeding, changing, and fondling the infant. Food, the case in point. is a primary positive reinforcer because it alleviates a state of physiological deprivation. The reinforcing food, however, is not delivered *in vacuo*; the occasion is a social one and in all probability the mother is smiling and talking to the child as it is fed. The smile and the mother's voice in no way reduce the child's hunger, but they are present when the reinforcing event of feeding occurs. Indeed, when food is delivered, the smile and voice are, almost invariably, associated with it until they and even the sight of the mother's face take on reinforcing capabilities. The smile, originally a neutral stimulus, has become a secondary or *conditioned* positive reinforcer capable of increasing the frequency of behaviors which precede it.

From this example and the previous discussion of discriminative stimuli it is possible to extract a general rule: In order to act as a conditioned reinforcer for any response, a stimulus must have status as a discriminative stimulus for some response (Keller and Schoenfeld, 1950). The rule states two things. First, in order to transform a neutral stimulus into a conditioned positive reinforcer it must be presented so as to become discriminative for reinforcement. Second, once it has become a conditioned reinforcer in one situation, it can function as a reinforcer in other situations.

The process of developing a neutral stimulus into a secondary reinforcer has extremely important social implications because reinforcement (or punishment) is seldom delivered in isolation—it is embedded in a matrix of social events, it is the stuff of social interaction. Under normal circumstances the conditioned reinforcers, developed through their association with primary or previously conditioned reinforcers, pyramid rather quickly. Consider the case of the feral children reported by Kingsley Davis (1947). Anna and Isabelle lacked virtually all of the behaviors typical of children their age and were not responsive to the attentions of other people. Since the history of association between primary reinforcement and social attention was lacking, smiles and adult vocalizations were not reinforcing for these girls and consequently were incapable of affecting their behavior.

In our culture, the smile and the word "GOOD" are generally established as effective conditioned reinforcers very early in an individual's life (Harris, Wolf, and Baer, 1964). As such, they can be used to strengthen a wide variety of culturally approved behaviors; and their opposite counterparts, the frown and "BAD," have wide use as conditioned positive punishers. It is in this way that the previously discussed "threat of punishment" comes to control the behavior of a well-socialized individual. The threat, as a conditioned punisher, can affect the behaviors which precede it so that the actual delivery of an unconditioned punishing stimulus such as a severe spanking is rarely necessary. Occasionally, however, individuals are observed who do not seem appropriately responsive to these stimuli; as a result, their behaviors present problems for the community. The autistic child is an extreme example, but the "culturally deprived" child, the delinquent, and other groups of so-called deviants also manifest behavioral deficits which can be attributed to the ineffectiveness of such culturally determined conditioned reinforcers as the words "GOOD" and "BAD." This topic will be discussed more fully in Part III, but in the present context it should be noted that money, the very general reinforcer which carries such weight in our society, simply is not effective in modifying the behavior of people who have not gone through the elaborate training process which establishes it as "valuable." Consequently, rather than lamenting the absence of a "Protestant ethic" or the appropriate quantity of "achievement motivation," we need to learn how to employ gains in money or status (another conditioned reinforcer of great importance) to strengthen "entrepreneurial" or "achievement" behavior.

These last examples have dealt with a special kind of conditioned reinforcer—the *generalized reinforcer*. Reinforcers of this type have great power and importance in social analyses because they retain their effectiveness in the absence of any specific deprivation. The term "generalized" refers to the fact that these stimuli stand for, represent, or provide access to a wide range of other reinforcers, both unconditioned and conditioned, which may differ from time to time and from person to person. Social status and money are excellent examples of generalized reinforcers, and both share a number of important characteristics. When received, money is typically a token of approval or an award for "good" service and thus would be expected to acquire reinforcing properties according to the discrimination process already discussed. Once in hand, however, money may set the occasion for the acquisition of a host of other conditioned reinforcers. Obviously, many states of physiological deprivation can be alleviated or avoided if the individual who is hungry, thirsty, or exposed can purchase food, drink, clothing, and shelter. Beyond this, however, the individual who has been taught to value (or be reinforced by) a late-model automobile, a fashionable address, an exclusive education, stylish dress, or a cordless electric carving knife will find the acquisition of these reinforcers intimately associated with the local monetary exchange unit. As money is discriminative first for one reinforcer and then another, it becomes more and more reinforcing in itself. Furthermore, because of the variety of associations, this generalized stimulus is not tied directly to any single deprivation state, a fact which also means that large amounts of money will not result in satiating the individual. Similarly, social status is such a broadly generalized reinforcer that it is hard to overemphasize its importance as a means for modifying social behavior.

SHAPING BEHAVIOR

Largely for linguistic reasons, the preceding discussion may have generated some misconceptions which now need to be reconsidered. In those instances where it appeared that a specific response was emitted because of the reinforcement which followed it, two things are incorrect. First, of course, independent variables do not follow dependent variables. A response does not occur because of the reinforcement that will follow; it occurs because in the past, under similar circumstances, a similar response has been followed by reinforcement. It is this past history which has altered the probability of a response occurring or not occurring under present conditions, and very little can be said about current behavior without considerable knowledge of that history.

The second difficulty is created by the word "response." When a response is reinforced, it is not a specific response that has been strengthened; rather, all responses in the same *class* have been strengthened. Behavior normally occurs with slight variations, and the reinforcement of one of these tends to strengthen many of the variations which make up the response class. A response class can be illustrated effectively by referring to the familiar curve of a binomial distribution. Consider the curve as a representation of the various probabilities of the different variations of a response class. In a given situation the highest point on the curve represents the most probable response, while the tails of the curve represent

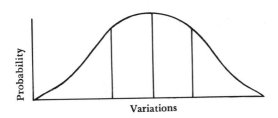

Variations

low-probability variations. In the event that the high-probability variation is emitted and reinforced, its probability is increased and so is the probability of the variations on either side. The generalization effect of the reinforcement, however, follows the same general curve, having its greatest influence on the more similar variations and less effect on the more extreme cases. Consequently, the end result of reinforcing the central variation is to make the entire probability curve alter its shape, becoming slightly more peaked and exhibiting reduced variability. An exaggerated illustration of this change would appear as follows:

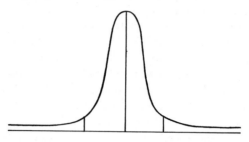

Precisely because of these characteristics it is possible to develop new response *classes* through operant procedures. Shaping, as the name suggests, is a procedure comparable to that employed by the artist who carefully molds an intricate form out of an undifferentiated lump of clay. The shaping of behavior is the differential reinforcement of successive approximations toward the terminal state desired. As an illustration, suppose that we wish to develop a behavior which lies completely outside the range of variations presently existing in the relevant response class. Schematically, such a situation might look like this:

Existing Response Class   Desired Behavior

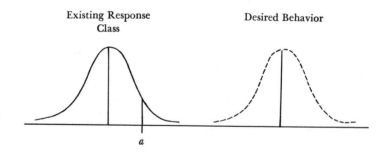

a

In the existing response class, some of the lower-probability variations are closer approximations of the desired behavior than the central or most probable variation. If one of these (for example, the low-probability but existing variation at *a*) is selected for differential reinforcement, its future probability will be increased. As before, reinforcing this particular variation also will increase the probability of similar variations and have less effect upon the extremes. Because the reinforcement is being provided differentially for the variation at *a*, it is being withheld from the original high-probability behavior at the center of the curve with the result that its probability is being reduced. After repeatedly selected variations which more and more closely approximate the terminal behavior, a vastly modified set of response probabilities (a new response class) is observed which centers on the desired terminal response.

This procedure of differential reinforcement allows complex behaviors to be developed out of simpler, less sophisticated responses. Consider, for example, the simple case of shaping up the vocal operant "WATER." Without going into an extensive operant

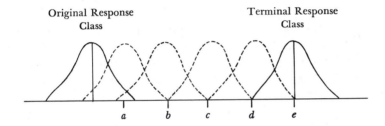

analysis of the development of verbal behavior (Skinner, 1957), it is reasonable to suppose that recording an infant's vocal behavior would reveal that the sound "ooo" was the most frequently emitted. Somewhere within this class of vocal operants, however, would lie the less frequent response "AW." From a knowledge of the infant's feeding schedule, a parent might be able to select times during the day when a drink of water would be an effective primary reinforcer. Wishing to develop the "AW" sound, the mother might provide repeated vocal examples, or she might simply sit and wait for the sound to be emitted. In either case, the desired "AW" would *immediately* produce a drink for the child together with effusive praise and laughter from the delighted mother. On subsequent occasions, represented by *c* in the illustration above, the water might be provided contingent upon "AWA," which stands as an approximation somewhere between the original "AW" and the desired response, "WATER." At about point *d* a baby sitter is present when the child starts emitting a variety of vocal responses centering around the sound "WAWA" but also including such variations as

"WANA," "WALA," and "WADA." In the event that the "WADA" response produces water fetching by the baby sitter whereas "WAWA" fails to, the former will, of course, be differentially reinforced and its future appearance will be more frequent. Subsequent training, either by prompting or simply because of quicker fetching of the water, may lead to the replacement of the approximation "WADA" by "WADUR" as the most likely in the presence of the twin discriminative stimuli of thirst and another person. The final step to "WATER" may also result simply because clearer enunciation produces a quicker response from the environment.

Unfortunately, skillful shaping is still closer to being an art than a science and many crippling errors can occur along the way. Happily, however, the normal environment often operates effectively to provide the necessary differential reinforcement. The thirsty child is understood more readily and thus more quickly reinforced the more closely he approximates the word "WATER." This also emphasizes the fact that, in shaping, the immediacy of the reinforcement is critical if it is to be differential. Thus the parent, teacher, executive training program director, or anyone who is assigned the task of shaping up certain defined behaviors in "unsocialized" individuals must be able to provide immediate differential reinforcement for appropriate approximations. If the parent withholds reinforcement while waiting for an approximation which is not contained within the existing response class, the gains up to that point may be lost through extinction and the entire sequence will have to be repeated. Such errors are not uncommon. The "culturally deprived" child who enters the first grade without benefit of special training may have to interact with a teacher who, as a result of her own past history, has very set expectations about the abilities of six-year-olds. If her standards are beyond the reach of the child, and if she reinforces only according to her standards, a situation is created in which the child is unable to receive any reinforcement from the teacher. Under these circumstances, high-probability behaviors from outside the classroom are likely to take over and undoubtedly meet with punishment from the teacher. In a setting where reinforcement is absent and punishment is present, "dropout" behavior is a form of self-preservation.

From the preceding illustration it may be concluded with good reason that the shaping process is a focal point of the behavioral model for learning. It is also a basic process in a new set of therapeutic techniques known as *behavior modification* (Ullman and Krasner, 1965; Krasner and Ullman, 1965). The general procedure for behavior modification, clearly outlined by Reese (1966), is adapted here both as a summary for many of the preceding points and as a lead-in to the chapters which follow.

1. The initial step in a program of behavior modification is to identify in very specific terms the final performance that is sought. Certainly, until the terminal response is defined, there is no way to recognize, much less reinforce, an approximation. Very different responses would have been reinforced in the previous example if the mother was trying to develop the response "DADDY" instead of "WATER."

2. It is necessary to determine the nature of the existing response classes or the operant level of the subject. The earlier assumption that the thirsty baby's response repertoire contained "AW" was needed in order to chart a course of approximations between the initial and terminal states. In actual practice, of course, operant levels are never assumed; they are measured with great care.

3. With a course of action in mind it is next necessary to construct or select a favorable situation for the training. This means eliminating distracting stimuli, the possibility of conflicting or incompatible behavior, and providing stimuli which are discriminative for the desired response. Rather than selecting a grocery store or a railroad station as the site for shaping the "WATER" response, a familiar room and a prominently displayed glass of water would be preferred. Though this may appear a bit of common sense not worthy of explicit mention, one has only to look at the typical classroom to appreciate that the creation of a favorable situation is often given less attention than it deserves.

4. When the foregoing conditions have been met, it is then necessary to consider the problem of establishing motivation in the subject: child, student, trainee, etc. This involves nothing more or less than locating and securing control of an effective reinforcer. Water solves the problem for a thirsty baby, but in most cases practicality militates for the use of a generalized reinforcer such as money, social attention, or status. This is true partly because inconvenience is involved in determining the deprivation state along a single dimension, and partly because an isolated deprivation may be quickly alleviated, thus bringing an end to the motivation and the training.

5. The shaping itself involves, as noted above, the differential

reinforcement of responses that are successively closer to the terminal state. The criterion for reinforcement must be raised gradually. Too high a criterion will result in extinction and necessitate backing up several steps to an earlier approximation. Failing to raise the criterion when it has been met can result in a single approximation receiving repeated reinforcement. Such an overdose can disproportionately strengthen a single variation and so narrow the distribution of other variations that the result is a highly stereotyped response. In the absence of considerable response variability, further shaping is extremely difficult.

6. In this abbreviated version of Reese's outline, the final step involves modifying the sustaining contingencies by thinning out to a more intermittent schedule or, in many cases, turning the reinforcement over to the "natural" environment. Many behaviors require careful shaping, but once established, they are maintained because they provide access to reinforcement not previously available. The reinforcers employed to shape bicycle riding, for example, may be qualitatively different from those which maintain it. Academic learning may require extensive support during the shaping or acquisition period; later, however, skillful intellectual performance may produce occasional reinforcers so subtle that the activity might, on the basis of casual observation, be called "self-reinforcing."

Other aspects of the shaping process will be illuminated in later chapters, but for the present it should be observed that the refinement of our knowledge about these procedures is particularly critical to sociology. To date, experimenters working with operant behavior have concentrated on the maintenance of behavior under various contingencies and have given us little that is systematic or lawful regarding the shaping process, although there are exceptions (Stoddard and Sidman, 1967). Unfortunately, most researchers often do not even turn on their recording apparatus until a response has been shaped and is present in some strength. The backgrounds which sociologists and social psychologists might bring to this problem from the fields of socialization, the development of values, and normative behavior could be of tremendous value in furthering study in this area.

Throughout the rest of this book numerous other possibilities for the mutually beneficial conjunction of sociological issues and behavioral analysis will be indicated. As Homans has already noted, there is nothing to be gained by charging reductionism. Behavioral analysis provides some new tools which sociologists are in a position to exploit in a unique way.

At this point it is advisable that the reader have the opportunity to encounter some of the empirical evidence generated by specific researches undertaken against the background provided by these behavioral principles. Thus the remainder of Part I consists of reports of a group of recent laboratory investigations reflecting, in varying degrees, a concern for the learning process which is far more explicit than is customary in small-group research. More importantly, these chapters demonstrate some of the basic principles of the experimental analysis of social behavior far more effectively than they can be explained by mere exposition.

In these five chapters the problems under study touch at the core of some extremely complex social processes. At the current state of the art, significant progress can often be made in such issues by distilling their essential ingredients for precise analysis under laboratory conditions. Whereas the investigators in Part I chose to bring the "outside world" into the laboratory, the contributors of the following Part took the opposite course by adapting laboratory practices to institutional settings. There is nothing inherent in the approach which restricts it to one arena or the other. The more fruitful course must be determined for each case as it arises.

Schmitt's opening article on worker supervision is, for instance, a laboratory study because the necessity for the delicate manipulation of supervisory behavior would have been highly disruptive to any regular production system. The further requirement for precisely measuring worker response would have so altered the environment of a normal factory that it would have looked like a laboratory anyway. It is the results of the study, however, rather than Schmitt's tactics, which are of central interest. One suggestive finding, for example, was that penalties for being off the job were effective in maintaining work behavior only when supervision occurred at variable intervals. Such a finding obviously has relevance to education and law enforcement, and to the processes of social control in general.

The following article by Baer, Peterson, and Sherman describes their work with three extremely retarded children in a hospital setting. In spite of the clarity of the writing this article may present some difficulties for the reader simply because of the complexity of its research design. Careful study will be rewarded, however, for the narrative recounts the process whereby the children were taught to imitate the behavior of others by a step-by-step program of differential reinforcement. These were children who had no imitative behavior at the beginning of the study; thus its development provides some fascinating insights into the general process of how social discriminative stimuli may be acquired. To some readers this will suggest new avenues for the empirical analysis of role models or the "significant other." In addition, Baer and his colleagues have made some provocative discoveries about the development of normative behavior. The well-socialized individual conforms to the behavioral norms of his community even though he has not been schooled in each specific normative requirement. The behavior of the subjects in the imitation study led the authors to hypothesize that the act of producing a response matching that of the model became a conditioned reinforcer for these children. Is this what we mean when we say that some people place a high "value" on conformity? If so, the relevance of this investigation extends well beyond the immediate problem of therapy for retarded children.

The three remaining studies in Part I employ group responses rather than individual or aggregate responses as their dependent variable. That is, a number of individuals must behave in concert before a response is defined. Two of these studies even required different but complementary behaviors from the cooperative group members before a response was recorded.

The results of the Mithaug and Burgess study indicate that holding reinforcement contingent upon the production of parallel cooperative responses (three subjects making the same response at the same time) was not effective in producing such behavior. Indeed, all the signs point to the fact that the practice of trying to shape cooperation by group reinforcement results in the extinction of cooperative responding because of ratio strain. It is just too big a step to take. If, however, the response is initially shaped by differentially reinforcing individual rather than group responding, cooperative behavior can apparently be maintained by a combination of group reinforcement and simple feedback to the individual.

The research by Wiggins experimentally evaluates the persistence and the changes which can be brought about in the reward distributions utilized by groups composed of persons having clearly differentiated roles. The results indicate that even as complex an activity as the distribution of scarce group resources is functionally related to the consequences following this distribution. It is of additional interest that the relationship between distribution and consequence held regardless of whether or not the subjects were "aware" of it.

The final study in Part I, by Burgess, represents an attempt to bring order to the previously diverse empirical findings of communication network studies. By recognizing the impact of learning principles it was discovered that group problem solving exhibits a substantial transition or acquisition period. As a result of controlling first for the variable effects of the acquisition or shaping period and subsequently for the variability generated by differential motivational factors, substantial order developed out of what had previously been a confusing array of conflicting results. Although differences in problem-solving rates did exist between the two networks studied during the initial acquisition phase, these differences were reduced when reinforcement was employed. Differences were still smaller if the groups were allowed to pass through the acquisition period to a steady state; and finally, when reinforcement was added to the steady-state period, performance differences between the two structures vanished.

An important test of any experimental technique is how much added leverage it affords in field situations. One of the bright promises of the experimental analysis of behavior is the way in which it has generated field-relevant techniques for changing behavior. Behavior modification in its worst (unscientific) form simply alters response frequencies by manipulating appropriate environmental consequences. No attempt is made at systemic data gathering. In its best form the modifications are carried out according to the basic tenets of laboratory observation. The fact that such field techniques are possible within this framework augurs well for the development of self-correcting procedures which will improve as data accumulate. With such a tight bond between the laboratory and the field, progress in each must surely be enhanced. Though this topic is dealt with in following chapters, it should be noted here that this is the path which Professor Homans pointed out as leading to the real task of behavioral sociology.

REFERENCES

Ayllon, T., and N. H. Azrin, 1966. Punishment as a discriminative stimulus and conditioned reinforcer with humans. *Journal of the Experimental Analysis of Behavior, 9,* pp. 411-419.

Azrin, N. H., and W. C. Holz, 1966. Punishment. In W. K. Honig (Ed.), *Operant Behavior: Areas of Research and Application.* New York: Appleton-Century-Crofts, pp. 380-447.

Bijou, S. W., and D. M. Baer, 1961. *Child Development: Vol. 1, Systematic and Empirical Theory.* New York: Appleton-Century-Crofts.

Burgess, R. L., and R. L. Akers, 1966. Are operant principles tautological? *The Psychological Record, 16,* pp. 305-312.

Davis, K. 1947. Final note on a case of extreme isolation. *American Journal of Sociology, 43,* pp. 432-437.

Harris, F. R., M. M. Wolf, and D. M. Baer, 1964. Effects of adult social reinforcement on child behavior. *Young Children, 20,* pp. 8-17.

Keller, F. S., and W. N. Schoenfeld, 1950. *Principles of Psychology.* New York, Appleton-Century-Crofts.

Krasner, L., and L. P. Ullman (Eds.), 1965. *Research in Behavior Modification.* New York: Holt, Rinehart & Winston.

Morse, W. H. 1966. Intermittent reinforcement. In W. K. Honig (Ed.), *Operant Behavior: Areas of Research and Application.* New York: Appleton-Century-Crofts, pp. 52-108.

Nurnberger, J. I., C. B. Ferster, and J. P. Brady, 1963. *An Introduction to the Science of Human Behavior.* New York: Appleton-Century-Crofts.

Reese, E. P. 1966. The analysis of human operant behavior. In J. Vernon (Ed.), *Introduction to Psychology: a Self-Selection Textbook.* Dubuque, Iowa: William C. Brown Company.

Skinner, B. F. 1957. *Verbal Behavior.* New York: Appleton-Century-Crofts.

Stoddard, L. T., and M. Sidman, 1967. The effects of errors on children's performance on a circle-ellipse discrimination. *Journal of the Experimental Analysis of Behavior, 10,* pp. 261-270.

Ullman, L. P., and L. Krasner (Eds.), 1965. *Case Studies in Behavior Modification.* New York: Holt, Rinehart & Winston.

2

Punitive Supervision and Productivity:
An Experimental Analog

David R. Schmitt

As is characteristic of a great many facets of complex human behavior, little is known about the parameters which determine its shape. Described in this chapter is an attempt to isolate in a laboratory situation behavioral variables which appear in a very frequent social setting—the supervision of one individual by another.

In organizations, relationships involving supervision form one of the primary bases of social control—the means that ensure that persons within the organization will act in the desired manner. Thus supervision may involve a number of diverse activities, such as job planning, delegation of duties, communication of orders, and enforcement of work rules, which bear directly or indirectly on the job performance of the supervised individual. The focus of a number of studies of supervision involving a variety of types of work groups has been the effects of the *presence* or *absence* of such activities or their combinations on worker productivity (e.g., Coch and French, 1948; Katz, Maccoby, and Morse, 1950; Katz, Maccoby, Gurin, and Floor, 1951; Gouldner, 1954; Argyle, Gardner, and Coifi, 1957, 1958; Likert, 1961; Day and Hamblin, 1964).

Reprinted in part from the *Journal of Applied Psychology*, 53 (1969), pp. 118-123, with permission of the author and the American Psychological Association.

The study was supported by The Cooperative Research Program of The Office of Education (Project No. S-319) and by The Graduate Research Committee of the University of Wisconsin. I wish to thank Lois Loddeke for her assistance in the research and L. Keith Miller and Robert Shotola for their suggestions and criticisms.

Supervision, however, is characterized by more than simply the presence or absence of various activities. The supervisor's choice of activities constitutes only one of the dimensions of what may be defined as his style of supervision. Of additional importance, although largely unexplored, may be the manner in which these activities are *scheduled*. Two characteristics define the schedule of an activity: its *frequency* and its *regularity*. Thus any supervisory activity can occur at various frequencies and at intervals which may be either regular or irregular.

The potential effects of different supervisory schedules would appear to be greater for some activities than for others. For those such as job planning which usually occur infrequently and involve little interpersonal contact, the effects may be slight. However, for others which occur often or involve direct contact between the supervisor and the worker, the effects may be substantial. For example, a common function of supervision is to control the amount of work activity on an assigned job. In many settings supervisors "check up" on a subordinate to ensure that he is following his assignment. The importance of the *frequency* of such check-ups has been suggested in research by Katz and his associates (1950, 1951) comparing the effects of close and general styles of supervision. In these studies supervisors of less productive workers were found to be more likely to use close supervision involving frequent check-ups and task instructions. In explanation, Kahn and Katz (1960) suggest that most workers desire maximum autonomy and that supervision in a manner that does not permit it leads to lower morale and motivation. Other research, however, suggests that these effects may be limited to certain types of settings and production technologies (Argyle et al., 1957; Dubin, 1965).

Although unexplored, the *regularity* of the supervisory activities may have other important effects on work patterns. For example, where supervisory check-ups are used, it might be predicted that regular check-ups will be less effective than irregular ones in ensuring job performance. With regular check-ups the worker may learn the periods during which he needs to be present in order to coincide with the appearance of the supervisor, and thus may spend little additional time on the job. With irregular check-ups, however, he may find such anticipation difficult or impossible, and thus must remain on the job for longer periods.

Such examples suggest the potentially important, diverse effects of the schedule of an activity in supervisory situations, and recommend its more systematic investigation in evaluating the effectiveness of various supervisory practices. The general lack of research on schedule as an element of supervision style may have been dictated in part by the field research techniques typically used in previous studies on supervision. In general, field methods do not permit the measurement and control necessary to determine the effects which this aspect of supervision may have on productivity, even though under some conditions such techniques may determine the effectiveness of the supervisory activity.

However, the effects of the schedules of various behavioral consequences, such as punishment, *have* been studied, but in another type of setting—the experimental laboratory, where sufficient measurement and control may be obtained. Thus it may prove desirable initially to describe the effects of various schedules of reinforcement or punishment experimentally, and then to determine the extent to which the results may be generalized to nonexperimental supervisory situations.

In the experimental study of task choice, a minimal task situation has been developed which permits the introduction of several conditions appearing to be functionally analogous to those in a nonexperimental situation involving the supervisor's use of checkups and sanctions to maximize the amount of time spent in work. The subject in the experimental setting is confronted by two concurrent operants: spatially distinct tasks or responses available simultaneously to him (Ferster and Skinner, 1957; Catania, 1966). As with single operants, these tasks are simple, readily repeatable, and easily measured, for example, pressing a lever or button, pulling a knob. Different schedules of reinforcement or punishment are generally programmed for each of the operants. In such a multitask situation, various consequences may be manipulated to attempt to eliminate an individual's behavior on one of these operants while increasing it on a second. Such a condition appears to be functionally equivalent to the supervisor's use of various means to attempt to maximize the amount of time a worker spends in task activity while minimizing various unauthorized behaviors. Although previous research in experimental psychology has explored some of the variables controlling concurrent behavior, unfortunately the combinations of conditions which might be generalized to a supervisory setting have not been studied.

The study described below attempts to demonstrate the manner in which the effects of one type of consequence, punishment, can be explored under conditions relevant to the study of the effectiveness of supervision. Punishment of various magnitudes was administered on two basic schedules for behavior on one of the two tasks.

PUNITIVE CONSEQUENCES AND TASK CHOICE

In its broadest sense punitive control includes a variety of punishing behaviors ranging from fines, threats, or physical abuse to more subtle acts such as criticism, ridicule, slights, snubs, or avoidance, and thus is manifest, at least to some degree, in almost all supervisory situations. The focus of this study was on two variables relevant to its use in affecting the choice of activities: the *magnitude* of the punitive consequences and the *schedule* with which they were administered. Two types of schedules, fixed and variable-interval, were explored. Earlier studies of two-task settings have not investigated the effects of interval punishment on task choice. Rather, in previous research involving concurrent operants (Reynolds, 1963) or two-choice risk-taking situations (Kogan and Wallach, 1967), punishment for one of the choices either was continuous or occurred for a particular proportion of the task responses. In general, such studies suggest a tendency toward the elimination of the punished behavior as the negative consequences become high. The effects of fixed and variable-interval schedules of punishment have been compared using a single operant (Azrin, 1956). The results indicate that variable-interval schedules tend to produce more response suppression.

METHOD

SETTING

The experimental setting in this study involved a choice of two activities, each of which was reinforced. Both activities were button-pressing tasks located at opposite ends of a small workroom. For each task, the subject was reinforced for pressing a large button mounted on an instrument panel. The reinforcer was money, and a counter mounted on the panel indicated how much money the subject had earned. The tasks differed in the amount of money that could be earned for them. The number of presses required before a reinforcement count was registered was greater for one of the tasks. To standardize the *rate* at which different subjects could work on either task, a 3-second time-out occurred after each response. The number of responses for each cent earned on the higher-paying task (Task B) was half that of the other (Task A). With four responses for each cent required on Task B, subjects could earn approximately $2.80 per hour; with eight responses required for each cent on Task A, subjects could earn $1.40. Thus, of the two, Task B was presumably the more attractive.

The effectiveness of the punitive consequences in changing task behavior was studied under conditions in which its interpretation would be relatively unambiguous. The consequences were evaluated regarding the degree to which they produced behavior on Task A, the less attractive task. Thus work on Task B, the more attractive task, was punished. In most nonexperimental settings the unauthorized activities which the supervisor punishes are probably not consistently more attractive than any other activity including the work itself, as was the case in this study. Thus, if the consequences are effective in eliminating an activity which is considerably more attractive than any other situational alternative, they are likely to be at least as effective in other situations where the alternatives are of more nearly equal attractiveness.

Work on Task B, the higher-paying alternative, was periodically penalized by a loss of money. Only one of the two tasks was operable at a time. A subject-controlled switch on Task A determined which task could be used. The time at which work on Task B would be penalized was indicated by the sounding of a buzzer, regardless of which task the subject was on. A penalty was administered only if the subject had Task B switched on when the buzzer sounded. A penalty count was added on a separate counter in the workroom; the amount of the penalty for that session was posted next to the counter. No consequences accompanied the buzzer if Task A was being operated. Since the change-over from work on Task B to Task A resulted in a delay of several seconds while the subject crossed the room and turned on Task A, frequent switching to avoid penalties resulted in reduced reinforcement on either task. A clock on the wall was visible at all times.

All events and measures were programmed and recorded by automated equipment in an adjacent room.

PROCEDURE

The subjects were college students who were informed before

volunteering that they would have an opportunity to make money on a laboratory task. Thereafter, they were told only how the tasks could be operated and that the sound of the buzzer would be followed by a loss of money if they were working on Task B.

The effects of penalty magnitudes were explored under both fixed-interval (FI) and variable-interval (VI) schedules of supervision. Different subjects were used for each of the schedules. Within a schedule, however, subjects were exposed to penalties of several different magnitudes. Changes in penalty were made only after the subjects evidenced stability in task work under a given condition. Since this investigation focused on the extensive study of several subjects in each variation, a statistical analysis of the performance was judged not to be appropriate. Rather, similar patterns of response were sought in response to changes in the experimental conditions.

The subjects worked in sessions of 1–4 hours several times a week. Payment was made at the conclusion of the total hours of work.

RESULTS

Fixed-Interval Supervision Schedules

Seven subjects worked over periods ranging from 4–14 hours on several fixed-interval schedules in which the buzzer sounded after time periods of equal length throughout a work session. The different schedules included time intervals of 1, 3, 5, or 10 minutes. Penalties from $0.02 to $2.00 were used. Subjects worked at least 1 hour under each penalty.

The results indicated that none of the fixed-interval punishment schedules was effective in producing a substantial amount of activity on Task A. Figure 1 shows the percentage of time spent by five subjects on Task A, working on one of the schedules (FI 3 minutes) under various penalty conditions. After less than 1 hour of work under any of the schedules and penalty magnitudes, none of the subjects spent more than 30 per cent of his time on Task A. With experience on a schedule subjects avoided virtually all penalties by switching from Task A immediately after the buzzer sounded and switching back again a few seconds before the next buzzer.

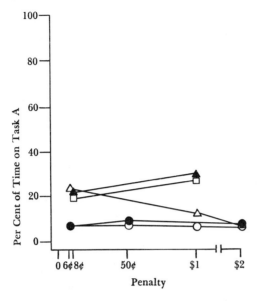

Fig. 1. Percentage of time spent on Task A under various penalty conditions using a fixed-interval schedule (FI 3 minutes.)

VARIABLE-INTERVAL SCHEDULE

Four subjects worked over periods ranging from 24–37 hours on variable-interval schedules in which the buzzer sounded after time periods of varying lengths. One schedule was used with an average of 4 minutes for each interval. The intervals varied between 10 seconds and 8 minutes. Penalties from $0.01 to $1.00 were used.

During the subjects' first 2 hours of work on this schedule no penalties were administered although the buzzer continued to sound at the various intervals. In the remaining hours for each subject, two progressions of penalties were used. Two subjects were begun on high penalties which were progressively decreased when intersession stability was achieved. The other two subjects were begun on low penalties which were progressively increased. Several penalty magnitudes were repeated after intervening periods of work under other penalties to determine the replicability of effects. Subjects worked at least 2 hours under each penalty condition.

Figure 2 shows the proportion of time that the subjects spent on Task A under the various penalty magnitudes. The results indicate that variable-interval punishment was effective in producing activity on Task A. For all subjects the proportion of time spent on Task A increased with rising penalty size. Small penalties (less than $0.03) had a slight effect on task behavior, while moderate penalties of $0.05 to $0.15 considerably increased the time spent on Task A. After several hours of work high penalties, of $0.25 or more, generally resulted in time spent only on Task A. No pronounced effects appear to be caused by penalty sequence. Task performance under the various penalty conditions showed considerable stability and replicability, particularly under the extremes. For example, hourly differences in proportion of time on Task A under a given penalty averaged 9 per cent.

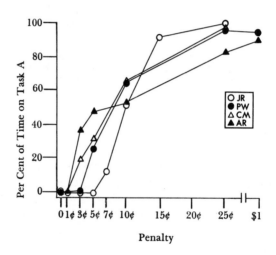

Fɪɢ. 2. Percentage of time spent on Task A under various penalty conditions using a variable-interval schedule (VI 4 minutes). Subjects JR and CM worked under progressively increasing penalties, while AR and PW worked under progressively decreasing ones.

DISCUSSION

The data clearly indicate the importance of different schedules in determining the effects of punishment on task choice. When penalties for work on one of the tasks were scheduled at equal intervals throughout a work period, subjects learned quickly to avoid them. Thus, regardless of their magnitude, the penalties proved relatively ineffective in increasing activity on the unpunished task. In contrast, when the penalties were scheduled at unequal intervals, none of the subjects could spend a large amount of time on the punished task without receiving a number of penalties. Under this condition, the larger the penalties the greater was the time spent on the unpunished task.

Importantly, however, the effectiveness of the variable-interval penalties was not predictable as a direct function of their influence on total earnings. Low and moderate penalties produced more than the predicted amount of work on the unpunished task. Subjects tended to avoid losses, often to the detriment of their total earnings. For example, subjects working on Task A earned approximately $1.40 per hour, on Task B $2.80 per hour. Thus, with an average of 14-15 penalties randomly distributed per hour, subjects could maximize their earnings by working only on Task A with penalties greater than $0.10 and only on Task B with penalties less than $0.10. With $0.10 penalties, remaining on either task would result in approximately the same earnings. The results, however, indicate that with $0.03 penalties only two of the subjects spent no time on Task A during these periods. The other subjects spent 20 and 38 per cent of their time, respectively, on the lower-paying task. With $0.05 penalties only one of the subjects spent no time on Task A, the other subjects spending 26, 32, and 49 per cent of their time, respectively, on that task. For each of these penalty magnitudes the rank-orders of the average amount earned by each subject and the proportion of time spent on the higher-paying task corresponded exactly. With $0.10 penalties, the point at which either task could be selected with little difference in earnings, all of the subjects spent more than half of their time on Task A.

The implication drawn from these findings appears to be an important one for an analysis of the effectiveness of supervision. The results strongly recommend the consideration of not only the type of supervisory activity but also the schedules with which it is performed. As the case of punitive control illustrates, schedule type in conjunction with the magnitude of the punishment may determine in large part the effectiveness of the activity. A generalization of these results to nonexperimental settings, however, should take note of the various limiting characteristics of this research in a "minimal" task situation. To what extent other variables such as task complexity, variety of consequences, number and type of available activities, or group sanctions alter the relationships found in this research will need to be determined.

An important attribute of the kind of experimental setting used in this research is that with little modification the effects of a number of additional variables relevant to the study of supervision may be explored. Examples include the following:

(a) Type of supervisory consequence. Reinforcing as well as punitive consequences for behavior can be readily introduced. For example, check-ups may be followed by monetary bonuses (reinforcement) if the subject is responding on Task A. Other non-monetary consequences, including breaks, praise, and desirable activities, can be programmed as well.

(b) Means of delivering consequences. In the setting described above, check-ups were indicated by a buzzer and were not accompanied by the appearance of a supervisor. The effects of the personal administration of consequences can be measured by having the supervisor himself appear.

(c) Knowledge of supervisory consequences. The presence or absence of stimuli indicating the magnitude of penalties or bonuses can be controlled.

(d) Task characteristics. Variations can be made in both the relative amounts that can be earned on the two tasks and the kinds of payment schedules used for the tasks. Several types of schedules contain contingencies which appear similar to those of piece and fixed-rate payment systems in industry. For example, the use of short-interval or ratio schedules necessitating frequent responses for reinforcement on the lower-paying task would be similar functionally to most piece-rate work, where pay is provided in proportion to the amount of work performed. Similarly, the payment of a fixed amount per session for a specified number of responses would be similar to fixed-rate (hourly or salary) work, where in the short run pay does not vary but a minimum level of performance is usually required for continued employment.

Research varying these conditions will lead to a greater understanding of the manner in which basic processes of control operate to shape or maintain various kinds of behavior in more complex situations.

REFERENCES

Argyle, M., G. Gardner, and F. Coifi, 1957. The measurement of supervisory methods. *Human Relations,* 10, pp. 295-313.

Argyle, M., G. Gardner, and F. Coifi, 1958. Supervisory methods related to productivity, absenteeism and labor turnover. *Human Relations,* 11, pp. 23-40.

Azrin, N. H., 1956. Effects of two intermittent schedules of immediate and nonimmediate punishment. *Journal of Psychology,* 42, pp. 3-21.

Catania, A. C., 1966. Concurrent operants. In W. K. Honig (Ed.), *Operant Behavior: Areas of Research and Application.* New York: Appleton-Century-Crofts, pp. 213-270.

Coch, L., and J. R. P. French, 1948. Overcoming resistance to change. *Human Relations,* 1, pp. 512-532.

Day, R. C., and R. L. Hamblin, 1964. Some effects of close and punitive styles of supervision. *American Journal of Sociology,* 69, pp. 499-510.

Dubin, R., 1965. *Leadership and Productivity.* San Francisco: Chandler Publishing Co., pp. 1-50.

Ferster, C. B., and B. F. Skinner, 1957. *Schedules of Reinforcement.* New York: Appleton-Century-Crofts.

Gouldner, A. W., 1954. *Patterns of Industrial Bureaucracy.* Glencoe, Ill.: Free Press.

Kahn, R. L., and D. Katz, 1960. Leadership practices in relation to productivity and morale. In Dorwin Cartwright and Alvin Zander (Eds.), *Group Dynamics,* 2nd ed., Evanston, Ill.: Row, Peterson Co.

Katz, D., N. Maccoby, G. Gurin, and L. G. Floor, 1951. *Productivity, Supervision and Morale Among Railroad Workers.* Ann Arbor: Survey Research Center, University of Michigan.

Katz, D., N. Maccoby, and N. C. Morse, 1950. *Productivity, Supervision and Morale in an Office Situation,* Part I. Ann Arbor: Survey Research Center, University of Michigan.

Kogan, N., and M. A. Wallach, 1967. Risk taking as a function of the situation, the person, and the group. In *New Directions in Psychology,* Vol. III. New York: Holt, Rinehart & Winston, pp. 113-278.

Likert, R., 1961. *New Patterns of Management.* New York: McGraw-Hill Book Company, pp. 93-94.

Reynolds, G. S., 1963. Potency of conditioned reinforcers based on food and on food and punishment. *Science,* 139, pp. 838-839.

3

The Development of Imitation by Reinforcing

Behavioral Similarity to a Model

Donald M. Baer, Robert F. Peterson, and James A. Sherman

DISCUSSION

The development of a class of behaviors which may fairly be called imitation is an interesting task, partly because of its relevance to the process of socialization in general and language development in particular, and partly because of its potential value as a training technique for children who require special methods of instruction. Imitation is not a specific set of behaviors that can be exhaustively listed. Any behavior may be considered imitative if it temporally follows behavior demonstrated by someone else, called a model, and if its topography is functionally controlled by the topography of the model's behavior. Specifically, this control is such that an observer will note a close similarity between the topography of the model's behavior and that of the imitator. Fur-

Reprinted from the *Journal of the Experimental Analysis of Behavior*, 10 (1967), pp. 405-416, with permission of the authors and the editors. Slightly edited. Copyright © 1967 by the Society for the Experimental Analysis of Behavior, Inc.

A portion of this research was presented at the biennial meeting of the Society for Research in Child Development, Minneapolis, Minnesota, March, 1965. This research was supported by PHS grant MH-02208, National Institute of Mental Health, entitled An Experimental Analysis of Social Motivation. Mr. Frank Junkin, Superintendent, Dr. Ralph Hayden, Medical Director, and other members of the staff of the Fircrest School, Seattle, Washington, made space and subjects available. We wish to thank Mrs. Joan Beavers for her help as a "new" experimenter in the tests of generalization and for assistance in the preparation of this manuscript. Reprints may be obtained from Donald M. Baer, Department of Human Development, University of Kansas, Lawrence, Kansas 66044.

thermore, this similarity to the model's behavior will be characteristic of the imitator in responding to a wide variety of the model's behaviors. Such control could result, for example, if topographical similarity to a model's behavior were a reinforcing stimulus dimension for the imitator.

There are, of course, other conditions which can produce similar behaviors from two organisms on the same occasion or on similar occasions at different times. One possibility is that both organisms independently have been taught the same responses to the same cues; thus, all children recite the multiplication tables in very similar ways. This similarity does not deserve the label imitation and hardly ever receives it; one child's recitation is not usually a cue to another's, and the similarity of their behavior is not usually a reinforcer for the children. Nevertheless, the children of this example have similar behaviors.

The fact that the world teaches many children similar lessons can lead to an arrangement of their behaviors which comes closer to a useful meaning of "imitation." Two children may both have learned similar responses; one child, however, may respond at appropriate times whereas the other does not. In that case, the undiscriminating child may learn to use this response when the discriminating one does. The term "imitation" still need not be applied, since the similarity between the two children's responses is not functional for either of them; in particular, the second child is not affected by the fact that his behavior is similar to that of the first. This arrangement approaches one which Miller and Dollard (1941) called "matched-dependent" behavior. One organism responds to the behavior of another merely as a discriminative stimulus with respect to the timing of his own behavior; many times these behaviors will happen to be alike, because both organisms will typically use the most efficient response, given enough experience.

It should be possible, however, to arrange the behavior of two organisms so that one of them will, in a variety of ways, produce precise topographical similarity to the other, but nothing else. A study by Baer and Sherman (1964) seemingly showed the result of such prior learning in several young children. In that study, reinforcements were arranged for children's imitations of three activities of an animated, talking puppet, which served both as a model and a source of social reinforcement for imitating. As a result of this reinforcement, a fourth response of the puppet was spontaneously imitated by the children, although that imitation had never before been reinforced. When reinforcement of the other three imitations was discontinued, the fourth, never-reinforced imitation also decreased in strength; when reinforcement of the original imitations was resumed, imitation of the fourth response again rose in rate, although it still was never reinforced. In short, these children apparently generalized along a stimulus dimension of similarity between their behaviors and those of a model: when similarity to the model in three different ways was reinforced, they thereupon displayed a fourth way of achieving similarity to the model. Thus, similarity between their behavior and the model's was a functional stimulus in their behavior.

Metz (1965) demonstrated the development of some imitative behavior in two autistic children who initially showed little or no imitative response. In this study, responses similar in topography to demonstrations by the experimenter were reinforced with the word "Good" and food. Metz found that, after intensive training, several imitative responses could be maintained in strength even when not reinforced with food, and that the subjects had a higher probability of imitating new responses after training than before. However, in one of the conditions used to evaluate the subjects' imitative repertoire before and after imitative training, "Good" was still said contingent upon correct new imitations. Thus, for one subject who initially showed a nonzero rate of imitation, it could be argued that the increased imitation in the test after training was due to an experimentally developed reinforcing property of "Good," rather than to the imitation training as such. Furthermore, in the Metz study, because of a lack of extinction or other manipulation of the behavior, it is difficult to specify that the higher probability of imitating new responses, and the maintenance of unreinforced imitative responses, were in fact due to the reinforcement of the initial imitative responses during training.

Lovaas, Berberich, Perloff, and Schaeffer (1966) used shaping and fading procedures to establish imitative speech in two autistic children. They reported that, as training progressed and more vocal behavior came under the control of a model's prior vocalization, it became progressively easier to obtain new imitative vocalizations. When reinforcement was shifted from an imitative-contingent schedule to a basically noncontingent schedule, imitative behavior deteriorated. In an additional manipulation, the model presented Norwegian words interspersed with English words for the children to imitate. Initially, the children did not reproduce the Norwegian words perfectly. However, the authors judged that the subjects gradually improved their imitations of the Norwegian words even though these imitations were not reinforced.

The studies by Baer and Sherman (1964), Metz (1965), and Lovaas et al. (1966), as well as other reports (Bandura, 1962), suggest that for children with truly imitative repertoires, induction has occurred, so that (1) relatively novel behaviors can be developed before direct shaping, merely by providing an appropriate demonstration by a model, and (2) some imitative responses can be maintained, although unreinforced, as long as other imitative responses are reinforced.

The purpose of the present study was to extend the generality of these findings and to demonstrate a method of producing a truly imitative repertoire in children initially lacking one.

METHOD

SUBJECTS

Three children, 9–12 years of age, were selected from several groups of severely and profoundly retarded children in a state school. They were chosen not because they were retarded, but because they seemed to be the only children available of a practical age who apparently showed no imitation whatsoever. (The success of the method to be described suggests that it may have considerable practical value for the training of such children.) The subjects were without language, but made occasional grunting vocalizations and responded to a few simple verbal commands ("Come here," "Sit down," etc.). They were ambulatory (but typically had developed walking behavior relatively late in their development, in the sixth or seventh year), could dress themselves, were reasonably toilet trained, and could feed themselves. Fair eye-hand coordination was evident, and simple manipulatory skills were present.

The subjects were chosen from groups of children initially observed in their wards from a distance over a period of several days. No instances of possible imitation were noted in the subjects finally selected. (That is, on no occasion did any subject display behavior similar to that of another person, except in instances where a common stimulus appeared to be controlling the behaviors of both persons—for example, both going to the dining area when food was displayed on the table.) Subsequently, an experimenter approached and engaged the subjects in extended play. In the course of this play, he would repeatedly ask them to imitate some simple response that he demonstrated, such as clapping his hands or waving. The children failed to imitate any of these responses, although they clearly were capable of at least some of them. Finally, during the training itself, every sample of behavior was initially presented to the child as a demonstration accompanied by the command, "Do this"; at first, none of these samples was imitated, despite extensive repetition.

FIRST TRAINING PROCEDURES

Each subject was seen at mealtimes, once or twice a day, three to five times a week. The subject's food was used as a reinforcer. It was delivered a spoonful at a time by the experimenter, who always said, "Good," just before putting the spoon into the subject's mouth. The subject and the experimenter faced each other across the corner of a small table, on which were placed the food tray and the experimenter's records. Elsewhere in the room were another small table on which were placed some materials used later in the study, a desk with a telephone on it, a coat rack holding one or more coats, a wastebasket, and a few other chairs.

The basic procedure was to teach each subject a series of discriminated operants. Each discriminated operant consisted of three elements: a discriminative stimulus (S^D) presented by the experimenter, a correct response by the subject, and reinforcement after a correct response. The S^D was the experimenter's command, "Do this," followed by his demonstration of some behavior. The response required was one similar to the experimenter's. Thus the operant learned was always topographically imitative of the experimenter's demonstration. The reinforcement was food, preceded by the word "Good."

Since none of the subjects was imitative, none of the initial S^Ds was followed by any behavior which resembled that demonstrated by the experimenter. This was true even for those behaviors which the subjects were clearly capable of performing. Subject 1, for example, would sit down when told to, but did not imitate the experimenter when he said, "Do this," sat down, and then offered her the chair. Hence the initial imitative training for all subjects was accomplished with a combination of shaping (Skinner, 1953) and fading (Terrace, 1963a, 1963b) or "putting through" procedures (Konorski and Miller, 1937).

The first response of the program for Subject 1 was to raise an arm after the experimenter had raised his. The subject was presented with a series of arm-raising demonstrations by the experimenter, each accompanied by "Do this," to which she made no response. The experimenter then repeated the demonstration, reached out, took the subject's hand and raised it for her, and then immediately reinforced her response. After several trials of this sort, the experimenter began gradually to fade out his assistance by raising the subject's arm only part way and shaping the completion of the response. Gradually, the experimenter's assistance was faded until the subject made an unassisted arm-raising response whenever the experimenter raised his arm. The initial responses for all subjects were taught in this manner whenever necessary.

Occasionally during the very early training periods a subject would resist being guided through a response. For example, with a response involving arm raising, Subject 3 at first pulled his arm downward whenever the experimenter attempted to raise it. In this case, the experimenter merely waited and tried again until the arm could be at least partially raised without great resistance; then the response was reinforced. After subjects had received a few reinforcements following the experimenter's assistance in performing a response, they no longer resisted. As the number of responses in the subjects' repertoire increased, the experimenter discontinued the guiding procedure and relied only on shaping procedures when a response did not match the demonstration.

A number of responses, each topographically similar to a demonstration by the experimenter, was taught to each subject. Training of most responses was continued until its demonstration was reliably matched by the subject. The purpose of these initial training procedures was to program reinforcement, in as many and diverse ways as practical, whenever a subject's behavior was topographically similar to that demonstrated by the experimenter.

FURTHER TRAINING PROCEDURES

Probes for Imitation
As the initial training procedures progressed and the subjects

began to come under the control of the experimenter's demonstrations, certain responses were demonstrated which, if imitated perfectly on their first presentation, were deliberately not reinforced on the first or any future occasion. These responses served as probes for the developing imitative nature of the subject's repertoire. A list of the responses demonstrated, including the reinforced ones for the initial training procedure and the unreinforced probe demonstrations, is given in Table 1 for Subject 1. These responses

TABLE 1

The Sequence of Responses Demonstrated to Subject 1
(*Asterisks indicate unreinforced responses.*)

1. Raise left arm.
2. Tap table with left hand.
3. Tap chest with left hand.
4. Tap head with left hand.
5. Tap left knee with left hand.
6. Tap right knee with left hand.
7. Tap nose.
*8. Tap arm of chair.
9. Tap leg of table.
10. Tap leg with left hand.
11. Extend left arm.
*12. Make circular motion with arm.
13. Stand up.
14. Both hands on ears.
15. Flex arm.
16. Nod yes.
17. Tap chair seat.
18. Extend both arms.
19. Put feet on chair.
20. Walk around.
21. Make vocal response.
22. Extend right arm sideways.
23. Tap shoulder.
24. Tap head with right hand.
25. Tap right knee with right hand.
26. Tap leg with right hand.
27. Tap left knee with right hand.
28. Raise right arm overhead.
29. Tap chest with right hand.
30. Tap table with right hand.
31. Move chair.
32. Sit in chair.
33. Throw paper in basket.
34. Pull up socks.
35. Tap desk.
36. Climb on chair.
37. Open door.
38. Move ash tray.
39. Put paper in chair.
40. Sit in two chairs (chained).
41. Tap chair with right hand.
42. Move paper from basket to desk.
43. Move box from shelf to desk.
44. Put on hat.
45. Move hat from table to desk.
46. Move box from shelf to desk.
47. Nest three boxes.
48. Put hat in chair.
49. Tap wall.
50. Move wastebasket.
51. Move paper from desk to table.
52. Stand in corner.
53. Pull window shade.
54. Place box in chair.

55. Walk around desk.
56. Smile.
57. Protrude tongue.
58. Put head on desk.
*59. Ring bell.
60. Nest two boxes.
61. Crawl on floor.
*62. Walk with arms above head.
63. Sit on floor.
64. Put arm behind back (standing).
65. Walk with right arm held up.
66. Throw box.
*67. Walk to telephone.
*68. Extend both arms (sitting).
69. Walk and tap head with left hand.
70. Walk and tap head with right hand.
*71. Walk and clap hands.
*72. Open mouth.
73. Jump.
74. Pat radiator.
*75. Nod no.
76. Pick up phone.
77. Pull drawer.
78. Pet coat.
79. Tear Kleenex.
80. Nest four boxes.
81. Point gun and say, "Bang."
*82. Put towel over face.
*83. Put hands over eyes.
*84. Tap floor.
*85. Scribble.
*86. Move toy car on table.
87. Place circle in form board.
88. Place circle, square, and triangle in form board.
*89. Crawl under table.
*90. Walk and clap sides.
*91. Lie on floor.
*92. Kick box.

*93. Put foot over table rung.
*94. Fly airplane.
*95. Rock doll.
*96. Burp doll.
*97. Tap chair with bat.
*98. Open and close book.
99. Work egg beater.
100. Put arm through hoop.
101. Build three-block tower.
*102. Stab self with rubber knife.
103. Put blocks in ring.
104. Walk and hold book on head.
105. Ride kiddie car.
106. Sweep with broom.
107. Place beads around neck.
108. Ride hobbyhorse.
*109. Put on glove.
110. Use whisk broom on table.
111. Work rolling pin.
*112. Push large car.
113. Put beads on doorknob.
*114. Put hat on hobbyhorse.
115. Sweep block with broom.
116. Place box inside ring of beads.
117. Put glove in pocket of lab coat.
118. Push button on tape recorder.
*119. Bang spoon on desk.
120. Lift cup.
121. Use whisk broom on a wall.
*122. Put a cube in a cup.
123. Rattle a spoon in a cup.
*124. Throw paper on the floor.
*125. Hug a pillow.
126. Tap pegs into pegboard with hammer.
*127. Wave a piece of paper.
*128. Shake a rattle.
*129. Hit two spoons together.
130. Shake a tambourine.

are listed in the order of first demonstration. Subject 1 had 95 reinforced and 35 unreinforced responses. Similar responses were used with Subjects 2 and 3. Subject 2 had 125 reinforced and 5 unreinforced probes; Subject 3 had 8 reinforced responses and 1 reinforced probe.

During the probes, the experimenter continued to present S^Ds for imitation. If the response demonstrated belonged to the group of reinforced responses and the subject imitated within 10 seconds, reinforcement ("Good" and food) was delivered and the next response was demonstrated. If the subject did not imitate within 10 seconds, no reinforcement was delivered and the experimenter demonstrated the next response. If it belonged to the unreinforced group of responses (probes), and if the subject imitated it, there were no programmed consequences and the experimenter demonstrated the next response no sooner than 10 seconds after the subject's imitation. If it was not imitated, the experimenter performed the next demonstration 10 seconds later. The purpose of the 10-second delay was to minimize the possibility that the subjects' unreinforced imitations were being maintained by the possible reinforcing effects of the presentation of an S^D for a to-be-reinforced imitative response. Demonstrations for reinforced and unreinforced responses were presented to subjects in any unsystematic order.

Nonreinforcement of All Imitation
After the probe phase, and after stable performances of reinforced and unreinforced imitative responses were established, nonreinforcement of all imitative behavior was programmed. The purpose of this procedure was to show the dependence of the imitative repertoire on the food reinforcement which was apparently responsible for its development.

Nonreinforcement of imitation was instituted in the form of reinforcement for any behavior other than imitation. Differential reinforcement of other behavior is abbreviated DRO (Reynolds, 1961). The experimenter continued to say, "Good," and to feed the subject, but not contingent on imitations. Instead, the experimenter delivered reinforcement at least 20 seconds after the subject's last imitation had taken place. Thus, for the group of previously reinforced responses, the only change between reinforcement and nonreinforcement periods was a shift in the contingency. For the group of unreinforced or probe responses there was no change;

food reinforcement still did not follow either the occurrence or the nonoccurrence of an imitative response. This procedure involved simultaneously the extinction of imitation and also the reinforcement of whatever other responses may have been taking place at the moment of reinforcement.

For Subject 1, the DRO period was 30 seconds. For Subject 2, DRO periods were 30, 60, and 0 seconds. (DRO 0-second meant that reinforcement was delivered immediately after the S^D, before an imitative response could occur.) This sequence of DRO intervals was used because, as shown later under "Results," Subject 2 maintained stable imitation under the initial DRO procedures, unlike the other subjects. For Subject 3, the DRO period was 20 seconds. After the DRO procedure for each subject, contingent reinforcement of imitation was resumed and the procedures described below were instituted.

Imitative Chains

After reinforcement for imitative behavior was resumed with Subjects 1 and 2, the procedure of chaining together old and new imitations was begun. At first only two-response chains were demonstrated; then three-response chains, after two-response chains were successfully achieved; and so on. During chaining, the experimenter demonstrated the responses that the subject was to imitate as an unbroken series. In all cases, the demonstrated chain contained both responses previously learned by the subject and relatively new ones. Walking from one locale to another in the process of performing these behaviors was not considered part of the imitative chain and was not judged for imitative accuracy.

Verbal Imitations

Late in the training program for Subjects 1 and 3, when virtually any new motor performance by the experimenter was almost certain to be imitated, vocal performances were begun with simple sounds. The experimenter, as usual, said, "Do this," but instead of producing some motor response made a vocal one, for example, "Ah." Subjects 1 and 3 repeatedly failed to imitate such demonstrations. Different procedures were then employed to obtain vocal imitations. For Subject 1, the vocal response to be imitated was set into a chain of nonvocal responses. For example, the experimenter would say, "Do this," rise from his chair and walk to the center of the room, turn toward the subject, say, "Ah," and return to his seat. To such a demonstration Subject 1 responded by leaving her seat, walking toward the center of the room, turning toward the experimenter, and then beginning a series of facial and vocal responses out of which eventually emerged an "Ah" sufficiently similar to the experimenter's to merit reinforcement. This coupling of motor and vocal performances was maintained for several more demonstrations, during which the motor performance was made successively shorter and more economical of motion; finally, the experimenter was able to remain seated, say, "Do this," say, "Ah," and immediately evoke an imitation from the subject. In this manner, simple sounds were shaped and then combined into longer or more complex ones and finally into usable words.

Subject 3, like Subject 1, initially failed to imitate vocalizations. In his case, the experimenter proceeded to demonstrate a set of motor performances which moved successively closer to vocalizations. At first the experimenter obtained imitative blowing out of a lighted match, then blowing without the match, then more vigorous blowing which included an initial plosive "p"; he then added a voiced component to the blowing which was shaped into a "Pah" sound. In this manner a number of vocalizations were produced, all as reliable imitations.

Generalization to Other Experimenters

When the imitative repertoire of Subject 1 had developed to a high level, new experimenters were presented to her, of the opposite or the same sex as the original male experimenter. These novel experimenters gave the same demonstrations as the original experimenter in the immediately preceding session. The purpose of this procedure was to investigate whether the subject's imitative repertoire was limited to demonstrations by the original male experimenter. During this procedure, the new experimenters delivered reinforcement in the same manner as the original experimenter, that is, previously reinforced imitations were reinforced and probes were not.

RESULTS

Reliability of Scoring Imitative Responses

Checks on the reliability of the experimenter's scoring of any response as imitative were made at scattered points throughout the study for Subjects 1 and 2. The percentage of agreement between the experimenter's scoring and the independent records of a second observer exceeded 98 per cent.

FIRST TRAINING PROCEDURES

The initial training procedure contained occasions when the extent of the developing imitative repertoire of each subject could be seen. These were occasions when behavior was demonstrated by the experimenter to the subject for the first time. Any attempt by the subject to imitate such new behavior before direct training or shaping could be attributed to the history of reinforcement for matching other behavior of the experimenter. Thus it was possible to examine the sequence of initial presentations to each subject to discover any increasing probability that new behavior would be imitated on its first presentation.

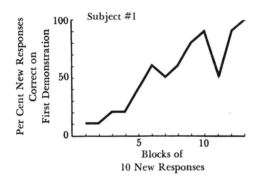

Fig. 1. The development of imitation in Subject 1.

The sequence of 130 responses in Subject 1's program was sufficient to increase her probability of imitating new responses from zero at the beginning of the program to 100 per cent at the end. This was demonstrated by grouping the 130 responses into 13 successive blocks of 10 each. As shown in Fig. 1, the proportion imitated on the first presentation within each block rose, not too steadily but nonetheless clearly, to 100 per cent by the thirteenth block.

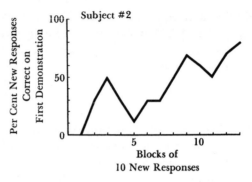

FIG. 2. The development of imitation in Subject 2.

The proportion of new responses successfully imitated by Subject 2 upon their first presentation rose from 0 to 80 per cent through a sequence of 130 new responses, as shown in Fig. 2.

Subject 2 displayed both more variable and less thorough imitation of new responses on their first presentation than did Subject 1, although the general form of the data is similar.

Subject 3 was taught only eight discriminated operants of imitative topography, which he acquired much more rapidly than did either Subject 1 or 2. He imitated the ninth spontaneously on its first presentation, although he had not imitated it before training.

The progressive development of imitation was apparent in other aspects of the data as well. The number of training sessions required to establish new imitations was displayed by plotting this number of sessions for each successive block of 10 new responses. The criterion for establishment of a new imitative response was that, for one trial, a subject displayed the response demonstrated by the experimenter with no shaping or fading procedures required for that trial. This is shown in Fig. 3 for Subject 1 and in Fig. 4 for Subject 2, as solid lines. Both graphs show a systematically decreasing number of sessions required to establish successive new imitations. The dotted portions of each graph represent deviations from the usual type of training procedure and thus are plotted differently. For Subject 1 the dotted portion represents a period in which verbal responses were introduced (not plotted as part of Fig. 3, but discussed later in this report). For Subject 2 the dotted portion represents a sequence of sessions in which few new

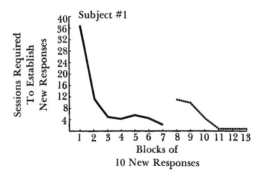

FIG. 3. The rate of development of imitation in Subject 1.

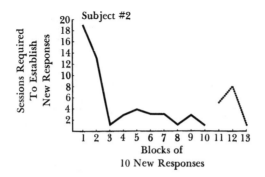

FIG. 4. The rate of development of imitation in Subject 2.

imitative responses were introduced. Rather, two previously established imitative responses of similar topography, which the subject no longer clearly displayed, were worked on intensively.

DRO PROCEDURES

For all subjects, both reinforced and unreinforced imitative behavior was maintained over continuing experimental sessions as long as food reinforcement was contingent upon at least some imitative behavior. When reinforcement was no longer contingent upon imitative behavior during the DRO periods, both the previously reinforced imitations and the never-reinforced probe imitations decreased markedly in strength.

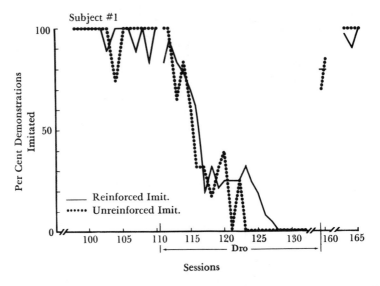

FIG. 5. The maintenance and extinction of reinforced and unreinforced imitation in Subject 1. (The breaks in the data before and after session 160 represents period of experimentation aimed at other problems.)

Figure 5 is a plot of the percentages of each type of imitative response by Subject 1. It shows that her probability of imitating the 35 probes varied between 80 and 100 per cent, as long as the other 95 imitations, within which the probes were interspersed, were reinforced. The application of the DRO 30-second procedure extinguished virtually all imitative behavior within about 20 hours. The previously reinforced imitations and the probe imitations extinguished alike in rate and degree. All imitative behavior recovered when, with a small amount of shaping, reinforcement was again made contingent upon imitative behavior.

Figure 6 is a similar plot of the imitative behavior of Subject 3. It shows the maintenance of the 1 probe imitation and 8 reinforced imitations during reinforcement of imitation, a marked decrease in both types of imitative behavior during the DRO 20-second period, and a recovery when contingent reinforcement of imitations was resumed.

Figure 7 is a plot of the imitative behavior of Subject 2. Her results were similar to those obtained for Subjects 1 and 3, in terms

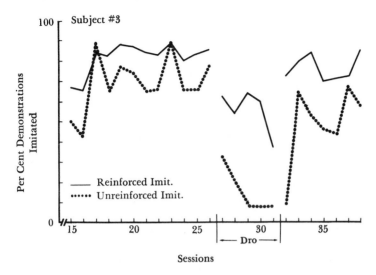

FIG. 6. The maintenance and extinction of reinforced and unreinforced imitation in Subject 3.

of the maintenance of 125 reinforced and 5 probe imitations, under conditions of reinforcement of imitations. However, her data depart from the others' during the DRO period. Initially, this subject showed no reliable signs of extinction after four sessions of DRO with a 30-second delay. Next, DRO 60-seconds was instituted for four sessions, still without any reliable effect. At that point, a procedure of DRO 0-second was begun, meaning that the experimenter demonstrated some behavior, and instantly, before the subject could respond, said, "Good," and delivered the food to her mouth. Thus reinforcement served to forestall the durable imitative responses this subject was displaying. Figure 7 demonstrates the immediacy of effect of this procedure. After four sessions of DRO 0-second, it was possible to resume the procedures of DRO 30-seconds and produce only a brief and partial recovery of the rate of imitation, which then declined to zero. A return to contingent reinforcement, with a small amount of shaping, quickly reinstated the high rate of imitation previously displayed.

In all cases, then, it is clear that the imitative repertoire depended on reinforcement of at least some of its members. It is noteworthy that the responses which had developed and been

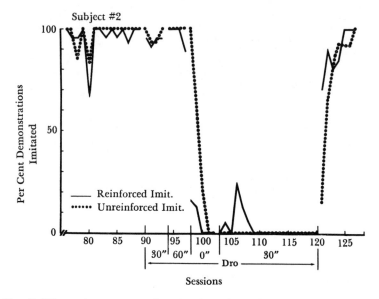

FIG. 7. The maintenance and extinction of reinforced and unreinforced imitation in Subject 2.

maintained previously without direct reinforcement could not survive extinction applied to the entire class of behaviors.

IMITATIVE CHAINS

Subjects 1 and 2 were exposed to the procedure of chaining together old and new imitative responses. At the end of 10 hours of the procedure for Subject 1, lengthy chains containing already established and new imitative responses became practical. It was possible to obtain perfect imitation on 90 per cent of the chains, some of which involved as many as five responses. Subject 2 received only 2 hours of training on chains. At the end of this time, she would imitate 50 per cent of the three-response chains demonstrated to her, and 80 per cent of the two-response chains.

VERBAL BEHAVIOR

Subjects 1 and 3 were used in the procedures for the development of verbal imitation. Verbal imitations were established for Subject

1 by chaining together motor and vocal behaviors and then fading out the motor components. Twenty hours of training resulted in 10 words which were reliably imitated, such as "Hi," "Okay," the subject's name, and the names of some objects. Subject 3's training in vocal imitations was accomplished by evoking a set of motor imitations which moved successively closer to vocalizations. Approximately 10 hours of training produced the reliable imitative vocalizations of seven vowel and consonant sounds.

GENERALIZATION TO OTHER EXPERIMENTERS

When Subject 1 was presented with new experimenters, of both the opposite and same sex as the original male experimenter, she showed approximately the same degree of imitation displayed to the original experimenter. That is, she imitated all of the 3 probe demonstrations given by one new male experimenter and 12 of 15 reinforced demonstrations by a second new male experimenter on the first demonstration and the remaining 3 by the third demonstration. On another occasion, the second new male experimenter re-presented the 15 demonstrations; all were imitated on their first demonstration. The subject also imitated all of a series of demonstrations by a female experimenter.

DISCUSSION

The procedures of this study were sufficient to produce highly developed imitation in the experimental subjects. However, a noteworthy point is the relative difficulty experienced in obtaining initial matching responses from a subject even when the response required (e.g., arm raising) clearly was in the subject's current repertoire. This suggests that the subjects were not so much learning specific responses as learning the instruction, "Do as the experimenter does." Initially, then, the procedures of this study seem to have involved bringing a number of the subjects' responses under the instructional control of the experimenter's demonstration.[1] To establish this type of instructional control by demonstration requires that the subjects either have or develop responses of observing their own behavior as well as that of the experimenter.

[1] The authors are indebted to Israel Goldiamond for his suggestions in clarifying this point.

As an increasing number of the subjects' behaviors came under the instructional control of demonstration, additional behavior, not previously observed in their repertoires, became increasingly probable, merely as a result of presenting an appropriate demonstration by a model. In the terminology suggested by Miller and Dollard (1941), a sufficiently extensive arrangement of one child's behavior into matched-dependent response with a model's behavior was sufficient to induce a tendency to achieve similarity in more ways than were originally taught.

The development of imitative repertoires, including the unreinforced imitation of probe demonstrations, could be accounted for by the effects of conditioned reinforcement. Conditioned reinforcement may have operated in the present study in the following way. The basic procedure was that of teaching the subject a series of responses, each of which was topographically similar to a demonstration just given by a model. Initially, each response had to be established separately. When established, such responses were imitative only topographically and would better be called matched-dependent behavior; the fact that a subject's response was similar to the experimenter's behavior at that point had no functional significance for any of the subject's other responses. Nevertheless, topographical similarity between child and experimenter was there to be attended to by the child, and this similarity was potentially discriminative with respect to the only reinforcement delivered in the experimental situation. One of the most effective ways of giving a stimulus a reinforcing function is to make it discriminative with respect to reinforcement. In these applications, the stimulus class of behavioral similarity was, in numerous examples, made discriminative with respect to positive reinforcement. Hence similarity could be expected to take on a positive reinforcing as well as a discriminative function. As a positive reinforcer, it should strengthen any new behavior that produced or achieved it. Behaviors that achieve similarity between one's self and a model are, of course, imitative behaviors; furthermore, they are imitative by function and not by coincidence.

This analysis is simple only at first inspection. In particular, it should be noted that "similarity" is not a simple stimulus dimension, like the frequency of sound or the intensity of light. Similarity must mean a correspondence of some sort between the stimulus output of the child's behavior and the stimulus output of the model's. A correspondence between two stimuli is not too esoteric a stimulus to consider as functional in controlling behavior. However, for an imitative repertoire to develop, a class of correspondences must become functional as stimuli. The child must learn to discriminate a correspondence between the appearance of his hand and the model's hand, his arm and the model's arm, his leg and the model's leg, his voice and the model's voice, etc. It would seem reasonable that each of these kinds of difference must require some prior experience on the child's part to appreciate. A scantiness of such experience may well be characteristic of retarded children, and makes them intriguing subjects for such studies. The ability to generalize similarities among a considerable variety of stimuli, which the children of these studies displayed, suggests that the training they were subjected to was adequate to the problem. An immediate next problem, it would seem, is the detailed analysis of these procedures to find out which of them accomplished what part of this generalization. Such analysis might yield a fair understanding of imitative behavior.

REFERENCES

Baer, D. M., and J. A. Sherman, 1964. Reinforcement control of generalized imitation in young children. *Journal of Experimental Child Psychology*, 1, pp. 37-49.

Bandura, A., 1962. Social learning through imitation. In M. R. Jones (Ed.), *Nebraska Symposium on Motivation*. Lincoln: University of Nebraska Press, pp. 211-269.

Konorski, J., and S. Miller, 1937. On two types of conditioned reflex. *Journal of General Psychology*, 16, pp. 264-272.

Lovaas, O. I., J. P. Berberich, B. F. Perloff, and B. Schaeffer, 1966. Acquisition of imitative speech by schizophrenic children. *Science*, 151, pp. 705-707.

Metz, J. R., 1965. Conditioning generalized imitation in autistic children. *Journal of Experimental Child Psychology*, 2, pp. 389-399.

Miller, N. E., and J. Dollard, 1941. *Social Learning and Imitation.* New Haven: Yale University Press.

Reynolds, G. S., 1961. Behavioral contrast. *Journal of the Experimental Analysis of Behavior,* 4. pp. 57-71.

Skinner, B. F., 1953. *Science and Human Behavior.* New York: Macmillan.

Terrace, H. S., 1963a. Discrimination learning with and without "errors." *Journal of the Experimental Analysis of Behavior,* 6, pp. 1-27.

Terrace, H. S., 1963b. Errorless transfer of a discrimination across two continua. *Journal of the Experimental Analysis of Behavior,* 6, pp. 223-232.

4

The Effects of Different Reinforcement

Contingencies in the Development

of Social Cooperation

Dennis E. Mithaug and Robert L. Burgess

THE EFFECTS OF DIFFERENT REINFORCEMENT
CONTINGENCIES IN THE DEVELOPMENT
OF SOCIAL COOPERATION

Under what conditions interaction patterns among individuals are established and maintained is a question that has been of interest to psychologists and sociologists alike. In a study by Azrin and Lindsley (1965) it was suggested that social behavior could be generated, maintained, and modified in the same way as individual behavior. In support of this contention these authors demonstrated that cooperative behavior could be developed, maintained, eliminated, and reinstated solely through the manipulation of the contingency between reinforcing stimuli and the cooperative act.

We attempted to replicate these findings in a somewhat more complex setting. Our subjects were groups of three children instead of two, who were faced with fourteen alternative responses each rather than three (Mithaug and Burgess, 1967). We were unable to generate a group response under such conditions simply by providing positive reinforcement contingent upon such response. Some sort of group "shaping," in which individual reinforcement for correct individual responses was provided, was necessary before

Reprinted from the *Journal of Experimental Child Psychology,* Vol. 5 (1968), pp. 441-454, with permission of the authors and editors. Slightly edited. Copyright © 1968 by Academic Press, Inc.

a *base rate* of group responses could be established. Once this base rate was established, however, group reinforcement was effective in increasing the frequency of social responses.

More precisely, our data suggested that group reinforcement alone is ineffective in establishing such a group response. Individual reinforcement for correct individual responses was effective in establishing a base rate of such group responses. However, the group responses that comprised the base rate were simply occasions when the subjects responded simultaneously by chance. But once this base rate was established, a combination of group *and* individual reinforcement was effective in strengthening the rate of the group response above the base level. Individual reinforcement appeared to be an important variable in generating the group response. Group reinforcement, which was subsequently added to the individual reinforcement, was important in the establishment of *social interaction*.[1]

The present investigation attempts to replicate the finding that the group response rate is higher under the condition of group and individual reinforcement than under the condition of individual reinforcement alone. In addition, the relative importance of individual "feedback," whereby the individual receives information that he has responded correctly, will be investigated more systematically. In all, the following conditions will be investigated: group reinforcement with individual feedback, individual reinforcement with feedback, and group and individual reinforcement with individual feedback. It should be noted that the major difference between the group reinforcement of the previous study and that of this study is the addition of *individual feedback* for correct individual responses. The two remaining conditions, individual reinforcement with feedback and group and individual reinforcement with individual feedback, are the same as the individual reinforcement condition and the group and individual reinforcement condition of the previous study. Here, the terms have been changed slightly to make it explicit that individual feedback is always present in these conditions.

---

[1] The base group response rate is not an adequate indicator of social behavior, that is, where the subjects attend to each others' actions. However, in order for the group response to rise above the base rate, the subjects must actively coordinate their responses in some way. The suggestion that *this* is social behavior will be discussed further later in the chapter.

METHOD

GROUP COMPOSITION

The subjects participating in this study ranged from 5 to 10 years of age. They were divided into three-member groups comprising various combinations of sex. In all, six separate groups participated.

APPARATUS

The apparatus consisted of three fourteen-key piano-keyboard instruments that were wired to a counting apparatus on the experimenter's desk. On top of each of the three instruments were two readily visible lights, one on the left end and one on the right. Electromechanical counters on the experimenter's desk recorded the number of times that a key representing a correct response was depressed. Likewise, electromechanical counters could be situated beside each instrument to record the correct key presses made on the respective instrument. The three keyboard instruments were aligned against a wall in a laboratory room. A 12 × 36-inch screen, on which were a series of lights, was hung in the center of the same wall. This light-screen was also wired to the apparatus on the experimenter's desk. The experimenter, by activating a switch on his desk, illuminated a light on the light-screen corresponding to a particular key on the subjects' keyboard instruments. Another series of switches on the desk enabled the experimenter to control the lights on the three keyboard instruments. If the enabling switches were placed at the "on" position, and if each of the subjects operating the instruments depressed the key corresponding to the light that the experimenter had flashed on the light-screen, the lights on the instruments were illuminated.

The general pattern of action here was as follows. The experimenter activated a switch controlling a particular light on the light-screen. The subjects would then press the key of their choice. If the chosen key was the correct one, that is, the key corresponding to the light illuminated on the light-screen, and if the enabling switches on the experimenter's desk were at the "on" position, the lights on the subjects' instruments flashed on. The electromechanical counters on the experimenter's desk and the counters situated beside the subjects' keyboard instruments recorded correct responses. The experimenter could make these latter counters inoperative by activating appropriate switches at his desk.

Finally, a single light and an electromechanical counter were situated in the center of the light-screen. The light and counter were activated (1) if the switches controlling the light and counter situated on the screen were in the "on" position; (2) if all three subjects pressed the key corresponding to the illuminated light on the light-screen; and (3) if each of the three subjects pressed the correct key at the same time, that is, within 0.5 second of each other. If all three subjects pressed the correct keys within this time interval, this "group response" was recorded by an electromechanical counter situated on the experimenter's desk and by a Gebrands' Cumulative Recorder also situated at the desk.

REINFORCEMENT CONDITIONS

INDIVIDUAL REINFORCEMENT WITH FEEDBACK VERSUS GROUP AND INDIVIDUAL REINFORCEMENT WITH INDIVIDUAL FEEDBACK

Experiment I
As noted above, we earlier found a higher group response rate under a condition in which *both* group reinforcements *and* individual reinforcements with individual feedback were provided than under the condition of individual reinforcement with feedback alone (Mithaug and Burgess, 1967). Experiment I represents an attempt to replicate that finding.

PROCEDURE
The subjects and procedures used in our previous study were also employed in this experiment. The three subjects were instructed, as before, that they could use only one finger and that they could press any one key as fast and as many times as they wanted to during a given trial. When the individual lights on a keyboard instrument flashed 100 times, the subject operating the instrument would receive 1 cent, and when the group counter situated on the light-screen reached 100 all three subjects would receive 1 cent. At the end of the session the subjects decided whether to purchase 5-, 10-, or 30-cent prizes, or to save their money and buy prizes at later sessions.

When the session commenced, a light flashed on the light-screen, indicating that the subjects were free to respond. The free response time was divided into 2-minute intervals.[2] As indicated by the instructions above, the subjects were permitted to press any of the keys as fast as they wanted, providing they pressed the keys only one at a time. A clock wired to the apparatus stopped when the note flashed off the screen and the apparatus was turned off. A Gebrands' Cumulative Recorder recorded the group responses that were emitted throughout the experiment.

The experimental session began with condition C, group and individual reinforcement with individual feedback. After a steady response rate was reached, condition B, individual reinforcement with feedback, was introduced. After a steady response rate was reached for condition B, condition C was reintroduced.

RESULTS

Figure 1 presents the data obtained in Experiment I. These data are similar to those obtained for the same group in our previous study (Mithaug and Burgess, 1967). Section C of the curve represents group and individual reinforcement with individual feedback, and section B represents individual reinforcement with feedback. During condition C, the group response rate is 46.0 responses per minute; for condition B, 23.0 responses per minute. And for C, again, the group response rate is 38.0 responses per minute.

Experiment IIa

The results of Experiment I are in accord with those obtained in Experiment IV of our previous study: the rate of the group response is higher under the condition of group and individual reinforcement with individual feedback than under individual reinforcement with feedback. Although this finding appears reliable, we have yet to state explicitly what may be producing it. What appears to be happening here is the following. The three subjects are responding in a noncoordinated and individualistic fashion in the condition of individual reinforcement with feed-

[2] In the previous study the subjects were allowed to respond for only 30 seconds. This increase in response time allowed for more stable response rates to be established.

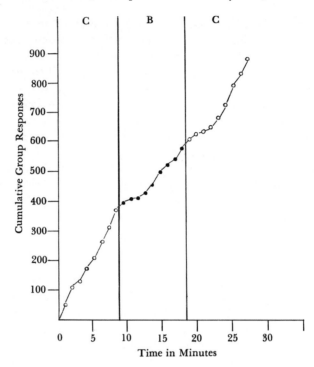

FIG. 1. A comparison of group and individual reinforcement with individual feedback (C) and individual reinforcement with feedback (B).

back. They make little effort to coordinate their key presses. However, during group and individual reinforcement with individual feedback the situation is different. The group counter situated in front of the subjects is tabulating simultaneous key presses. Group points may be more reinforcing to the members because they can see them being tabulated. With the three subjects focusing their attention on the group counter that tabulates every coordinated key press, it is little wonder that the rate of coordinated key press increases above the base rate. The group counter, with its points exchangeable for money, is a visible conditioned reinforcer for group responses; no comparable conditioned reinforcer for individual responses is visible to the subjects (Whitlock and Bushell, 1967).

This line of reasoning suggests that, if a conditioned reinforcer for individual responses were visible to the subjects, the group response rate in the group and individual reinforcement with individual feedback condition might be reduced and the differences between the two conditions thereby eliminated. In short, if individual counters tabulating correct individual key presses are placed beside the keyboard instruments so that they can be observed as readily as the group counter situated in front of the group, the subjects may attend to the group counter *less*, making fewer efforts to coordinate their respective key presses, and attend to their individual counters and individual key presses *more*. Therefore the group response rate in group and individual reinforcement with individual feedback may not be any higher than the base rate established in individual reinforcement with feedback. Experiments IIa and IIb were designed to investigate this interpretation.

PROCEDURE

The procedure for this experiment differed from that in Experiment I only in the placement of the individual counters. The counters tabulating individual points were now situated beside the subjects' respective instruments. The subjects from Experiment I were used again. The reinforcement system remained the same.

RESULTS

Figure 2 presents the data obtained in this experiment. These results differ from the findings of the previous experiments. The differences between the group response rates for the two conditions of group and individual reinforcement with individual feedback and individual reinforcement with feedback are not as great. In section C of the curve, representing group and individual reinforcement with individual feedback, the group response rate is 29.0 responses per minute; in section B (individual reinforcement with feedback), 23.0 responses per minute; and in section C, again, 31.0 responses per minute.

Experiment IIb

The results of Experiment IIa are in the direction one might expect if the presence of the individual counters has the importance that we have suggested. However, although the differences

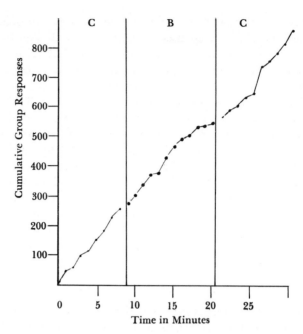

Fig. 2. A comparison of group and individual reinforcement with individual feedback (C) and individual reinforcement with feedback (B).

in group response rates between the two conditions decreased, they did not vanish completely. This may be due to the fact that the same group has been used for Experiments I and IIa, and these subjects have learned to attend to the group counter. Consequently, when the individual counters are placed beside their instruments, the established pattern of attending to the group counter may inhibit the acquisition of the potentially new response of attending to the individual counters. In order to avoid this possible complication, Experiment IIb was conducted.

PROCEDURE

The procedure here was similar to that in the previous experiment. However, three naive subjects were used to avoid the possible effects of previously learned response patterns. In addition, the subjects were given 1 cent for every 100 points that they accumulated on their individual counters and 1 cent for every 100 points that the group accumulated on the group counter. The experimenter no longer provided prizes that could be exchanged for the pennies.

RESULTS

Figure 3 presents the data obtained for this new group. There are no differences in group response rates between the conditions of group and individual reinforcement with individual feedback and individual reinforcement with feedback alone. In section C of the curve, representing group and individual reinforcement with individual feedback, the group response rate is 20.0 responses per minute; in section B (individual reinforcement with feedback), 22.0 responses per minute; and in section C, again, 23.0 responses per minute.

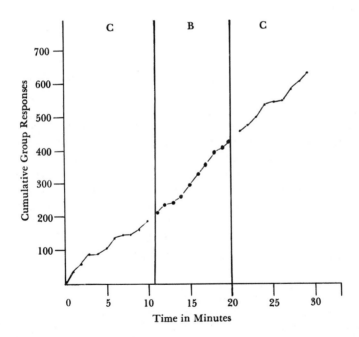

FIG. 3. A comparison of group and individual reinforcement with individual feedback (C) and individual reinforcement with feedback (B).

Discussion of Experiments I, IIa, IIb

The purpose of these three experiments was to replicate and explain the finding of our previous study in which the group response rate was higher under the condition of group and individual reinforcement with individual feedback than under individual reinforcement with feedback. Experiment I replicated that finding, and Experiments IIa and IIb were designed to test the interpretation that the presence or absence of a *conditioned reinforcer* for correct individual responses might account for the differences obtained. When the subjects had a choice of attending to the group counter (conditioned reinforcer for group responses) or their respective individual counters (conditioned reinforcers for individual responses), they chose the latter. This is shown in the results of Experiments IIa and IIb. These findings suggest that, if coordinated activity is to be strengthened above the base rate, some sort of salience must again be given to the group counter. This could be accomplished in at least two ways: (1) by removing the individual counters as before, or (2) by increasing the payoff of the group counter over that of the individual counters.[3]

GROUP REINFORCEMENT WITH INDIVIDUAL FEEDBACK VERSUS
GROUP AND INDIVIDUAL REINFORCEMENT WITH INDIVIDUAL FEEDBACK

Experiment III

The next two experiments, Experiments III and IV, were designed to investigate a different reinforcement condition, group reinforcement with individual feedback. In our previous study, the group reinforcement condition was found to be ineffective in generating a group response. The question of the effectiveness of group reinforcement *with individual feedback* remains to be investigated. Experiment III will investigate the relative effectiveness of group reinforcement with individual feedback and group and individual reinforcement with individual feedback; Experiment IV will in-

---

3 A new series of investigations is currently underway in which an attempt is made to strengthen the group response rate in the condition of group and individual reinforcement with individual feedback by manipulating the relative amounts of reinforcement from the group and individual counters. The preliminary data indicate that the group response rate can be strengthened in this condition if the amount of reinforcement from the group counter is sufficiently greater than that from the individual counters.

vestigate the relative effectiveness of group reinforcement with individual feedback and individual reinforcement with feedback.

PROCEDURE

Twelve new subjects participated in this experiment. These subjects, ranging in age from 6 to 10 years, were divided into groups of three members per group as in the previous experiments. They were instructed that they would be playing some games that would enable them to win money. For every 100 points that each member was able to accumulate on his individual counter, situated beside his keyboard instrument, he would receive 1 cent, and for every 100 points that the group was able to accumulate on the counter situated on the light-screen, each group member would receive 1 cent. Thus each subject had two possible sources from which to earn money; his own counter situated beside his keyboard instrument and the counter situated on the light-screen.

A light was flashed on the light-screen by the experimenter. The subjects would press the keys of the instruments one at a time for 2-minute intervals. At the end of each interval, the light flashed off the light-screen, the apparatus was shut off, readings were taken by the experimenter, and pennies were given to the subjects.

The reinforcement conditions manipulated in this experiment were group reinforcement with individual feedback and group and individual reinforcement with individual feedback. During the group-reinforcement-with-individual-feedback condition, lights on the keyboard instruments flashed for correct individual responses but the individual counters did not operate; they did not tabulate correct key responses, and consequently, the subjects did not receive pennies for correct individual responses. The light and counter situated on the light-screen, however, were in operation, tabulating correct group responses. The subjects received pennies for these responses.

During the condition of group and individual reinforcement with individual feedback, the lights on the keyboard instruments flashed for correct individual responses, the individual counters tabulated correct individual key presses, and the group counter on the light-screen tabulated correct group responses. The subjects were able to earn money for correct individual responses as well as for correct group responses.

The session began with group reinforcement with individual feedback (condition D), changed to group and individual reinforcement with individual feedback (condition C), and then returned to condition D.

RESULTS

Figures 4–7 present the data obtained for the four groups. Each figure is divided into two sections. The lower section presents two graphs, the mean correct individual responses per minute and the number of correct group responses per minute. The upper section also presents two graphs, the mean individual response rate per condition and the mean group response rate per condition. For all groups, the *individual* response rate is higher under group and individual reinforcement with individual feedback (C) than under group reinforcement with individual feedback (D), while the *group* response rate is higher under group reinforcement with individual feedback (D) than under the combination of group and individual reinforcement with individual feedback (C).

GROUP REINFORCEMENT WITH INDIVIDUAL FEEDBACK VERSUS
INDIVIDUAL REINFORCEMENT WITH FEEDBACK

Experiment IV
Experiment III raised the question of whether group reinforcement with individual feedback could increase the group response rate above the base rate that can be observed in the group-and-individual-reinforcement-with-individual-feedback condition. The data from that experiment provided an affirmative answer: group reinforcement with individual feedback was effective in strengthening the group response rate above the base rate.

If our results from Experiments IIa and IIb are reliable, that is, that we should obtain the same group response rates under the two conditions of individual reinforcement with feedback and group and individual reinforcement with individual feedback, we should expect to obtain the same results in this experiment that we obtained in Experiment III. In other words, group reinforcement with individual feedback should effectively strengthen the group response rate above the base rate established through individual reinforcement with feedback.

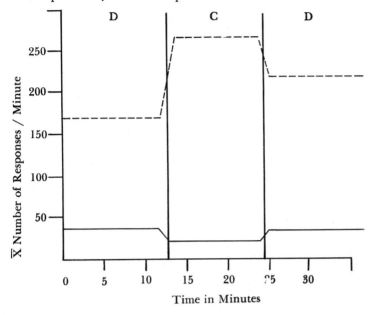

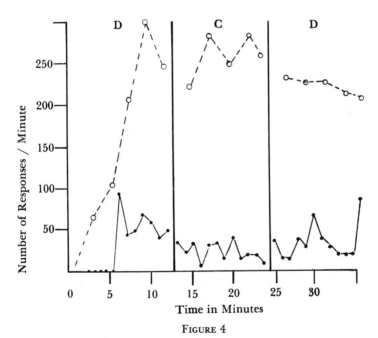

FIGURE 4

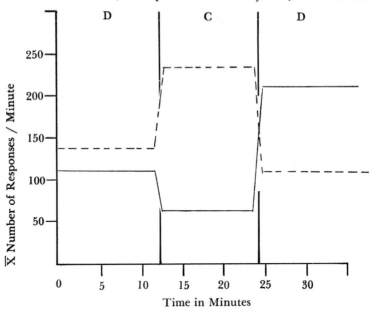

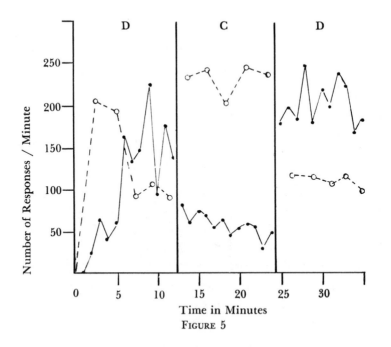

FIGURE 5

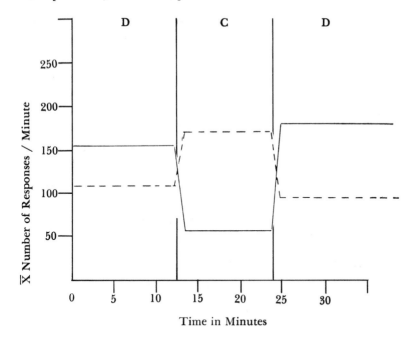

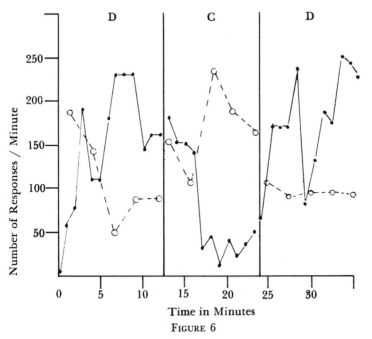

FIGURE 6

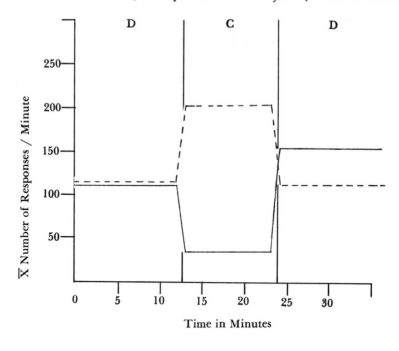

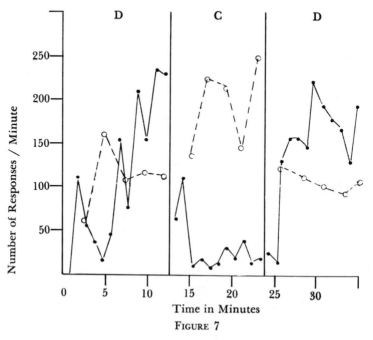

FIGURE 7

Figs. 4–7. A comparison of group reinforcement with individual feedback (D) and group and individual reinforcement with individual feedback (C). The solid line represents the correct *group* response rate, and the broken line represents the mean correct *individual* response rate. The lower graph represents the mean correct individual responses *per minute* and the number of correct group responses per minute. The upper graph presents the mean correct individual response rate *per condition* and the mean correct group response rate per condition.

Note: In Figs. 5–12 during group reinforcement with individual feedback (condition D) the mean group response rate is sometimes higher than the mean individual response rate. This reflects the coordinated response pattern of a group; *at any one time,* only one subject is "pressing," while the other two are "holding." Hence, the mean number of correct responses *per individual* can be less than the number of correct group responses. On the other hand, when all three subjects are pressing rapidly, the mean number of responses *per individual* may be larger than the number of group responses.

PROCEDURE

The procedures here were similar to those followed in Experiment III. The reinforcement conditions manipulated were group reinforcement with individual feedback and individual reinforcement with feedback. During the group-reinforcement-with-individual-feedback condition, lights on the keyboard instruments flashed for correct individual responses but the individual counters did not operate. The light and the counter situated on the light-screen did operate, however, tabulating correct group responses. Points on the counter were exchanged for pennies at a ratio of 100 points for 1 cent.

During the condition of individual reinforcement with feedback, the lights on the keyboard instruments flashed for correct individual responses and the individual counters tabulated correct individual responses. Points on the individual counters were exchangeable for pennies at a ratio of 100 to 1. The group counter and group light situated on the light-screen did not operate during this condition.

For two groups the session began with group reinforcement with individual feedback (condition D), changed to individual reinforcement with feedback (condition B), and then returned to condition D. For the other two groups the sequence was reversed, that is, the sequence was B-D-B.

RESULTS

Figures 8–11 present the data obtained for the four groups. As in the previous experiment, the figures are divided into two sections, the lower section presenting the mean correct individual responses per minute and the number of correct group responses per minute, and the upper section presenting the mean individual response rate per condition and the mean group response rate per condition. For all groups the individual response rate is higher under individual reinforcement with feedback (condition B), than under group reinforcement with individual feedback (condition D); concomitantly, the group response rate is higher under group reinforcement with individual feedback than under individual reinforcement with feedback.

It is important to note that the data for Group 6 in Fig. 8 present less striking differences between conditions than the data for the other three groups in Figs. 9-11. The reason seems to lie in the methods that the group used in order to obtain group points. Although this topic will be elaborated on in the discussion, a brief comment is needed here. Group 6 attempted to obtain group points by having each member press the same key at the same time. Group 7, 8, and 10 used a different method. For these groups two members held their keys down while the third member pressed his key at a high rate. This method was much more effective in obtaining group points.

Later, in a different series of experiments, Group 6 discovered this "presser-holder" method. Experiment IV was then replicated for this group. The procedures were the same as before, but this time pen recorders were also utilized to record on tape each correct individual response. With this new measuring device the holders (members who were simply holding down their keys) and the pressers (members pressing their keys) could be identified.

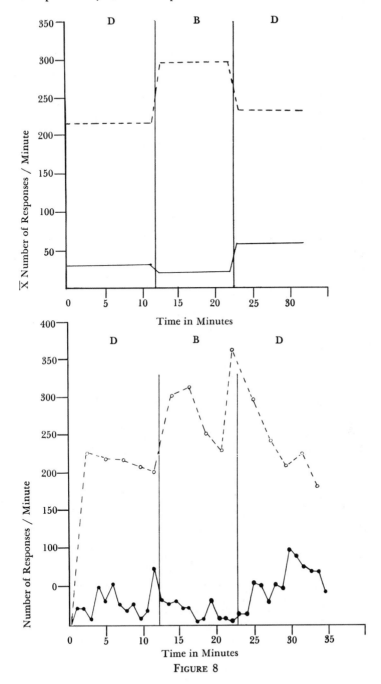

FIGURE 8

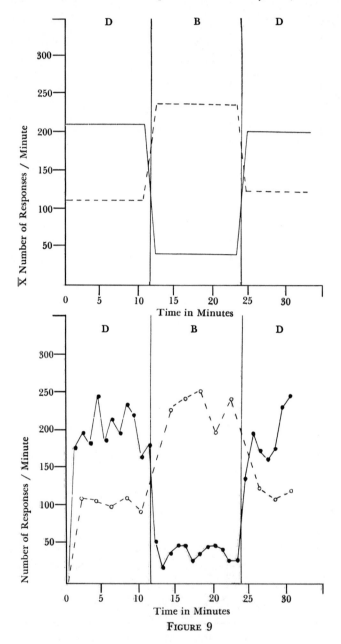

FIGURE 9

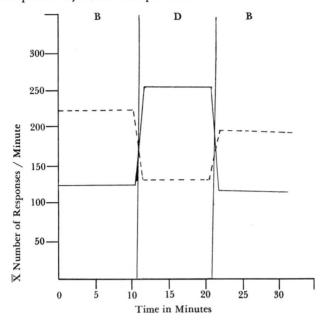

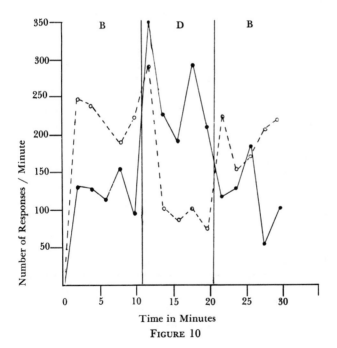

FIGURE 10

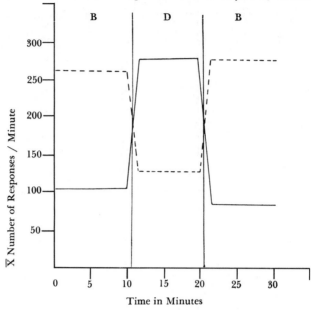

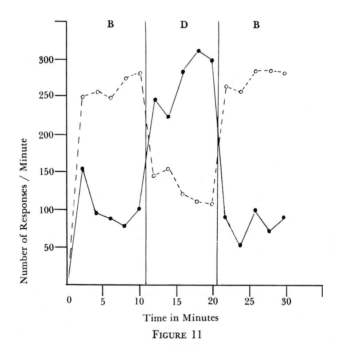

FIGURE 11

FIGS. 8–11. A comparison of group reinforcement with individual feedback (D) and individual reinforcement with feedback (B). The solid line represents the correct group response rate, and the broken line represents the mean correct individual response rate. The lower graph presents the mean correct individual responses per minute and the number of correct group responses per minute. The upper graph presents the mean individual response rate per condition and the mean group response rate per condition.

Figure 12 presents the data obtained for Group 6. The differences between conditions for group and individual response rates are now as striking as the differences already obtained for the other three groups. Figure 13 presents the record of individual responses from the pen recorder. On each tape are three response lines, one for each member of the group. A hatch mark indicates a key press. During condition B, individual reinforcement with feedback, all three response lines are filled with hatch marks, indicating that the members are pressing their keys at a high rate. There seems to be little coordination here. During condition D, group reinforcement with individual feedback, *only one* response line is hatch-marked at any one time; the other two response lines are displaced downward, indicating that keys are being held down. By closely examining the second tape one can see changes in the presser and holder roles. The hatch marks indicate a presser, and a displaced line indicates a holder. During condition B again, the response pattern changes back to what it was at the beginning of the session.

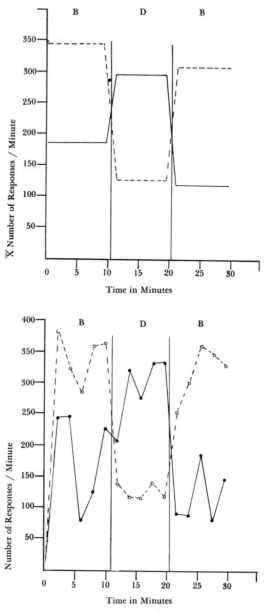

Fig. 12. A comparison of individual reinforcement with feedback (B) and group reinforcement with individual feedback (D) for Group 6 using the "presser-holder" response pattern.

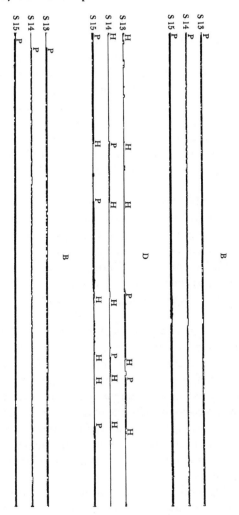

Fig. 13. A comparison of individual reinforcement with feedback (B) and group reinforcement with individual feedback (D). A straight line deflected downward represents a key being held down, while a series of hatch marks represents a key being pressed repeatedly. In condition D, the "presser-holder" response pattern can be seen; at any one time, only one of the three response lines is marked with hatch marks, indicating that there is only one "presser" and two "holders."

Note: The pens for the three subjects did not record with equal distinction. The recordings for Subjects 13 and 14 are noticeably lighter than those for Subject 15.

Discussion

In Experiment I one finding from our previous study was replicated: group and individual reinforcement with individual feedback was effective in strengthening the group response rate above the base rate. Experiments IIa and IIb accounted for this result. When conditioned reinforcers for individual responses (individual counters) were visible to the subjects along with the already visible conditioned reinforcer for group responses (group counter), the group-and-individual-reinforcement-with-individual-feedback condition was ineffective in generating the group response above the base rate.

Experiment III evaluated the possibility that, by adding individual feedback to the previously ineffective group reinforcement condition (Mithaug and Burgess, 1967), the group response could be strengthened above the base rate established under group and individual reinforcement with individual feedback. It was found that group reinforcement with individual feedback was consistently effective in strengthening the group response rate above this base rate.

Experiment IV compared group reinforcement with individual feedback with the condition of individual reinforcement with feedback. If, as the data from Experiments IIa and IIb indicated, there are no differences in group response rates between the conditions of individual reinforcement with feedback and group and individual reinforcement with individual feedback, we should have obtained results similar to those for Experiment III: the group response rate should have been higher under the condition of group reinforcement with individual feedback. The data were in accord with this reasoning.

It should be noted that different behavior patterns were clearly distinguishable during the experiments. During the individual-reinforcement-with-feedback condition and the group-and-individual-reinforcement-with-individual-feedback condition, each subject attended to his own counter while ignoring the group counter and light. During these two conditions, we observed what might be called competition. The subjects appeared intensely concerned with the points the other subjects were obtaining vis-à-vis their own. In general, each subject pressed his own correct key as fast as was physically possible.

When the group-reinforcement-with-individual-feedback condition was introduced, two different behavior patterns emerged.

One group (Group 6) developed a system of chanting "1, 2, 3, 4" in a rhythm that apparently aided the members in coordinating their efforts to press the correct key at the same time. Although this solution was more effective for obtaining group points than each pressing his own key as fast as possible, it was not so effective as another method discovered by the other three groups. This consisted of having two members of the group hold down their keys while the third member pressed his correct key at a high rate. The three groups that used this method were able to acquire group points as fast as the "presser" could press his key. For these groups a system was usually worked out to distribute the work load. When one member stopped pressing, he held down his key while another member took over. Usually one member of each group emerged as the fastest "presser" and ended up doing most of the work, probably because he could produce the greatest reinforcement for the group. That this method was more efficient than the chanting method developed by Group 6 was revealed clearly in the data. Figures 4 and 8 present the data for the group using the chanting method. For this group the group response rate was lower than the group response rates for the other three groups, and the differences between conditions were also less striking.

In any case, now we can understand the social processes that are reflected by the data in Figs. 4-13. During the group-reinforcement-with-individual-feedback condition, the subjects are highly reinforced not for pressing their own keys at a high rate, but for cooperating with other group members and for developing an efficient means for obtaining group points. Consequently, the subjects begin attending to each others' behavior in a way that enables them to coordinate their respective responses. The form of this coordination can be seen more clearly in Fig. 13.

During the group-and-individual-reinforcement-with-individual-feedback condition, the subjects are reinforced for both correct individual responses and correct group responses. Our data indicate that group responses and the concomitant amount of group reinforcement decrease during this condition while the individual response rate and individual reinforcement increase, resulting in a less coordinated and more individualistic response pattern. Hence, probably the most effective way to establish and maintain social cooperation, in general, is to provide positive reinforcement to each of the members, contingent upon the cooperative act, as well as some form of individual feedback for appropriate individual responses.

SUMMARY OF MAJOR FINDINGS

1. Group reinforcement *without individual feedback* was ineffective in generating a group response (Mithaug and Burgess, 1967).
2. Individual reinforcement with feedback and group and individual reinforcement with individual feedback were effective in generating a base group response rate or operant level of group responses.
3. Group reinforcement *with individual feedback* was effective in strengthening and maintaining a group response above the base rate or operant level.
4. When conditioned reinforcers were visible to the subjects for group responses, but not for individual responses, group and individual reinforcement with individual feedback was effective in strengthening and maintaining the group response above the base rate.
5. Differential response patterns, a division of labor, were produced only under the condition of group reinforcement with individual feedback.

REFERENCES

Azrin, N. H., and O. R. Lindsley, 1965. The reinforcement of cooperation between children. *Journal of Abnormal and Social Psychology, 52,* pp. 100-102.

Cohen, D. J., 1962. Justin and his peers: an experimental analysis of a child's social world. *Child Development, 33,* pp. 697-717.

Lindsley, O. R., 1966. Experimental analysis of cooperation and competition. In Thom Verhave (ed.), *The Experimental Analysis of Behavior,* New York: Appleton-Century-Crofts.

Mithaug, D. E., and R. L. Burgess, 1967. The effects of different reinforcement procedures in the establishment of a group response. *Journal of Experimental Child Psychology, 5,* pp. 441-454.

Whitlock, C., and D. Bushell, Jr., 1967. Some effects of "back-up" reinforcers on reading behavior. *Journal of Experimental Child Psychology, 5,* pp. 50-57.

5

Status Differentiation, External Consequences,
and Alternative Reward Distributions

James A. Wiggins

Social science has interested itself in how the distribution of rewards within social systems, large and small, affects the social structure of a system as well as the behavior of its individual members.
Because of such an interest, it has also concerned itself with the
antecedent question of how such distributions evolve. The investigations of the latter problem can be divided into an oversimplified
classification of (1) those concentrating on structural factors which
immediately precede the distribution of rewards and (2) those concentrating on factors which follow such distributions, yet are said
to affect future distributions.

The first set of explanations emphasizes such determinants as
structural differences in status, influence, scarcity, and investment.
Individuals or "classes" of individuals receive greater rewards because they are leaders, control scarce resources, invest more in the
system and consequently have more to lose, etc. Generally, such
investigations interpret these system responses as emanating from
the system's normative prescriptions for such distributions. Thus
the determinants of the reward distribution are viewed as occurring some time before the distribution itself.

The second set of explanations examines the consequences of
reward distributions. If a particular distribution has a positive con-

Reprinted from *Sociometry*, Vol. 29, No. 2 (June, 1966), pp. 89-103, with
permission of the author and The American Sociological Association. Slightly
edited.

sequence for a social system, the distribution will continue to be operative. If it has a negative consequence, it will be discontinued. For example, the traditional functionalist argues that an unequal or stratified distribution in a society is a result of the distribution's effectiveness in getting people to perform certain functionally important roles.[1] Then again, Schwartz, a not-so-traditional functionalist, argues that another kind of distribution (egalitarian) may have the same positive consequence and, as a result, persist as part of the system.[2] In both cases, however, the determinant of the distribution is viewed as actually following the distribution in time.

One rather traditional link which may be drawn between the two approaches is that, while the consequences may initially determine the distribution, they may also produce, in time, a normative structure with its own "emerging" consequences. The normative structure will then, with *some* autonomy, determine the distribution. A shorter link might involve the assumption that the "real" forces behind the normative structure are the consequences it implies.

Although the second class of explanations has concerned consequences, it has emphasized those that are internal rather than external to the system (i.e., role performances of system members). Although there is usually some rather unspecified hypothesis as to the importance of the "survival value" of the reward distribution which might include external consequences, this hypothesis is presently too impractical to be open to investigation—at least at the level of analysis for which it was initially designed, the society. There are not many occasions in which one can observe a society "die" several times (or even "die" or survive in varying degrees) and observe the effect on the society's distribution of rewards. To even define and operationalize "survival value" is extremely problematic. However, at another level of analysis, the "microstructure" or the group, such an investigation is more feasible. In addition, it is similarly easier to examine the effect of external consequences other than those which directly imply some survival value for the group.

---

[1] Kingsley Davis and Wilbert E. Moore, "Some Principles of Stratification," *American Sociological Review*, 10 (April, 1945), pp. 242-249.

[2] Richard D. Schwartz, "Functional Alternatives to Inequality," *American Sociological Review*, 20 (August, 1955), pp. 424-430.

The present investigation attempts to examine simultaneously the two explanations of reward distribution just discussed: (1) the frequency of status differentiation increases the frequency of a differential reward distribution, and the frequency of undifferentiated status (the absence of status differentiation) increases the frequency of an egalitarian reward distribution; (2) the frequency of positive consequences increases (and of negative consequences decreases) the frequency of a given reward distribution. Of primary concern is *which proposition is more powerful*. What happens when the status differentiation which precedes the reward distribution "contradicts" the external consequences which follow, that is, when a differential reward distribution following a status differentiation is in turn followed by *negative* consequences? Will the reward distribution continue its conformity to the status differentiation proposition, or will it change to conform to the external consequences proposition? In accordance with the previously mentioned assumption that the "real" power behind normatively based status structures are the consequences they imply, it is predicted that the external consequences are the more powerful. As this proposition refers to process (frequency over time), it does not negate the possibility that status differentiation might be *momentarily* more powerful. This investigation confirms just such a possibility. However, the proposition does suggest that external consequences will become a more powerful determinant of reward structures if they occur consistently over a period of time.

METHOD

Ten groups, each composed of three persons, were randomly assigned to one of two experimental variations. Within each group, the subjects were unacquainted with one another. All were volunteers from sociology classes at Northwestern University, who had been told they would be taking part in a study of problem solving in small groups. Their involvement would require 1 hour each day for 12 days. It was emphasized that anyone who volunteered could not drop out in the middle of the experiment but must participate for the full 12 days.

Each group was ushered into an experimental room and seated around a table. Once seated, each subject was given an instruction sheet. The experimenter read the instructions aloud:

You will be working as a group on a problem involving a matrix (7 × 7) of plus and minus units. The matrix is on the blackboard which you now face. The task involves, first of all, the experimenter's choice of a column of the matrix identified by a color—red, blue, yellow, etc. He will not announce his choice, however, until your group has agreed on a row of the matrix identified by "Able," "Baker," "Charley," etc. The intersecting cell of the experimenter's column-choice and your row-choice indicates your payoff for that trial—either a plus or minus unit.

Each unit is worth 30 cents and you will be paid at the end of each trial. You will also have to invest some money at the beginning of each trial. I will discuss this in one moment. In addition, if your group does become particularly proficient at this task, you will be excused 2 days earlier than the originally scheduled 12 days. You will have 30 trials on each day of your participation. If your intersecting cell indicates a plus value, you will receive 30 cents but, of course, lose your investment. The money won will be put in a "player-pool." If the cell indicates a minus value, you will not receive the 30 cents and will also lose your investment.

On each trial, your group will have a minute and a half to make a decision as to your choice of rows. You will have an additional half minute to decide what you want to pay yourselves for that trial. This money will come from the player-pool. You do not have to pay yourselves any particular *amount* of money, but you must pay yourselves something at the end of the trial. It is not necessary that each of you be paid an equal amount of money on each trial. The player-pool will be lent $5.00 to begin the task. This must be repaid at the end of the experiment. Your investments will come from your own money, not from the player-pool. Each of you will be lent $2.50 to begin the task. This must be repaid at the end of the experiment.

Finally, I would like to assign each of you a task.

Number 1, you will be the "leader." Your function will be to make the final decision in matters on which the members of the group cannot agree within the time allotted. You will invest 7 cents at the beginning of each trial.

Number 2, you will be the "secretary" and keep track of the experimenter's column-choices and the group's row-choices. You will also have certain information that the other two members will not have. You will have a paper that tells you two columns that the experimenter will not choose on each particular trial. If you want to show this information to the others, you may; but it is not necessary that you do so. You will invest 4 cents at the beginning of each trial.

Number 3, you will be the "treasurer." You will collect the investments from each member at the beginning of each trial and give them to the experimenter. You will also distribute the money from the player-pool to each of the group members after each trial according to the group's decision. You will invest 4 cents at the beginning of each trial.

Finally, one very important point. The experimenter will be using a complex system in determining his choice of columns. Your major task will be to detect this system and to coordinate your choice of rows with his choice of columns. Then you will be able to achieve a plus unit rather than a minus unit.

Now, are there questions concerning what you are supposed to do?

After the question period, the experimenter took his seat at a small table containing a stack of papers and five boxes of pennies. He gave each subject one box containing 250 pennies. The player-pool box containing 500 pennies was given to the "treasurer." A paper containing two "incorrect" columns for each trial was given to the "secretary." The subjects were then asked to begin by collecting the investments for the first trial and giving them to the experimenter. They then continued by guessing the experimenter's first choice of columns and picking what they thought would be a "profitable" row.

MANIPULATION OF STATUS DIFFERENTIATION

Since one of the major potential problems for the present investigation was the general lack of differentiation generated in informal experimental groups, the premanipulation design was, in part, an attempt to structure such status differentiation. As described in the instructions to the subjects, this was accomplished by three techniques: (1) power differences of the "leader," "secretary," and "treasurer"; (2) scarcity of resources differences embodied in the "secretary's" control over important information; (3) investment differences (that is, the "leader's" investment of 7 cents compared to the others' 4-cent investments). A fourth basis of differentiation which was expected to develop involved differences in "expertness" in terms of the subjects' "apparent" abilities to predict the experimenter's column-choices. "Expertness" was measured in terms of the percentage of times a subject's verbalized prediction as to the correct row was "confirmed." If during any day of experimentation (30 trials) the difference between any two subjects' percentages was as large as 25 per cent, expertness differences were said to exist.

At the macro-level of analysis, Davis and Moore have suggested only two clues as to what constitutes the "functional importance" of positions in society: (1) the degree to which a position is functionally unique, there being no other positions that can perform the same function satisfactorily; (2) the degree to which other positions are dependent on the one in question. At least three of the structural differentiations operating in the present experiment involve positions of "uniqueness." There is only one "leader," one "secretary," and one "high investor." It is also possible that there be only one "expert." The differentiations also meet the second criterion in that the group members are dependent on the "leader" for decisions, the "secretary" for important information, and the "expert" for intelligence and skill. Davis and Moore also associated investments of time, energy, and money in training with positions of functional importance. Although this experiment does not involve investments as a result of training, it does utilize differential monetary investments per se in the "high" and "low investors."

MANIPULATION OF EXTERNAL CONSEQUENCES

To effect the desired manipulation of the external consequence variable, the "correctness" of the group's choices and the resulting payoff were determined not by the group's row-choices, but by its distribution of rewards at the end of the previous trial. For the first 5 days (150 trials), groups in Variation I received a "correct" indication and 30-cent payoff (positive consequences) each time they distributed their player-pool money equally on the preceding trial (egalitarian distribution) and received an "incorrect" indication and no payoff (negative consequences) each time they distributed their player-pool money unequally on the preceding trial (differential distribution). Concerning the latter situation, it did not matter what kind of differential distribution they used as long as one or more members received an amount differing from that received by any of the other members. (A more rigorous interpretation of the procedures would state that, in the case of the egalitarian distribution, the consequences follow a single behavior; while for the differential distribution, the consequences follow a "class" of behavior.) For the remaining 5 days (150 trials) the procedure was reversed. Groups in Variation I received a "correct" indication and 30-cent payoff (positive consequences) each time they distributed their player-pool unequally on the preceding trial (differential distribution) and received an "incorrect" indication and no payoff (negative consequences) each time they distributed their player-pool money equally on the preceding trial (egalitarian distribution).

In order to control possible order effects, the treatment of the groups in Variation II was the opposite of that for Variation I. During the first 5 days, the groups received positive consequences for differential distributions and negative consequences for an egalitarian distribution. For the last 5 days, they received positive consequences for an egalitarian distribution and negative consequences for differential distributions.

All groups were dismissed at the end of the tenth day. At this time, the subjects were informed as to the real nature of the experiment, shown data gathered from their session, and asked for their cooperation in not discussing the experiment with anyone. If their "earnings" proved to be less than $10.00, they were paid the difference.

The experiment attempted to manipulate three external consequences. However, it was anticipated that they would have their effect at different times. Two of the consequences, the "correctness" of the group's prediction and the 30-cent payoff, would be most effective during the first part of the experiment. If, however, the subjects became tired or bored with the task toward the end of the experiment, the consequence that each "correct" prediction brought them closer to being dismissed from the experiment 2 days early would become effective.

The experimenter coded the following information: (1) the money distributed to each member on each trial; (2) the times that the "leader" made the decision for the group; (3) the "expertness" of the group members in terms of their apparent ability to predict the experimenter's column-choice; (4) the times that the "secretary" withheld the scarce information.

RESULTS

EFFECTIVENESS OF MANIPULATIONS
The effectiveness of the *status differentiation* manipulations may be viewed in two ways—the differentiation *structure*, with its normative prescriptions, which is instituted in the experiment and the differentiation *performances* which, in some cases, are not experimentally controlled. Of course, the latter is the one subject to effectiveness measures.

1. Power differentiation performances (final decision-making in matters on which the group members cannot agree) were made on an average of 37 times during the 300 trials (range: 23–61). An average of 25 such decisions involved the row-choice of the group, while an average of 12 involved the player-pool distributions. Although this does not represent the most effective manipulation of power differentiation, it does provide a more effective manipulation of external consequences. If the leader-decisions involving the reward distributions were frequent, the results of the experiment would be subject to the interpretation that they are not a function of the effect of external consequences on *group* behavior but rather a function of the effect of such consequences on the *leader's* behavior.

2. Investment differentiation performances (investing 7 or 4 cents on each trial) were made on each of the 300 trials. Power and investment differentiation performances always overlapped because of the experimental manipulations.

3. Resource differentiation performances (withholding knowledge of two incorrect columns) were made on the average of 8 trials per group (range: 0–13). Although this itself does not indicate effective manipulation, the threat of such behavior as a result of the differential structure and a few actual instances of information withholding may still have produced the desired effect. During a postexperimental discussion, all but two groups indicated that throughout most of the experiment they had felt the possibility of such behavior. (Of the two groups, one indicated they had such feelings during only the first part of the experiment.)

4. Expertness differentiation performances occurred on the average of 67 trials (range: 41–72). This differentiation overlapped the investment and power differentiations an average of 26 times (range: 20–36) and the scarce-resources differentiation an average of 32 times (range: 22–39). The postexperimental discussions indicated that all groups felt there were differences in percentage of predictions "confirmed." However, five groups agreed that "confirmation" was more a matter of luck than of skill.

The major question concerning the effectiveness of the *external consequences* manipulation is whether the subjects became aware of the true determinant of the consequences they received—their reward distribution. This is a very difficult question to answer. Patterson found no significant relationship between awareness of such contingencies and changes in the performance of children.[3] Spielberger, however, found that verbal conditioning occurs primarily when the subjects become aware of the consequence contingencies.[4] He also found that the subjects reported their awareness only after intensive interviewing. An intensive interview may itself increase the subject's awareness of the contingencies, and, not wanting to appear fooled by the experimenter, the subject may report he knew about them all the time. The present investigation used only a brief postexperimental interview, in which the groups did not report being aware of the real determinants. Three of the groups indicated they suspected their row-choices were not determining the consequences. However, they could not decide what was actually causing them. A more valid indicator of awareness may be the subject's behavior during the session. If one subject became aware of the contingency, he might communicate this finding to the other subjects in the group in order to (1) win more money and be excused from the experiment sooner or (2) simply foul up the experimenter (something all deceptors deserve). There was no such communication in any of the groups in this investigation. However, not all subjects may communicate their findings if (1) they are interested in the welfare of the experiment and think revealing the information would be detrimental to it or (2) they think their discovery of the experimenter's deception will terminate their opportunity to win more money.[5]

During the pretest, three groups discovered the true contingencies. In one case, the session was terminated. In the other two, sessions were continued to observe what would develop. Both groups discontinued the task, ribbed the experimenter, walked around the room, and intermittently returned to the task "to see if their system still worked." The members of one group stacked pennies as high as they could. After 15–20 minutes, they returned to the task for the remainder of the session. A greater attempt was then made to prevent subjects' awareness of the contingency by

3 G. R. Patterson, "Parents as Dispensers of Aversive Stimuli," *Journal of Personality and Social Psychology*, 2 (December, 1965), pp. 844-851.

4 C. D. Spielberger, "The Role of Awareness in Verbal Conditioning," in Charles Eriksen (Ed.), *Behavior and Awareness*, Durham, N. C.: Duke University Press, 1962.

5 James A. Wiggins, "Valid Inference and Experimental Laboratory Research," in Hubert M. and Ann B. Blalock, (Eds.), *Methodology in Social Research*, New York: McGraw-Hill Book Company, 1968.

diverting their attention from the reward distribution. Emphasis on the complexity of the experimenter's system of column-choices, the size of the task-matrix, and the time between the group's reward distribution and the payoff on each trial were increased. In addition, volunteers who had attended courses in social psychology were eliminated from the sample.

Even if the subjects were aware of the contingency, there still remain several theoretical questions. Do the external consequences or the awareness explain the group's behavior? What is the difference between not being aware of the contingency while learning a behavior and not being aware of it once the behavior has been performed enough to become "habit?" Is unawareness a necessary prerequisite for the test of the hypothesis? Each is an empirical question yet to be investigated. The fact that this investigation attempts to use unawareness is not meant to represent a support of that position.

TEST OF THE HYPOTHESIS

Figure 1 shows the cumulative differential distribution of the groups in Variation I. (As this distribution is the reciprocal of the egalitarian distribution, only one distribution is presented.) The data show that all five groups initially used egalitarian distributions. Next, each group began to vacillate in its uses of the two types of distributions. After this vacillation, all groups began the consistent use of the egalitarian distribution. The time of the consistency before the 151st trial (where the manipulation of the consequences was changed) varied from that of Group 9, which used the egalitarian distribution consistently for 38 trials (76 minutes or 1¼ days) to that of Group 8, which did similarly for 66 trials (132 minutes or 2 days).

After the manipulation of the independent variable (151st trial) all groups continued to use the egalitarian distribution for a period of time. Then again, they began to vacillate in their type of reward distribution. Finally, all five groups returned to consistent use of a particular distribution until the end of experimentation, but now it was the differential distribution. This time the groups' consistency ranged from that of Group 8, which used a differential distribution for 40 trials (80 minutes or over 1 day), to that of Group 6, which did similarly for 76 trials (152 minutes or 2½ days).

Cumulative Differentiated Distributions of Groups
in Variation I: (Egalitarian to Differentiated)

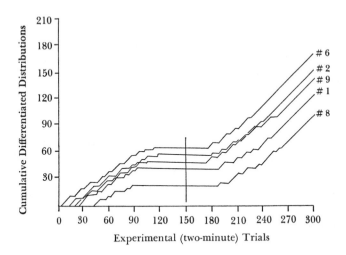

FIG. 1. The figure shows the cumulative increase in the number of differential distributions over 300 trials. If the line moves in an oblique direction, it means that on that trial the group used a differential reward distribution. If the line moves in a horizontal direction, the group did not use a differential distribution. The vertical line at the 151st trial indicates the time at which experimental contingencies were changed.

Figure 2 shows the cumulative differential distribution of the five groups in Variation II. As was true in Variation I, the groups began by using an egalitarian distribution. Each group then vacillated between distribution types. Then, before the 151st trial, all groups began the consistent use of a differential distribution. The groups varied in the length of this consistency from Group 7, which consistently used a differential distribution for 44 trials (88 minutes or 1½ days), to Group 3, which did similarly for 59 trials (118 minutes or 2 days).

After the manipulation of the independent variable, the above-mentioned consistency continued in all five groups. Next, a second period of vacillating between the egalitarian and differential distributions occurred. Finally, for a second time, all groups consistently employed one type of distribution, only this time it was the egalitarian distribution. The time of this consistency varied from that of Group 7, which consistently used this distribution for 32 trials (64 minutes or just over 1 day), to Group 10, which did similarly for 52 trials (104 minutes or close to 2 days).

Table 1 shows the number of egalitarian distributions per day of experimentation for the five groups in each variation. True, the number of egalitarian distributions was significantly more on days 4, 5, and 6, but significantly less on days 9 and 10. The statistical analysis also shows a significant difference between days within each variation. In Variation I, the number of egalitarian distributions decreased significantly between days 1 and 2, 6 and 7, and 8 and 9. The number also increased between days 3 and 4. Within Variation II, the number of egalitarian distributions decreased significantly between days 1 and 2, 3 and 4, and 4 and 5. The number increased between days 6 and 7, 8 and 9, 9 and 10.

Throughout the experiment, the high-status subjects failed to receive the largest amount of the player-pool in only 109 of the

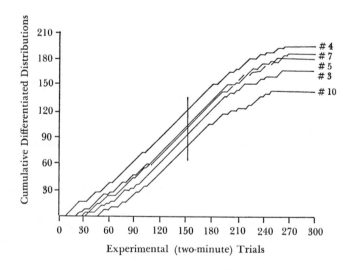

Cumulative Differentiated Distributions of Groups
in Variation II: (Differentiated to Egalitarian)

Fɪɢ. 2. See description for Figure 1.

TABLE 1

Number of Egalitarian Distributions for Each Group
on Each Day of Experimentation

Variation and Group		Day of Experimentation									Between-Day Differences	
		1	2	3	4	5	6	7	8	9	10	Days	p
Var. I													
Gr.	1	22	10	18	28	30	30	17	14	2	0	1–2	.007
	2	21	6	18	26	30	23	12	7	0	0	2–3	.352
	6	12	10	11	22	30	24	13	3	0	0	3–4	.002
	8	30	20	17	30	30	30	16	17	5	0	4–5	.024
	9	24	13	9	16	30	28	15	12	7	0	5–6	.043
												6–7	.001
$\overline{X}$		21.8	11.8	14.6	24.4	30.0	27.0	14.6	10.6	2.8	0.0	7–8	.144
SD		33.7	21.8	14.6	24.6	0.0	8.8	3.4	25.0	7.8	0.0	8–9	.007
												9–10	.044
Var. II													
Gr.	3	26	17	12	2	0	0	7	18	21	30	1–2	.003
	4	14	8	3	4	0	0	13	13	21	30	2–3	.238
	5	30	7	8	2	0	0	10	8	24	30	3–4	.009
	7	22	11	10	5	0	0	6	14	16	30	4–5	.001
	10	30	20	12	7	0	5	12	13	26	30	5–6	.318
												6–7	.001
$\overline{X}$		24.4	12.6	9.0	4.0	0.0	1.0	9.6	13.2	21.6	30.0	7–8	.118
SD		35.8	25.8	11.2	3.6	0.0	4.0	7.4	10.2	11.4	0.0	8–9	.001
												9–10	.001
Between-variation differences													
p		.535	.818	.028	.001	*	.001	.024	.424	.001	*		

* Without some variance, the significance of the difference is statistically uncomputable.

2030 trials on which some differential rewarding was made. Although in the beginning of the experiment the reward distribution corresponded closely to both the power-investment and the expertness differences, as the session progressed the distributions showed a decreasing correspondence to the expertness differences. This is compatible with the postexperimental reports that five groups felt the "expertness" to be more a matter of luck than of skill.

DISCUSSION AND CONCLUSIONS

Every group began the experiment using an egalitarian reward distribution. The groups varied in the number of periods in which this distribution was used consistently. One explanation might be that the laboratory, the experimental situation, and the fellow subjects were unfamiliar to most of the subjects. At first, they did not know how they *should* behave. They probably suspected that because it was an experimental laboratory many things were operating in the experiment (and on their behavior) which were not pointed out by the experimenter or which were not obvious to them. As a result of this unfamiliarity, the subjects may have relied on their expectation of the expectations of the experimenter and other subjects as they are representative of the larger university community. With the current sentiment of the university favoring egalitarian social policies, unequal distributions of rewards generally have to be justified. Having no frame of reference for the experiment, the subjects may have used that of the larger community. It may also be that the small groups with which the subjects had experience (i.e., family and peer groups) used egalitarian distributions. Older subjects may have more experience with formal groups and as a consequence have a frame of reference more compatible with differential distributions. Since individuals within the university vary as to (1) their commitment to the egalitarian philosophy and (2) their experience in egalitarian small groups, the groups varied within each variation as to the length of time they maintained the egalitarian distribution. Thus the following proposition might account for the initial period of egalitarian reward distribution: given the unfamiliarity of the experimental situation, (1) the egalitarian philosophy of the university community, (2) the subject's experience with egalitarian small groups, and (3) the frequency of positive consequences following egalitarian reward distributions will increase the frequency of an egalitarian reward distribution during the initial phases of an experiment.

After this period, all groups began to vacillate between the two styles of reward distribution. This effect may be the result of competition between the subjects' prior experiences (pre-experimental variables mentioned above) and the various experimental manipulations. If the above suggestions are correct, the status differentiation manipulations competed with the prior experiences in both experimental variations. The external consequences manipulations competed with the prior experiences in Variation II, but they reinforced them in Variation I. Under these conditions, it might be expected that the period of vacillation would be longer in Variation I. The average length of the vacillation period was 82 trials in Variation I and 73 trials in Variation II. It might also be expected that the number of vacillations would be greater in Variation I. The average number of vacillations was 15 in Variation I and 12 in Variation II. In neither case is the difference statistically significant. However, a more rigorous test *might* support the following proposition: contradictions (1) between pre-experimental variables and experimental manipulations (*particularly if some of the latter contradict the former while others reinforce them*) and (2) between status differentiation manipulations and external consequences manipulations will increase the vacillation between reward distribution alternatives.

All groups then entered a period of consistent use of a particular reward distribution (Variation I, $\bar{X} = 76$; Variation II, $\bar{X} = 88$). In Variation II, the occurrence of the differential reward distribution followed the predictions of both the status differentiation proposition and the external consequence proposition. Both predicted a differential distribution, while the former specified that this distribution would correspond with the status differences contained in the structure. However, in Variation I, the development of the egalitarian reward distribution conflicted with the prediction of the status differentiation proposition, but it confirmed the external consequences proposition. As a result, the evidence suggests that the external consequences proposition is more powerful when considering process and that *under status differentiation/external consequences conflict the frequency of positive consequences will increase (and of negative consequences will decrease) the frequency of a given reward distribution.*

The importance of the process assertions is amply demonstrated by the groups' continued use of a particular reward distribution *after* the change in experimental conditions at the 151st trial. Here, for a time, existing external consequences appear to lose their control. In Variation II, the continuous occurrence of the differential reward distribution is compatible with the status differentiation but not with the external consequences. However, the process assertions were that the distributions would be controlled by the frequency of external consequences. Immediately after the manipulation change, the distributions were determined by the frequency of consequences having occurred before the change. Some degree of frequency following the change is required before the new consequences gain control. The "some degree" is probably a function of the prior frequency: the greater the frequency of external consequences while establishing a given reward distribution, the greater the frequency required to change this distribution. This proposition is also equivalent to part of the proposition explaining the use of a distribution system at the beginning of the experimental sessions. The more the "egalitarian philosophy of the university community" and the more "the subjects' experience with egalitarian small groups" may be interpreted as the "frequency of external consequences while establishing a given reward distribution" (egalitarian) before the subjects' participation in the experiment. As no attempt was made to vary the frequency of external consequences during the establishment of the reward distribution, the proposition cannot be tested.

A second period of vacillation then occurred. As proposed in the case of the first period, it was probably the result of the decreasing strength of the external consequence manipulations before the manipulation change and the increasing control of the manipulations after the change. However, different from the first period of vacillation, the external consequences manipulations conflicted with the prior experiences in both variations, but the status differentiation manipulations conflicted with the prior experiences in Variation I while reinforcing those in Variation II. As a result, the vacillation proposition would predict a greater degree of vacillation in Variation II than in Variation I. The data show that the average length of the vacillation period was 71 trials in Variation II and 66 trials in Variation I. The average number of vacillations was 14 in Variation II and 12 in Variation I. Again, the differences are not statistically significant.

The second period of consistent use of a reward distribution provided the second test of the major proposition (Variation I, $\overline{X} = 54$ trials; Variation II, $\overline{X} = 41$ trials). In Variation I, the data conformed to both status differentiation and external consequences propositions. However, in Variation II, the data supported the external consequences proposition while contradicting the status differentiation proposition. At the same time, the second test eliminated the possible effect of the order of the experimental manipulations.

In summary, the data strongly support the proposition that,

under status differentiation/external consequences conflict, the frequency of positive consequences will increase (and that of negative consequences will decrease) the frequency of a given reward distribution. Thus the status differentiation proposition appears to be conditional. If the group's differential distribution is followed by positive consequences, the distribution will continue to persist and conform to the structural proposition. Under the present experimental situation, the differential distribution corresponded most closely to the power-investment aspect of the status differentiation. However, if the group's differential distribution is followed by negative consequences, the distribution of rewards will not conform to the structural proposition; instead it will be determined solely by external consequences. (It would be interesting to see whether external consequences favoring differential distribution, but a differential distribution not compatible with the status differentiation proposition, could gain complete determinance of the distribution.)

The experimental proposition may also account, in part, for the inconsistencies that are sometimes found among indices of social status. For example, in this investigation, the correlation between the "status structure dimension" and the "reward distribution dimension" of the stratification system of a group is a function of the external consequences following the associations. Therefore, one might predict there would be little stress to change inconsistent-status situations in which such inconsistencies are followed by positive consequences for the group.[6] Similarly, it could be predicted there would be stress to change consistent-status situations in which such consistency is followed by negative consequences for the group. This might be particularly true when the group has a task which is most effectively solved by a division of labor.

At least four important questions arise concerning the generalizability of these findings.

1. If the group members had been allowed to leave the group, would they have done so—possibly because the group's reward

[6] It has also been proposed with some experimental evidence that little stress results from inconsistent-status situations in which the inconsistencies were expected by the group members. See the following: Edward E. Sampson, "Status Congruence and Cognitive Consistency," *Sociometry*, 26 (June, 1963), pp. 146-162; and Arlene C. Brandon, "Status Congruence and Expectations," *Sociometry*, 28 (September, 1965), pp. 272-288.

distribution did not correspond to existing structural differences such as status, leadership, investment? And would the group be unable to refill the vacated position, thereby creating additional pressure to adopt a differential distribution? Does such "status incongruence" prevent the complete determinance by external consequences in situations where alternative courses of behavior are available, perhaps where such incongruence or conflict is absent?

2. As most of the world is composed of groups already using differential distributions, would an emerging group, being more or less dependent on existing groups, experience external consequences other than those contingent on differential distributions? This may be the reason behind the apparent universalism of the stratification of reward distributions. If an emerging group could avoid the consequences provided by groups already differentiated on the basis of reward distribution, the probability of its developing an egalitarian distribution might be greater.

3. Probably most of the external consequences "operating" on groups are not as clear, immediate, or regular as those existing in the present experiment. What effect does this have? Does it simply take longer to establish the determinance achieved in this experiment? Or are the effects more dramatic?

4. Can "consequences" be identified in all situations? Is the concept too general to be useful in most research situations, particularly using more macro-units of analysis?

6

Communication Networks: An Experimental
Re-evaluation

Robert L. Burgess

Social psychology is often defined as the study of social interaction (Swanson, 1965). In view of this fact, it is not surprising that many social psychologists have been concerned with exploring the effects of different patterns or forms of interaction upon other features of group processes such as member satisfaction or group productivity. These patterns of interaction are usually termed *networks* or *structures*. Alex Bavelas (1950) and his associates have contributed probably the most elegant operationalization of interaction networks or structures yet available. In his design, each individual in a group is given certain information. The group is assigned the task of assembling this information, using it to make a decision, and then issuing orders based on this decision. The critical feature of the design is that the group members are separated from one another and can communicate only through channels which may be opened or closed by the experimenter.

Research employing this design has been in progress for the past 18 years. Unfortunately, the research has not produced consistent and cumulative results. Indeed, the results are contradictory as well as inconclusive. Table 1 summarizes some major experiments conducted to date with regard to the dependent variable "productivity" or "solution rate." One independent variable which

Reprinted from the *Journal of Experimental Social Psychology*, Vol. 4, (1968), pp. 324-337, with the permission of the editors. Slightly edited. Copyright © 1968 by Academic Press, Inc.

many experimenters have considered to be important is problem complexity. Hence the results are presented for both "simple" and "complex" problems.[1]

Looking first at the studies that employed the "simple" task, we see that seven out of thirteen reported that the Wheel network produced the highest solution rate. The *Wheel* is a net in which organizational problems are kept to a minimum. All information is directed toward the individual occupying the central position. Typically, this individual, upon receiving the information provided by the other group members, solves the problems and sends out directives to the others in the group. However, the All-channel network was found to produce the highest rate in three cases. The All-channel is a net which permits direct communication between all members. In three instances there were found to be no significant differences between the networks.

Of the studies that used the "complex" task we see that one of ten reported the Wheel to be most proficient, six the All-channel, and three found no significant differences between the networks. The most obvious conclusion is that the variables underlying the relative effectiveness of different communication networks have not been isolated as yet. This conclusion, difficult to avoid, is quite simple to articulate. The more difficult task, yet the one which must be accomplished if we are to further our knowledge of social structure, is to specify and improve upon the deficiencies of previous studies. We shall take up this issue in the next section.

EXPERIMENT I

METHOD

The present investigation was designed in the anticipation that these inconsistent and contradictory findings could be resolved. In

---

[1] The "simple" problem, sometimes called the Leavitt-type problem, is utilized in this study and described below. The "complex" problem refers to a variety of arithmetic problems such as the following:

A small company is moving from one office building to another. It must move (1) chairs, (2) desks, and (3) typewriters. How many trucks are needed to make the move in one trip? For a three-member group, six items of information would be needed to solve the problem and these would usually be equally divided over the group members. For example, the company owns 12 desks, 48 chairs, and 12 typewriters, and one truckload consists of 12 typewriters or 3 desks or 25 chairs.

TABLE 1

Synopsis of Communication Network Findings

Author	Date	Size	Network Solution Rate (in descending order)	Task
Leavitt	1951	5	Wheel (fastest trial)	Simple
Heise and	1951	3	All-channel: Wheel	Simple
Miller			Wheel: All-channel	Complex
Hirota	1953	5	No significant difference	Simple
Shaw	1954a	4	No significant difference	Complex
Shaw	1954b	3	No significant difference	Complex
			No significant difference	Simple
Guetzkow and	1955	5	Wheel: All-channel: Circle	Simple
Simon			(Stable nets—no signif. diff.)	
Shaw	1956	4	All-channel: Wheel	Complex
Shaw and				
Rothschild	1956	4	All-channel: Wheel	Complex
Guetzkow and				
Dill	1957	5	All-channel: Circle	Simple
Shaw, Rothschild,				
Strickland	1957	4	All-channel: Wheel	Complex
Shaw	1958	4	All-channel: Wheel	Complex
Mulder	1959	4	Wheel	Simple
Mulder	1960	4	No significant difference	Simple
			No significant difference	Complex
Mohanna and				
Argyle	1960	5	Wheel	Simple
Cohen, Bennis,				
Wolkon	1961	5	Wheel	Simple
Cohen, Bennis,				
Wolkon	1962	5	Wheel	Simple
Lawson	1964a	4	(NR)* All-channel: Wheel: Circle	Simple
			(R) Wheel: All-channel: Circle	
Lawson	1964b	4	(NR) All-channel: Circle: Wheel	Complex
			(R) All-channel: Circle: Wheel	

*NR = nonreinforced; R = reinforced.

this experiment, the four members comprising a group were separated from one another by partitions. The members could communicate with one another by means of interconnected slots in the
partitions through which written messages could be passed. These
slots could be closed at any time by the experimenter in order to
create any desired communication structure. As with earlier studies,
the practice here was to permit free and continuous communication within the limits imposed by the various networks under investigation. Two networks were investigated. One network, the
Wheel, was described in the previous section. The other network,
the *Circle*, makes imperative some sort of relay system within the
group; no member has channels open to all other members. This
is a net which permits the emergence of one form or several forms
of patterned communication. Yet, unlike the All-channel net, it is
not possible for the members in the Circle to simulate completely
the pattern found in the Wheel. The comparison of these two
rather extreme networks should provide us with a crucial test of
the effects of different communication networks.

Several criticisms may be leveled against communication network experiments. For example, data from psychology have indicated that during individual learning there is an initial transition
or acquisition period, a period marked by an acceleration in the
response rate, leading to a "steady state." Once the steady state is
reached, the behavior typically remains stable for long periods of
time. None of the previous communication network experiments
was designed in such a way that we could observe steady-state periods. This state of affairs is, unfortunately, typical of most social-
psychological investigations. By being overly concerned with tests
of significance, we incorporate large samples with short periods of
observation. The reverse strategy is called for if, as the data of individual psychology suggest, such transitional states are the rule
rather than the exception. In the present investigation, a small
number of groups (15) was investigated for a relatively extended
duration of time. In previous experiments, groups were required
to solve only 25–60 problems. As a consequence, the groups were
still learning to organize and solve the tasks presented *when the
experiments were terminated*. In the present investigation, the
groups were required to solve 900–1100 problems.

Another defect in previous studies is that, with one or two
exceptions, they relied entirely upon control by randomization. It
may be argued that this method increases rather than decreases

random error variance (Sidman, 1960). Here, control by constancy was employed wherever possible; all groups were run under both experimental conditions. Each group was "its own control." One half of the groups began under the Circle net and were subsequently changed to a Wheel net and back again in an A-B-A design. For the other half of the groups the pattern was Wheel-Circle-Wheel.

Another major criticism of previous studies is that they failed to include one basic property of social life, namely, behavioral consequences, either positive or negative. This is particularly critical since recent research seems to indicate that most social behavior exists precisely because of its environmental, especially social, consequences (Staats and Staats, 1964). Hence in this experiment "reinforcement" was provided contingent upon correct problem solving, and "punishment" was provided contingent upon errors.

APPARATUS

In front of each member was a panel on which five letters of the alphabet were placed vertically with a light and a banana jack next to each letter. For each problem a different light was illuminated on each member's panel. The task was to determine, through written communication, which light was not illuminated on any subject's panel. Once the group had determined the answer, all members inserted their plugs into the selected answer jacks. If the answer was correct an amber light on the panel was illuminated. The subjects then took their plugs out of the answer jacks and inserted them into a neutral jack below the amber light. With this accomplished, electromechanical relays automatically set up the next problem and the process began all over again.

PROCEDURES

For Experiment I, 20 subjects from the experimenter's class in introductory sociology volunteered for 10 hours of experimental work in lieu of an assigned term paper. The groups were randomly assigned to either the Circle or the Wheel network.

Each experimental session began with the subjects being ushered into the experimental room and seated around a table. It will be recalled that they were separated from one another by four vertical partitions. Their communications were restricted to writ-

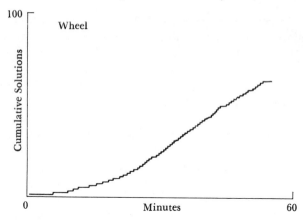

FIG. 1. This figure represents the cumulative record of the first hour of a group under the Wheel network. Note the accelerating slope.

ten messages which they could pass through slots in the partitions. During the operating trials, they interchanged messages on pre-coded cards. Blank cards were provided also for organizational purposes or for any other need the subjects might have. The first session for each group was preceded by a training period in which the group worked through two problems to make sure that the basic mechanics were understood.

RESULTS[2]
During the first sessions especially, but also during succeeding sessions, there was a gradual yet steady acceleration in solution rates. Eventually, all groups reached a steady state. An example can be seen in Figs. 1 and 2. By the hour six the group had reached a steady state. It took the five groups in this experiment, on the average, some 500 problems to reach a steady state. Consequently, one must question the generalizability of the findings from previous investigations, particularly since the maximum number of required solutions before this was 60. If it took this long to reach a steady state with the "simple" problems, the findings from studies incorporating "complex" problems should be especially questionable. One would expect the attainment of a steady state in such

[2] For a more detailed presentation of the data from this study see R. L. Burgess, 1968.

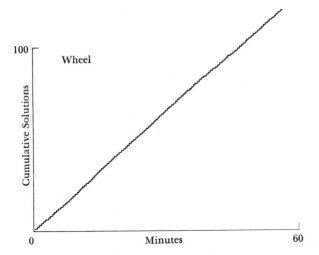

Fig. 2. This is the cumulative record of the sixth hour of the group seen in Fig. 1. It is plainly evident that the group no longer is exhibiting the erratic, relatively slow but accelerating solution rate. The group had reached a "steady state."

circumstances to be attenuated drastically. These results strongly suggest that, in order to compare properly the effects of communication structures, a group should have enough experience as an operating unit to reach a steady state.

Observation of the five groups in this experiment revealed wide differences in motivation. One group, for example, was very concerned with working as quickly as possible, even though the experimenter's instructions were only to "work at your own speed." But by being so concerned with speed, this group was making a remarkable number of errors. In contrast, another group was concerned not with speed but with minimizing errors. As a consequence this group worked at a steady but slow rate. Still another group was concerned with maximizing speed as well as minimizing errors. It became quite apparent that, despite random assignment, this motivational factor would confound the evaluation of the effects of the communication network variable.

In an attempt to reduce this variability, control by constancy was employed. The error-rate dimension was tackled first. Now, whenever an error occurred, a raucous buzzer would sound for 15 seconds and the subjects' panels would be shut off for the same period of time. Upon the onset of the buzzer and the "time-out" period, there was an immediate decline in the solution rate as well as in the error rate. But whereas the error rate remained at a low level, the solution rate recovered. The other major effect of this manipulation was that the error rates declined to a level which mitigated against their previous contaminating effects. The error rates for the five groups also became much more comparable. For Groups 1–5 the number of errors per hundred problems was, before the manipulation, 24, 40, 11, 15, and 30, respectively. After the change the rates were 2.2, 4.3, 2.3, 3.0, and 3.2 errors per hundred problems.

The other aspect of behavioral consequences involves positive reinforcement or incentives, contingent upon solution performance. In this case, the experimental situation was altered so that the groups could reduce their time in the experiment by working quickly. This turned out to be a substantial incentive, as can be seen in Fig. 3. Looking at this figure, we see a typical pattern. At the beginning of this session the group was operating under the

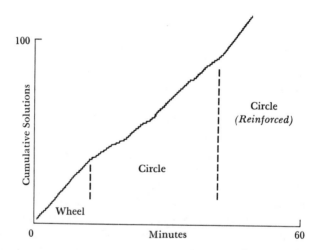

Fig. 3. This figure presents the behavior of a group under three experimental conditions: the Wheel net, the Circle net, and reinforcement under the Circle net. The pattern is typical. When the network is changed to a Circle pattern, there is a noticeable deterioration in the group's performance. After reinforcement is introduced, the behavior becomes much less erratic and the solution rate increases, even surpassing the rate under the Wheel network.

Wheel network. During this period the members were working at a relatively high and steady rate, 2.7 solutions per minute. When the net was changed to the Circle, however, there was an immediate deterioration in performance, in term of both solution rate, now 1.9 per minute, and overall consistency in performance. But note the effects of the onset of the reinforcement contingency: there was an immediate increase in the solution rate to 3.1 per minute, and an elimination of the variability in the group's behavior. This pattern was observed in each of the five groups; only before the introduction of the reinforcement variable was the solution rate lower and more erratic under the Circle net.

Two major findings have emerged so far from Experiment I. First, as with individual learning, groups exhibit an initial transition period during which their response rates steadily increase until a steady state is reached. Second, the introduction of reinforcement and punishment consequences, contingent upon group behavior, alters the behavior in the predicted directions.

But what are the effects of the two networks upon a group's solution rate? Here we find that without reinforcement in effect performance under the Wheel is significantly higher than under the Circle initially. But, once a steady state has been reached *and* con-

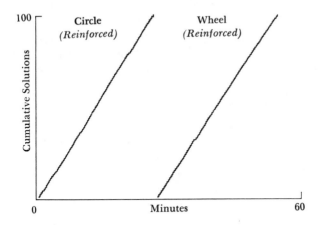

Fig. 4. This represents the last two sessions of a group. These cumulative records highlight one important finding in this study. That is, once groups have reached a steady state and there are contingencies upon their behavior, there are no differences in solution rates for the two networks under investigation.

tingencies of reinforcement are in operation, there are no significant differences between the two networks with regard to the variable "solution rate." Indeed, under these conditions the solution rates are, for most purposes, identical. An example can be seen in Fig. 4.

This experiment, however, leaves certain issues unresolved. For while there may be no *ultimate* differences in solution rates between the two networks, there do appear to be some *initial* differences between the networks. The communication structure may affect the behavior of groups indirectly by either handicapping or facilitating the group members in their attempts to organize themselves for efficient task performance. There may be, for example, a difference in the networks with regard to the time it takes to reach a steady state.

In this connection, certain structural characteristics stand out. For instance, the Wheel net is structured in such a way that all "unnecessary" channels are blocked. The very structure itself largely determines who the group leader will be. Furthermore, the other members of the group cannot communicate directly with anyone but the person in the centralized position. Thus it is not surprising that the behavior of the group members operating under such a structure is devoted entirely to the problem-solving task. That the solution rate under the Wheel net is relatively stable was seen in both Figs. 2 and 3. The Circle net, at least before contingent reinforcement is introduced, produces a very different pattern, as also was seen in Fig. 3. This particular communication structure, besides requiring a relay system of some sort, is of such a nature that it permits the group members to communicate directly and at will with their respective "neighbors." Such a structure increases the possibility of non-task-related behavior. And, in the absence of behavioral consequences, this is precisely what happens.

The major problem yet to be answered is whether there are differences between the two networks in the transitional stages leading to the steady states. To answer this question would require one to look in detail at the developmental behavior of such task groups. The next experiment was designed in an attempt to answer this question, as well as to provide a replication of the results of Experiment I with regard to the failure to find any difference in the solution rates during the steady-state periods for the two networks.

EXPERIMENT II

METHOD

For this experiment 40 additional subjects were recruited and divided into ten groups. After random assignment, half of the groups began under the Circle net and were kept there until they reached a steady state. At this point the network was changed to a Wheel. After the groups had solved at least 100 problems at a steady rate, the network was changed back to a Circle. For the other five groups this procedure was reversed to a Wheel-Circle-Wheel pattern. From the very beginning, contingencies were in operation in this experiment. Though the subjects volunteered for ten 1-hour sessions, they were instructed at the beginning of the experiment that they could reduce this time by working quickly. A session would be terminated upon the completion of 100 problems. In actuality, it took a few of the groups slightly longer than 1 hour to complete 100 problems at first. But with practice they were able to solve the required number of problems in less than half an hour. They were, in effect, getting back almost 5 of the 10 hours for which they had volunteered.

RESULTS

The entire experimental history of a group under these conditions can be seen in Fig. 5. Here we see under the Circle net a transitional stage of almost 500 problems leading to a steady-state period. Then, when the network was changed to a Wheel, there is a decrease in the solution rate. But after this transition period a steady state again is reached. The network was then changed back to the Circle. As in the previous experiment, the rates for the two nets during the steady-state periods are for all purposes identical. This was true for each of the ten groups investigated.

Theoretically, Wheel and Circle groups can be equally efficient. That is, there are no *physical* limitations favoring one net over another. If there were, any observed *behavioral* differences would result from this experimental artifact and hence be social-psychologically uninteresting. As it stands, if the groups were to perform optimally, they could solve problems by using a minimum of only six message units under both networks. One way to com-

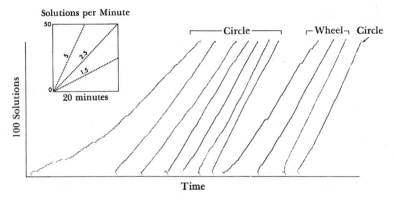

FIG. 5. This figure shows the entire experimental history of a group under both networks. The members had reached a steady state under the Circle network during the sixth and seventh sessions. At that point, the network was changed to a Wheel. Note the decline in the members' solution rate and their subsequent recovery during the next two sessions. The rates under the two networks were, during the steady state periods, essentially identical.

pare the networks is, then, to measure how long it takes the groups to reach an optimally efficient organization. And here we find that all of the groups that began under the Wheel net immediately used only the minimum number of message units. In contrast, none of the Circle groups developed such an organization at the very beginning. Indeed, one group never did reach this level of efficiency. Four of the five groups that began operation under the Circle net required, on the average, 40 problems to reach an optimum message-unit system. Consequently, one possibly important and significant difference between the networks during the transitional period is the amount of experience required to attain an optimally efficient organization. It should be remembered, however, that each of these four groups eventually attained an optimum organization.

The fifth group is an interesting case in itself. Throughout the entire experiment, it employed an each-to-each communication pattern while operating under the Circle net. What evolved within this group was essentially a three-step flow of information *for each member*. In other words, the members of this group developed a very complex relay system. They took much longer to reach a steady state than any other group. But once this group did reach a steady state it performed as well under the Circle net as it did under the Wheel net. If this experiment had not been designed to allow groups to reach steady states, we never would have been able to determine that this particular difference between the networks is only temporary in nature.

Though the groups that began under the Wheel network were from the very beginning using only the minimum number of message units, it took them on the average over 200 problems to reach a steady state. In contrast, groups under the Circle net required a little over 300 problems to reach a steady state. Something more than simply minimizing redundant messages is involved here. In actuality, the solution of these group tasks involves a wide range of component behaviors. The group members, for example, must *learn* how to manipulate the experimental apparatus properly and efficiently, how to organize and collate the incoming information, and how to transfer messages efficiently to persons in the position or positions with whom they are linked. In short, there is not just one behavior here. Rather, there are a number of relatively complex interconnected behaviors; and these behaviors must be learned. This is one reason why the contingent reinforcement variable is so important. These behaviors, in other words, are subject to the principles of learning, and the experimenter can ignore such principles only at the expense of inconclusive, artificial, and inaccurate results.

One final point should be made: steady states and optimum organizations may vary independently of one another. For example, a group may reach a steady state that fails to employ an optimum organization, as we found to be the case with one group. Likewise, a group can attain an optimum organization before reaching a steady state, as was the case for a time with nine groups.

CONCLUSION

The present investigation, consisting of two experiments, was designed in the anticipation that inconsistent and inconclusive findings could be resolved. Four-member groups under two rather extreme networks were studied. In one network, the Wheel, the communication restrictions reduce the difficulty of organizational problems to a minimum. The other net, the Circle, makes imperative some sort of relay system within the group.

In Experiment I, it was determined that group problem-solving behavior within such communication networks exhibits a substantial transition period indicated by an acceleration in the solution rate leading to a steady state. It also was determined that contingencies of reinforcement substantially increase the solution rate for such groups. The reinforcement variable was introduced by altering the experimental situation so that groups could reduce their time in the experiment by working quickly. It was also found that punishment for errors effectively reduced the error rate and eliminated a large portion of the intergroup variability along this dimension. Finally, it was discovered that only without contingencies of reinforcement in effect does the Wheel network produce a significantly higher solution rate than the Circle. But groups in natural settings invariably will have some form of reinforcement system in operation. Any experiment not incorporating this variable would be needlessly artificial.

Experiment II was designed to explore systematically the transition periods leading to the steady states. The two networks were found to differ during these transition periods. For example, the Wheel initially performed at a slightly higher rate than the Circle; the Circle net generally required more problems to reach a steady state than the Wheel; and it took the Circle longer than the Wheel to reach an optimum organization.

Looking at the entire experimental history of these task groups, we observe an orderly progression toward smaller differences between the networks. The differences between the nets are greatest during the acquisition period without reinforcement in effect, are less marked with reinforcement in effect, and are still smaller during the nonreinforced steady-state period; finally, during the steady-state periods, with reinforcement in effect, there are no differences between the networks.

On the methodological side, these findings argue for the design of social-psychological experiments to permit the observation and analysis of the entire developmental histories of groups from their transition to their steady-state periods. The findings also suggest that one important variable which must be included in order to explore properly the effects of various communication networks, and possibly social structures in general, is motivation. This can be appreciated especially in light of the fact that the introduction of reinforcement eliminated previous differences in solution rates between the networks.

One conclusion suggested by these data is that previously asserted "differences" in solution rates between communication structures, in which no physical limitations favored one network over the other, were a function of experimental artifacts. Had previous experimenters included reinforcement contingent upon performance, and had they observed their experimental groups over sufficient time periods, the collection of a vast array of contradictory findings could have been avoided. It remains to be seen whether presumed differences in member satisfaction under such networks also are temporary phenomena.

REFERENCES

Bavelas, A., 1950. Communication patterns in task-oriented groups. *Journal of the Acoustical Society of America*, 22, pp. 725-730. Reprinted in D. Cartwright and A. F. Zander (Eds.), *Group Dynamics: Research and Theory*, 2nd ed. New York: Row, Peterson and Co., 1960, pp. 660-683.

Burgess, R. L., 1968. Communication networks, behavioral consequences and group learning. Unpublished Ph.D. dissertation, Washington University, St. Louis.

Cohen, A. M., W. G. Bennis, and G. H. Wolkon, 1961. The effects of continued practice on the behaviors of problem-solving groups. *Sociometry*, 24, pp. 416-432.

Cohen, A. M., W. G. Bennis, and G. H. Wolkon, 1962. Changing small-group communication networks. *Administrative Science Quarterly*, 6, pp. 443-462.

Guetzkow, H., and W. R. Dill, 1957. Factors in the organizational development of task-oriented groups. *Sociometry*, 20, pp. 175-204.

Guetzkow, H., and H. A. Simon, 1955. The impact of certain communication nets upon organization and performance in task-oriented groups. *Management Science*, pp. 233-250. Reprinted in A. H. Rubenstein and C. J. Haberstroh, *Some Theories of Organization*. Homewood, Ill.: Richard D. Irwin and Dorsey Press, 1960, pp. 259-277.

Heise, G., and G. Miller, 1955. Problem solving by small groups using various communication nets. In A. P. Hare, E. F. Borgatta, and R. F. Bales (Eds.), *Small Groups: Studies in Social Interaction.* New York: Alfred A. Knopf, pp. 353-367.

Hirota, K., 1953. *Japan Journal of Psychology,* 24, pp. 105-113.

Lawson, E. D., 1964a. Reinforced and non-reinforced four-man communication nets. *Psychological Reports,* 14, pp. 287-296.

Lawson, E. D., 1964b. Reinforcement in group problem-solving with arithmetic problems. *Psychological Reports,* 14, pp. 703-710.

Leavitt, H., 1958. Some effects of certain communication patterns in group performance. In E. E. Maccoby, T. M. Newcomb, and E. L. Hartley (Eds.), *Readings in Social Psychology,* 3rd ed. New York: Henry Holt and Co., pp. 546-564.

Mohanna, A. I., and M. Argyle, 1960. A cross-cultural study of structured groups with unpopular central members. *Journal of Abnormal and Social Psychology,* 60, pp. 139-140.

Mulder, M., 1959. Group-structure and performance. *Acta Psychologica, the European Journal of Psychology,* 16, pp. 356-402.

Mulder, M., 1960. Communication structure, decision structure and group performance. *Sociometry,* 23, pp. 1-14.

Shaw, M. E., 1954a. Group structure and the behavior of individuals in small groups. *Journal of Psychology,* 38, pp. 139-149.

Shaw, M. E., 1954b. Some effects of problem complexity upon problem solution efficiency in different communication nets. *Journal of Experimental Psychology,* 48, pp. 211-217.

Shaw, M. E., 1956. Random versus systematic distribution of information in communication nets. *Journal of Personality,* 25, pp. 56-69.

Shaw, M. E., 1958. Some effects of irrelevant information upon problem-solving by small groups. *Journal of Social Psychology,* 47, pp. 33-37.

Shaw, M. E., and G. H. Rothschild, 1956. Some effects of prolonged experience in communication nets. *Journal of Applied Psychology,* 40, pp. 281-286.

Shaw, M. E., G. H. Rothschild, and J. F. Strickland, 1957. Decision processes in communication nets. *Journal of Abnormal and Social Psychology,* 54, pp. 323-330.

Sidman, M., 1960. *Tactics of Scientific Research: Evaluating Experimental Data in Psychology.* New York: Basic Books.

Staats, A. W., and C. K. Staats, 1964. *Complex Human Behavior: A Systematic Extension of Learning Principles.* New York: Holt, Rinehart & Winston.

Swanson, G. E., 1965. On explanations of social interaction. *Sociometry,* 28, pp. 101-123.

PART II

The Experimental Analysis of Social
Process in the Field

It is apparent from the preceding research reports that the methods employed in the analysis of operant behavior are somewhat different from the familiar practices of the social sciences. Those who have developed the custom of evaluating social research according to the sophistication of its statistical design and the levels of significance achieved in differences between experimental and control group scores may have found the research in this collection a bit disconcerting. Consequently, a review of the methods of the experimental analysis of behavior is necessary to clarify their relation to current research practices in the social sciences.

The general subject of methodology in the social sciences is frequently discussed as though it were synonymous with statistics. In contrast, Goode and Hatt (1952) state, "Techniques are thought of as comprising the specific procedures by which the sociologist gathers and orders his data *prior* to their logical or statistical manipulation" (p. 5, italics added). Aspects of the research enterprise may be separated, at least analytically, in order to facilitate a closer inspection of each, and, though it is an oversimplification, the present discussion tends to separate techniques of data *collection* from the techniques of data *analysis*. The latter deal primarily with the logical operations, including statistical manipulation, which are employed in order to draw some sort of conclusion. The techniques of data collection, on the other hand, deal primarily with the operations associated with observing a phenomenon. It follows that performing operations that will render an event recordable is a central problem in any research design. However, textbooks on methodology give comparatively little attention to this problem.

The statistical methods appropriate to social science data are discussed in a number of excellent books. Unfortunately, with the exception of survey research, there are relatively few treatments of how to go about the basic process of obtaining useful data. In part this paucity may be due to the fact that the techniques for collecting social science data are not considered to be highly problematic. Webb, Campbell, Schwartz, and Sechrest (1966) illustrate this by observing, "Today, some 90 per cent of social science research is based upon interviews and questionnaires" (p. 1). With such a limited array of collection techniques, it is entirely reasonable that procedures at that level should be well standardized, and consequently most of the researcher's attention is given to problems at the level of analysis. The present collection, however, is not concerned with interview or questionnaire procedures. It deals with some portion of the remaining 10 per cent.

Much of Chapter 7 is based on Campbell and Stanley's (1963) article, "Experimental and Quasi-experimental Designs for Research on Teaching," which is an excellent foundation for evaluating the relative merits of the research designs generally employed in the social sciences. Of the sixteen designs which these authors present and evaluate, three are designated as "true experimental designs," yet none of these adequately portrays the strategies employed by most of the contributors to the present collection. The procedures of the "experimental analysis" constitute a fourth experimental design worthy of explicit consideration.

REFERENCES

Campbell, D. T., and J. C. Stanley, 1963. Experimental and quasi-experimental designs for research on teaching. In N. L. Gage (Ed.), *Handbook of Research on Teaching*. Chicago: Rand McNally, pp. 171-246.

Goode, W. J., and P. K. Hatt, 1952. *Methods in Social Research*. New York: McGraw-Hill Book Company.

Webb, E. J., D. T. Campbell, R. D. Schwartz, and L. Sechrest, 1966. *Unobstrusive Measures: Nonreactive Research in the Social Sciences*. Chicago: Rand McNally.

7

Characteristics of the Experimental Analysis

Don Bushell, Jr. and Robert L. Burgess

> We can reach knowledge of definite elementary conditions
> of phenomena only by one road, viz., by experimental
> analysis. Analysis dissociates all the complex phenomena
> successively into more and more simple phenomena, until
> they are reduced, if possible, to just two elementary condi-
> tions. Experimental science, in fact, considers in a phe-
> nomenon only the definite conditions necessary to produce it.
>
> CLAUDE BERNARD, 1865

Comparison, the identification of similarities and differences between phenomena, is unquestionably the basis of all scientific evidence. From this process, common to all modes of inquiry, widely
different methodologies emerge, distinguished by the manner in
which they present information for comparison. Bernard recognized two gross approaches by differentiating passive and active
observation. The passive observer draws comparisons between
events as they are presented by nature, while the active observer
(the experimenter) creates the phenomena to be compared. Such
a distinction does not mean to imply that some types of problems
can be approached in only one of these modes and not the other.
Meteorology has been largely a science of passive observation, but
the next few decades will probably see the beginnings of an experimental science of meteorology, the active changing of atmos-
pheric conditions. Anthropologists trained under Boaz were taught
to record what they saw in great detail, making every effort not to
modify the setting by their presence, but a growing number of contemporary anthropologists are engaged in what can reasonably be
termed cultural experimentation. The question of whether a topic
is approached actively or passively appears to be most closely related to the technological sophistication of the science involved.

The experimental analysis seeks to gain sufficient control of
its subject matter to be capable of drawing direct comparisons between phenomena which are different by virtue of the experimenter's actions. When successful, this is indeed a powerful form

of analysis, for the clearest way to account for a phenomena lies in the ability to control its appearance.

An account offered by Bernard so clearly exemplifies many aspects of the experimental analysis that it is repeated here as grist for further discussion even though it is over 100 years old.

> One day, rabbits from the market were brought into my laboratory. They were put on the table where they urinated, and I happened to observe that their urine was clear and acid. This fact struck me, because rabbits, which are herbivora, generally have turbid and alkaline urine; while on the other hand carnivora, as we know, have clear and acid urine. This observation of acidity in the rabbits' urine gave me an idea that these animals must be in the nutritional condition of carnivora. I assumed that they had probably not eaten for a long time, and that they had been transformed by fasting, into veritable carnivorous animals, living on their own blood. Nothing was easier than to verify this preconceived idea or hypothesis by experiment. I gave the rabbits grass to eat; and a few hours later, their urine became turbid and alkaline. I then subjected them to fasting and after twenty-four hours, or thirty-six hours at most, their urine again became clear and strongly acid; then after eating grass their urine became alkaline again, etc. I repeated this very simple experiment a great many times, and always with the same result. I then repeated it on a horse, an herbivorous animal which also has turbid and alkaline urine. I found that fasting, as in rabbits, produced prompt acidity of the urine, with such an increase in urea that it spontaneously crystallizes at times in the cooled urine. As a result of my experiments, I thus reached the general proposition which then was still unknown, to wit, that all fasting animals feed on meat, so that herbivora then have urine like that of carnivora (p. 152).
>
> But to prove that my fasting rabbits were really carnivorous, a counterproof was required. A carnivorous rabbit had to be experimentally produced by feeding it with meat, so as to see if its urine would then be clear, as it was during fasting. So I had rabbits fed on cold boiled beef (which they eat very nicely when they are given nothing else). My expectation was again verified, and as long as the animal diet was continued, the rabbits kept their clear and acid urine (p. 153).

The events described by Bernard provide an outline of the basic tactics of the experimental analysis which can be broken into the following steps.

Step 1. The inquiry was initiated when Bernard observed an event which did not fit the circumstances. As a physiologist, Bernard had had experience with rabbits that led him to view the appearance of clear and acid urine as an anomaly—it just didn't fit the patterns he had come to expect. The event *did* conform, however, to his experience with carnivorous animals. For Bernard these factors combined to foster a series of experiments, whereas, for most of us, having a rabbit urinate on the table would probably cause only mild embarrassment. This is what Bachrach (1962) calls the "prepared mind" to emphasize the fact that a thorough familiarity with one's subject matter is undoubtedly a necessary prerequisite to significant achievement. Or, in other words, a lengthy and complex history would be required before an isolated event such as the one that Bernard observed could become a discriminative stimulus controlling the subsequent complex behaviors of experimental research.

Step 2. The idea (hypothesis) which struck Bernard is presented in the form of a functional relationship between the appearance of the urine and the nature of the rabbits' diet. "I assumed that they had probably not eaten for a long time, and that they had been transformed by fasting, into veritable carnivorous animals, living on their own blood." Not only is the relationship between diet and urine a clear one, but the means for examining both elements of the proposition are also straightforward. Both the appropriate measures and the necessary manipulations are strongly indicated by his statement of the problem.

Step 3. At this point Bernard becomes an experimenter and intervenes to act upon the objects of his study to produce, if possible, a phenomenon not currently observable. He feeds the rabbits grass. Sure enough, "a few hours later, their urine became turbid and alkaline." Bernard had executed what Campbell and Stanley (1963) call a "one-group pretest-post-test design." He had, in effect, before and after measures of his dependent variable surrounding an experimental manipulation and presumably reflecting its influence.

Such a sequence must, unquestionably, be the first step in any experimental procedure. Unfortunately, it is the only step in a great many social science inquiries. This procedure is similar to the case study method frequently employed in which it is presumed that full control of the critical variables lies beyond the reach of the investigator. "What were the effects of the 1929 market crash upon the loan policies of rural land-holding banks west of the Mississippi?" illustrates a problem which might be attacked in this way. Consider also the report by Wolf, Birnbrauer, Williams, and Lawler (1965) of an institutionalized child who frequently vomited in the classroom and was, as a result, removed to spend the remainder of the day in her room. On the assumption that the vomiting behavior was an operant maintained by the consequent escape from the classroom, it was decided that future vomiting would result in a matter-of-fact cleaning up of the mess and continuation of the class with the girl present. When the normal routine was changed accordingly, so that the girl stayed in the classroom even when she vomited, the rate of vomiting was gradually reduced to zero. In another case Ayllon and Michael (1959) observed a mental patient who disrupted the ward nurses by entering their office sixteen times a day. Assuming that the behavior was being maintained by the reinforcing consequence of the nurses' attention as they hustled the patient out of the office, Ayllon directed them to change their procedures and completely ignore the woman each time she entered the office. Within two months of this new procedure the patient was entering the office only twice each day. Both of these illustrations suggest that a particular behavior was being maintained by the social consequences (attention) which it produced, because the removal of that attention corresponded to a marked decline in the frequency of the behavior. Similarly, Bernard's act of feeding the rabbits grass corresponded to a changed appearance in their urine, but in all of these cases the drawing of firm conclusions is a very risky business. Some of these risks need to be examined.

FOUR THREATS TO INTERNAL VALIDITY

As suggestive as the above experiments are, all suffer from a very low degree of *internal validity*. Internal validity is referred to by Campbell and Stanley as "the basic minimum without which any experiment is uninterpretable: did in fact the experimental treatments make a difference in this specific experimental instance?" To the extent that alternative explanations of the changes in behavior can be offered, the effect of the changed procedures remains in doubt. Such rival hypotheses are broken into several types by Campbell and Stanley, the first of which is *history*. During the time that the mental patient's visits to the nurses' office were being recorded several other events might have occurred in addition to the procedural changes instituted by Ayllon. The patient might have developed a sore foot which made it inconvenient to walk to the office so frequently. A color television set may have been installed in the dayroom which occupied a greater share of her time than the old black and white set.

An additional rival hypothesis which constantly threatens the case study is termed *maturation* ("biological or psychological processes which systematically vary with the passage of time, independent of specific external events"). For example, the vomiting girl may have simply "outgrown" her unfortunate habit at the same time that the classroom procedures were changed. *When multiple hypotheses are plausible, none of them can carry any explanatory power.*

A third threat to the internal validity of an experiment is found in the possible effects of the observations themselves. This, of course, is the problem of *reactive measures*, a chronic headache in the social sciences (Webb, Campbell, Schwartz, and Sechrest, 1966). It may have been, for instance, that the nurses' action of tallying the patient's visits to the office constituted a stimulus which was effective in reducing the frequency of these visits. The administration of IQ tests may alter an individual's future performance on tests of this type. Being subjected to socioeconomic scales may alter respondents' behavior by making them more conscious of their "class" position. The questions of election pollsters may stimulate a voter to take a stand on an issue.

A fourth problem is identified by Campbell and Stanley as *instrumentation* or *instrument decay*. If we are dealing with before and after measures taken by observers, these observers may be more or less attentive on the second occasion. Perhaps the novelty of the observing situation affected their reports in the first instance. Instead, a change in observer personnel during the course of the study may account for reported differences. A vomiting response is probably clear enough that the possibility of serious instrument decay in its measurement seems unlikely, but it is possible that a change in the nursing staff could have altered the reporting of the patient's visits to the office.

For these reasons, and others which will be discussed later, Bernard's initial act of feeding his rabbits grass was a promising beginning which produced results in conformity with his hypothesis, but it falls far short of demonstrating a functional relationship between his two critical variables. A diagram of his experiment to this point might look something like the following graph. Another form in which such data might appear is the familiar fourfold table, indicating the results of ten urinalyses on four rabbits.

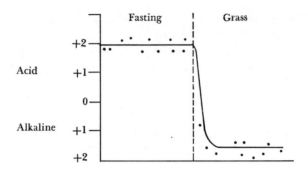

	Fasting	Grass
Acid	20	0
Alkaline	0	20

The data could even be pressed to the point of computing some measure of association which would certainly produce a comforting coefficient of 1.00. Having enumerated several reasons why the relationship portrayed could be entirely spurious, let us assume that the "perfect" coefficient would be treated with appropriate modesty.

Step 4. The next step in Bernard's experiment substantially increases confidence in the hypothesized relationship and correspondingly reduces the tenability of several of the rival hypotheses discussed above. Bernard attempted to restore the original conditions in order to observe the reappearance of the initially clear and acid urine. He stopped feeding the rabbits. "I then subjected them to fasting and after twenty-four hours, or thirty-six hours at most, their urine again became clear and strongly acid."

Notice that with this check for the reversibility of effect the rival hypothesis of history is weakened seriously, but not eliminated entirely. Recall that in the case of the Ayllon and Michael (1959) study it was suggested that the advent of a color television set or a sore foot might have accounted for the patient's reduced visits to the nurses' office. Both of these alternative explanations of the observations are still theoretically possible, but it stretches credulity to hold out for a perfect coincidence between historical events and *two* experimental manipulations. This would require that, on the same day the original procedures were resumed, the patient tired of color TV or her foot healed as abruptly as it had become troublesome—possible, but not likely.

The maturation hypothesis fares even worse as a plausible rival hypothesis in the face of reversibility. If getting older accounted for the disappearance of vomiting in the first place, growing yet a little older cannot also account for its reappearance.

The testing (reactive) hypothesis is also severely damaged by the demonstration of reversibility. If the nurses' behavior in recording visits to the office, rather than the removal of attention, was a stimulus producing a reduction in that behavior, the resumption of the attention should not alter the depressing effect of the record keeping. It is, however, an outside possibility that the depressing influence of the record keeping was transitory and became ineffective at the same time that the original attending procedures were reinstituted. Similarly, serious consideration of the instrumentation or instrument decay hypothesis depends upon the existence of some highly unlikely circumstance in the face of reversibility.

The graph of the rabbits' urinalysis to this point might now look something like this:

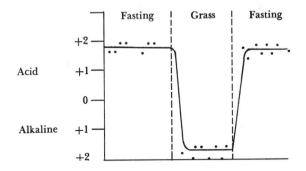

Step 5. Bernard was not through. He reports that he fed his rabbits grass, recorded his observations; let them fast, recorded his observations; fed them grass, recorded his observations; etc. "I repeated this very simple experiment a great many times, and always with the same result." Coincidence can no longer support the

plausibility of any of the rival hypotheses: history, maturation, reactive measures (testing), or instrumentation. The relationship must exist between the acidity of the urine and the dietary regimen as hypothesized.

At this point the graph of Bernard's experiment might have the following appearance:

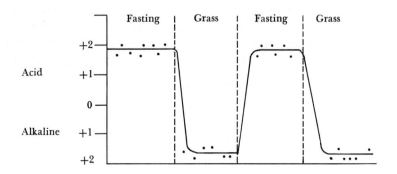

Step 6. The original hypothesis, however, posited a relationship between the acidity or alkalinity of urine and diet in herbivora. Bernard had tested only rabbits, and at this point his conclusions could not be extended to the entire class of mammals. Consequently, "I then repeated it [the experiment] on a horse, an herbivorous animal which also has turbid and alkaline urine. I found that fasting, as in rabbits, produced prompt acidity of the urine, with such an increase in urea that it spontaneously crystallizes at times in the cooled urine." The suspected relationship could now be phrased as a general proposition: "all fasting animals feed on meat, so that herbivora then have urine like that of carnivora."

Notice the phrase, *"like* that of carnivora." What Bernard suspected at the outset was that the rabbits had *become* carnivorous (living on their own blood), but he had demonstrated only the relationship between the *absence* of grass and the presence of acid urine. In order to complete his investigation, it was necessary to demonstrate that the acid urine would also be produced by a meat-eating rabbit, not just a noneating rabbit.

Step 7. To prove that fasting is the functional equivalent of a carnivorous diet, Bernard fed his hungry rabbits cold boiled beef. "My expectation was again verified, and, as long as the animal diet was continued, the rabbits kept their clear and acid urine." The final graph of the experiment might look something like this:

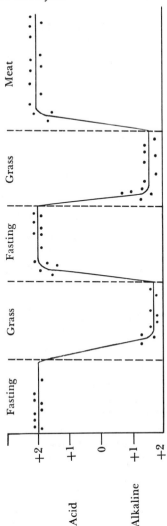

ADDITIONAL THREATS TO INTERNAL VALIDITY

Campbell and Stanley (1963) specify other threats to internal validity beyond those already discussed. The first of these is *statistical regression*, that phenomenon which is to be expected when groups (experimental and control) have been selected by virtue of their extreme scores on a pretest measure. When an extreme case is used, an interesting process results from the fact that a full range of variation is no longer possible. To illustrate, consider the group of students who have been selected from a classroom because they all

scored 100 on a particular examination. Obviously their performance cannot be improved upon—the only variation they can display
is to get worse, to regress toward the overall mean of the class as
a whole. As long as human behavior displays variability, regression of this type is inevitable. Bernard's work, however, did not
rely on the custom of using two groups, one control and the other
experimental. Instead, he modified the environment of a single
group and, by *repeated* manipulations on one environmental variable, controlled for all other factors by keeping them constant. Statistical regression presents no problem when the experimental
group is used as its *own control*.

One of the most intractable problems in the methodologies
of sociology has been that of achieving equivalent groups through
randomization processes. All too often we are interested in dealing
with natural groups, such as families, classrooms, communities, or
businesses, that are not available in sufficient quantity to allow for
randomization. Inevitably, then, questions arise—usually after the
fact—concerning biases resulting in differential selection of respondents for the comparison groups. Campbell and Stanley put
it this way:

Selection is ruled out as an explanation of the difference to the extent
that randomization has assured group equality at time R. This extent is
the extent stated by our sampling statistics. Thus the assurance of equality is greater for large numbers of random assignments than for small.
To the extent indicated by the error term for the no-difference hypothesis,
this assumption will be wrong occasionally. . . . This means that there
will occasionally be an apparently "significant" difference between the
pretest scores. Thus, while simple or stratified randomization assures
unbiased assignment of experimental subjects to groups, it is a less than
perfect way of assuring the initial equivalence of such groups (p. 185).

In spite of this, they go on immediately to say, "It is nonetheless
the *only* way of doing so, and the *essential* way" (italics added).
Thus selection bias can occur when we must deal with small numbers of cases, when our units are not amenable to sampling, and
even when random sampling is employed. In contrast, using a
group as its own control does not require that sampling techniques
be utilized, and it is particularly appropriate when the objects of
study need to be dealt with as complete units.

The differential loss of subjects from the comparison groups,
or *experimental mortality*, stands as an additional threat to the
internal validity in customary research designs. Such a problem

would also obtain in a single-group design if all the subjects with low pretest scores (baselines) were lost before the end of the study. This would not, however, tarnish the results yielded by the subjects that remained. At worst, it would simply mean that additional sessions would be advised for new subjects who were similar to those lost. In the case of comparison groups, on the other hand, the differential loss of subjects may well toll the fruitless end of the study.

EXTERNAL VALIDITY

A consideration of external validity reflects the scientist's concern over whether the relationship that he discovered between his independent and dependent variables meets the criterion for being a *generalization*. Will the observed relation hold *whenever and wherever the originally stipulated conditions are in effect?* Generalization, then, requires the precise specification of the conditions under which a relationship will obtain. Does Avogadro's law, stating that equal volumes of gases contain the same number of molecules, when measured under the same conditions of temperature and pressure (the relevant conditions in this case), hold for all gases; if not, to which gases does it apply? Do the several laws of operant behavior, when all conditions are met, generalize to all social actions; if not, to which social acts do they apply? Does the relationship that Schmitt discovered (see Chapter 2) between supervisory sanctions and productivity, when all conditions are satisfied, apply to all instances of productive activity; if not, to which does it apply? From the standpoint of the philosophy of science this issue involves the development and testing of *epistemic derivations* (Hamblin, 1966).

A decidedly different problem is reflected in the concern with the extent to which the *conditions* specified in a generalization are actually represented in situations or populations other than those in which they were originally observed. This is a concern for the *representativeness* of a particular set of conditions. That Bernard established a positive relationship existing between a meat diet and the amount of acid in the urine of herbivora does not imply that herbivora frequently have a high acidic content in their urine, even though Bernard was unable to produce this phenomenon. Similarly, Galileo's law, $D = cT^2$, would rarely, if ever, be found to exist outside the laboratory precisely because the conditions under which this relation obtains will probably never be duplicated in natural settings. These points may be clarified by returning to a consideration of Schmitt's analysis of the effects of supervision on worker productivity.

The research objective of the supervision study, it will be recalled, was to determine the conditions under which a worker would remain at a given task when more attractive alternatives were available. By manipulating the magnitude of the penalty risked by being away from the less attractive of the two tasks, Schmitt found a uniform curvilinear positive relationship between size of penalty and proportion of time spent on the work task. How much external validity has this finding? Will a behavioral regularity found among several University of Wisconsin undergraduates apply to a group of San Diego longshoremen?

To deal with these questions great effort is expended to make sure that the composition of the experimental sample is isomorphic with some greater population. This is accomplished by sampling from the total population of interest so that all of the relevant variables describing that population are proportionately represented in the sample. This entire process is necessary precisely because we are not able to identify all of the variables which may influence the behavior under study. For purposes of description such procedures are appropriate, and it is in the descriptive sense that they are generally employed. Consider again the question of whether a behavioral regularity found among several University of Wisconsin undergraduates will apply within known limits to a group of San Diego longshoremen. With the question stated in this way, few would agree that accurate predictions could be made about longshoremen's behavior on the basis of students' behavior. This is not, however, the question to which Schmitt's research is directed. His primary focus at this time is not to generalize from one group of *subjects* to another group or to a definable population because he is not studying people per se but rather the precise *conditions* under which a specified *behavior* will occur with predictable frequency. The concern is not with the social and behavioral characteristics of the subjects, but with the stimulus properties of the environment and with the lawful behavioral effects of specified reinforcement and punishment contingencies.

Thus Schmitt's research does not deal with the complexities of the social reality containing Wisconsin students and San Diego longshoremen; he has, instead, constructed a simplified *model* of reality from which he was able to extract a series of "if-then" statements. Blalock (1963) has pointed out that this approach defines some of the important advantages enjoyed by physicists, but he also observes:

In the social sciences, the formulation of propositions involving only a small number of variables is likely to meet with the skeptical argument that such a formulation is far too simple to be realistic. But by beginning with grossly oversimplified models a cumulative process can be set in motion in which one successively modifies the model or theory until it becomes more and more complex and provides a better fit to reality.

Blalock goes on to say that "a concern with indicating the *specific* population to which one can generalize may be a blinder which prevents one from attempting to spell out theoretical conditions more exactly." The dominant methodologies of the social sciences reflect the assumption that their concepts and variables must apply to real-life situations (Nagel, 1961), and it is because of this assumption that the question of representativeness exists. The question does not arise for the physicist because he deals with simplified models of reality from which he extracts relationships that hold *under specified conditions.* If these conditions were originally isolated in a laboratory, the associated relationship should hold *to the extent* that the limiting conditions are approximated in a more complex situation.

In his studies of acceleration, Galileo chose to work with a carefully shaped sphere rolling down a grooved, inclined plane that was lined with parchment. He did not seek a generalization that would pertain directly to the problem of predicting the maximum outrun of a boulder rolling down a mountain. The latter case is completely defeating, for even if it were possible to mount probability on top of probability so as to deal with the various exigencies created by the shape of the rock; the other rocks, trees, and bushes that it might encounter; the differential effects of discrete undulations on the mountainside; and the manner of initial release—even if this were possible, the resulting statement would apply only to a particular rock on a particular mountain. The generalizations he did discover hold to the extent that his experimental conditions are achieved.

By the same token, the relationship revealed by Schmitt's analysis of the behavior of Wisconsin students will hold for longshoremen to the extent that the foreman employs a variable supervisory schedule and exacts penalties contingent upon off-the-job behavior. The fact that union practices or other considerations may prohibit the exercise of such authority, and thus limit the representatives of the observed relationship, does not alter the behavioral regularity described by the supervision proposition or detract from its status as a possible generalization.

It is in this same context that questions frequently arise concerning the notable absence of correlation coefficients and significance tests in experimental analysis studies. The reason for these absences is that many statistical procedures are inappropriate when dealing with data resulting from the experimental analysis. Sociology tends to rely on a limited number of statistical operations which, while they may be valid for that 90 per cent body of questionnaire research, were never intended to embrace all empirical data. In the article already cited, Blalock (1963) points to this difficulty in the following way:

Presumably, the aim of the scientist is to formulate *laws* which specify the nature or form of a relationship between two or more variables under given conditions. This aim would be reflected in a focus on slopes, types of nonlinearity, and the like. Instead, we find in sociology a much greater interest in the magnitude of correlation coefficients and how well we can predict from one variable to another. Such a concern is of course due to the high degree of unexplained variation with which we must deal. We are indeed happy if we can explain any variation at all, witness the emphasis on simple tests of the null hypothesis (p. 403).

The search for small but consistent effects is far different from the statement of a relationship which will hold under specified conditions. In the experimental analysis every effort is made to bring the dependent variable under control so that it will persist through time at a stable level. Once this is achieved, the experimental variable is shifted to a new value and the resulting changes in the dependent variable are measured. If the values of the dependent variable are stable but different before and after the manipulation, statistical analysis will add little information. Correlational analysis might be employed, but it is difficult to see what, if any, gain would be achieved in the clarity of the results.

There are still further problems. Most of the statistics, both parametric and nonparametric, which have some currency in sociology are based on an assumption which many types of data cannot meet. That is the assumption that the data under consideration derive from *independent observations*. Given the nature of the learning process, there is no way in which an individual's thirtieth response in a given situation may be considered to be independent of the preceding twenty-nine responses. Neither is it possible to consider one child's behavior independent of another's when both are operating in the same environment. This problem, however, is not unique to data derived by the experimental analysis. Consider, for example, the demographer who violates the independence assumption by computing significance tests for differences in data from the 1950 census and the 1960 census. The 1960 population is simply not independent of the population ten years earlier. Though it will not be dealt with here, the existence of the assumption of independent observations stands as a serious barrier to the statistical analysis of the social scientists' central problem—social change.

One line of attack on this general problem is illustrated by Samuel H. Revusky's article, "Some Statistical Treatments Compatible with Individual Organism Methodology" (1967). His work is oriented toward developing procedures to be followed in the experimental analysis of behavior which will produce data capable of meeting randomization assumptions and thus be amenable to the procedures of inferential statistics. Revusky's approach, like others previously discussed, depends upon the availability of multiple subjects.

There should be no misunderstanding. Experimental data and statistical procedures are not inherently antithetical. The continued development of time-series analysis by econometricians promises potential solutions to many of the problems just cited. Time-series data do not assume independent observations and are instead specifically intended to deal with trends over time. The analysis of changes in the cost of living index, for example, presents many of the same characteristics as are found in the continuing observation of individual behavior. Present trend analysis procedures, however, are best suited to data that present recurrent cycles of values in a relatively smooth fashion. They, too, are handicapped when faced with very sharp discontinuities in trend lines. These are technical problems, and such problems are typically short lived in science.

Having gone rather far afield, we will conclude this discussion by reiterating that the extent to which a laboratory finding has field relevance is, in the final analysis, an empirical question to be resolved by additional research. Using rabbits as subjects, Bernard demonstrated a relationship between relevant variables and hypothesized that the relationship should hold for all herbivora. A greater proportion of his audience is willing to accept his hypothesis *after* observing that the procedures used on rabbits produced the same results when applied to horses. The first five articles of this book have demonstrated that response-contingent stimuli control behavior. According to the definition we have been using, the next five articles in this Part test the external validity of that proposition.

TECHNIQUES OF EXPERIMENTAL CONTROL

REVERSIBILITY AS REPLICATION

Bernard's encounter with a group of nervous rabbits can be used to illustrate additional properties of the experimental analysis. Much of the strength of his experimental finding derives from the fact that, through time, he repeatedly demonstrated the ability to produce and eliminate the phenomenon originally observed. "Indeed," he said, "proof that a given condition always precedes or accompanies a phenomenon does not warrant concluding with certainty that a given condition is the immediate cause of that phenomenon. It must still be established that, when the condition is removed, the phenomenon will no longer appear" (Bernard, 1957, p. 55).

Thus Bernard's experiment was not one experiment, but an entire series of linked investigations each one of which contributed to a cumulative understanding of a particular relationship. Each time Bernard reversed conditions by switching from grass to fasting, he was replicating his original study, not once, but several times for each rabbit in the group. When an experimenter can exert such control over his subject matter in a consistent fashion, there is little doubt that he has the relevant variables under control.

Series of replications of this sort entail more than simply getting a dependent variable to oscillate like a yo-yo. Genuine reversibility is the alternation from one condition to another and back again as a direct and *stable* function of the presence or absence of the independent (or experimental) variable. Exactly what constitutes stability will vary from situation to situation, but the burden is on the experimenter to eliminate the possibility that the change in the dependent variable is transitory, occurring only briefly with the presentation or removal of the independent variable.

In order to make meaningful comparisons it is imperative that experimental control be adequate to maintain a given value of the dependent variable under specified conditions over repeated observations. This is very different from what is obtained with a one-shot pretest and calls for a degree of control over variables well beyond what we are accustomed to seeing. There is no other recourse, however, if clear results are to be obtained. For this reason the first step in the execution of an experimental analysis is the construction of a stable baseline, a series of observations which describe within narrow limits the quality of the dependent variable under a stable set of carefully identified conditions. A change in one of these conditions, holding all others constant, may then be made so as to create a new set of conditions, a new environment. Changes in the quality of the dependent variable which persist through repeated observations within narrow limits may tentatively be judged to be under the control of the manipulated variable. The relationship is strengthened if a return to the original conditions results in the recovery of the original value of the dependent variable which, as before, persists through repeated observations within narrow limits.

Clearly, requirements such as these must alter many of our perspectives toward research. The so-called one-shot manipulation is out of the question if these canons are embraced. Instead it is necessary to think along the lines of long-term research which is patient enough to defer experimenter manipulation until the many problems associated with constructing a stable baseline are mastered.

INTERSUBJECT VARIABILITY

Although human subjects present variations imposed by the genetic and physiological uniqueness of each individual, these factors pale in contrast to the variability imposed by each individual's completely unique history of experience. If we present a standard stimulus to ten individuals, there will probably be ten different reactions, governed by the past experiences each has had with similar stimuli in like or different situations. The previously discussed baseline technique is the procedure used in operant research to develop experimental control in the face of such variability.

Since behavioral variability under a standard set of conditions is largely a function of the variability of individual reinforcement histories, an important task of baseline procedures is to construct a common reinforcement history for an array of individuals in a given situation. In the following chapters, for example, several authors report the use of one form or another of "token" reinforcement. To oversimplify, tokens are in many respects similar to money. They provide a monetary exchange unit which can be given for a variety of behaviors and can be spent by the earner according to his own individual preferences. In a preschool situation it might be fairly assumed that three-year-old children do not have an elaborate prior history of earning and spending. Other subjects, however, have personal histories which have created considerable variability in their attitudes toward earning and spending in any form.

Consequently, the first step in developing a token economy in an experimental situation (even in a preschool) involves the establishment of a clear set of rules governing economic exchanges that will hold for all the individuals in the group. Through time, as more and more experience is acquired by each individual, economic behavior *within that setting* will become highly predictable. That is, the particular contingencies of the specific environment shape up particular forms of behavior appropriate to that setting and, perhaps, appropriate to no other setting in which a given individual operates. The problem of getting a particular set of behaviors to come under the appropriate control of environments other than the experimental one is considered later; at this point the emphasis is on establishing uniform stimulus control for a group of individuals within a common research environment.

Rather than lamenting the variability which individuals always bring to an experimental situation or attempting to control for it statistically, operant research typically begins by constructing stable patterns of behavior within the setting so that a high degree of predictability (the opposite of what we usually mean by variability in this context) is achieved *before* experimental manipulations are initiated. The implications of this practice for changing our time perspectives on research have already been mentioned, but it should be noticed that frequently weeks or months and thousands of responses may go into the development of such a pretreatment baseline. Baseline construction is not an easy task, but its successful execution will often teach the experimenter as much about the behavior in which he is interested as will the actual experimental manipulations.

MULTIPLE BASELINE

The discussion of Bernard's experiment in this chapter has illustrated the advantages which result from controlled reversibility. When an experimenter can predictably produce and eliminate a behavior by manipulating environmental events, he can claim substantial knowledge of the phenomenon he is studying. Elegant and convincing as this strategy is, however, there are several situations where it is impractical or undesirable. One would not, for example, be inclined to teach a mute to talk and then recover his mutism just to prove a point. Moral and ethical considerations, as well as therapeutic objectives, in many field settings may conflict with reversibility demonstrations.

Frequently, where reinforcement contingencies are systematically designed to improve an individual's control over his environment, the therapist will shape behavior so it will come under the control of the existing environmental contingencies. Initially, the therapist may use special contingencies and prosthetic devices, analogous to training wheels on a bicycle, which are eliminated when they are no longer necessary. In such cases, reversibility is the antithesis of the desired objective.

Reversibility has been described as a technique for reducing the probability that the observed variation in the behavior under study could be attributed to chance or to uncontrolled variables. Another technique for reducing such threats to internal validity is the *multiple baseline*.

The multiple baseline strategy can be illustrated with a description of a hypothetical predelinquent boy. A predelinquent generally displays a number of different behaviors which are considered socially undesirable without being sufficiently antisocial to warrant institutional confinement. In the present example, the boy in question does not carry out his family responsibilities, his behavior in school is described as "quarrelsome," "uncooperative," "hostile," "aggressive," and "immature." More specifically, a number of behaviors may be identified which need direct attention. Among these are that he does not clean his room, he is late for meals, he fights with his sister, he talks back to his parents and teachers, he damages property, he picks fights at recess, he does not complete his homework assignments, and he frequently cuts school.

In order to correct these problems the decision is made to employ a token reinforcement system. Under this system tokens will be given contingent on desirable behavior. Once he has earned them, the boy is to be allowed to exchange his tokens for a variety of privileges or back-up reinforcers. For twenty tokens he can obtain a license to ride his bicycle for one week. Fifteen tokens can be exchanged for the opportunity to stay out until 10:00 P.M. Friday night. Twenty-five will provide the opportunity to use the telephone for a week. He can rent a radio for his room for twenty tokens per week, and he can earn a movie ticket for thirty tokens.

It is then decided that careful records will be kept of four specific behaviors which need improvement: (1) room cleaning, (2) homework assignments, (3) fighting with other children, and (4) truancy. Before tokens were given, the records show that he cleans his room once every three weeks, does twenty minutes of homework per week, has an average of three fights a week, and cuts school five times each month. The records of these behaviors are kept for five weeks and indicate that there is little reason to expect spontaneous improvement.

At the beginning of the sixth week the token system is introduced, and the boy is told that he will be given five tokens each day his room is found to be clean. Although there are other ways in which he can earn tokens, *none* are given at this point for homework or the other behaviors for which baseline records have been kept. The records of the next four weeks indicate that room cleaning increases rapidly and stabilizes at six out of every seven days, but the other behaviors have not changed during this period.

In the fifth week of the token period the system is expanded so that ten tokens are given for each homework assignment completed. Within three weeks, he is earning ninety tokens per week for homework and his room is still generally clean, but fighting and truancy remain unaffected. Subsequent expansions of the token system provide that every reported fight will result in the loss of sixty-five tokens; and five tokens may be earned for each day of school attended, while unauthorized absence will cost twenty-five tokens. The figure describing the effects of the token system might have the following appearance.

In four distinct instances the introduction of token contin-

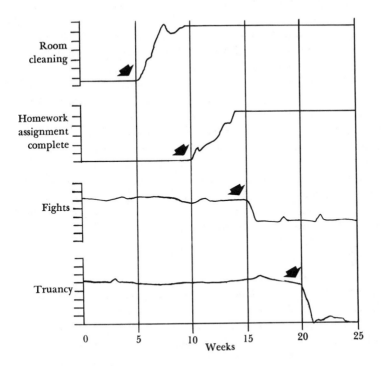

gencies has corresponded with a shift in the treated behavior. If only a single behavior had been examined, a variety of hypotheses could be advanced to account for the observed change as was done in the case mentioned earlier of the patient visiting the nurses' station. When four behavioral changes correspond to four discrete changes in contingencies, the number of plausible alternative explanations is greatly reduced, and the probability of such changes being attributed to "chance" is virtually eliminated.

Because it does not require a demonstration of the reversibility of effect, the multiple baseline strategy may be expected to occur with increasing frequency in the experimental analysis of social situations.

PREFERENCE PROCEDURES

Another experimental strategy well suited to social situations which prohibit straight reversibility is illustrated in the following report by Wolf, Giles, and Hall. In this analysis of token reinforcement in a remedial classroom, they arranged different point contingencies on work done in three different workbooks. By varying the number of points available for reading, arithmetic, and English problems, they were able to establish the effects of the point contingency quite clearly. Alternative explanations of their results would be hard to come by, and, at the same time, they avoided the problems which might have resulted if they had elected the reversibility strategy employed by Bushell, Wrobel, and Michaelis which is presented in Chapter 10. There are a variety of situations in which the effects of a particular reinforcement contingency can be established by shifting it from one behavior to another rather than withdrawing it entirely. If the subjects in such a situation are free to engage in different behaviors according to their own "preference," correspondence between changes in contingencies and changes in behavior allows for rather firm conclusions.

THE SIMPLE RESPONSE

Another recurrent characteristic of operant research is that the dependent variable takes the form of a simple, easily repeated response. It will become eminently clear in the rest of Part II that this concern with a small precise response does not impede or detract from the experimental analysis of extremely complicated social behavior. Quite the contrary, this form of response definition has several advantages in complex situations (Verhave, 1966).

In order to meet the requirements previously discussed for an initial stable baseline of behavior, it is necessary to deal with a response that can be emitted repeatedly over a relatively long period of time without appreciable subject fatigue. Such a response is, of course, much easier to define and record than a more complex behavior. But even more important is the fact that a response of this type can occur with a wide range of frequencies. As a result, rate of response is the most frequently encountered dependent variable in operant research. For simple repeatable responses, it has proved to be an extremely sensitive measure capable of reflecting subtle changes over long periods of time.

RATE OF RESPONSE AS A DEPENDENT VARIABLE

At the very outset, it was noted that various behavioral processes were defined in terms of increases or decreases in the rate of responding. Mention of the response rate variable earlier in the book would probably require a lengthy apologia, but at this point only an additional comment or two is in order.

One of the difficulties encountered in discussing response rates is that they do not convey to some audiences many of the qualities of behavior which are of interest. Skinner (1966) refers to this point in the following:

Behavior is often interesting because of what might be called its *character*. Animals court their mates, build living quarters, care for their young, forage for food, defend territories, and so on, in many fascinating ways. These are worth studying, but the inherent drama can divert attention from another task. Even when reduced to general principles, a narrative account of *how* animals behave must be supplemented by a consideration of *why*. What is required is an analysis of the conditions which govern the probability that a given response will occur at a given time.

Furthermore, response rate as a dominant measure enjoys all the properties common to *ratio* measures. That is, response rates can vary quantitatively from an absolute zero through discrete increments which are equivalent. For this reason, response rates may be treated mathematically according to the usual operators for integers. A rate of twenty responses per minute really is twice as fast as one of ten responses per minute. This offers decided advantages over nonratio or noninterval measures, which allow only for statements of ordinal position. It would be difficult to contend, for example, that a position score of twenty on the North-Hatt (1949) scale offered only half the prestige of a position score of forty.

Small N_s, Large N_r

Habit, past experience, and graduate training have combined to leave most of us with the impression that the confidence we can place in an experimental finding is directly proportional to the number of subjects involved. Certainly such a proposition is sound if the problem at hand is public opinion polling. A very small fee would be commanded by a pollster trying to forecast national elections with a sample group of twenty respondents. This, however, recalls Skinner's earlier comment, for opinion polling deals primarily with *how* individuals behave and generally restricts itself to a limited number of speculative statements about the *why* of such things as voting behavior. The questions of how and why are not, of course, entirely unrelated, but there is certainly no reason to adhere to a single methodology for dealing with both of them.

The great bulk of social science research to date has been largely ethnographic or descriptive in nature. So long as this proclivity persists, large N studies will continue to be appropriate, and more and more answers to the *how* question will be obtained. Bernard, however, did not require large numbers of rabbits to convince us that he had managed to obtain a real purchase on the question of why the rabbits' urine was clear and acid. In fact, probably few of the most cautious would fail to be convinced of the validity and generality of his finding if he had performed his simple experiment on only four subjects with consistent results: a rabbit, a horse, a sheep, and a cow.

Experimental evidence is established when the experimenter is able to *produce* the phenomenon he wishes to observe. If sufficient control is established so that a particular behavior may be selectively developed or eliminated in one subject, the chances are greatly increased that it can be developed in another subject. On the other hand, observing that a certain behavior is found in ten thousand individuals does not increase our confidence that it is a behavioral imperative. Neither does it explain *why* the behavior is there.

Although operant research typically involves only a limited number of subjects, it is also characterized by very large volumes of responses. These are a product of the previously discussed use of simple, repeatable responses as the dependent variable. Although a questionnaire may contain one hundred discrete items which are responded to once before an experimental manipulation, or intervention, it is not uncommon to observe premanipulation operant baselines composed of many thousands of responses. For all of the reasons previously mentioned in the discussions of variability and validity, high-density baselines provide a much sounder foundation from which to make comparative judgments. This is particularly true in the analysis of social behavior, which invariably involves an acquisition, or learning, phase.

SUMMARY

Because the various elements of the experimental analysis have been discussed in the context of social science methods in general, some clarification may be achieved by assembling the final product in the form of a highly simplified and idealized scheme.

1. The initial step in the experimental analysis requires the construction of a stable baseline which describes the operant level of the behavior (dependent variable) to be studied. To permit precise measurement, the behavior is operationalized in the form of a small, easily emitted, repeatable response. This response is then continuously monitored within a stable environment to the point that its occurrence is highly predictable over time.

2. After a stable baseline, or operant level, has been achieved, a single independent variable is modified. The response is again continuously monitored until it achieves a new stable and predictable value. The difference between the second and baseline values of the dependent variable may be tentatively attributed to the experimental manipulation.

3. To check for the reversibility of effect, the original environmental conditions are restored. Continuous monitoring of the response is again conducted until it achieves a stable pattern. If this stable pattern is the same as that of the original baseline, the assumed relationship between the dependent variable and the independent variable is greatly strengthened. If, however, the initial value of the dependent variable is not recoverable under the original conditions, it is not possible to identify the factors involved in the change in the response. In this circumstance, additional experimental control is required before the response-environment relationship may be stated precisely.

4. In those cases where reversals are impossible or undesirable, several (multiple) baselines are established simultaneously. The independent variable, or experimental manipulation, is then brought to bear on each baseline behavior, one at a time. Correspondence between shifts in the several dependent variables and each application of the independent variable establishes the relationship between the independent variable and the dependent variables.

EXTENSIONS TO THE FIELD

Over the years sociologists and social psychologists have been subjected to a variety of arguments concerning whether or not the subjects of interest to them could or should be brought into the laboratory for analysis. Generally speaking, small-group advocates concluded that you could and should, while survey researchers contended that you could not and should not. The debate has occasionally generated some refreshing excitement in otherwise dour academic corridors, but it has done little to advance either discipline.

During the last six or seven years operant research has emerged from its laboratory habitat and moved into field settings. There are at least three reasons why a scientist might move into the field. One is that he is attempting to use the field as a testing ground for established principles. He will, at least implicitly, construct epistemic derivations of these principles in the attempt to *extend* their generality. A second reason for moving into the field is to exploit the natural ecology in an attempt to formulate new relationships or further refine existing ones. A third reason is to *apply* already existing generalizations to the solution of practical problems. Goldiamond, Dyrud, and Miller (1965) have suggested a close bond between practice and research.

This view states that first we have practice. By *practice* we mean the attempt to solve by our behavior certain problems of an empirical nature. In their solution, whatever skills, artistry, and knowledge we have are put to use. The critical thing is to get the job done. Another stage, which may develop out of such problems, is science. In *science*, we may attempt to systematize our procedures and knowledge. Such systematization may suggest an application to other problems, and we shall limit the term, *technology*, to such applications of science. The technician, having demonstrated some success in the areas of his application, may be asked to solve problems for which his technology is only partly sufficient. He may then in addition call upon unformulated skills, procedures from other disciplines, intuition, and artistry; and we have practice again. This practice may lead to further science, to further technology, to further practice, to further science, and so on. In each case, the practice incorporates more and more scientific elements and the sciences incorporate more and more from the problem areas and technologies, so that the relationship between the three is an ascending spiral rather than a circle or a unidirectional arrow (p. 111).

There is probably widespread agreement with the notion that the individual scientist can be concerned with extension, discovery, and application, *simultaneously.*

In any case, if it is true that operant research has been accumulating a growing store of basic behavioral principles, then an important test of these principles is their ability to ameliorate some of the serious human problems which surround us. These principles exist in the form of statements of relationship between behaviors on the one hand and environmental reactions on the other. Thus extensions to the field depend upon our ability to modify behavior by reprogramming selected portions of the environment.

Clearly, man's institutions are his own and of his own making, so it is not to be expected that they approach perfection to any important degree. They have developed in a Topsy-like fashion with the result that they often show a remarkable ability to reinforce undesirable behavior and simultaneously extinguish behaviors that would be preferable. In the face of such difficulties, institutional reform has virtually become an institution itself, with various philosophies of education, child rearing, penology, and marital relations changing as frequently and extremely as women's skirt lengths—and apparently with equal effect. No scientist would ever accept the type of data presented by a particular reform group as the basis for overthrowing its predecessor, and by now it is clear that the truly functional modification of social institutions will come about most directly if we employ techniques which are self-correcting because they are responsive to their own data. A program such as Project Head Start should not be abandoned if it fails to cure all of the remedial problems of disadvantaged children during its first three years. Instead, it might profit by taking a leaf from the operant researcher's handbook and selecting a manageable number of well-defined responses in need of strengthening. These responses could be shaped until they reached the desired level and then stabilized. If accurate records were kept—and they are essential —the various shaping techniques could be evaluated accurately as to their consequences and retained or rejected for reasons of efficiency and effectiveness rather than vogue.

In the process of taking the techniques and procedures of operant research to the field, however, its experimental foundations and the canons of the experimental analysis must not be left behind. Such was the fate of programmed instruction not too long ago. During the meteoric rise of the self-instructional program, the product unfortunately became separated from its experimental foundations. As a result, a significant proportion of the programs on the commercial market were of poor quality (i.e., did not follow the operant principles on which they were presumably based), and they failed to teach in the way that the brochures promised they would. When the bright promise of this new medium failed to materialize, the market for the product fell, and a number of small companies went out of business.

The techniques of operant conditioning are still quite new, but they are amazingly powerful. It is entirely possible to use them without regard for their scientific origins or without attempting to meet the rigorous criteria for objectivity and cumulative replication. In such cases the raw application of behavior modification techniques will be judged, in the short run, by the expedient, "Does it work? If so, use it; if not, forget it." Any science is likely to produce such by-products, and every science must police itself against abuse of this type.

The chapters which immediately follow constitute some initial fruits of what promises to be a most exciting and profitable venture —the experimental analysis of social behavior in its customary field setting. The study by Hawkins and his colleagues (Chapter 9) deals with the problem behaviors of an unsocialized boy. In virtually every respect, this study meets the standards of the experimental analysis. The premanipulation baseline consisted of 10-second observations taken for 1 hour in 16 consecutive sessions, or 57,600 discrete observations. A check for the reversibility of effect was employed successfully, and the stability of the behavioral change was established by follow-ups. In a laboratory such a study would undoubtedly be a sound piece of research, but the setting for this work was the boy's own home. The environmental change that was effected was a modification in the behavior of the mother, which, in turn, resulted in desired changes in the boy's behavior. In short, his problem behavior was being maintained by the response-contingent behavior of his mother.

The report by Montrose Wolf and his associates at the University of Kansas (Chapter 11) is of special interest for at least two reasons. First, this work is a direct attack on one of the pressing social problems of our society, the undereducation of the underprivileged; and, second, the research employs a complimentary combination of control-group/experimental-group comparisons with the customary single-subject design of operant research.

John Burchard's research is particularly significant because of the population involved—delinquent retardates. Of even greater interest to many sociologists, however, is the fact that this project has begun the careful design of a social system on the basis of operant principles.

Work of the sort which Part II illustrates is not the exclusive domain of any academic discipline. It is firmly based on the experimental foundations provided by psychologists and sociologists, but its very existence is opening up a host of new theoretical and research problems to challenge economists and political scientists as well. These researchers are dealing with ongoing social behavior in its natural setting, and doing so according to the best articles of experimental science. In each case contingencies are being modified in order to learn what is maintaining the behavior. "The *cause* of a behavior may be described as the variables which are currently maintaining it" (Goldiamond et al., 1965, p. 126). By attempting to change behavior, we can gain basic theoretical knowledge about that behavior. The contributors to Part II are simultaneously providing suggestive solutions to practical problems and extending the generality of behavioral principles.

REFERENCES

Ayllon, T., and J. Michael, 1959. The psychiatric nurse as a behavioral engineer. *Journal of the Experimental Analysis of Behavior,* 2, pp. 323-334.

Bachrach, A. J., 1962. *Psychological Research: an Introduction.* New York: Random House.

Bernard, C., 1957. *An Introduction to the Study of Experimental Medicine.* New York: Dover (originally published in French, 1865).

Blalock, H. M., 1963. Some important methodological problems for sociology. *Sociology and Social Research,* 47, pp. 398-407.

Campbell, D. T., and J. C. Stanley, 1963. Experimental and quasi-experimental designs for research on teaching. In N. L. Gage (Ed.), *Handbook of Research on Teaching.* Chicago: Rand McNally, pp. 171-246.

Goldiamond, I., J. E. Dyrud, and M. D. Miller, 1965. Practice as research in professional psychology. *Canadian Psychologist,* 6a, pp. 110-128.

Goode, W. J., and P. K. Hatt, 1952. *Methods in Social Research.* New York: McGraw-Hill Book Company.

Hamblin, R. L., 1966. Ratio measurement and sociological theory: a critical analysis. Paper read at the Annual Meetings of the American Sociological Association, Miami Beach, August.

Nagel, E., 1961. *The Structure of Science.* New York: Harcourt, Brace & World.

North, C. C., and P. K. Hatt, 1949. Jobs and occupations: a popular evaluation. In L. Wilson and W. Kolb, *Sociological Analysis.* New York: Harcourt, Brace.

Revusky, S. H., 1967. Some statistical treatments compatible with individual organism methodology. *Journal of the Experimental Analysis of Behavior,* 10, pp. 319-330.

Skinner, B. F., 1966. Operant behavior. In W. K. Honig (Ed.), *Operant Behavior: Areas of Research and Application.* New York: Appleton-Century-Crofts, pp. 12-32.

Verhave, T., 1966. An introduction to the experimental analysis of behavior. In T. Verhave (Ed.), *The Experimental Analysis of Behavior.* New York: Appleton-Century-Crofts, pp. 1-47.

Webb, E. J., D. T. Campbell, R. D. Schwartz, and L. Sechrest, 1966. *Unobtrusive Measures: Nonreactive Research in the Social Sciences.* Chicago: Rand McNally.

Wolf, M. M., J. S. Birnbrauer, T. Williams, and J. Lawler, 1965. A note on apparent extinction of the vomiting behavior of a retarded child. In L. P. Ullmann and L. Krasner (Eds.), *Case Studies in Behavior Modification.* New York: Holt, Rinehart & Winston, pp. 364-366.

8

A Method to Integrate Descriptive and
Experimental Field Studies at the
Level of Data and Empirical Concepts

Sidney W. Bijou, Robert F. Peterson, and Marion H. Ault

INTRODUCTION

Psychology, like the other natural sciences, depends for its advancement both upon descriptive accounts and functional analyses of its primary data. Descriptive studies answer the question "How?" They may, for example, report the manner in which a Bantu mother nurses her child, or the way in which the yellow shafted flicker mates. Experimental studies, on the other hand, provide the answer to "Why?" They may discuss the conditions which establish and maintain the relationships between the mother and the infant, between the male and female birds.

It has been claimed that progress in the behavioral sciences would be enhanced by more emphasis on descriptive studies. This may be true, but one may wish to speculate on why descriptive accounts of behavior have been de-emphasized. One possibility is the difficulty of relating descriptive and experimental data. For example, a descriptive study of parent-child behavior in the home may have data in the form of ratings on a series of scales (Baldwin,

Reprinted in part from the *Journal of Applied Behavior Analysis,* Vol. 1 (1968), pp. 175-191, with the permission of the authors and editors. Slightly edited. Copyright © 1968 by the Society for the Experimental Analysis of Behavior, Inc.

The formulation presented here was generated from the research conducted under grants from the U. S. Public Health Service, National Institute of Mental Health (M-2208, M-2232, and MH-12067), and from the U. S. Office of Education, Handicapped Children and Youth Branch (Grant No. 32-23-1020-6002, Proposal No. R-006).

Kalhorn, and Breese, 1949), while an experimental study on the same subject may have data in the form of frequencies of events (Hawkins, Peterson, Schweid, and Bijou, 1966). Findings from the first study cannot reasonably be integrated with the second at the *level of data and empirical concepts.* Anyone interested in relating the two must resort to imprecise concepts like "permissive mother," "laissez-faire atmosphere," "controlling child," and "negativism." This practice is unacceptable to psychologists who believe that all concepts must be firmly based on or linked to empirical events.

It is the thesis of this chapter that descriptive field studies (which include cross-cultural, ecological, and normative investigations) and experimental field studies can be performed so that the data and empirical terms in each are continuous, interchangeable, and mutually interrelatable.

Barker and Wright (1955) state that one of the aims of their ecological investigations is to produce data that may be used by all investigators in child behavior and development. Their study of "Midwest" and its children is in part devoted to the development of a method which provides raw material (which they compared to objects stored in a museum) amenable to analyses from different theoretical points of view. There are two considerations which make this doubtful. First, their data consist of "running accounts of what a person is doing and his situation on the level of direct perception or immediate inference" with "minor interpretations in the form of statements *about* rather than descriptions *of* behavior or situations" (Wright, 1967). Therefore their method is serviceable only to those who accept in the raw data nonobservable phenomena defined according to their prescription. Investigators who prefer to define their hypothetical variables in some other way or who wish to exclude nonobservables cannot integrate data from Barker and Wright studies with their own. Second, final data in the form of running narrations cannot reasonably be transformed into units describing interactions between behavioral and environmental events, such as duration, intensity, latency, or frequency. Any attempt to convert such verbal accounts into one or more of the interactional dimensions would require so many arbitrary decisions that it would be doubtful whether another investigator interested in duplicating or extending the study could even come close to producing the same operations and the same results.

If, however, frequency-of-occurrence measures of environmental and behavioral events were used in both descriptive and field experimental studies, data and empirical concepts could be made congruous. The measure of frequency is preferable to that of duration, intensity, and latency for several reasons (Skinner, 1953). First, this measure readily shows changes over short and long periods of observations. Second, it specifies the *amount* of behavior displayed (Honig, 1966). Finally, and perhaps most important, it has been demonstrated to be applicable to operant behaviors across species. Hence a methodology based on frequency of events would be serviceable for both experimental and descriptive studies of both human and infrahuman subjects. This versatility has been illustrated by Jensen and Bobbitt (1967) in a study on mother and infant relationships of the pigtailed macaques.

With the use of frequency measures, the work of the ecological psychologist and that of the experimental psychologist would both complement and supplement each other. Descriptive studies would reveal interesting relationships among the raw data that could provide provocative cues for experimental investigations. On the other hand, field experimental studies would probably yield worthwhile leads for descriptive investigations by pointing to the need for observing new combinations of behavioral classes in specified situations. Ecological psychologists would show, in terms of frequency of events, the practices of a culture or subculture, or an institutional activity of a subculture; experimental investigators working with the same set of data terms and empirical concepts would attempt to demonstrate the conditions and processes which establish and maintain the interrelationships observed.

THREE BASIC ASSUMPTIONS
Before considering the procedures for conducting a descriptive study using frequency measures, it may be well to make explicit three basic assumptions.

The first assumption: For psychology as a natural science, the primary data are the observable interactions between a biological organism and environmental events, past and present. These interrelationships constitute the material to be recorded. This means that the method does not include accounts of behavior *isolated from related stimulus events* ("Jimmy is a rejected child"; "Johnny is a highly *autistic* child"; "First Henry makes swimming movement, then he crawls, then he lifts himself to the upright position holding on, then he stands with support, . . ."). Furthermore, it means that the method excludes statements of *generalizations about behavior and environmental interactions* ("This is an extremely aggressive child who is always getting into trouble"). Finally, it means that the method excludes accounts of interactions between *behavioral and environmental events intertwined with hypothetical constructs* ("The preschool child makes errors in describing the water line in a jar because of his undeveloped cognitive structure").

The second assumption: Concepts and laws in psychology are derived from raw data. Theoretical concepts evolve from empirical concepts, and empirical concepts from raw data; theoretical interactional laws are derived from empirical laws, and empirical laws from relationships in the raw data.

The third assumption: Descriptive studies provide information only on events and their occurrence. They do not provide information on the functional properties of the events or the functional relationships among the events. Experimental studies provide that kind of information.

PROCEDURES

We move on to consider the procedures involved in conducting a descriptive field investigation. They include (1) specifications of the situation in which a study is conducted, (2) definitions of behavioral and invironmental events in observable terms, (3) measurements of observer reliability, and (4) procedures for collecting, analyzing, and interpreting the data. We terminate the chapter with a brief illustration of a study of a four-year-old boy's behavior in a laboratory nursery school.

SPECIFYING THE SITUATION IN WHICH A STUDY IS CONDUCTED

We define the situation in which a study is conducted in terms of its physical and social setting and the *observable events* that occur within its bounds. The physical setting may be part of the child's home, a hospital or residential institution, a store, or a playground in the city park. It may be a nursery school, a classroom in an elementary school, or a room in a child guidance clinic.

The specific part of the home selected as a setting may consist of the living room and kitchen if the design of the home precludes flexible observation (Hawkins, Peterson, Schweid, and Bijou, 1966). In a hospital it may be the child's bedroom, the dining room, or the dayroom (Wolf, Risley, and Mees, 1964). In a state school for the retarded, it may be a special academic classroom (Birnbrauer, Wolf, Kidder, and Tague, 1965); in a regular elementary school, a classroom (Becker, Madsen, Arnold, and Thomas, 1967); and in a nursery school, the schoolroom and the play yard (Harris, Wolf, and Baer, 1965).

During the course of a study, changes in the physical aspect of the situation may occur despite efforts to avoid them. Some will be sufficiently drastic to prevent further study until restoration of the original conditions (e.g., power failure for several days). Others will be within normal limits (e.g., replacement of old chairs in the child's bedroom) and hence will not warrant disrupting the research.

The social aspect of the situation in a home may consist of the mother and the subject's younger sibling (Hawkins et al., 1966); in a child guidance clinic, the therapist and the other children in the therapy group. In a nursery school it may include the head teacher, the assistant teacher, and the children (Johnston, Kelley, Harris, and Wolf, 1966).

Sometimes the social situation changes according to routines, and the investigator wishes to take records in the different situations created by the changes. For example, he may wish to describe the behavior of a preschool child as he engages in each of four activities in the morning hours of the nursery school: show-and-tell, music and games, snack, and pre-academic exercises. Each would be described as a field situation, and data would be taken in each case as if it were a separate situation. The events recorded could be the same for all the activities (e.g., frequency of social contacts), or they could be specific to each, depending upon the nature of the activity. They could also be a combination of both types (e.g., frequency of social contacts and sum total of prolonged productive activity in each pre-academic exercise).

Major variations in social composition in a home study that would be considered disruptive could include the presence of other members of the family, relatives, or friends. In a nursery school, such a variation might be the absence of the head teacher, the presence of the child's mother, or the absence of many of the children. These and other events like them would probably call a halt to data collection until the standard situation returned.

Temporary social disruptions may take many forms. For example, in the home the phone may ring, a salesman may appear, a neighbor may visit; in the nursery school the disrupting event may be a holiday preparation or a birthday party for a member of the group.

In summary, the physical and social conditions in which an ecological study is conducted are specified at the outset. Whether the variations occurring during the study are sufficient to disrupt data collection depends, in large measure, on the interactions to be studied, practical considerations, and the investigator's experience in similar situations in the past. However, accounts of changes in physical and social conditions, whether major or minor, are described and noted on the data sheets.

DEFINING BEHAVIORAL AND STIMULUS EVENTS IN OBSERVABLE TERMS
In this method we derive definitions of behavioral and stimulus events from preliminary investigations in the actual setting. Such pilot investigations are also used to provide preliminary information on the frequencies of occurrences of the events of interest and the feasibility of the situation for study.

A miniature episode in the life of a preschool boy, Timmy, will serve as an example. We start with having the observer make a running description of Timmy's behavior in the play yard in the style she would use if she were a reporter for a magazine.

Timmy is playing by himself in a sandbox in a play yard in which other children are playing. A teacher stands nearby. Timmy tires of the sandbox and walks over to climb the monkeybars. Timmy shouts at the teacher, saying, "Mrs. Simpson, watch me." Timmy climbs to the top of the apparatus and shouts again to the teacher, "Look how high I am. I'm higher than anybody." The teacher comments on Timmy's climbing ability with approval. Timmy then climbs down and runs over to a tree, again demanding that the teacher watch him. The teacher, however, ignores Timmy and walks back into the classroom. Disappointed, Timmy walks toward the sandbox instead of climbing the tree. A little girl nearby cries out in pain as she stumbles and scrapes her knee. Timmy ignores her and continues to walk to the sandbox.

To obtain a clearer impression of the time relationships among antecedent stimulus events, responses, and consequent stimulus events, the objective aspects of the narrative account are transcribed into a three-column form and each behavioral and stimulus event is numbered in consecutive order.

Setting: Timmy (T.) is playing alone in a sandbox in a play yard in which other children are playing. T. is scooping sand into a bucket with a shovel, then dumping the sand onto a pile. A teacher, Mrs. Simpson (S.), stands approximately 6 feet away but does not attend to T.

Time	Antecedent Event	Response	Consequent Social Event
9:14		1. T. throws bucket and shovel into corner of sandbox.	
		2. . . . stands up.	
		3. . . . walks over to monkeybars and stops.	
		4. . . . turns toward teacher.	
		5. . . . says, "Mrs. Simpson, watch me."	
			6. Mrs. S. turns toward Timmy.
	6. Mrs. S. turns toward Timmy.	7. T. climbs to top of apparatus.	
		8. . . . looks toward teacher.	
		9. . . . says, "Look how high I am. I'm higher than anybody."	
9:16			10. Mrs. S. says, "That's good, Tim. You're getting quite good at that."
	10. Mrs. S. says, "That's good Tim. You're getting quite good at that."	11. T. climbs down.	
		12. . . . runs over to tree.	
		13. . . . says, "Watch me climb the tree, Mrs. Simpson."	

Time	Antecedent Event	Response	Consequent Social Event
			14. Mrs. S. turns and walks toward classroom.
	14. Mrs. S. turns and walks toward classroom.	15. T. stands, looking toward Mrs. S.	
9:18	16. Girl nearby trips and falls, bumping knee.		
	17. Girl cries.		
		18. T. proceeds to sandbox.	
		19. . . . picks up bucket and shovel.	
		20. . . . resumes play with sand.	

Note that a response event (e.g., 5. . . . says, "Mrs. Simpson, watch me.") may be followed by a consequent social event (e.g., 6. Mrs. S. turns toward Timmy.) which may also be the antecedent event for the next response (e.g., 7. T. climbs to top of apparatus.). Note, too, that the three-column form retains the temporal relationships in the narration. Note, finally, that only the child's responses are described. Inferences about feelings, motives, and other presumed internal states are omitted. Even words like "ignores" and "disappointed" do not appear in the table.

On the basis of several such running accounts and analyses a tentative set of stimulus and response definitives is derived and criteria for their occurrence are specified. This material serves as a basis for a provisional code consisting of symbols and definitions. Observers are trained to use the code and are tested in a series of trial runs in the actual situation.

Consider now the problems involved in defining behavioral and stimulus terms, devising codes, and recording events. But first let us comment briefly on the pros and cons of two recording methods.

When discussing the definitions of events and the assessment of observer reliability, we refer to observers who record with paper and pencil. In each instance the same purpose could be accomplished by electromechanical devices. The investigator must decide which procedure better suits his purpose. For example, Lovaas used instruments to record responses in studies on autistic behavior. He and his co-workers have developed apparatus and worked out procedures for recording as many as twelve responses in a setting. The following is a brief description of the apparatus and its operation Freitag, Gold, and Kassorla, 1965b).

The apparatus for quantifying behaviors involved two units: an Esterline-Angus twenty-pen recorder and an operating panel with twelve buttons, each button mounted on a switch (Microswitch: "Typewriter pushbutton switch"). When depressed, these buttons activated a corresponding pen on the Esterline recorder. The buttons were arranged on a 7 ×14-inch panel in the configuration of the fingertips of an outstretched hand. Each button could be pressed independently of any of the others and with the amount of force similar to that required for an electric typewriter key (p. 109).

An electromechanical recording device has certain advantages over a paper-and-pencil system. It requires less attention, thus allowing the observer to devote more of his effort to watching for critical events. Furthermore, instruments of this sort make it possible to assess more carefully the temporal relationships between stimulus and response events, as well as to record a large number of responses within a given period. On the other hand, paper-and-pencil recording methods are more flexible. They can be used in any setting since they do not require special facilities, such as a power supply.

Defining and Recording Behavioral Events

The main problem in defining behavioral events is establishing a criterion or criteria in such a way that two or more observers can agree on their occurrences. For example, if it is desired to record the number of times a child hits other children, the criteria of a hitting response must be clearly given so that the observer can discriminate hitting from patting or shoving responses. Or if it is desired to count the number of times a child says, "No," the criteria for the occurrence of "no" must be specified to discriminate this word from others the child utters, and from nonverbal forms of negative expressions. Sometimes definitions must include criteria of loudness and duration. For example, in a study of crying behavior (Hart et al., 1964), crying was defined to discriminate it from whining and screaming, and it had to be (a) "loud enough to be heard at least 50 feet away, and (b) of 5-seconds or more duration."

The definitions of complex behavioral events are treated in the same way. Studies concerned with such intricate categories of behavior as isolate behavior, fantasy play, aggressive behavior, and temper tantrums must establish objective criteria for each class of responses included in the category. We shall elaborate on defining multiple response classes in the following discussion on recording behavioral events.

There are two styles of recording behavioral events in field situations: one consists of logging the incidences of responses (and in many situations, their durations); the other, of registering the frequencies of occurrences and nonoccurrences within a time interval.

Sometimes frequencies and the durations are recorded (Lovaas, Freitag, Gold, and Kassorla, 1965b).

Recording the frequencies of occurrences and nonoccurrences in a time interval requires the observer to make a mark (and only one mark) in each time interval in which the response occurred. It is apparent that in this procedure the maximum frequency of a response is determined by the size of the time unit selected. If a 5-second interval were used, the maximum frequency would be 12 responses per minute; for a 10-second interval, 6 responses per minute; and so on. Thus, in studies with a high frequency of behavioral episodes, small time intervals are employed to obtain high correspondence between the actual and the recorded frequencies of occurrences.

There are several approaches to defining and recording single- and multiple-class responses. One method consists of developing a *specific observational code* for each problem studied. For example, in studies conducted at the Child Behavior Laboratory at the University of Illinois, codes were prepared for attending-to-work behavior, spontaneous speech, and tantruming. The attending-to-work or time-on-task code was employed with a distractible 7-year-old boy. It included (1) counting words, (2) looking at the words, and (3) writing numbers or letters. When any of these behaviors occurred at any time during a 20-second interval, it was scored as an interval of work. In a second study involving a 6-year-old boy with a similar problem, this code was used with one additional feature: in order for the observer to mark occurrence in the 20-second interval, the child had to engage in relevant behavior for a minimum of 10 seconds. The reliability on both codes averaged 90 per cent for two observers over 12 sessions. (See pp. 191-192 for our method of determining reliability.)

A code for spontaneous speech was developed for a 4-year-old girl who rarely spoke. Incidences of speech were recorded whenever she uttered a word or words which were not preceded by a question or a prompt by a peer or teacher. Although this class of behavior was somewhat difficult to discriminate, reliability averaged 80 per cent for two observers over 15 sessions.

Tantrum behaviors exhibited by a 6-year-old boy were defined as including crying, whining, sobbing, and whimpering. The average reliability for this class of behavior was 80 per cent for two observers over 11 sessions.

In contrast to this more or less vocal form of tantrum behavior, a code developed in another study on temper tantrums centered around the gross motor responses of an autistic child (Brawley, Harris, Allen, Fleming, and Peterson, 1968, in press). Here a tantrum was recorded whenever the child engaged in self-hitting in combination with any one of the following forms of behavior: (1) loud crying, (2) kicking, or (3) throwing himself or objects about.

Another method of defining and recording responses is to develop a *general observational code,* one that is inclusive enough to study many behaviors in a given field situation. An example of such a code is the one prepared by the nursery school staff at the University of Washington. In essence, verbal and motor responses are recorded in relation to physical and social events, using a three- or four-track system. In Table 1, each box represents an interval of 15 seconds (Allen, Reynolds, Harris, and Baer, 1967). In Table 2, each box represents an interval of 10 seconds (Allen, 1967).

In Table 1, which is a segment of a data sheet for a nursery school boy who changed activities with high frequency, entries were made in the boxes in the top row to indicate occurrences of vocalizations (V). Entries were made in the middle row to show proximity (P) or physical contact (T) with another person, and in the bottom row to indicate simply being in or on the same piece of equipment with another person (E) or engaging in parallel (A) or cooperative (C) play. Other marks and symbols are added in accordance with the problem studied. For example, each single bracket in Table 1 indicates leaving one activity and embarking on another. During the 6-minute period in which records were

Table 1

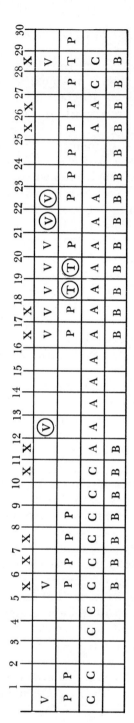

Table 2

taken (24 15-second intervals), the child changed his activity 12 times. During that time the teacher gave approval 5 times contingent upon the child's verbal or proximity behavior as indicated by X's above the top line (10, 11, 16, 17, and 18). A tally of the data indicated that he spent most of the 6-minute period alone or in close proximity to another child, sometimes on the same piece of play equipment. During 3 intervals (16, 17, and 18) he talked (V), touched (T), and engaged in physical interaction with another child (C). Even though rate of activity change, and not peer interaction, was the subject of the study, the other data on social behavior provided interesting information: decline in rate of activity change was related to an increase in rate of appropriate peer behavior.

This code can be readily modified to handle more complex interactions. For example, it was used to record the behavior of a nursery school boy who shouted epithets, kicked, and hit other children. Ordinarily these aggressive acts would appear in the record sheets undifferentiated from a nonaggressive interaction. To differentiate them from other behaviors the symbol letter was circled if the behavior met the criteria of an aggressive act. As shown in Table 2, intervals 13, 22, and 23 contain a V with a circle, Ⓥ, which indicates aggressive verbalizations, while intervals 19 and 20 contain a T with a circle, Ⓣ, which indicates physical "attack" (actual hitting, kicking, or pinching). Another bit of information was incorporated in the recording system. The letter B was entered in the fourth row to indicate that the child was playing with or being aggressive to a specific nursery school boy named Bill. This additional notation was made midway in the study when teachers observed that the subject and Bill usually behaved aggressively toward each other. Data collected before this change served as a baseline against which to judge the effects of changing social contingencies. Subsequently, teachers gave approval contingent on nonaggressive interactions between these boys, as shown by the X's above intervals 6, 7, 8, 11, 12, 17, 18, 26, 27, and 29.

Another *general observational code*, tailored for analysis of pupils' behavior in the elementary school classroom, has been devised by Becker and Thomas (1967). Like the nursery school code, it consists of symbols and definitions designed to cover the range of interactions that may take place in the field situation defined by the classroom.

Defining and Recording Stimulus Events

The ease or difficulty of defining a stimulus class is related to its source. It has been pointed out (e.g., Bijou and Baer, 1961) that some stimuli originate in natural and man-made things, some in the biological make-up of the subject himself, and some in the behavior of people and other living organisms. Consider briefly each source in turn.

Defining stimuli from physical sources does not pose a difficult problem since physical objects are usually available for all to see. All that is required is that these stimuli be described in the usual physical dimensions of space, time, size, velocity, color, texture, and the like.

Defining stimuli which originate in the biological make-up of the subject is beset with difficulty, mainly because of their obscurity under any circumstance and particularly under field conditions. Consider what must be available to an observer if he is to record in objective terms the duration, intensity, or frequency of stimuli involved in a toothache, "butterflies" in the stomach, general bodily weakness, dizziness, or hunger pangs. Instruments would be needed to make visible all sorts of internal biological events, and for the most part these devices are not yet available in practical forms. It seems clear that, at present, field methods of research, especially with human beings, are not appropriate for describing biologically anchored variables. Research on these variables must be postponed until it is practical to monitor physiological actions through cleverly designed telemetric devices. But it should be stressed that the exact role of specific biological variables *must* be studied at some time for a thorough functional analysis of psychological behavior (defined here as the interaction of a total functioning biological individual with environmental events).

In difficulty of definition, social stimuli, or stimuli which evolve from the action of people, range between physical and biological events. This is so because social events, like physical and biological ones, must in many instances be described in terms of their physical dimensions, and, as is well known, the components of social stimuli can be terribly subtle and complex. For the reader interested in a further analysis of social events within the framework of a natural science, Skinner's discussion (1953, pp. 298-304) is recommended.

In field studies, the procedure for defining and recording social stimuli is the same as that for defining and recording response events, since social events are treated as the responses of people in antecedent or consequent relationships to the behavior of the subject. Therefore the entire previous section on defining and recording behavioral events pertains also to defining and recording social events.

Some social stimuli, like response stimuli, may consist of a single class of behavior on the part of an adult or a child and may be recorded on the basis of frequency or of occurrence or nonoccurrence within a time interval. Examples of single-class antecedent stimuli are simple commands and requests: "Start now," "Gather around in a circle," "Come, let's ride the trikes." Examples of single-class consequent stimuli are confirmations ("Right"), disconfirmations ("Wrong"), approval ("Good"), and disapproval ("You play too rough").

Other social stimuli may be composed of several classes of behavior stemming from one person or several in concert. As in the case of defining multiple response classes, criteria for each subclass in the group may constitute a code. A *specific observational code* may be developed to describe social events in a specific situation for a specific study. For example, in a study of autistic behavior, adult attention was defined as "(1) touching the child; (2) being within two feet of and facing the child; (3) talking to, touching, assisting or going to the child" (Brawley, Harris, Allen, Fleming, and Peterson, 1969). With such criteria the investigators catalogued the types of behaviors which constituted social interaction involving attention and excluded other stimuli originating in the behavior of an adult in contact with the subject.

General observational codes for social events, like those for response events, have also been devised to study many problems in a general type of field setting. For example, Becker and Thomas (1967) have developed a comprehensive code for recording the teacher's behavior in an elementary classroom situation.

Which classes of behavior-environment interactions will be selected for study will depend on the purpose of the investigation; the maximum number, however, will be limited by the practical considerations. Studies requiring detailed analyses of many response classes may be planned as a series, the first dealing with grossly defined classes and the others with more and more progressively refined categories. For example, the first study may be concerned with the frequency of social contacts with adults and peers, and the second with specific verbal and motor responses directed to specific adults (teachers and parents) and peers (boys and girls).

Assessing Observer Reliability

Disagreements between observers may be related to inadequacies in (1) the observational code, (2) the training of the observers, or (3) the method of calculating reliability.

The Observational Code

Problems of defining and recording behavioral and stimulus events have been discussed (pp. 188–189). We need only add here that observer reliability is directly related to the comprehensiveness and specificity of the definitions in the observational code. Generally it is advisable to devise codes with mutually exclusive event categories, each definition having criteria that do not occur in any other definition.

Training of Observers

Even when a code is completely serviceable, two observers may not necessarily record the occurrence of the same event at the same time unless each has been adequately trained in using the code and in controlling his behavior while observing and recording.

For example, training might begin by familiarizing the observer with the tools for recording, for example, the clipboard, the stopwatch, and data sheets. This might be followed by an orientation to the code and exercises in recording events, first alone and then with a second observer. A film or video tape of sequences similar to those in the actual situation might be used to provide supplementary experiences.

It is often helpful to have a second observer to record along with the first observer. During trial recordings the observers can indicate to each other the behaviors being scored and uncover misunderstandings regarding the nature of the code or ambiguities in the definition of particular responses. Such a procedure reduces interpretation on the part of the observer and can contribute to an improved code.

Since it is relatively easy for the observers to slip an interval in the course of a long recording session, they should be instructed to note the beginning of certain activities, *e.g.*, story time, snack, nap, *etc.* This allows them to determine easily when they are out of phase with one another. Slips may also result from inaccurate stopwatches. Watches should be periodically tested by starting them simultaneously and checking them a few hours later.

After training on the proficient use of the code the observer might be given instruction on how to conduct himself while observing and recording. Thus he might be told how to refrain from interacting with the subject, for example, ignore all questions, avoid eye contact, and suppress reactions to the subject's activities as well as those associated with him. He might also be instructed in moving about to maintain a clear view of the subject without making it obvious that he is following him.

Method of Calculating Reliability

The reliability index is to some degree a function of how it is calculated. Suppose that we have data from two observers showing the frequency of a class of events taken over one hour. Unless the sums obtained by each observer are equal, the smaller sum is divided by the larger to obtain a percentage of agreement. If the sums are identical, the reliability index will be 100. This method is often used when the investigator is interested in frequencies per se, since the measure obtained gives only the amount of agreement over the total number of events observed. It does not indicate whether the two observers were recording the same event at exactly the same time. Thus it might be possible that one observer was recording few behaviors during the first half hour and many during the second, whereas the second observer was doing just the opposite. To ascertain whether this is the case, one could divide the period of observation into small segments and calculate the reliability of each. Agreements over progressively smaller segments would give confidence that the observers were scoring the same event at the same time. One may assess the agreement over brief intervals such as 5 or 10 seconds. Reliability is calculated by scoring each interval as agree or disagree (match or mismatch) and dividing the total number of agreements by the number of agreements plus the number of disagreements. Note that one may score several agreements or disagreements in an interval if a number of events are being recorded simultaneously, as shown in Tables 1 and 2. In this case the interval is broken down according to the number of different events recorded, with each event scored as a match or mismatch.

The reliability index may also be influenced by the frequency of response under study. When a behavior is displayed at a very low rate, the observer will record few instances of occurrence and many of nonoccurrence. In this situation the observers could disagree on the occurrence of the behavior yet still show high reliability due to their agreement on the large number of intervals where no behavior was recorded. A similar problem exists with regard to high-frequency behaviors. Here, however, the observers may disagree on the nonoccurrence of the behavior and agree on occurrence, because of the frequency of the latter. The problem may be resolved by computing not one but two reliability coefficients, one for occurrence and one for nonoccurrence.

In some cases the requirement of perfect matching of intervals may be relaxed slightly. Thus, behaviors recorded within one interval (especially if the interval is short) may also be considered as instances of agreement for reliability purposes. A technique of noncontinuous observing may also increase reliability (O'Leary, O'Leary, and Becker, 1967). In this procedure the observers record for shorter portions of time. For example, instead of taking continuous 10-sec observations, the observer might record for 10 out of every 15 sec, or for 20 out of every 30 sec. During the period in which the observer is not attending to the child, he should be recording the behaviors just observed.

The use of a second observer does not ensure high reliability of recording; it is possible for both observers to agree on the scoring of certain events and at the same time be incorrect (Gewirtz and Gewirtz, 1964). Both observers might record some events which should not be noted and ignore others which should be included. Hence a third observer might be used on occasion to determine whether this possibility exists.

COLLECTING, ANALYZING, AND INTERPRETING DATA

Data Collection

Final data collection is begun as soon as it is evident that the observers are adequately trained, the field situation is feasible, and the subject has adapted to the presence of the observers.

Whether the investigator collects data during all of the time available for observation or takes time samples will depend upon many factors, including the purpose of the study, the nature of the data, and the practical considerations. Regardless of the frequency with which observations are made, it is recommended that the data be plotted at regular intervals to provide a kind of progress chart. A visual account of the fluctuations and trends can help the investigator to make important decisions, for example, setting up the time for the next reliability evaluation or establishing the termination time for a phase of the study.

Data Analysis

Up until now we have discussed the investigator's activities in relation to the interactions between the observer and the field events. The investigator was viewed as a critic, watching the observer record the events in a natural ecology. Thus in the data collection phase of a study the investigator's role is somewhat similar to that of a motion picture director—evaluating what the camera is recording in relation to the scene as he sees it. In this section on data analysis and in the next on interpretation, we shall consider what the investigator does, not in relation to the recording equipment and field events, but in relation to the data collected.

Basically, in data analysis the investigator looks at the data collected to "see what is there." Usually he finds that making one or several transformations in the raw data helps him to see more clearly the relationships among the events observed. Transformational procedures may consist of converting the frequency counts into graphic, tabular, verbal, arithmetical, or statistical forms. Exactly which operations he performs on the data will depend on the purpose of the study, the nature of the data, and his theoretical assumptions about what can or cannot be demonstrated by a descriptive field study.

Usually, data analysis begins when data collection ends. However, as noted previously, an investigator may graph the data while the study is in progress. Under these circumstances data analysis may consist of revising and refining the graphs and making other transpositions to show the relationships among the subparts of the data.

Data collected in terms of rate are usually plotted in a graphic form with responses on the vertical axis and time on the horizontal axis. Points on the chart may represent either discrete or cumulative values. Discrete values are the sums or means for each successive session; cumulative values are the sums or means for all previous sessions. Therefore, curves with discrete values may go up, stay at the same level, or go down; cumulative curves may also go up or stay at the same level, but they do not go down. A decrease in the frequency of a response is shown in the curve as a deceleration in rate (bends toward the horizontal axis), an increase in frequency as an acceleration (bends toward the vertical axis), a constant frequency as no change in rate, and a zero frequency as a horizontal line.

In most instances graphic presentations are made more meaningful when accompanied by percentage values. In addition, it is often advantageous to show percentages of occurrences in the different conditions and subconditions of the field situation.

By viewing the interactions in selected time periods (early morning and late morning) or around certain events (before and after mealtime) as populations, statistical analyses may be made to assess the nature and the reliability of differences observed.

Interpretation of Findings

Essentially, interpretation of findings consists of the investigator's statements on what is "seen" in the data together with his conception of their generality. Such statements are the *raison d'être* of an investigation.

Obviously, an investigator is free to interpret his findings in any way he chooses. The investigator who accepts the assumptions of a natural science approach to psychology seeks to limit his interpretations to empirical concepts and relationships consistent with his observations and the analytical operations made upon the products of these observations. Hence in a descriptive field study his interpretations will usually consist of a discussion of what was found in the situation with comparisons to other findings obtained under functionally similar conditions. Conclusions on the similarities and differences uncovered in these comparisons will be incorporated in his argument for the generality of his findings. Interpretations in an experimental field study would depend on the number and type of manipulations employed and would usually be limited to describing the functional relationships obtained.

ILLUSTRATIVE STUDY

By means of the procedures previously described, a study was undertaken to obtain a descriptive account of a boy in a laboratory nursery school at the University of Illinois. The nursery school curriculum and the practices of the teaching staff of this school were based on behavioral principles (Skinner, 1953; Bijou and Baer, 1961).

SUBJECT AND FIELD SITUATION

In the judgment of the teachers the subject, Zachary, was typical of the children in the nursery school. He was 4½ years of age, of high average intelligence (Peabody IQ 116), and from a family of middle socioeconomic class. On the Wide Range Achievement Test he scored kindergarten 3 in reading, prekindergarten 5 in spelling, and kindergarten 6 in arithmetic.

The nursery school consists of a large room, approximately 21 × 40 feet. Evenly spaced along one wall are three doors which lead to three adjacent smaller rooms. One of these rooms was a lavatory; the second contained paints, papers, and other equipment, and the third a variety of toys. Nearby were a large table and several chairs, used for art activities and snack. Opposite these rooms along the other wall were several tables separated by brightly colored, movable partitions. In these booths, the children worked on academic subjects.

The school was attended by 12 children, 6 boys and 6 girls, between 4 and 5 years of age. The teaching staff consisted of a full-time teacher, an assistant teacher and, depending on the time of day, 1–3 undergraduates who assisted in administrating new programs in reading, writing, and arithmetic.

In general, the morning program was as follows:

9:00–10:00   Art, academic, and pre-academic work
10:00–10:30   Free play
10:30–11:00   Snack
11:00–12:00   Academic work, show-and-tell, and storytime

A typical morning might begin with art. At this time, 8–10 children sat around a large table working with various materials. During this activity each child in turn left the group for 10–20 minutes to work on writing or arithmetic with a teacher in one of the booths. After completing his assigned units of work, he returned to his art activity and another child left the group to work on his units of writing or arithmetic. After all the children had participated in these academic subjects, the art period was terminated and was followed by play. During play, the children were free to move about, often spending much of the time playing with blocks or other toys in either of the smaller schoolrooms. After approximately 30 minutes of play, the youngsters returned to the large table for a snack of juice and cookies. While eating and drinking they talked spontaneously and informally with their teachers and peers. After snack time some of the children participated in reading, while the others gathered for show-and-tell or storytime. During storytime the children sat on the floor in a group while the teacher read and discussed the story. In show-and-tell, instead of the teacher leading the group, each child had a chance to stand by the teacher in front of the group and to show an object he had brought from home and tell about it. As they did during the art period, the children left the group one at a time for a period of reading. Because of variations in the amount of time spent on academic subjects, a child did not engage in all of these activities every day.

BEHAVORIAL AND STIMULUS EVENTS RECORDED

The behaviors recorded were of two general categories: social contacts and sustained activities. Social contacts included verbal interchanges and physical contacts with children and teachers. Sustained activities involved behaviors in relation to the school tasks. The specific observational code developed for the study is presented in Table 3.

Observation began 3½ weeks after the start of the school year and covered a 3-hour period in the morning. The observations were taken on 28 school days. The observer sat a few feet from her subject and discreetly followed him as he moved from one activity to another in the nursery schoolroom. Every 10 seconds she recorded the occurrence or nonoccurrence of events defined in the code. The data sheet was similar to that shown in Table 1; however, only the first and second rows were used.

OBSERVER RELIABILITY

The reliability of observation and the adequacy of the behavioral code were evaluated several times throughout the study by having a second observer record stimulus and response events. Reliability was calculated by scoring each interval as a match or mismatch and dividing the total number of agreements by the number of agreements plus disagreements. Four checks on social contacts showed agreements of 75, 82, 85, and 87 per cent. Three checks on sustained activity yielded agreements of 94, 95 and 97 per cent. Thus average agreement on social contacts exceeded 82 per cent, while average agreement of sustained activity exceeded 95 per cent.

TABLE 3   Observational Code for Describing the Behavior of a Boy
in a Laboratory Nursery School

Symbol	Definition
	First Row **(Social Contacts)**
◻	*S* verbalizes to himself. Any verbalization during which he does not look at an adult or child or does not use an adult's or child's name. Does not apply to a group situation.
◻○	*S* verbalizes to adult. *S* must look at adult while verbalizing or use adult's name.
◻	*S* verbalizes to child. *S* must look at child while verbalizing or use child's name. If in a group situation, any verbalization is recorded as verbalization to a child.
S	Child verbalizes to *S*. Child must look at *S* while verbalizing or use *S*'s name.
△	Adult verbalizes to *S*. Adult must look at *S* while verbalizing or use *S*'s name.
S	Adult gives general instruction to class or asks question of class or makes general statement. Includes storytelling.
⊟	*S* touches adult. Physical contact with adult.
⊟	*S* touches child with part of body or object. Physical contact with child.
V	Adult touches *S*. Physical contact with adult.
T	Child touches *S* with part of body or object. Physical contact with child.

Symbol	*Definition*

Second Row
(Sustained Activity)

Sustained activity in art. S must be sitting in the chair, facing the material and responding to the material or the teacher within the 10-second interval. Responding to the material includes using pencil, paint brush, chalk, crayons, string, scissors, or paste or any implement on paper, or working with clay with hands on clay or hands on implement which is used with clay, or folding or tearing paper. Responding to the teacher includes following a command made by an adult to make a specific response. The behavior must be completed (child sitting in his chair again) within 2 minutes.

Sustained activity in storytime. S must be sitting, facing the material, or following a command given by the teacher or assistant. If S initiates a verbalization to a peer, do not record sustained activity in the 10-second interval.

Sustained activity in show-and-tell. S must be sitting, facing the material, or following a command given by the teacher. If S initiates a verbalization to a peer, do not record sustained activity in that 10-second interval.

Sustained activity in reading. S must be sitting in the chair, facing the material and responding to the material or the teacher with the 10-second interval.

Sustained activity in writing. S must be sitting in the chair, facing the material and responding to the material or the teacher within the 10-second interval. Responding to the material includes using the pencil (making a mark), or holding the paper or folder. Responding to the teacher includes responding verbally to a cue given by the teacher.

Symbol	Definition
	Sustained activity in arithmetic. S must be sitting in the chair, facing the material and responding to the material or the teacher within the 10-second interval. Responding to the material or teacher includes using the pencil or eraser or holding the paper or folder or responding verbally to cue.
	Sustained activity did not occur in interval.

ANALYSIS OF DATA

Social Contacts

Data were gathered on Zachary's social behaviors in informal activities of art, play, snack, storytime, and show-and-tell. They will be described and samples of the detailed accounts in art and snack will be presented in graphic form. The youngster's dominant behavior during the art period, shown in Fig. 1, was talking to others (14 per cent of the time). Teachers and peers talked with him about equally, an average of 8 and 7 per cent, respectively. Physical contacts between Zachary, teachers, and peers were low, about 1–2 per cent. The child's verbal behavior to peers was higher during play than in the art period. He talked to his friends on an average of 38 per cent; they talked to him on an average of only 10 per cent. Verbal exchanges with teachers were low (an average of 2.5 per cent). Zachary touched other children 7 per cent of the time on the average, and they reciprocated on an average of 3 per cent. Physical contacts with teachers were relatively infrequent.

As in the art and play periods, Zachary's social interactions during snack time, as shown in Fig. 2, consisted mostly of talking to his classmates, an average of 21 per cent. They in turn talked to him only an average of 7 per cent. During this period the teacher's general commands (instructions addressed to the group) were relatively high, an average of 7 per cent in contrast to 2 per cent during art and play. Physical contacts with other children were low, as in art and play: about 3 per cent.

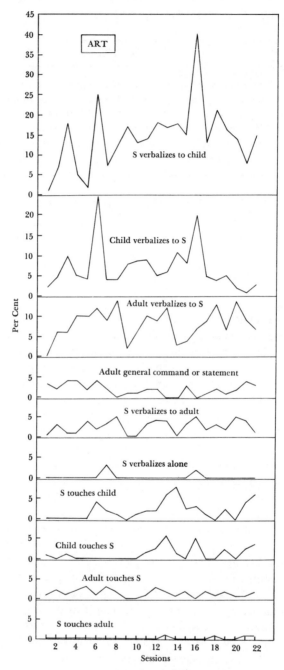

FIG. 1. Social contact during art.

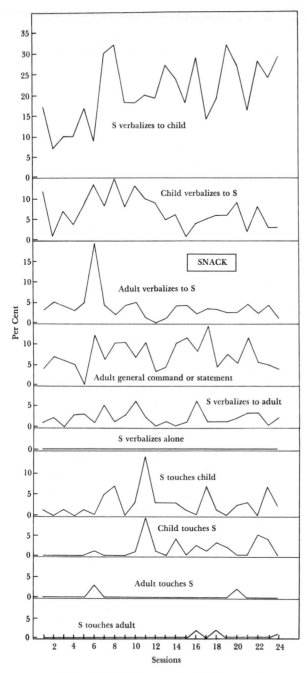

Fig. 2. Social interaction during snack.

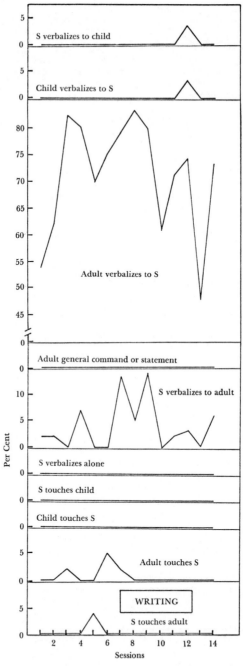

FIG. 3. Social behavior during writing.

Compared to those of the art, play, and snack periods, Zachary's verbalizations to peers and to teachers were low (8 and 4 per cent, respectively), and the numbers of times he touched children (10 per cent) and children touched him were also relatively low (2 per cent). Storytime had a high frequency of teacher's general commands and statements (average of 73 per cent), since this category was scored when the teacher read and discussed the stories.

In show-and-tell, Zachary's social behavior was similar to that during storytime. He talked to other children 14 per cent of the time and touched them 9 per cent of the time. Zachary touched teachers about 1 per cent of the time, and they reciprocated about 3 per cent of the time.

In respect to Zachary's social behavior during the academic periods, these data clearly indicate that the teacher talked to Zachary a great deal during the reading (an average of 69 per cent), writing (an average of 71 per cent), and arithmetic periods (an average of 58 per cent), and the child talked to the teacher with high frequency, particularly in reading (an average of 44 per cent) and arithmetic (an average of 41 per cent). In writing he talked to the teacher only 3 per cent of the time. There were also a few instances in which the teacher touched Zachary and rare occasions on which Zachary interacted socially with other children. Figure 3 is a detailed graphic account of his social behavior during the writing period.

Sustained Activity
For the observer to mark the occurrence of sustained activity, Zachary had to respond in a manner appropriate for a particular school activity. (See "Second Row" in Table 3.) For example, during art, the child had to be sitting in his chair, facing the art materials and manipulating them during each 10-second interval. Similar definitions were used for other situations and periods. Given these definitions, the results show a generally high level of sustained activity in all phases of the morning program. Daily rates of sustained activities in art, storytime, and show-and-tell range between 70 per cent and 99 per cent with an average of 89 per cent for art, 95 per cent for storytime, and 88 per cent for show-and-tell. See Fig. 4 for variations from session to session and Zachary's sustained behavior during art. Sustained activity in reading, writing, and arithmetic ranges from 90 per cent to 100 per cent over the days observed with an average of 97, 95, and 96 per cent, respec-

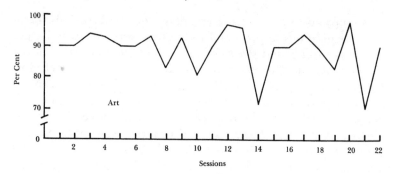

FIG. 4. Sustained activity during art.

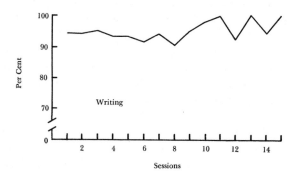

FIG. 5. Sustained activity during writing.

tively. See Fig. 5 for variations in the child's sustained behavior and writing. Because of the limited availability of the observer and the fact that not every activity occurred every day, the number of observations on each activity varied.

DISCUSSION

A descriptive account of the behaviors of a boy during the morning hours in a laboratory nursery school was obtained in terms of the frequency of occurrence of objectively defined stimulus and response of events. The account shows rates of changes in social interactions (verbal and physical contacts) and sustained activities during eight periods of the school morning.

In the informal activities of the nursery school in which the youngster performed on an individual basis, as in art, free play, and snack time, the subject talked to his peers and teachers to a moderate degree. His peers and teachers responded to him verbally to lesser extent. And over the period of the study his verbal output increased. Physical interactions with peers and teachers in these situations were at a relatively low level. Finally, the youngster's sustained activity in the art period was high (between 70 and 98 per cent) and become more variable, on a day-to-day basis, during the second half of the study. In the other two informal activities, storytime and show-and-tell, the child participated as a member of a group in which the teacher's verbal behavior was prominent, especially during storytime. In these two situations the child talked to others less; but, as in art, free play and snack time, he talked more than he listened. In storytime and show-and-tell he engaged in some body contacts with peers and teachers, yet his sustained activity on nursing school tasks was high with a range of 90–99 per cent for the former and 70–95 per cent for the latter.

In the more structured activities of reading, writing, and arithmetic the teacher's verbal behavior to the child was at a high level and his verbal behavior to her was correspondingly high, particularly in reading and arithmetic. During academic exercises all other social interactions were zero or near zero, and the child's sustained activities were consistently high, ranging from 90 to 100 per cent of the time.

The data gathered in this study can serve two main purposes. First, they can provide normative information on behavior in a laboratory preschool. Thus it might be interesting to compare this child's rates of response as obtained in this study after $3\frac{1}{2}$ weeks of school with his rates during the last month of the school year. It might also be interesting to compare this child's behavior with that of another child in the same nursery school. Such a comparison might be especially valuable if someone claimed that the second child's behavior was deviant. In addition, it might be informative to compare this child's behavior with that of a comparable child in a community-operated nursery school. Second, the data suggest certain relationships between the behavior of the subject, the teacher, and other children. Thus the investigator might use the data as a baseline for an experimental study in which conditions are manipulated to test for possible functional relationships.

SUMMARY

Psychology, like the other natural sciences, depends for its advancement upon both descriptive field accounts from ecological and cross-cultural studies, as well as from functional analyses of its primary data. It would be advantageous to have findings from descriptive field and experimental field studies that could be related to each other at the *level of data and empirical concepts*. For the most part, integration of findings of this sort has not been possible because data have been collected in the two types of investigation in irreconcilable ways. It is the thesis of this chapter that data from descriptive and experimental field studies can be interrelated if both sets were derived from frequency-of-occurrence measures.

The methodology proposed for a descriptive field study is predicated on three assumptions. (1) The primary data of psychology are the observable interactions of a biological organism and environmental events, past and present. (2) Theoretical concepts and laws are derived from empirical concepts and laws, which in turn are derived from the raw data. (3) Descriptive field studies describe interactions between behavioral and environmental events; experimental field studies provide information on their functional relationships.

The ingredients of a descriptive field investigation using frequency measures consist of (1) specifying in objective terms the situation in which the study is conducted, (2) defining and recording behavioral and environmental events in observable terms, and (3) measuring observer reliability.

Field descriptive studies following the procedures suggested here would reveal interesting new relationships in the usual ecological settings and would also provide provocative cues for experimental studies. On the other hand, field experimental studies using frequency measures would probably yield findings that would suggest the need for describing new interactions in specific natural situations.

REFERENCES

Allen, K. Eileen, 1967. Elimination of disruptive classroom behaviors of a pair of preschool boys. Paper presented at the American Educational Research Association, Boston.

Allen, K. Eileen, Nancy J. Reynolds, Florence R. Harris, and D. M. Baer, 1967. Control of hyperactivity by social reinforcement of attending behavior. *Journal of Educational Psychology,* 58, pp. 231-237.

Baldwin, A. L., J. Kalhorn, and F. H. Breese, 1949. The appraisal of parent behavior. *Psychological Monographs,* 63, No. 299.

Barker, R. G., and H. F. Wright, 1955. *Midwest and Its Children: The Psychological Ecology of an American Town.* New York: Harper & Row.

Becker, W. C., C. H. Madsen, Jr., Carole Revelle Arnold, and D. R. Thomas, 1967. The contingent use of teacher attention and praise in reducing classroom behavior problems. *Journal of Special Education,* 1, pp. 287-307.

Becker, W. C., and D. R. Thomas, 1967. A revision of the code for the analysis of a teacher's behavior in the classroom. Unpublished manuscript.

Bijou, S. W., and D. M. Baer, 1961. *Child Development: A Systematic and Empirical Theory,* Vol. 1. New York: Appleton-Century-Crofts.

Birnbrauer, J. S., M. M. Wolf, J. D. Kidder, and Cecilia Tague, 1965. Classroom behavior of retarded pupils with token reinforcement. *Journal of Experimental Child Psychology,* 2, pp. 219-235.

Brawley, Eleanor R., Florence R. Harris, K. Eileen Allen, R. S. Fleming, and R. F. Peterson, 1969. Behavior modification of an autistic child. *Behavioral Science,* 14, pp. 87-96.

Gewirtz, Hava, and J. L. Gewirtz, 1964. A method for assessing stimulation behaviors and caretaker-child interaction. Unpublished manuscript.

Harris, Florence R., M. M. Wolf, and D. M. Baer, 1964. Effects of adult social reinforcement on child behavior. *Young Children,* 20, pp. 8-17.

Hart, Betty M., K. Eileen Allen, John S. Buell, Florence R. Harris, and M. M. Wolf, 1964. Effects of social reinforcement on operant crying. *Journal of Experimental Child Psychology,* 1, pp. 145-153.

Hawkins, R. P., R. F. Peterson, Edda Schweid, and S. W. Bijou, 1966. Behavior therapy in the home: amelioration of problem parent-child relations with parent in a therapeutic role. *Journal of Experimental Child Psychology,* 4, pp. 99-107.

Honig, W. K., 1966. Introductory remarks. In W. K. Honig (Ed.), Operant behavior: *Areas of Research and Application.* New York: Appleton-Century-Crofts.

Jensen, G. D., and Ruth A. Bobbitt, 1967. Implications of primate research for understanding infant development. In J. Hellmouth (Ed.), *The Exceptional Child*, Vol. 1. Seattle: Special Child Publications.

Johnston, Margaret S., C. Susan Kelley, Florence R. Harris, and M. M. Wolf, 1966. An application of reinforcement principles to development of motor skills of a young child. *Child Development,* 37, pp. 379-387.

Lovaas, O. I., G. Freitag, Vivian J. Gold, and Irene C. Kassorla, 1965a. Experimental studies in childhood schizophrenia: analysis of self-destructive behavior. *Journal of Experimental Child Psychology,* 2, pp. 67-84.

Lovaas, O. I., G. Freitag, Vivian J. Gold, and Irene C. Kassorla, 1965b. Recording apparatus and procedure for observation of behaviors of children in free play settings. *Journal of Experimental Child Psychology,* 2, pp. 108-120.

O'Leary, K. D., Susan G. O'Leary, and W. C. Becker, 1967. Modification of a deviant sibling interaction pattern in the home. *Behavior Research and Therapy,* 5, pp. 113-120.

Skinner, B. F., 1953. *Science and Human Behavior.* New York: The Macmillan Company.

Wolf, M. M., T. R. Risley, and H. L. Mees, 1964. Application of operant conditioning procedures to the behavior problems of an autistic child. *Behaviour Research and Therapy,* 1, pp. 305-312.

Wright, H. F., 1967. *Recording and Analyzing Child Behavior.* New York: Harper & Row.

9

Behavior Therapy in the Home: Amelioration of Problem Parent-Child Relations with the Parent in a Therapeutic Role

Robert P. Hawkins, Robert F. Peterson,
Edda Schweid, and Sidney W. Bijou

In recognition of the important part parents play in the behavioral (or personality) development of the child, various agencies dealing with child behavior problems have often utilized techniques whose goal is to modify parent-child relationships. For example, the parent of a child who exhibits deviant behavior may, himself, be given psychotherapy in order to change his behavior toward the child. Alternatively, the parent may merely be given advice as to how he should react differently toward the child, or both parent and child may be given psychotherapy and/or counseling. The technique employed is likely to depend on the type of therapist consulted and the therapist's theoretical orientation. A general discussion of therapeutic techniques with children has been presented by Bijou and Sloane (1966).

Traditional types of therapy have a number of deficiencies. First, the child's behavior is seldom observed by the therapist, leaving definition of the problem and description of the child's behavior totally up to the parent. Second, the behavior of the parent toward the child is seldom observed. Thus considerable reliance is placed on the verbal reports of the parent and child and on the imagination of the therapist. Third, when "practical suggestions"

Reprinted from *Journal of Experimental Child Psychology,* 4 (1966), pp. 99-107, with permission of the authors and the editors. Slightly edited. Copyright © 1966 by Academic Press, Inc.

This research was supported in part by a grant from National Institute of Mental Health (MH-2232), U. S. Public Health Service.

are made by the therapist, they may be so general or technical that it is difficult for the parent to translate them into specific behavior. Fourth, since no objective record is kept of behavior changes over short intervals, (e.g., minutes, hours, days), it is difficult to judge the effectiveness of the treatment.

Wahler, Winkel, Peterson, and Morrison (1965) have developed a technique for effectively altering mother-child relationships in a laboratory setting, with objective records being kept of the behavior of both mother and child. The present study was an investigation of the feasibility of treatment in the natural setting where the child's behavior problem appeared—the home. As in the studies of Wahler et al., the mother served as the therapeutic agent. She received explicit instructions on when and how to interact with the child. The behaviors of both the mother and child were directly observed and recorded.

METHOD

Subject

The child in this study was a 4-year-old boy, Peter S. He is the third of four children in a middle-class family. Peter has been brought to a university clinic because he was extremely difficult to manage and control. His mother stated that she was helpless in dealing with his frequent tantrums and disobedience. Peter often kicked objects or people, removed or tore his clothing, called people rude names, annoyed his younger sister, made a variety of threats, hit himself, and became very angry at the slightest frustration. He demanded attention almost constantly and seldom cooperated with Mrs. S. In addition, Peter was not toilet trained and did not always speak clearly. Neither of these latter problems was dealt with in the study.

Peter had been evaluated at a clinic for retarded children when he was 3 years old and again when he was $4\frac{1}{2}$. His scores on the Stanford Binet, form L-M, were 72 and 80, respectively. He was described as having borderline intelligence and as being hyperactive and possibly brain-damaged.

Procedure

The experimenters (Es), observing the mother and child in the home, noted that many of Peter's undesirable behaviors appeared to be maintained by attention from his mother. When Peter behaved objectionably, she would often try to explain why he should not act thus; or she would try to interest him in some new activity by offering toys or food. (This "distraction" method is often put forth by teachers as a preferred technique for dealing with undesirable behavior. Behavior theory suggests, however, that, although distraction may be temporarily effective in dealing with such behaviors, repeated employment of such a procedure may increase the frequency of the unwanted set of responses.) Peter was occasionally punished by the withdrawal of a misused toy or other object, but he was often able to persuade his mother to return the item almost immediately. He was also punished by being placed on a high chair and forced to remain there for short periods. Considerable tantrum behavior usually followed such disciplinary measures and was quite effective in maintaining the mother's attention, largely in the form of verbal persuasion or argument.

Before the study, the child's difficulties were discussed thoroughly with his mother. She was told that therapy might take several months, was of an experimental nature, and would require her participation. She readily agreed to cooperate.

Treatment consisted of two to three sessions per week, each approximately 1 hour in length. Peter's mother was instructed to go about her usual activities during these sessions. His younger sister was allowed to be present and to interact with him in her usual way. Peter was permitted to move freely through the main part of the house—the recreation room, laundry room, dinette, kitchen, and living room—because the wide openings between these areas made it possible to observe his activity with a minimum of movement on the *E*s' part. The *E*s never responded to Peter or his sister. When the children asked questions about them or spoke to them, they were told by the mother, "Leave them alone; they are doing their work."

Initial observations showed that the following responses made up a large portion of Peter's repertoire of undesirable behavior: (1) biting his shirt or arm, (2) sticking out his tongue, (3) kicking or hitting himself, others, or objects, (4) calling someone or something a derogatory name, (5) removing or threatening to remove his clothing, (6) saying "No!" loudly and vigorously, (7) threatening to damage objects or persons, (8) throwing objects, and (9) pushing his sister. These nine responses were collectively termed "Objectionable behavior" (O behavior), and their frequency of occurrence was measured by recording, for each successive 10-second interval, whether or not an O behavior occurred. This same method was used to obtain a record of the frequency of all verbalizations Peter directed to his mother and of the frequency of her verbalizations to him.

In order to assess interobserver reliability, two *E*s were employed as observers on eight occasions and three *E*s on one occasion. Since it was sometimes possible for an observer to detect when another observer had scored a response, the obtained reliability scores may be overestimated. For every session of observation each observer obtained total frequency scores for the O behaviors, the child's verbalizations, and the mother's verbalizations. When two observers were employed, proportion of agreement in any one of these three classes of behavior was calculated by dividing the smaller score by the larger. When three observers were employed, the three proportions for a class of behavior were averaged to obtain the mean proportion of agreement. Agreement on O behaviors ranged from .70 to 1.00, with a mean of .88. Agreement on mother's verbalizations to Peter ranged from .82 to .98, with a mean of .94. Agreement on Peter's verbalizations to his mother ranged from .90 to .99, with a mean of .96.

Treatment was divided into five stages: the first baseline period, the first experimental period, the second baseline period, the second experimental period, and a follow-up period.

First Baseline Period

During this period Peter and his mother interacted in their usual way. Their behaviors were recorded by the *E*s; and after some 16 sessions, when an adequate estimate of the pretreatment rate of O behavior had been obtained, the next stage was begun.

First Experimental Period

Before the beginning of this period, the mother was informed of the nine objectionable behaviors which would be treated. She was shown three gestural signals which indicated how she was to behave toward Peter. Signal A meant she was to tell Peter to stop whatever O behavior he was emitting. Signal B indicated she was immediately to place Peter in his room and lock the door. When signal C was presented, she was to give him attention, praise, and affectionate physical contact. Thus every time Peter emitted an O behavior, Mrs. S. was either signaled to tell him to stop or to put him in his room. On the first occurrence of a particular O behavior during the experimental session, Mrs. S. was merely signaled to tell Peter to stop; but if he repeated the same response at any subsequent time during that session, she was signaled to place him in his room. (This isolation period may be viewed as a period of "time-out" from stimuli associated with positive reinforcement. See Ferster and Appel, 1961.) Occasionally, when *E* noticed that Peter was playing in a particularly desirable way, Signal C was given and his mother responded to him with attention and approval. Mrs. S. was asked to restrict the application of these new behavioral contingencies to the experimental hour. She was told to behave in her usual way at all other times.

The period of Peter's isolation was not counted as part of the experimental hour, so each session consisted of 1 hour of observation in the main living area of the house. When placed in his room, Peter was required to remain there for a minimum of 5 minutes. In addition, he had to be quiet for a short period before he was allowed to come out (a technique employed by Wolf, Risley, and Mees, 1964). Since all objects likely to serve as playthings had been previously removed from the room, he had little opportunity to amuse himself. Neither Mrs. S. nor Peter's sister interacted with him during time-out. On two occasions, however, it was necessary to deviate from this procedure. These deviations occurred when Peter broke windows in his room and called out that he had cut himself. The first time Mrs. S. entered his room, swept up the glass, reprimanded him for breaking the window, noted the (minor) nature of his injury, and left. The second time she bandaged a small cut and left immediately. Peter broke a window on one other occasion, but since no injury was apparent, the act was ignored.

Second Baseline Period
When, after 6 experimental sessions, the frequency of O behaviors appeared stable, contingencies were returned to those of the earlier baseline period. Mrs. S. was told to interact with Peter just as she had during previous (nonexperimental) observation sessions. This second baseline period consisted of 14 sessions.

Second Experimental Period
After the second baseline period, the experimental procedure was reintroduced and continued for 6 sessions. Contingencies were

identical to those of the first experimental period except that special attention for desirable play was excluded, save one accidental instance.

Follow-up

For 24 days after the second experimental period there was no contact between the *E*s and the S. family. Mrs. S. was given complete freedom to use any techniques with Peter that she felt were warranted, including time-out, but she was given no specific instructions. After this 24-day interval (whose length was limited by the impending departure of one *E*) a 3-session, posttreatment check was made to determine whether the improvements effected during treatment were still evident. These 1-hour follow-up sessions were comparable to earlier baseline periods in that Mrs. S. was instructed to behave in her usual manner toward Peter.

RESULTS AND DISCUSSION

The frequency of Peter's O behaviors in each treatment condition is shown in Fig. 1. Asterisks mark sessions in which observer re-

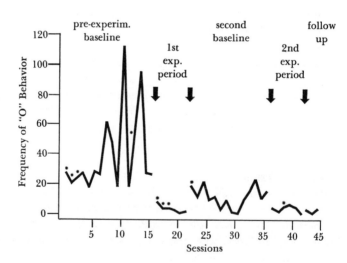

FIG. 1. Number of 10-second intervals, per 1-hour session, in which O behavior occurred. Asterisks indicate sessions in which reliability was tested.

liability was assessed. These 9 reliability sessions are plotted in terms of the mean of the frequencies obtained by the different observers. During the first baseline period, the rate of O behavior varied between 18 and 113 per session. A sharp decrease occurred in the first experimental period; the rate ranged from 1 to 8 per session. In the course of this period, Peter was isolated a total of four times, twice in session 17, once in session 18, and again in session 22. He received special attention twice in session 17, six times in session 18, and once each sessions 20 and 21.

During the second baseline period, the rate of O behaviors varied between 2 and 24 per session. Although this was an increase over the previous experimental period, the frequency of response did not match that of the first baseline period. This failure to return to earlier levels may have occurred for several reasons. For example, midway through the second baseline, Mrs. S. reported considerable difficulty in responding to Peter as she had during the first baseline period. She stated that she felt more "sure of herself" and could not remember how she had previously behaved toward her son. It was apparent that Mrs. S. now gave Peter firm commands when she wanted him to do something and did not "give in" after denying him a request. The Es also noted that Peter was receiving more affection from his mother. This increased affection, however, seemed to be due to a change in Peter's behavior rather than his mother's, since Peter has recently begun to approach her with affectionate overtures.

The rate of O behaviors in the second experimental period was comparable to that of the first experimental period, from 2 to 8 per session. Special attention was (accidentally) given once in session 38.

Data obtained during the follow-up period show that Peter's O behaviors remained low in rate after the passage of a 24-day interval. Mrs. S. reported that Peter was well behaved and much less demanding than he had previously been. She stated that she had been using the time-out procedure approximately once a week. (It was the E's impression that not only the quantity but also the quality, i.e., topography, of O behaviors had changed. As early as the second baseline period it had been observed that O behaviors frequently lacked components which had been present earlier, such as facial expressions, voice qualities, and vigor of movement that typically constitute "angry" behavior.) Thus it would appear that

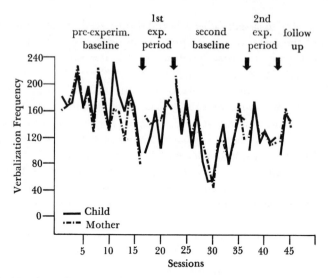

Fig. 2. Number of 10-second intervals, per 1-hour session, in which Peter spoke to his mother or the mother spoke to Peter.

not only were the treatment effects maintained in the absence of the *E*s and the experimental procedures, but also they had generalized from the treatment hour to the remaining hours of the day. These developments were being maintained by the use of occasional isolation (contingent, of course, on the occurrence of an O behavior) and other alterations in the mother's behavior.

Evidence that Mrs. S.'s behavior toward her child did change during the course of treatment is presented in Fig. 2, which shows the verbal interaction between Peter and his mother. It can be seen by comparing Figs. 1 and 2 that the frequency of O behavior and the frequency of the mother's verbalizations to Peter sometimes covaried. A positive correlation is particularly evident during the second baseline period, and a negative correlation during the follow-up. The correlation between O behavior and mother verbalization was determined for each of the five stages of the experiment. During the first and second baseline periods the correlations were .17 and .47, respectively, while for the experimental and follow-up periods they were −.41, −.20, and −.71 in that order. None of these correlations differs significantly from zero. Combining these figures into nontreatment (baseline) and treatment (experimental and follow-up) periods yields correlations of .39 for the former, and —.41 for the latter. These coefficients were found to be significantly different from one another ($z = 2.48, p = .007$). This finding may indicate that Mrs. S., when left to her usual way of interbehaving with Peter, attended to (and thus maintained through social reinforcement) his undesirable behaviors while ignoring (extinguishing) desirable (non-O) responses. A number of studies (Allen, Hart, Buell, Harris, and Wolf, 1964; Harris, Johnston, Kelley, and Wolf, 1964; Hart, Allen, Buell, Harris, and Wolf, 1964; Wahler et al., 1965) have demonstrated that social reinforcement in the form of adult attention can influence the behavior of the young child. It is interesting to note that Mrs. S.'s proclivity to respond to Peter's O behaviors was reversed during the two experimental periods and thereafter.

Besides showing a relationship between the mother's verbalizations and Peter's O behaviors, a comparison of Figs. 1 and 2 indicates that the time-out procedure operated in a selective manner. Even though the isolation technique reduced the rate of undesirable responses, other classes of behavior such as verbalizations were not affected. This is shown by the fact that Peter's verbalization rate during the combined treatment periods did not differ significantly from his rate during nontreatment periods ($F = 2.24$; $df = 1, 43; .25 > p > .10$).

The results of this study show that it is possible to treat behavioral problems in the home, with the parent as a therapeutic agent. Home treatment may, in some cases, be more effective than treatment in the clinic, particularly when the undesirable responses have a low probability of occurrence in settings other than the home. Since it is widely held that many of a child's problems originate in the home environment, direct modification of this environment (including the behavior of other family members) may arrest the difficulty at its source. One limitation of this type of study, however, is the requirement of a cooperative parent. If this requirement can be met, not only can the use of the parent as therapist free the professional for other duties, but also the parent, in learning to use techniques of behavioral control, may become generally more skillful in dealing with the responses of the developing child and more capable of handling any future difficulties that may occur.

REFERENCES

Allen, K. Eileen, Betty M. Hart, Joan S. Buell, Florence R. Harris, and M. M. Wolf, 1964. Effects of social reinforcement on isolate behavior of a nursery school child. *Child Development,* 35, pp. 511-518.

Bijou, S. W., and H. N. Sloane, 1966. Therapeutic techniques with children. In L. A. Pennington and I. A. Berg (Eds.), *An Introduction to Clinical Psychology,* 3rd ed. New York: Ronald Press.

Ferster, C. B., and J. B. Appel, 1961. Punishment of S△ responding in matching to sample by time-out from positive reinforcement. *Journal of the Experimental Analysis of Behavior,* 4, pp. 45-56.

Harris, Florence R., Margaret K. Johnston, C. Susan Kelley, and M. M. Wolf, 1964. Effects of positive social reinforcement on regressed crawling of a nursery school child. *Journal of Educational Psychology,* 55, pp. 35-41.

Hart, Betty M., K. Eileen Allen, Joan S. Buell, Florence R. Harris, and M. M. Wolf, 1964. Effects of social reinforcement on operant crying. *Journal of Experimental Child Psychology,* 1, pp. 145-153.

Wahler, R. G., G. H. Winkel, R. F. Peterson, and D. C. Morrison, 1965. Mothers as behavior therapists for their own children. *Behavior Research and Therapy,* 3, pp. 113-124.

Wolf, M., T. Risley, and H. Mees, 1964. Application of operant conditioning procedures to the behaviour problems of an autistic child. *Behavior Research and Therapy,* 1, pp. 305-312.

10

Applying "Group" Contingencies to the Classroom Study Behavior of Preschool Children

Don Bushell, Jr., Patricia Ann Wrobel,
and Mary Louise Michaelis

The experimental analysis of behavior has concentrated on the examination of responses emitted by a single subject. Recently, extensions of this research have begun to deal with groups of individuals. Behavioral research with adult psychiatric patients (Ayllon and Azrin, 1965) and retarded children (Birnbrauer, Wolf, Kidder, and Tague, 1965) has indicated that certain operant techniques can be applied effectively well beyond the "artificial" conditions of the experimentally isolated subject.

In most group situations it is not practical to program individually special contingencies for the responses of each group member. Uniform criteria must be designed according to which a number of individuals are to be rewarded or punished. Schools,

Reprinted from the *Journal of Applied Behavior Analysis*, Vol. 1, 1968, pp. 55-61, with permission of the authors and the editors. Slightly edited. Copyright © 1968 by the Society for the Experimental Analysis of Behavior, Inc.

This study was carried out as a part of the program of the Webster College Student Behavior Laboratory, and preparation of the report was supported in part by the Institute for Sociological Research, The University of Washington. The authors gratefully acknowledge the able assistance of the observers who made this study possible: Alice Adcock, Sandra Albright, Sister Eleanor Marie Craig, S. L., Jim Felling, and Cleta Pouppart. We are particularly indebted to Donald M. Baer, who encouraged us to commit this study to paper and subsequently gave thoughtful criticism to the manuscript. Reprints may be obtained from Don Bushell, Jr., Dept. of Human Development, University of Kansas, Lawrence, Kansas 66044.

prisons, hospitals, business, and military organizations all maintain systems of response contingencies which are quite similar for all the individuals of a certain category within the organization. The objective of this research was to determine whether operant techniques may be applied to a group of individuals with effects similar to those expected when a single subject is under study. The specific behavior under analysis was the study behavior of a group of preschool children.

The dependent variables were behaviors such as attending quietly to instructions, working independently or in cooperation with others as appropriate, remaining with and attending to assigned tasks, and reciting after assignments had been completed. Counter examples are behaviors such as disrupting others who are at work, changing an activity before its completion, and engaging in "escape" behaviors such as trips to the bathroom or drinking fountain, or gazing out the window. To the extent that the first constellation of behaviors is present and the second is absent, a student may be classified as industrious, highly motivated, or conscientious; in short, he has good study habits.

METHOD

CHILDREN AND SETTING

The subjects were 12 children enrolled in a summer session. Three other children were not considered in this report because they did not attend at least half of the sessions because of illness and family vacations. Four of the 12 children were 3 years old, 2 were 4 years old, 5 were 5 years old, and 1 was 6 years old. These 10 girls and 2 boys would be described as middle class; all had been enrolled in the pre-school the preceding spring semester, all scored above average on standardized intelligence tests, and all had experienced some form of token system during the previous semester.

Classes were conducted from 12:45 to 3:30 P.M., 5 days a week for 7 weeks. A large room adjoining the classroom afforded one-way sight and sound monitoring of the class. The program was directed by two head teachers who were assisted for 25 minutes each day by a specialist who conducted the Spanish lesson. All of the teachers were undergraduates.

DAILY PROGRAM

Data were collected in three phases during the first 75 minutes of each of the last 20 class days of the summer session. During the first 20 minutes individual activities were made available to the children for independent study, and the amount of social interaction, student-student or student-teacher, was very slight. The next 25 minutes were devoted to Spanish instruction. The interaction pattern during this period was much like that of a typical classroom, with the teacher at the front of the assembled children, sometimes addressing a specific individual but more often talking to the entire group. The remaining 30 minutes were given over to "study teams," with the children paired so that the one more skilled at a particular task would teach the less skilled. Composition of the groups and their tasks varied from day to day according to the developing skills of the children.

After this 75 minutes, a special event was made available to the children. Special events included a short movie, a trip to a nearby park, a local theater group rehearsal, an art project, a story, or a gym class. The special event was always 30 minutes long and was always conducted outside the regular classroom. The children were not told what the activity would be for the day until immediately before it occurred.

TOKEN REINFORCEMENT

The tokens, colored plastic washers about 1.5 inches in diameter, served as a monetary exchange unit within the classroom. As the children engaged in individual activities, Spanish, and study teams, the teachers moved about the room giving tokens to those who appeared to be actively working at their various tasks, but not to those who were judged to be not attending to the assignment at the moment.

To minimize unproductive talking about the tokens, the teachers avoided mentioning them. Tokens were never given when requested. If a child presented a piece of work and then asked for a token, the request was ignored and additional work was provided if needed. Similarly, the presentation of tasks was never accompanied by any mention of tokens, such as, "If you do thus and so, I will give you a token." The tokens were simply given out as the children worked, and, where possible, the presentation was accompanied by such verbal statements as "Good," "You're doing fine: keep it up," and "That's right." The teachers avoided a set pattern in dispensing the tokens so that their approach would not become discriminative for studying. They would watch for appropriate behavior, move to that child, present a token and encouragement, then look for another instance not too nearby. During Spanish, the two teachers were able to present tokens for appropriate responding to the children who were assembled in front of the Spanish teacher. During study teams the teachers presented tokens as they circulated from group to group, and also at a checking session at the end of the period. Here, the student-learner recited what had been learned and both children were given tokens according to the performance of the learner. Each teacher distributed from 110 to 120 tokens during the 75 minutes.

The tokens could be used to purchase the special-event ticket. The price varied from 12 to 20 tokens around an average of 15 each day so that the children would not leave their study activities as soon as they acquired the necessary number. Children who did not earn enough to purchase the special-event ticket remained in the classroom when the others left with the teachers. There were no recriminations or admonishments by either the teachers or the students, and the one or two children left behind typically found some toy or book to occupy themselves until the rest of the class returned. After the special event, additional activities enabled the children to earn tokens for a 3:00 P.M. snack of cookies, ice cream, milk, or lemonade, and a chair to sit on while eating. Tokens could be accumulated from day to day.

As tokens became more valuable, theft, borrowing, lending (sometimes at interest), hiring of services, and a variety of other economic activities were observed. No attempt was made to control any of these except theft, which was eliminated simply by providing the children with aprons which had pockets for the tokens.

OBSERVATION AND RECORDING PROCEDURES

The four principal observers were seated in an observation room. Each wore earphones which enabled audio monitoring of the class and also prevented interobserver communication. On a signal at the beginning of each 5-minute period, each observer looked for the first child listed on the roster and noted his behavior on the data sheet, then looked for the second child on the list and noted his behavior, and so on for each child. All observers were able to complete the total observational cycle in less than 3 minutes. During the 75 minutes of observation, the children's behavior was described by noting what the child was looking at, to whom he was talking, and what he was doing with his hands. Fourteen daily observations of each child by each observer produced 672 times of data each day.

Criteria were established by which each behavioral description on the data sheets could be coded as either "S," indicating study behavior, or "NS," indicating nonstudy behavior. Behaviors such as writing, putting a piece in a puzzle, reciting to a teacher, singing a Spanish song with the class, and tracing around a pattern with a pencil were classified as S if they were observed in the appropriate setting. Descriptions of behaviors such as counting tokens, putting away materials, walking around the room, drinking at the fountain, looking out the window, rolling on the floor and attending to another child were classified as NS. Singing a Spanish song was scored S if it occurred during the Spanish period when called for, but NS if it occurred during an earlier or later period. Similarly, if one child was interacting with another over instructional materials during the study teams period, the behavior was labeled S, but the same behavior during another period was classified NS.

If a given child's behavior was described 14 times and 8 of these descriptions were coded S, the amount of study time for that child was $8/14$ for that day. The amount of study behavior for the entire class on a given day was the sum of the 12 individual scores.

TIME-SAMPLING VALIDITY CHECK

Time sampling assumes that, in a given situation, the behavior observed at fixed spacings in time adequately represents the behavior occurring during the total interval. To check the validity of this assumption, a fifth observer described the behavior of only three children much more frequently. At the beginning of each 15-second interval an automatic timing device beside the fifth observer emitted a click and flashed a small light. The observer then described the ongoing behavior of the first of the three target children of the day, noting essentially the child's looking, talking, and hand behaviors. The procedure was repeated for the second child, then the third. At the onset of the next 15-second interval, the sequence was repeated. The tape ran continuously. Consequently, during the same interval when the principal observers made 14 observations, the fifth made slightly more than 300 observations of each of the three children. This procedure was used during nine of the twenty experimental sessions, and the three children chosen for this type of observation varied.

The data sheets completed by the four regular observers and the tapes recorded by the fifth observer were coded each day by the four principal observers, who assigned either an S or NS to each description. Coding was accomplished independently by each observer without consultation. The fifth observer did not participate in classifying any of the tape descriptions.

DESIGN

The study, a within-group design, consisted of three stages. During the first stage, participation in the special event was contingent upon purchase of the necessary ticket with tokens. After 9 days under these conditions, participation in the special event was made noncontingent. During the 7 days of the noncontingent stage, the children were presented with special-event tickets and snack tickets as they arrived for school. Tokens and verbal statements of praise and encouragement were still given for the same behaviors as during the first phase, but the tokens no longer had any purchasing power. All the privileges of the classroom were available to every child regardless of how much or how little study behavior he or she displayed.

The decision to continue dispensing tokens but devalue them by providing everything free was made in order to retain all of the original procedures except the contingent special event. Had the tokens been given on a noncontingent basis at the beginning of each session, or eliminated entirely, the behavior of the teachers toward the children throughout the remainder of the session might have been altered.

After the sixteenth day of the study, the aprons containing the accumulated tokens were "sent to the cleaners" and all of the tokens were removed. As the children arrived the next day and asked where their tickets were, they were told they would have to buy them. When the children noted that they couldn't because they had no tokens, the teachers responded by saying, "Perhaps you can earn some. Your (activity—name) is over there." Thus, for the final 4 days, the last days of the summer session, the initial conditions were restored with special-event and snack tickets again being made contingent upon tokens acquired by the students for study behavior.

RESULTS

Figure 1 shows that study behavior was influenced by whether or not the special event was contingent upon it. During the first 9-day stage, offering the special event contingent on study behavior resulted in an average score for the class as a whole of 67 per cent. During the noncontingent stage, the observed study behavior declined 25 percentage points over 7 days to a low of 42 per

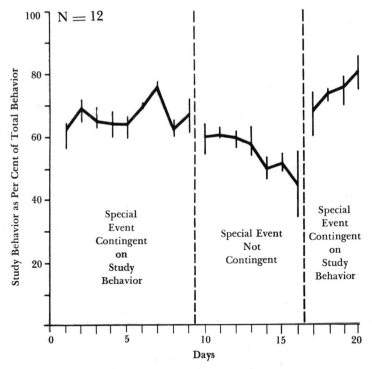

FIG. 1. Mean per cent of 12 children's study behavior over 20 school days. Vertical lines indicate the range of scores obtained by the four observers each day.

cent. Restoring the original contingencies on Day 17 was associated with a 22 per cent increase in study behavior over that of the previous day.

Because the study behavior data were derived from observational measures, a number of checks were made to establish the reliability of the procedures. First, the total class score obtained by each observer for each day was compared to the scores of the other three observers. The vertical lines at each point in Fig. 1 describe the range of group scores obtained by the four observers each day. Inspection of these lines indicated that the same pattern was described even if the summary class score for any given day was drawn at random from the four available scores. Indeed, the data of any one, or any combination, of the four observers presented the same pattern with respect to the effects of contingent reinforcement upon study behavior.

The fact that the behavior descriptions of each day were coded within a few hours after they were obtained might have been an additional source of error. A description might have been coded NS on Day 15 and S on Day 19 simply because the observer expected study behavior to increase during the final contingent stage. To check for such effects, four new coders were empaneled 9 months after the study was completed. These new coders had no knowledge of the details of the original investigation. They were trained to read behavioral descriptions like those appearing on the original data sheets and to assign an S or NS to each according to the criteria outlined in the previous section. Once they agreed within 5 per cent on the independent scoring of a given data sheet, they were each given nine of the original sheets.

The data sheets given to the new coders were in scrambled order with all dates and other identifying marks obscured so that they had no way of determining which stage a sheet came from even if they understood the significance of the experimental conditions. Sheets from Days 3, 4, 5, 12, 13, 14, 18, 19, and 20 (three from each stage) were recoded in this fashion. The procedure guaranteed that the expectations of the coder would not influence the scores obtained. The comparison of the original scores and those obtained by the new coders are shown in Fig. 2.

As a further check on coding bias, two of the original observers were recalled after a 9-month interval to recode one set of four

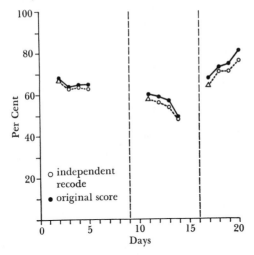

FIG. 2. Mean study behavior scores obtained by original observers compared with scores obtained by a panel of coders nine months after the completion of the study. Δ indicates scores obtained by two of the original observers who recoded the original data sheets nine months after completion of the study.

data sheets from each of the three stages of the study, twelve sheets in all, also presented in random order. Each of these two observers recoded the descriptions of one of the other observers and his own data sheet completed at the time of the original study. The results are also shown in Fig. 2 for Days 2, 11, and 17. These points, marked Δ, indicate that the results obtained by having the original observers recode their own and someone else's data do not differ from those obtained when newly trained coders score the original data. In all cases the scores obtained described the effects of contingent and noncontingent reinforcement in the same way.

The comparison of the total score for the three target children obtained by the regular method and the tapes is shown in Fig. 3 and supports the validity of the 5-minute time-sampling technique.

The data describing the effects of the different contingencies upon each of the three instructional styles (individual activities, group instruction, teams), failed to demonstrate that this dimension was important in the present study. Day-to-day variability was

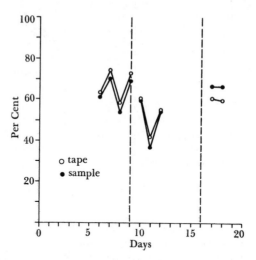

FIG. 3. Mean study behavior of various trios of children based on taped observations each day compared with written time-samples during the same period.

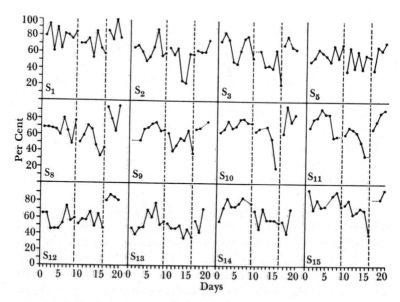

FIG. 4. Percentage of each individual child's behavior classified as study behavior under all conditions. Dotted lines without points indicate absence.

greater for the smaller periods than for the entire session, but in all cases the proportion of study behavior dropped similarly in the absence of the contingent special event and rose during the final 4 days.

Just as the day-to-day variability increased as the analysis moved from the whole class to periods within each day's class, individual study behavior was more variable than the aggregate data for all twelve children. It is to be expected that students of different age, sex, and educational background will perform differently in comparable settings, but all twelve records shown in Fig. 4 indicate that noncontingent reinforcement was less effective in sustaining study behavior than contingent reinforcement. In no case did an individual student display more study behavior during the second stage of the study than during the first and third stages.

DISCUSSION

The results indicate that the contingent special event controlled much of the study behavior. In the time available it was not possible to continue the noncontingent stage until study behavior stabilized. With such an extension, study behavior might have gone lower.

A token system has much to recommend it from a practical standpoint, for there are many school activities (recess, early dismissal, extracurricular events) which might be employed to develop and maintain higher levels of study behavior. Furthermore, the classroom teacher responsible for the behavior of many students can manage a token system but faces some difficulty in relying solely on verbal praise and attention as reinforcers. Behavior modification with social reinforcement requires constant monitoring of the subject's responding (Baer and Wolf, 1967). This can be done only on a very limited scale in a classroom by a single teacher.

The day-to-day variability in individual records requires further study. At first glance it would appear that the individual fluctuations could indict the smoother curve of the group as resulting from the canceling effect of numerous measurement errors at the individual level. However, the several measurement checks suggest that other factors may have been more important in explaining the variability. For example, the practice of allowing the children to accumulate tokens from day to day may have produced some variability. It allowed the children to work hard and lend one day, loaf and borrow the next; work hard and save one day, loaf and spend their savings the next. This would tend to produce a smooth curve for the group, since not everyone could lend at the same time nor could all borrow at once. The present practice in the preschool is to remove all tokens from the children's pockets after each day's session.

The next approximation toward a useful classroom observational technique will require additional measures to determine the effects of the students' changing behavior on the attending and helping behavior of the teachers. This work is now in progress.

It may be concluded that (1) practical reinforcement contingencies can be established in a classroom; and (2) the effects of various contingencies can be ascertained by direct observational techniques when the use of automated recording equipment is not practicable.

REFERENCES

Ayllon, T., and N. H. Azrin, 1965. The measurement and reinforcement of behavior of psychotics. *Journal of the Experimental Analysis of Behavior,* 8, pp. 357-383.

Baer, D. M., and M. M. Wolf. The reinforcement contingency in preschool and remedial education. In Robert R. Hess and Roberta Meyer Bear (Eds.), *Early Education: Current Theory, Research, and Practice.* Chicago: Aldine.

Birnbrauer, J. S., M. M. Wolf, J. D. Kidder, and C. E. Tague, 1965. Classroom behavior of retarded pupils with token reinforcement. *Journal of Experimental Child Psychology,* 2, pp. 219-235.

11

Experiments with Token Reinforcement in
a Remedial Classroom

Montrose M. Wolf, David K. Giles, and R. Vance Hall

Token reinforcement systems have now been used many times to develop and maintain useful human behavior in institutional settings (e.g., Ayllon and Azrin, 1965; Birnbrauer, Wolf, Kidder, and Tague, 1965; Cohen, Filipczak, and Bis, 1965; Lent, 1966; and Staats and Butterfield, 1965). In the present research, we created a token economy designed to develop and maintain the academic behavior of low-achieving children in a community setting. This report describes the results from the first year of an after-school, remedial education program for low-achieving fifth and sixth-grade children in an urban poverty area. The remedial program incorporated standard instructional materials, mastery of which was

Reprinted from *Behavioral Research and Therapy*, Vol. 6 (1968), pp. 51-64, Pergamon Press Limited, England, with permission of the authors and the editors. Slightly edited.

The authors wish to express their appreciation for the help and encouragement given by Ted Gray, Director of Special Education, Kansas City, Kansas Public Schools; Alonzo Plough, Principal of Grant Elementary School; David Glass, Principal of Stowe Elementary School; and Reverend David Gray, Pastor of Pleasant Green Baptist Church. We are also indebted to Mrs. Janet McCormick and Mrs. Natalie Barge, who were the assistant teachers; to Todd Risley and Donald Baer, who provided valuable counsel throughout the course of the investigation; to Donald Baer and Stephanie Stolz for their critical readings of the manuscript; and to Dick Schiefelbusch and Fred Girardeau, who did a great deal to facilitate this research. The research was partially supported by grants: OEO-KANS CAP-694/1 7-9, Bureau of Child Research, Kansas University Medical Center and NICHHD-HD-00870-(02-03), Bureau of Child Research, University of Kansas.

supported by token reinforcement. Experimental analyses of the function of the tokens were carried out with individual students. The effects of the program were evaluated by comparing the academic achievement and report card grades of the remedial group with those of a control group who had no remedial program.

GENERAL PROCEDURES

STUDENTS

Pupils from two elementary schools located in a low-income neighborhood of Kansas City, Kansas, attended a remedial education program during the summer of 1965, the 1965–1966 school year, and the summer of 1966. Fifteen of the 16 students entered the sixth grade and 1 student entered the fifth grade in the fall of 1965. All of the students had scored at least 2 years below the norm for their grade level on the reading section of the Stanford Achievement Test (SAT) administered by the public schools during the 1965 spring term, which preceded our program.

According to the pupils' school records, their median IQ was 88 (range 73–104), the median SAT reading grade-level score was 3.4, and the median SAT Total Battery grade-level score was 3.6. Their median 6-week report card average from the previous year was 4.1, on a scale where A = 1.0 and F = 5.0.

The program began with 5 children during the summer of 1965. After 5 weeks, 5 more children were added. In the fall, 1 more student[1] (the fifth grader) was enrolled at the beginning and 5 additional students added at the end of the first 6-week period. The last student was enrolled at the end of the second 6 weeks.

In most instances the children belonged to families of more than 5 children who received welfare support. In the majority of the homes no father was present.

The children's parents were visited by a social worker who explained the program and gave the parents the opportunity to have their children attend. All of the parents enrolled their children, usually during the first visit. (One parent, however, was visited four times before he made his decision.)

---

[1] The one fifth-grade student was added because her parent refused to let her sixth-grade sister attend unless the fifth-grader could take part as well. The fifth-grade girl was 2 years below the norm in her SAT reading score.

TOKEN REINFORCEMENT SYSTEM

The reinforcement procedure resembled a trading stamp plan (e.g., S & H Green Stamps). Each child was given a folder containing groups of four different-colored pages, each page approximately 3 × 3 inches in size. Blue, yellow, and pink pages were divided into 100 quarter-inch squares; green pages were divided into 60 quarter-inch squares. After a child completed an assignment correctly, he was given points by the teacher, who marked the squares of the appropriately colored pages with a felt pen.

When a child first joined the program, points were often given after each problem that was worked correctly. As the student acquired a higher rate and more accurate output, the amount and/or difficulty of work required to obtain points was gradually increased. The number of points to be given a child for particular work was decided by the teacher. This decision sometimes was determined partially through negotiation with the child.

Filled pages of points were redeemable, according to their color, for a variety of goods and events:

Blue pages: weekly field trips, such as circus, swimming, zoo, picnic, sporting events, movies.

Green pages (the 60-square pages): a daily snack of sandwich, milk, fruit, and cookie.

Pink pages: money and items available in the "store," such as candy, toiletries, novelties, and clothing.

Yellow pages: long-range goals which might take several weeks or months to obtain, such as clothes, inexpensive watches, and second-hand bicycles. Any child who had accumulated $2.00 worth of yellow tickets was eligible for a shopping trip to local department stores on a designated night of each week.

The face value of a filled page was 25 cents. However, the actual value of a page usually was something less. Many of the field trip events were free to the project, although the children needed from four to eight filled blue pages to be able to go. Also, snacks and store items were purchased wholesale and marked up to approximate typical store prices.

The children received an approximately equal number of points for each of three areas:

1. Work completed and/or corrected in regular school and brought to the classroom, such as seat work, corrected homework, and tests. For a grade of A the students received 100 points; for B, 75 points; for C, 50 points; and for D, 25 points.

2. Homework assignments and remedial work completed in the remedial classroom. The number of points given for items in an assignment varied widely as a function of the *characteristics of the items* and *the repertoire of the particular child*. Since these interacted to determine the probability of correct answers and the length of time necessary for completion, both had to be considered beforehand when deciding the point values of items. These values ranged from as little as half a point to as high as 20 to 30 points for items that were especially difficult for a particular child.
3. Six-weeks report card grades. The students were given grades by their regular school teacher in five academic subjects each 6 weeks. For each grade of A most students received 1,600 points; for B, 800 points; for C, 400 points; and for D, 200 points. Three children who had made almost all failing marks the preceding year, however, received double the above amounts.

MATERIALS

A folder of remedial work was always to be found on each student's desk. This folder consisted primarily of exercises in the student's weakest area, graded at an appropriate level of difficulty. The reading materials included the Science Research Associates' *Reading Laboratory* and the *New Practice Reader* by the McGraw-Hill Book Company. The arithmetic workbooks were *Arithmetic for Today* by Charles E. Merrill Books, Inc.; *The Practice Workbook of Arithmetic* by Treasure Books, Inc.; *Adventures in Arithmetic* by the American Book Company; and *Practice for Arithmetic* of the Lard Law Mathematics Series. Language materials included *Individual Corrective English* workbooks by the McCormick-Mathers Publishing Company; and '3' *in One* workbooks by Charles E. Merrill Books, Inc.

The students' regular school texts were relied upon for academic materials in the areas of social studies and spelling. When suitable materials could not be found, teachers devised their own.

PROGRAM

The remedial group attended the classroom each weekday after school for 2½ hours, on Saturday mornings during the public school year, and each morning except Sundays for 3 hours during the summer months.

The summer program concentrated on reading, language, and arithmetic deficiencies indicated by the California Achievement Test. With the onset of the public school year, work relevant to the ongoing curriculum was also included. Emphasis was placed on homework assigned by the public school teacher, such as solving arithmetic problems, learning spelling lists, writing theme assignments, and preparing social studies projects. After the student completed such assignments, he engaged in remedial work in his deficient areas.

FACILITIES

The remedial classroom was located in the basement of a church near the students' elementary schools. Inexpensive card tables served as desks. These were placed along the walls of a large room and were enclosed on two sides by 4 × 4-foot wooden partitions. Two adjoining rooms were used to keep academic materials and some of the back-up reinforcers (the "store").

PERSONNEL

The classroom was administered by one head teacher and, as the number of students increased, by two more teaching assistants. All are referred to below as instructors. Each instructor worked with five or six students, moving from one to another for short periods of individualized tutoring when necessary. Students were told to raise their hands when they had questions or had materials ready for scoring. There was almost no formal lecturing; however, group participation activities often were led on Saturday morning.

Two Neighborhood Youth Corps employees assisted in the classroom. Their duties included scoring completed assignments, distributing the snack, and exchanging the tokens in the "store" at the end of the day.

EXPERIMENTAL ANALYSIS OF THE TOKEN
REINFORCEMENT PROCEDURE

Experimental analysis of the relationship between the rate of certain academic behavior in the classroom and the token system was accomplished in a number of ways. These involved either the modification or discontinuation of the token system and its contingency with achievement.

EXPERIMENT I

The students usually had a wide choice of materials in the remedial classroom and varied markedly in their selections of these materials. The purpose of this experiment was to determine whether the choice of materials by two students was at least partially a function of the distribution of the points.

Students

Two boys, identified as KT and AS, both in the sixth grade, were chosen for this experiment. Both had the same remedial instructor; one had a high rate and the other a low rate of completing reading sections in their *New Practice Readers.*

Response

The response consisted of completed units in the *New Practice Reader.* Each unit consisted of a story of approximately 200 words and a set of 12 or 13 questions. Half the questions were designed to test the student's comprehension of the reading material; half, to prepare the student's vocabulary for the story in the next reading section. The questions were multiple-choice, true-false, and fill-in-the-blank in form. A dictionary was provided for the vocabulary portion. The number of points available for correct answers varied, but a 10-point bonus was given uniformly for a perfect score on either half of the questions. However, no points were given for any half unit if less than 50 per cent of the questions were correct. Also, unless it met the 50 per cent criterion, a half unit was not recorded as a response in the data analysis. In a unit where half was not counted, the other half was still recorded if it met the criterion.

Procedure

For several weeks of class sessions the number of points that the students could obtain from reading the story and answering the questions in the *New Practice Reader* was manipulated as shown in Table 1. For student KT, after 19 days which established a base-line rate against which to compare the effects of subsequent point manipulations, the maximum number of points which could be obtained from each reading unit was changed from 90 to 52 points. After 7 sessions, the number was shifted back to 90 points for 8 sessions; then again to 52 points for 5 sessions; and finally back again to 90 points for 10 sessions. Points for student AS were increased from 60 possible points per reading unit to 120 points for 20 sessions and then back to 60 points for 6 sessions. The differences in design between KT and AS were necessary because AS had never had a rate of reading under previous conditions.

TABLE 1.

Experimental Conditions and Number of Sessions for Each Subject in Experiment 1

Subject	Number of Possible Points per Reading Unit	Number of Sessions
KT	90	19
	52	7
	90	8
	52	5
	90	10
AS	60	19
	120	20
	60	6

Each of the students was informed about the number of points that he could obtain for correct answers to questions whenever (1) the number of points was changed, (2) the student inquired about what number of points could be earned, or (3) the student completed an assignment.

Results and Discussion

Experimental manipulation of the number of points earned by reading drastically modified the reading rates of both students, as shown in Fig. 1. Each time KT's points for reading were decreased, his rate fell to almost zero. Doubling the number of points that AS could receive produced a modest rate of behavior, even though he had done no reading during the previous month. The results of

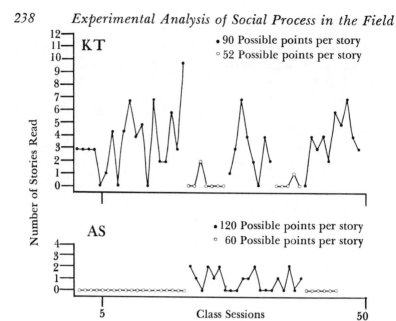

Fig. 1. A record of completing reading units by two students, KT and AS. Each dot represents the number of units completed during a class session.

Experiment I indicated that the points functioned as strong reinforcers for KT and AS.

EXPERIMENT II

In Experiment I there were no observations of the effect of changing the reading rate on the rates of other academic behavior. The second experiment was designed to determine the effects of point manipulations on three alternative types of behavior (responses in three workbooks) and, at the same time, to extend the experimental analysis of the token reinforcement system to all of the students in the remedial program.

Students

The second experiment took place during the 2-month summer session which followed the school year program. Eleven students began the summer remedial program 2 days after the spring remedial program ended.[2] The summer program extended over 47 meetings: 39 weekday classes and 8 Saturday sessions. Systematic data were recorded only on weekdays, since Saturdays were devoted primarily to group participation activities.

Responses

The responses consisted of completed units in any of three standard workbooks: *The New Practice Reader, The Practice Workbook and Arithmetic,* and *Individual Corrective English.* The characteristics of the *New Practice Reader* were described in Experiment I. The response criterion was the same as in that Experiment.

In *The Practice Workbook of Arithmetic* and *Individual Corrective English,* each page was considered to be a unit. Directions were given at the top of the page, and the problems to be worked appeared immediately below. The number of arithmetic problems on each page varied from about 40 *regular computations* to about 15 *"story problems."* In *Individual Corrective English,* a unit consisted usually of 20–25 sentence-items. Each unit involved a topic such as punctuation, proper nouns, or complete and incomplete sentences. Points were given for each correct sentence-item, regardless of the number of components involved in a particular sentence. A few sections did not follow the above format; for example, one set of directions instructed the student to write a friendly letter. These few sections were deleted in order to keep the remaining units as uniform as possible.

In order for points to be earned or for a response (a completed unit) to be counted in the data, a criterion of 75 per cent correct had to be met for units in both books.

Procedures

Classes during the summer program lasted 3 hours. The first hour involved a variety of activities, such as writing themes and letters or looking up identification questions in reference books. The third hour consisted of group participation activities, such as oral reports,

2 At midyear 16 students were enrolled in the program. However, for various reasons only 11 attended the summer sessions: 1 girl had married during the spring term, 2 students were out of town for the summer, 1 boy was required to stay home and "work" for his mother during the summer, and 1 student who had moved across town and was supposed to ride the bus to class failed to attend after the first week of summer session.

oral reading, and academic games. During the middle hour, the daily experimental session was held. It was described to the students as "free choice time." They were instructed that they could work on any material they pleased but that they would receive points only for working in the three workbooks described above. They were not allowed to work in these books at any other time.

During a baseline period all of the 11 students received the same number of points for working in the three books. Each correct answer in the reader earned 5 points. Each correct arithmetic *computation problem* earned 2 points, and each correct arithmetic *"story" problem* earned 5 points. Each correct sentence in the English workbook earned 2 points. The distribution of points, the percentage-correct criteria, and the particular workbooks which could be worked to earn points were advertised by a poster in the classroom. When changes in point contingencies occurred, the students were told and a 3 × 5-inch card with the new point schedule was tacked to the wall of their cubicles.

After a student's behavior in the three workbooks appeared to stabilize, the number of points which he could earn in each of the books was shifted in an attempt to increase the rate of the workbook behavior which occurred least frequently. For example, if after five or more sessions a student had steady rates of reading and English but a very low frequency of arithmetic, the distribution of points would be shifted in an attempt to increase the rate of arithmetic. On occasions when the initial shift in the points did not result in an increment, a second adjustment of the points was made. After changes in the workbook behaviors did occur for several sessions, the points were again shifted, either back to baseline values or to new values. Representative records are presented below.

Results

The design of this experiment makes each student a separate and independent miniature investigation. However, the students responded in either of two very typical ways, with one exception. Consequently, the results of two prototypical students and of the single exception will be presented as a summary of the experimental outcome.

Student GP's baseline response pattern was similar to that of about a third of the students. All of the students recorded responses in the three workbooks during the first few days of the baseline condition. However, the behavior of four of the eleven students (including GP) quickly dropped to zero in two of the workbooks but continued in the third. GP and one other student worked primarily on English, one student did nothing but read, and another worked almost exclusively on arithmetic. When the number of points which could be earned in the workbooks was shifted, their rates of working in the three books shifted correspondingly.

For GP, baseline condition (6 sessions) allowed reading responses to earn 5 points (R 5), arithmetic responses to earn 2 or 5 points, depending on whether they were computation or story problems (A 2, 5), and English responses to earn 2 points. During these sessions GP worked primarily on English. His reading and arithmetic rates fell to zero after the second session. These rates are shown in Fig. 2.

Then, for 12 sessions, the points were changed, so that reading responses earned 8 points (R 8), arithmetic responses earned 2 or 5 points (A 2, 5), and English responses earned ½ point (E ½). This

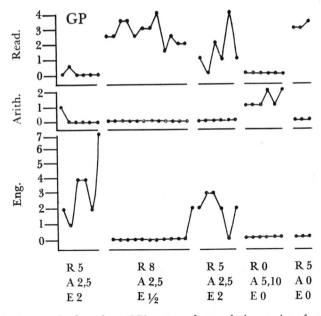

Fig. 2. A record of student GP's rates of completing units of reading, arithmetic, and English in three workbooks. Each dot represents the number of units completed during the experimental hour each class session. The letter and number captions describe the number of points to be earned for reading (R), arithmetic (A), and English (E) under each condition. Two numbers are given for arithmetic, the first for computation problems and the second for story problems.

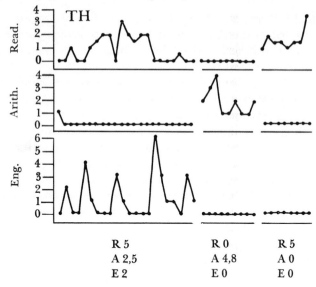

FIG. 3. A record of student TH's rates of completing units of reading, arithmetic, and English in three workbooks during the experimental hour.

shift produced a substantial increase in reading, no effect on arithmetic, and a significant drop in English.

The point contingencies were then returned for 6 days to the baseline conditions, where reading earned 5 points, arithmetic 2 or 5 points, and English 2 points (R 5; A 2, 5; E 2). On this occasion the baseline point value maintained a higher rate of reading and a lower rate of English than previously. The arithmetic rate remained at zero.

The fourth condition, lasting 6 sessions, changed reading to zero point, arithmetic to 5 or 10 points, and English to zero point (R 0; A 5, 10; E 0). During this phase, the first arithmetic in over a month occurred, and reading and English fell to zero.

The final condition was reading at 5 points and arithmetic and English at zero point (R 5; A 0; E 0). It produced a decrease in arithmetic, held English to zero, and re-established reading.

Student TH was one of seven students who normally worked in at least two of the workbooks. Extensive baselines were taken in some cases. The record of TH was typical, showing the alternation among the workbooks which often occurred.

TH remained under baseline conditions, where reading responses earned 5 points, arithmetic 2 or 5 points, and English 2 points (R 5; A 2, 5; E 2) for 22 sessions. During baseline, TH generally alternated between English and reading, arithmetic remaining at zero after the first day as shown in Fig. 3. When the points were changed to zero for reading, 4 or 8 for arithmetic, and zero for English (R 0; A 4, 8; E 0) for 9 sessions, her arithmetic rate was increased to an average of about 2 units a session; meanwhile, her English and reading rates were consistently zero.

The final condition lasted 8 sessions. Reading responses earned 5 points, and arithmetic and English earned zero point. This produced zero rates of arithmetic and English, and a reasonably steady rate of reading.

Student CH was unusual: he worked in all three notebooks for an extended period of time. His baseline condition lasted for 4 weeks. The first change in condition shifted reading to 8 points, and arithmetic and English to zero point (R 8; A 0; E 0), making all his points contingent upon reading. As in the case of GP and TH above, the announcement of "no points" reduced arithmetic and English workbook rates to zero. However, when the baseline condition was reinstated, the pattern of behavior observed under

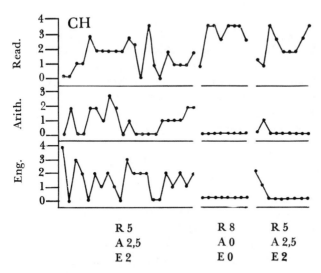

FIG. 4. A record of student CH's rates of completing units of reading, arithmetic, and English in three workbooks during the experimental hour.

the baseline condition (work in all three books) returned only temporarily; CH then returned to reading exclusively.

Discussion of Experiments I and II

In every case, shifts in the point contingencies led to shifts in the workbook behavior of the students. Shifts in point values to zero produced immediate cessation of behavior. Lesser shifts produced intermediate and more variable changes. Again, it is clear that the token reinforcement system functioned as such.

One type of irregularity did occur in the data of several of the subjects. As with GP and CH, when the points were shifted to produce a high rate of reading, a return to baseline condition often did not restore the reading behavior to its original level. Apparently, exposure to reading changed the operant level of the reading behavior. No similar effect was observed for arithmetic or English.

OTHER CONTINGENCIES

A number of other contingencies were provided in the program. Their functions were not systematically analyzed; however, they did seem to operate as intended. They are included here to provide a complete description of the program.

Contingency for the Instructors

In an effort to encourage maximally effective instruction, a monetary contingency was arranged for the instructors which was linked to the productivity of the students within their charge. Every 6 weeks, for each child whose 6-week report card grade average improved over his previous 6-week report, a bonus of $10.00 was given to the two assistant instructors.

Contingencies Involving Further Academic Work

Favorite subjects or popular academic activities were in some instances reserved for presentation only after completion of work in a less favored subject area. One boy, for example, who asked for junior high arithmetic materials, was told that as soon as he correctly spelled all of his current spelling words, he would receive instruction in the desired area. Children were often given their choice of activities following the completion of material in a deficient area with less than 5 per cent error.

Academic productivity was often followed by permitting the productive student to instruct other students in their deficient areas. Good students were allowed to check materials completed by other students. Students frequently asked to continue their academic work after the 2½-hour remedial session. For good work, they were given additional assignments to take home.

Contingency for Attendance

A 100-point bonus was given each month to every student who had perfect attendance for that period. The bonus was cumulative, in that 200 points were given after 2 months of perfect attendance, 300 after 3 months, and so on.

Contingency for Good Behavior

A blackboard containing the names of all the children was placed in front of the classroom. An alarm clock was set to go off at variable intervals during the remedial session, usually about three times during the 2½-hour period. Any child who was out of his seat for any reason when the alarm sounded received a mark after his name on the blackboard. Any other disruptive behavior, such as hitting another student, resulted in a mark being placed after the offender's name. At the end of each day, the child with the *fewest* marks received a 60-point award in his ticket booklet. The others received a number of points between 60 and zero, depending upon their position in the hierarchy of blackboard marks. The student with the highest number of marks received no points at all in this way. When more than four marks were received during any one day, some privilege was lost, for example, being denied use of the "store" at the end of the day.

Contingency for Report Card Average Improvement

A party was held shortly after the end of each 6-week report card period for all students whose grade average improved over that of the previous 6 weeks. Maintenance of a B average or better also qualified students for the party. The parties consisted of such activities as dining out at a restaurant, camping, and going on an airplane ride.

Contingencies from the Regular School Teachers

Teachers in the public school classroom were given the opportunity to give points to, or remove the store privilege from, the students in their classrooms. A form was distributed to the public school teachers on which they could indicate occasions of academic excellence or inappropriate classroom behavior. The children brought the reports to the remedial classroom in sealed envelopes. A report of excellence (the criterion of which was left to the teacher's discretion) resulted in 50 bonus points. A report of inappropriate conduct resulted in denying the use of the store to the student until the following day.

Contingencies for Members of the Student's Family

Items which could be used as gifts for members of a student's family were available in the store and could be purchased with pink tickets. Shaving lotion, safety razors, shampoo, toys particularly appealing to primary-level children, and clothing in a variety of sizes were included. Such gifts were intended to interest the members of the family in the student's academic achievements and his participation in the program.

Contingencies from the Natural Environment

Token rewards were often effective in bringing about the acquisition of behavior, but whenever possible the goal of this program was to bring the behavior under the control of the natural consequences of such behavior.

Purchases made either with tickets or real money, and the calculations necessary before the distribution of points, required a functional use of newly acquired arithmetic skills. Reading skills were to some extent maintained by requiring the students to do exactly as the directions of an assignment required in order to receive points for their responses. Comics and other high-interest reading materials were made available to the students in an effort to maintain reading skills by consequences other than points.

Contingencies for Teams of Students

Token contingencies were arranged for subgroups of the students. On Saturdays, group games similar to television's "College Bowl" were conducted to encourage cooperation among students as well as to increase group participation skills. Several teams, consisting of two individuals each, competed against one another for a 40-point bonus to be given to the team accumulating the most correct responses. Such members of a team received points for every correct response by either of them. It was necessary for each member of the team to emit at least one correct response in order to qualify for the bonus given to the winning team. The students were permitted to choose their partners. This was done in an effort to place students who responded well in these activities in a situation similar to that of the athlete who does well in games during recess: he is sought out as a hero and a desirable teammate by his peers.

Each group of five or six students who worked regularly with one of the instructors competed with the other two groups in accumulating tests with A grades from the public school. An announcement was made to the whole class each time that a student brought in such a paper. The A paper itself was thumbtacked to one of the partitions at the side of the student's desk. At the end of the week the team receiving the highest number of A papers was treated to candy bars of their choice.

EVALUATION OF THE TOTAL REMEDIAL PROGRAM

A primary goal of the program was to help the students make larger than usual gains in their academic skills. In order to evaluate the progress of the students in the program, indications of their academic achievement during the year were compared with those of a control group. The control group went to regular school and had no remedial program at all.

STUDENTS

The sixth-grade students for the remedial program and for the control group were chosen in the following manner. The names of students were placed in rank order according to their degree of reading deficiency as measured by the SAT. The lowest-scoring student was assigned to the remedial classroom group, the next lowest to the control group, etc. This procedure was continued until 15 students had been assigned to each group. As described earlier, for special reasons 1 fifth-grade girl was enrolled in the classroom. A fifth-grade girl with the same reading score and a similar report card grade average was added to the control group.

One of the sixth graders in the classroom group was lost during the spring term. She married and dropped out of school and out of the remedial program. The control group had also been reduced to 15 during the spring term as a result of a child moving. Thus the comparisons made at the end of the year involved only 15 students in each group.

The median characteristics of the control group were the same as those of the remedial classroom group described earlier, except that the average 6-week report card grade of the control group was slightly higher, at 3·7, as compared to 4·1 for the classroom group (A= 1·0 and F = 5·0).

Procedures and Results

Stanford Achievement Test

During each of the preceding 2 years the median gain made by the experimental and control groups on the SAT administered by the public school had been 0·6 year. The gains during the year of the remedial program made by the experimental and control groups were compared by using the Mann–Whitney U Test, one tailed (Siegel, 1956). The median gain of the remedial group on the Total Battery of the SAT was 1.5 years, as compared to a median gain of 0.8 for the control group. Thus, the rate of gain for the remedial group was almost twice that of the control group. The remedial group gains were significantly greater (at better than .01 level of confidence).

Report Card Grades

Gains in report card grades of the remedial and control groups were analyzed using the Mann–Whitney U Test, one tailed (Siegel, 1956). The last 6-week report card grade averages of the year of the remedial program, and of the previous year, were compared. The median gain of the remedial group was 1.1 grade points from slightly below a D to a C average, while the gain by the control group was 0.2 grade point. The gain of the remedial group was significantly greater (at better than the 0.005 level of confidence).

Attendance

The attendance in the remedial program averaged 85 per cent, with a range from 65 to 100 per cent, though the program met on Saturdays and most regular school holidays. (The decision to work on regular school holidays was determined by a vote of the students. If a majority voted that the remedial program be held on a holiday, class was conducted on that day. Without exception, the children chose to have class every holiday that a choice was given. The only holidays on which class was not held were the Thanksgiving and Christmas holidays, when the instructors somewhat undemocratically chose not to work.)

Cost

The students earned an average of $225.00 in points during the school year. The range was from $167.05 to $278.08. These amounts did not include the cost of the improvement parties. The costs of the points and the improvement parties combined averaged about $250.00 per student during the school year.

DISCUSSION

The results indicate that the students benefited substantially from the remedial program. Not only did they gain, on the average, a full year's advancement in their achievement level; they also gained an additional half year in their previously accumulated deficit.

The comments by the regular school teachers (for what they are worth) suggest that the remedial program benefited the regular school classroom as well. They stated that not only were the children in the program helped, but also the increased participation and "changed attitudes" of these children increased the productivity of the other children in the regular school classrooms.

Although the control group, on the average, made only about half the gain of the remedial group, individual children in the control group acquired significant gains. One sixth-grade boy in the control group made the highest gain in report card grades of all the children. However, perhaps very significantly, some of the control group children regressed in their standard achievement test scores and made lower report card grade averages than during the previous year. No child in the remedial group showed any such regression.

The remedial program's effectiveness in maintaining the children's participation was indicated by the high attendance record, and the fact that whenever the opportunity was given them the children chose to attend class on regular school holidays.

The cost of the program, which was substantial, must be contrasted with the long-term cost to society in terms of human as well as economic resources lost by not educating these children adequately. The cost could be reduced significantly by utilizing the potential reinforcers which already exist in almost every educational setting. Properly used, such events as recess, movies, and athletic and social activities could be arranged as consequences for strengthening academic behavior.

REFERENCES

Ayllon, T., and N. H. Azrin, 1965. Measurement and reinforcement of the behavior of psychotics. *Journal of the Experimental Analysis of Behavior,* 8, pp. 357-383.

Birnbrauer, J. S., M. M. Wolf, J. D. Kidder, and C. E. Tague, 1965. Classroom behavior of retarded pupils with token reinforcement. *Journal of Experimental Child Psychology,* 2, pp. 219-235.

Cohen, M. L., J. A. Filipczak, and J. S. Bis, 1965. *Case Project: Contingencies Applicable for Special Education.* Brief progress report, Institute of Behavioral Research, Silver Spring, Md.

Lent, James R., 1966. *A Demonstration Program for Intensive Training of Institutionalized Mentally Retarded Girls.* Progress Report, Bureau of Child Research, University of Kansas, February.

Siegel, S., 1956. *Non-parametric Statistics for the Behavioral Sciences.* New York: McGraw-Hill Book Company.

Staats, A. W., and W. H. Butterfield, 1965. Treatment of non-reading in a culturally deprived juvenile delinquent: an application of reinforcement principles. *Child Development,* 36, pp. 925-942.

12

Systematic Socialization: a Programmed Environment for the Habilitation of Antisocial Retardates

John D. Burchard

With respect to the treatment of the individual who repeatedly displays antisocial behavior, several programs claim to have achieved behavioral change by using the dynamics of the interpersonal relationship and group interaction occurring within the institutional setting (Aichorn, 1935; Bettelheim, 1950; McCorkle, Elias, and Bixby, 1958; Polsky, 1962; Redl and Wineman, 1957). Although these programs differ, they all have some characteristics in common. In the first place each is derived from, or closely associated with, psychoanalytic theory. The emphasis clearly is placed on psychic or psychodynamic processes rather than overt behavior. Second, it is felt that internal disturbances can be modified through the establishment of close, accepting interpersonal relationships enabling the individual to "work through" his problems. Thus the programs involve considerable permissiveness, acceptance, and reward (reinforcement). Individuals are encouraged to express themselves freely and openly and within very broad limits; punishment and censure are avoided. It is hypothesized that, since the internal conflict developed out of previous punitive interpersonal

Reprinted from *The Psychological Record*, Vol. 17 (1967) with permission of the author and editors. Slightly edited. Copyright (1967) © by Denison University, Granville, Ohio.

This project is supported by a Mental Health Project Grant (1 R20 MH02270-01) from the Department of Health, Education, and Welfare, and by Murdoch Center, a state institution for the mentally retarded in North Carolina.

relationships, any response to antisocial behavior which involves punishment will make the individual more defensive (suspicious, hostile) and less capable of developing adaptive interpersonal relationships. Thus it is assumed that antisocial behavior must occur with impunity.

These treatment programs which rely heavily on the use of reinforcement and permissiveness are in sharp contrast to "programs" they replaced. With respect to punishment the pendulum has swung to the opposite side. In the past most efforts to modify or eliminate antisocial behavior involved punishment. Whether for purposes of revenge, deterrence, or social protection, the individual was punished either by inflicting physical pain (flogging, mutilation, branding, etc.) or by being placed in an institutional environment where most sources of gratification and reward were removed. Although punishment may be justified logically on the grounds of seeking revenge, there is a dearth of empirical evidence to support the claim that punishment serves the purpose of deterrence. Recent studies show that observation of a model receiving punishment for socially unacceptable behavior has a deterrent effect on the subsequent behavior of college and nursery school students in a similar situation (Bandura, Ross, and Ross, 1963; Lefcourt, Barnes, Parke, and Schwartz, 1966; Walters, Leat, and Mezei, 1963). Such studies do not, however, provide objective evidence that punitive treatment of delinquents and criminals deters delinquent or criminal behavior in others.

Preventive detention or imprisonment does offer social protection against the life prisoner who remains in prison. The majority of individuals sent to correctional institutions and prisons, however, are later returned to society to continue their depredations. Furthermore, many individuals who receive punishment are likely to be more hostile and bitter after serving sentences and are returned to society more criminally competent and dangerous than before their commitment. Hence, some of the new treatment programs have attempted to eliminate punishment and establish permissive, accepting institutional environments.

It generally is agreed that an institutional setting which creates a punitive atmosphere or one in which all but undesirable behavior is ignored (custodial prison or correctional institution) generates hostility to, and lack of cooperation with, rehabilitative goals. That is not to say, however, that all forms of punishment are ineffective or fail to render the results for which they were intended. Recent evidence indicates that, while punishment can eliminate certain behaviors, consistency, intensity, timing, and duration are important (Azrin and Holz, 1966; Church, 1963; Solomon, 1964).

In considering whether or not to use punishment or reinforcement the main consideration should be the effect that each has on the behavior being modified. Programs which indiscriminately reinforce or punish behavior do little to prepare the individual to meet the exigencies of the social environment and its contingencies outside the institution. Case histories of many delinquents suggest that the previous conditioning history of antisocial behavior is characterized by indiscriminate punishment (rejection, disapproval, whipping, etc.) and indiscriminate reinforcement (love, affection, attention). Although permissive treatment programs may result in a positive reinforcement contingency (relationship) between the resident and the therapist, it does not necessarily follow that the resident learns from this relationship how to cope more effectively with the contingencies that will occur in the noninstitutional environment (Eysenck, 1964).

If antisocial behavior is conceptualized as behavior acquired, maintained, and modified by the same principles as other learned behavior, it is conceivable that an individual can learn constructive, socially acceptable behavior by being placed in an environment where the behavioral consequences are programmed according to principles of operant conditioning. Instead of administering an excess of reinforcement or punishment on an indiscriminate, noncontingent basis, behavior would be punished or reinforced systematically on a response-contingent basis. This has been the objective of the Intensive Training Program at Murdoch Center.

The Intensive Training Program is an experimental, residential program in behavior modification for mildly retarded, delinquent adolescents. Utilizing techniques based on principles of reinforcement, punishment, and programmed instruction, a standardized program involving mostly nonprofessional staff has been developed to teach delinquent retardates practical skills (personal, social, recreational, educational, and vocational) which are essential for an adequate community adjustment and for reducing or eliminating antisocial behavior.

RESIDENTS AND STAFF

Residents are selected for the Intensive Training Unit (ITU) on the basis of age (10-20 years), IQ (above 50), and the amount of antisocial behavior displayed in the institution. Twelve residents presently are in the ITU. Table 1 lists age, years at Murdoch Center, months in the ITU, and a brief description of characteristic antisocial behaviors which occurred prior to transfer into the ITU.

The staff consists of nine unit instructors, workshop instructor,

TABLE 1

Age, Years at Murdoch Center, Months in Intensive Training Unit, Approximate Academic Level and Previous Antisocial Behavior of Residents in the Intensive Training Unit

Resident	Age	Years at Murdoch Center	Months In ITU	Approximate Academic Level
1	18	6	16	5th grade
2	16	2	16	Pre 1st grade
3	13	5	15	1st grade
4	17	3	16	Pre 1st grade
5	16	4	16	Pre 1st grade
6	12	1¼	13	Pre 1st grade
7	15	5	11	Pre 1st grade
8	19	4	9	Pre 1st grade
9	16	¼	3	5th grade
10	13	1	4	Pre 1st grade
11	15	¼	1	3rd grade
12	17	7	1	2nd grade

Note: All the residents have obtained intelligence quotients within the mildly retarded range (50–70) with the exception of one (9) whose IQ was within the borderline range. One (4) was attending school on a regular basis. The residents who were assigned institutional jobs (1, 2, 3, 4, 5, 7, 8, 11, 12) were classroom instructor, research assistant (all classified as attendants), project director, teacher, and social worker. University students participate in the program periodically. There are two unit instructors on duty each day from 6:30 A.M. until 11:00 P.M., and one on duty at night. The remaining staff works on weekdays between 8:00 A.M. and 5:00 P.M.

A high school education is required for the position of instructor. Some instructors have further education, but none has completed a full year of college. Instructor training consists of one week of class lecture and discussion, and one week of demonstration

TABLE 1 *(Continued)*

Characteristic Forms Antisocial Behavior Displayed at Murdoch Center During Year before Transfer to ITU

Property damage in excess of $1000, AWOL 11 times, fights, excessive profanity, expelled from school and job assignment

Stealing from staff cars and residents' lockers, AWOL 3 times, arson with minor property damage, expelled from school and job assignment

Arson with minor property damage, breaking and entering, theft from staff and peers, expelled from school

Arson with minor property damage, theft from staff and peers, AWOL 1 time, expelled from job assignment

Theft of straight razors, radio, and tractor, property damage, choking residents with rope, fights, breaking and entering, expelled from job assignment

Constantly disobeying staff, no major infractions, expelled from school

Constantly disobeying staff, no major infractions, expelled from school

Theft of tent, hatchet, knives, bicycle, and cigarettes, breaking and entering, arson causing property damage in excess of $1000. AWOL 5 times, expelled from job assignment

Knocking down older resident causing broken leg,* constantly disobeying staff

Theft from staff, masturbating dog, attempt to set residents' clothes afire, hitting CP with wet towel, refusal to attend school

AWOL 3 times, accomplice in theft of two cars†

Breaking and entering, theft from staff, property damage, AWOL 4 times, frequently truant from school, expelled from job assignment

either expelled for displaying antisocial behavior or worked on an irregular basis because of behavior problems displayed elsewhere.

   * while in state mental hospital

   † while living in community

and participation in reinforcement techniques.[1] Informal, on-the-job training involving individual discussion and biweekly meetings of the staff is a continuing process.

REINFORCEMENT PROCEDURES

Reinforcement procedures are based on operant conditioning principles (Ferster and Skinner, 1957; Michael and Meyerson, 1966; Skinner, 1953) used to develop voluntary behaviors of human beings in a variety of institutional settings (Atthowe and Krasner, 1968; Ayllon and Azrin, 1964, 1965; Birnbrauer, Wolf, Kidder, and Tague, 1965; Burchard and Tyler, 1965; Cohen, Filipczak, and Bis, in press; Girardeau and Spradlin, 1964). The steps included defining the behaviors to be reinforced, selecting an effective reinforcing stimulus, and programming the reinforcement contingencies.

There are two independent criteria for selecting behavior to be reinforced. One involves selecting behaviors which produce a physically identifiable change in the environment that can be reliably observed and reinforced. To facilitate observation and reinforcement of these behaviors the environment is arranged so that these responses can occur only during a specified time interval and within a designated area (Ayllon and Azrin, 1965). Examples of such behaviors are the time that a resident spends sitting in his seat during the school or workshop periods. The purpose of this criterion is to permit an analysis of the effects of a given reinforcer.

Because of the complexity of the situation and the limitations on the staff it is impossible to record and reinforce the occurrence of many behaviors which are necessary as part of the habilitation of the resident. Therefore the second criterion is to select behaviors which provide the resident with a behavioral repertoire that will produce reinforcement in a community environment. Behaviors which are selected are maintaining a job, staying in school, budgeting money, buying and caring for clothes, buying food and meals, cooperating with peers and adults, and so on. For these behaviors an analysis of specific effects of reinforcing stimuli was not performed.

Previous studies have demonstrated that verbal reinforcement (praise, approval, etc.) is not an effective reinforcer for individuals frequently displaying antisocial behavior (Cleckley, 1968; Johns and Quay, 1962; Quay and Hunt, 1965). Therefore, immediate

[1] The author would like to express his appreciation to Julia Lawler for her participation in this training program.

reinforcing stimuli are nonverbal conditioned reinforcers consisting of aluminum tokens. Tokens are delivered promptly by staff members upon the occasion of selected responses and can be exchanged for various items and privileges listed in Table 2.

To minimize stealing, pressuring, and the development of undesirable reinforcement contingencies between residents, each resident is assigned a number, and only tokens stamped with his number can be exchanged for reinforcement. Most reinforcing items and privileges are available for all residents in the institution on an infrequent, noncontingent basis. Generally the reinforcement schedule is as nearly continuous as possible.

PUNISHMENT PROCEDURES

Punishment procedures are based on the operant conditioning principles of punishment developed from previous research (Azrin and Holz, 1966). The objective was to develop a punishing stimulus which could be administered immediately following the response, and which was of short duration but of sufficient intensity to decrease the frequency of response. This is in contrast to some institutional situations in which responses are not punished until they become extreme, and then the punishment is of long duration (restriction or seclusion) and involves much litigation and reconciliation (attention) on the part of staff.

Steps in developing punishment procedures were similar to those involved in the development of reinforcement procedures and consisted of defining behaviors to be punished, selecting effective punishing stimuli, and programming punishment contingencies. Behaviors selected for punishment are those which usually meet punishment in the community; these include fighting, lying, stealing, cheating, physical and verbal assault, temper tantrums, and property damage.

Unlike objective behaviors selected for reinforcement, specific behaviors to be punished are not defined in terms of specific, identifiable change in the physical environment that occurs within a specifically designated time or place.[2] It is impossible to observe the

2 The behaviors which have been selected for punishment are under the control of a wide variety of stimuli, most of which would not be present at any arbitrarily designated time or place. However, it would be possible to program the environment so that some of those stimuli were present and then analyze the effects of the punishing stimulus as specific identifiable responses occurred. This is presently being done under laboratory control.

TABLE 2

Reinforcement Available for Tokens*	Number of Tokens†
Meals	5
Commissary	
Food items: candy, cake, coffee, crackers, gum, peanuts, pies, potato chips, and soda pop	5-10
Smoking articles: cigarettes, cigars, flints, lighters and lighter fluid, matches, pipes, and pipe tobacco	2-100
Grooming and hygienic articles: combs, deodorant, hair cream, shampoo, shaving cream, shoe shine equipment, soap, talcum powder, toothbrushes, and toothpaste	3-30
Other commissary items: books, fishing equipment, key chains, kites, models, locks, string, and writing accessories	2-100
Clothing articles: shoes, pants and shirts	25-1000
Recreation activities: ball games, riding bicycles and go-carts, fishing, hiking, recreation with non-ITU residents (unsupervised by ITU staff), movies, skating, swimming, and trampoline‡	10-190
Miscellaneous: bus tickets for trips to town and visits home	90-1500

* In most instances the value of a token is equivalent to the value of a penny. With the exception of meals and some recreational activities, the number of tokens required for an item or activity is roughly equivalent to its monetary cost.

† Upon making each purchase a resident is required to fill out a purchase order with his name, the date, the day, the time, the items, and the appropriate cost. If the purchase order is filled out correctly, one token is subtracted from the cost of each item.

‡ Residents may exchange tokens for money and make any "reasonable" purchases while they are in town.

occurrence of all punishable behavior, and even if all such behavior were observed, it would not be punished with perfect consistency. It was felt, however, that the consistency was sufficient to proceed with an analysis of the punishing stimuli that were utilized.

The punishing stimuli consist of two verbal responses, "time-out" and "seclusion," which signify the loss of positive reinforcers (tokens) and removal from the immediate environment—a combination of response cost (Weiner, 1962) and time-out from positive reinforcement (Wolf, Risley, and Mees, 1964). The difference between time-out and seclusion is primarily one of intensity with seclusion involving a greater loss of tokens and a more extreme and prolonged removal from the environment.

Time-out is contingent upon most offenses which cannot be ignored but which do not involve violence. Whenever a staff member says "time-out" to a resident, he is charged four tokens and is required to sit in the time-out area, a row of chairs at one side of the dayroom. Minor disruptive behavior while in time-out is ignored; however, the resident remains in time-out until his behavior is appropriate for 3-5 minutes.

Seclusion is contingent upon fights, physical assault, significant property damage, disruptive behavior in time-out which cannot be ignored, or refusal to go to the time-out area. Whenever a staff member says "seclusion," the resident is charged 15 tokens and taken out of the unit to a nearby seclusion room. This is an empty room approximately 8 x 16 feet with one outside window. The window is covered by a heavy metal screen with the shade behind the screen drawn. The resident remains in seclusion until he is quiet for approximately 30 minutes. If the resident goes to seclusion in an orderly fashion and stays there the minimum period of time, he is reinforced with five tokens upon his return to the unit.

The staff is instructed to administer the punishing stimuli in a matter-of-fact manner, and all litigation is ignored until after the termination of the time-out or seclusion period to minimize any uncontrolled reinforcement contingencies that might exist (i.e., attention). The punishing stimuli are administered immediately after each punishable response occurs and are programmed on a continuous basis as much as possible.

In order to effect the response cost which is charged at the presentation of the punishing stimuli, the Behavior Credit System was devised. A behavior credit (BC) sheet similar to those shown in Table 3 is posted on the bulletin board in the unit for each resident. The columns represent days of the week, and the rows represent number of BCs. In order to earn a BC or to maintain the maximum number of BCs (seven), a resident has to pay the response cost he has been charged during the day. Each resident has until the end of the day to pay the debt he has accumulated during the day. If he does not do so, he loses one BC.

In order to create incentive to earn BCs and thus to pay the response cost associated with his punishment, prices and privileges

Table 3

Sample behavior credit sheets for two consecutive weeks

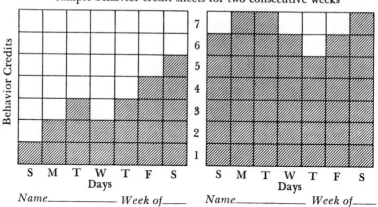

are partially determined by the number of BCs a resident has. If he has seven (the maximum number), all reinforcers cost their regular price (see Table1), the resident has free access to the yard area outside the unit, and he can buy the following privileges: (*a*) a trip to town (90 tokens), and (*b*) 1 hour of recreation time with non-ITU residents (girls). Each hour costs 15 tokens; 10 are returned to the resident upon his prompt return to the unit at the end of the hour.

Residents with 3, 4, 5, or 6 BCs are required to pay an additional 5 tokens for every item they purchase (e.g., each meal costs 10 tokens). Residents with 0, 1, 2 BCs are required to pay an additional 10 tokens for each item (e.g., each meal costs 15 tokens). Residents with fewer than 7 BCs are not eligible for "outside" privileges.

EXPERIMENT I

The purpose of the first experiment was to analyze the effect of the reinforcing stimulus (the token) on the frequency of two specific responses. Although all residents express a desire to have tokens, which they readily exchange for a variety of items and privileges, this does not demonstrate that administration of the token, contingent on a given response, actually increases the frequency of that response.

RESPONSE

The two responses selected for this experiment consisted of sitting at a desk during workshop and during school. There were four reasons for selecting these particular responses. (1) The responses could be recorded reliably by a relatively untrained person who merely started a clock when a resident was in his chair, and stopped it when he was not. (2) The responses could not take place without the observer being present. Both school and workshop sessions were 2 hours each weekday, with school taking place in the morning (9-11 A.M.) and workshop in the afternoon (2:45-4:45 P.M.). (3) The environment could be arranged so that the response was a free operant. Within each 2-hour time interval the response was free to occur for any duration. Attendance in both school and workshop was voluntary. However, the only way a resident could earn tokens during that time was by going to school (workshop). (4) The responses were similar to behavior which occurred outside the ITU with relatively low frequency. As noted above, only one resident was attending school on a regular basis and none of the residents had worked satisfactorily or regularly on a job assignment.

PROCEDURE

The design of the experiment was based on an A-B-A type of analysis with reinforcement contingent on the response during the first phase, noncontingent during the second phase, and then contingent again during the third phase. Each phase lasted 5 consecutive days. The experiment was conducted on two separate occasions, first for school behavior and later for workshop behavior.

The schedule of reinforcement for Phases 1 and 3 was twofold in both the workshop and the school. One schedule was based on the amount of time the resident spent sitting in his assigned seat. He received one token for every 15 minutes accumulated on his clock. Because the school and workshop were in session for 2 hours each day the maximum daily number of tokens a resident could earn for each session was 8.

The second schedule was based on specific tasks which the resident could perform while he was in the school or workshop, such as completing a page of arithmetic problems or assembling a certain number of objects. Although the type of school task varied from day to day, the type of tasks performed in the workshop remained constant each day. The number of tokens a resident earned on this schedule varied between 0 and 50.

On each day in Phase 2 each resident received the average number of tokens he had received each day during the 5 days of the first phase. On the first day of Phase 2 all the residents were told the following: "From now on you will receive your school (workshop) tokens 5 minutes before you go to school (workshop). You will receive about the same number you have been earning in the past. We would like you to keep going to school (workshop) but you will not receive any tokens while you are there. Here is the number of tokens each of you will receive." (The amounts were read, and the list was posted on the bulletin board.)

Phase 3 was similar to Phase 1 with the administration of tokens contingent upon the time each resident spent in school (workshop) and the number of tasks he completed while he was there.[3]

RESULTS AND DISCUSSION

The lower graphs in Figs. 1 and 2 show that when reinforcement was noncontingent (Phase 2) decline in school and workshop performance was immediate and near zero throughout the 5-day period. The reinstatement of contingent reinforcement in Phase 3 resulted in an immediate increase in school and workshop performance to a level similar to that in Phase 1. The upper graphs show that reinforcement was relatively constant across all three phases.

The absence of overlap between the contingent phases (1 and 3) and the noncontingent phase (2) demonstrates that the token had a reinforcing effect which was greater than any other reinforcement that occurred in either the school or the workshop. The generality of the reinforcing effect of the token is further demonstrated by the fact that individual graphs are very similar to the graphs for the entire group. For each resident there was a marked decline in school and workshop performance in Phase 2, followed by an increase in performance during Phase 3 that is similar to the level obtained in Phase 1.

With respect to the reactions of residents during the experiment, the instructions preceding Phase 2 seemed to coincide with their definition of happiness. During the last 2 days of Phase 2,

[3] Because of home visits and transfers into the program after the experiment was underway the residents who contributed to the school data (1, 2, 3, 4, 7, 8, 9, 10, 11) were not the same as those who contributed to the workshop data (1, 3, 4, 7, 9, 10, 11, 12).

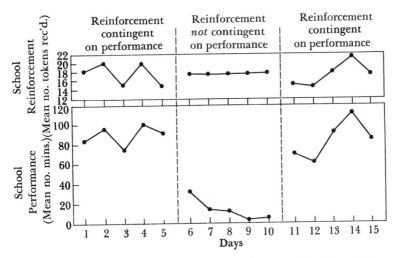

Fig. 1. Mean number of minutes of school performance by nine residents.

however, several residents asked if they could go back to earning their tokens in school (workshop) because they thought they could earn more tokens in that way.

EXPERIMENT II

The purpose of this experiment was to analyze the effects of a punishing stimulus (response cost) on the behaviors which were punished. If punishment is defined as the removal of a positive reinforcer contingent on a given response (Skinner, 1953), the data provided in Experiment I demonstrate that contingent removal of tokens (response cost) does involve punishment. If, however, punishment is defined in terms of a consequence of a behavior that reduces the future probability of that behavior (Azrin and Holz, 1966), it is uncertain whether or not response cost, as used in the ITU, is punishing. Therefore this experiment attempts to ascertain the effects of response cost on the future probability of certain responses.

RESPONSES

The responses consisted of various antisocial behaviors (stealing, lying, cheating, fighting, property damage, and physical and verbal

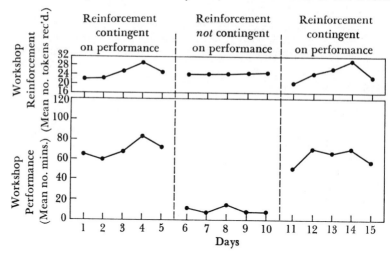

FIG. 2. Mean number of minutes of workshop performance by eight residents.

assault). The staff was instructed to use time-out whenever a particular response could not be ignored, and to use seclusion whenever time-out was inappropriate. The staff was also instructed to ignore such behaviors as disobeying the request of a staff member, name calling, and profanity unless this behavior precipitated a fight.

Except for extreme instances of violence and rage the time-out procedure was used first. If a particular response in time-out could not be tolerated or if a resident refused to go to time-out, seclusion was used. Although responses were not defined as objectively as those in Experiment I, the staff had been using time-out and seclusion for approximately 1 year before this study and was familiar with the procedures involved.

PROCEDURE

The design is the A-B-A type of analysis used in Experiment I. Each of the three phases lasted 7 consecutive weekdays. During Phase I response cost was contingent upon the antisocial responses which resulted in time-out (a loss of 4 tokens) and seclusion (a loss of 15 tokens). Therefore, the number of tokens each boy had to pay each day for his behavior credit depended upon the number of times he went to time-out and seclusion that day. During Phase 2 the response cost was noncontingent. The number of tokens each boy had to pay for his behavior credit during this phase did *not* depend upon the number of times he went to time-out and seclusion each day. Rather, the daily behavior credit cost for each resident was the average number of tokens he had paid each day for his behavior credit during Phase 1.

At the beginning of Phase 2 the residents were told that they would be paying a fixed number of tokens for their behavior credits. Although they kept the staff busy by asking many questions about the procedure, the initial statement made to them was as follows: "From now on the number of tokens you have to pay for your behavior credit will be the same each day. Each of you will be charged about the same amount you have been paying in the past. Here is the amount each boy will have to pay. (The charge for each boy was read and the list was posted on the bulletin board.) It doesn't matter how many times you go to seclusion or time-out; your behavior credit will always cost you that many tokens each day."

Phase 3 was similar to Phase 1 with response cost contingent upon the antisocial responses which resulted in time-out and seclusion. Eight residents contributed to the data in this experiment.

Results and Discussion

Figure 3 shows that time-out and seclusion responses were not brought under complete experimental control by the manipulation of the response cost contingency. Although responses generally increased during the noncontingent phase, there was some overlap between contingent and noncontingent phases, indicating that other uncontrolled variables were influencing the occurrence or the recording of the responses.

Variables which may have contributed to the uncontrolled effect could be a function of the data collection system (responses too subjectively defined, staff inconsistency, etc.) or of the punishment contingency (too much delay between response and response cost). Nevertheless, effects of these variables should have been relatively constant across all three phases. A more plausible explanation for the overlap between the contingent and noncontingent phases is that the verbal discriminative stimuli which defined the change

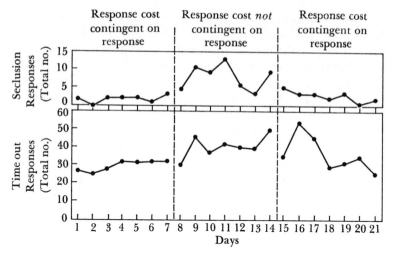

FIG. 3. Total number of seclusion and time out responses by eight residents.

from one phase to another were ineffective. Although the residents were told that the cost of their behavior credit would or would not depend upon the number of times they went to time-out or seclusion, it may be that they had to experience the change before it affected the frequency of the responses. Also, the increase in the frequency of responses resulting in seclusion during Phase 2 probably prevented the occurrence of a greater number of responses which would have resulted in time-out. As the amount of time that a resident spends in seclusion increases, the opportunities to go to time-out decrease.

Without further experimental manipulation additional speculation regarding the incomplete experimental control seems unwarranted. Nevertheless, the data that were obtained in Experiment II, together with data demonstrating the reinforcing effects of the token, provide evidence in support of response cost as a punishing stimulus.

CONCLUSION

The overall objective of the Intensive Training Program is to develop effective techniques for teaching the antisocial retardate a repertoire of socially acceptable behavior which will enable him to survive outside of an institutional environment. The first step was to determine effective reinforcing and punishing stimuli which could be used to increase or decrease the future occurrence of behaviors. Experiments I and II provide evidence in support of the contingent presentation or removal of tokens as reinforcing and punishing stimuli, respectively. Further research is being done to enhance the effectiveness of these stimuli, especially with respect to their influence on different individual behaviors. At the same time programs are continually being developed which utilize the contingent presentation and removal of tokens to teach a wide variety of practical behaviors (reading, writing, time telling, using public transportation, buying and washing clothes, and using a telephone).

Thus far the emphasis in the program has been on the acquisition or elimination of specific behaviors by trying to place the resident in an environment where maximal behavior modification can occur. A second objective is to develop methods for bringing modified behaviors under the control of more natural contingencies. Although frequent and immediate administration of a material reinforcer (token) may be an effective way to increase or maintain behavior, the probability of such a consequence occurring outside of the ITU is extremely remote for most behaviors. The same is true for behaviors which result in the removal of tokens. Although it is impossible to determine the uncontrolled contingencies which will exist outside of the ITU, it is probable that the presentation and removal of material reinforcers (money) will occur only after a considerable amount of behavior (vocational) and/or time (weeks) has taken place. Therefore, if behavior is to persist in the community, other consequences will have to become reinforcing, such as infrequent praise and social approval or performing a behavior which is part of a chain of behaviors that has resulted in reinforcement in the past.

As behavior is modified in the ITU, the contingencies gradually are modified in the direction of those which would exist if the resident were living in the community. Obviously, it is not completely possible to simulate a noninstitutional environment within an institution. Therefore, as soon as the contingencies within the ITU have become as "natural" as the situation will permit, the resident will be placed in environmental settings (work placement, halfway house, boarding house, etc.) which provide a closer approximation of the community.

The preceding outline for phasing the residents into the community is largely theoretical. Contingencies and schedules of reinforcement and punishment will be modified on an individual basis, depending upon a resident's response to a given program.

Whether or not the controlled environment and the systematic reinforcement and punishment contingencies which exist in the Intensive Training Program will facilitate the habilitation of antisocial retardates must await further experimental analysis. The program has demonstrated, however, that specific behaviors can be modified, at least on a temporary basis. It is also apparent that gross antisocial behavior can be brought under control and that a variety of practical behaviors can be learned.

REFERENCES

Aichorn, A., 1935. *Wayward Youth*. New York: Viking Press.

Atthowe, J. W., and L. Krasner, 1968. A preliminary report of the application of contingent reinforcement procedures (token economy) on a "chronic psychiatric ward." *Journal of Abnormal Psychology*, 73, pp. 37-43.

Ayllon, T., and N. Azrin, 1964. Reinforcement and instructions with mental patients. *Journal of the Experimental Analysis of Behavior*, 7, pp. 327-331.

Ayllon, T., and N. Azrin, 1965. The measurement and reinforcement of behavior of psychotics. *Journal of the Experimental Analysis of Behavior*, 8, pp. 357-383.

Azrin, N. H., and W. C. Holz, 1966. Punishment. In W. H. Honig (Ed.), *Operant Behavior: Areas of Research and Application*. New York: Appleton-Century-Crofts.

Bandura, A., Dorothea Ross, and Sheila A. Ross, 1963. Vicarious reinforcement and limitation. *Journal of Abnormal and Social Psychology*, 66, pp. 3-11.

Bettelheim, B., 1950. *Love Is Not Enough*. Glencoe, Ill.: The Free Press.

Birnbrauer, J. S., M. M. Wolf, J. D. Kidder, and C. E. Tague, 1965.

Classroom behavior of retarded pupils with token reinforcement. *Journal of Experimental Child Psychology*, 2, pp. 219-235.

Burchard, J. D., 1966. A residential program of behavior modification. Paper read at the annual meeting of the American Psychological Association, New York, September.

Burchard, J. D., and V. O. Tyler, Jr., 1965. The modification of delinquent behavior through operant conditioning. *Behavior Research and Therapy*, 2, pp. 245-250.

Church, R. M., 1963. The varied effects of punishment on behavior. *Psychological Review*, 70, pp. 369-402.

Cleckley, M., 1964.*The Mask of Sanity*. St. Louis: Mosby.

Cohen, H. L., J. A. Filipczak, and J. S. Bis. In press. CASE Project: Contingencies applicable for special education. To appear in R. E. Weber (Ed.), A book on education and delinquency, Office of Juvenile Delinquency and Youth Development, Dept. of Health, Education, and Welfare.

Eysenck, H. J., 1964. *Crime and Personality*. Boston: Houghton Mifflin.

Ferster, C. B., and B. F. Skinner, 1957. *Schedules of Reinforcement*. New York: Appleton-Century-Crofts.

Girardeau, F., and J. Spradlin, 1964. Token rewards in a cottage program. *Mental Retardation*, 2, pp. 275-279.

Johns, J. H., and H. C. Quay, 1962. The effect of social reward on verbal conditioning in psychopathic and neurotic military offenders. *Journal of Consulting Psychology*, 26, pp. 217-220.

Lefcourt, H. M., K. E. Barnes, L. D. Parke, and F. S. Schwartz, 1966. Anticipated social censure and aggression-conflict as mediators or response to aggression induction. *Journal of Social Psychology*, 70, pp. 251-263.

McCorkle, L. W., A. Elias, and F. L. Bixby, 1958. *The Highfields Story*. New York: Henry Holt.

Michael, J., and L. Meyerson, 1966. A behavior approach to human control. In R. Ulrich, T. Stachnik, and J. Mabry (Eds.), *Control of Human Behavior*. Glenview, Ill.: Scott, Foresman & Company.

Polsky, H. W., 1962. *Cottage Six*. New York: Russell Sage Foundation.

Quay, H. C., and W. A. Hunt, 1965. Psychopathy, neuroticism and verbal conditioning: A replication and extension. *Journal of Consulting Psychology*, 29, p. 283.

Redl, R., and D. Wineman, 1957. *The Aggressive Child*. Glencoe, Ill.: The Free Press.

Skinner, B. F., 1953. *Science and Human Behavior*. New York: The Macmillan Company.

Solomon, R. L., 1964. Punishment. *American Psychologist*, 19, pp. 239-253.

Walters, R. H., 1966. Implications of laboratory studies of aggression for the control and regulation of violence. *The Annals*, 364, pp. 60-72.

Walters, R. H., Marion Leat, and L. Mezei, 1963. Inhibition and dis-
inhibition of responses through empathetic learning. *Canadian Journal
of Psychology,* 17, pp. 235-243.

Weiner, H., 1962. Some effects of response cost upon human operant behavior. *Journal of the Experimental Analysis of Behavior,* 5, pp. 201-
208.

Wolf, M., T. Risley, and H. Mees, 1964. Application of operant conditioning procedures to the behavior problems of an autistic child.
Behavior Research and Therapy, 1, pp. 305-312.

PART III

Theoretical Extensions of the Experimental Analysis of Social Process

The purpose of this book is to draw together a number of articles describing the experimental analysis of behavior in terms which might recommend its further consideration by sociologists and social psychologists. The laboratory and field studies contained in Parts I and II have made suggestive forays into a variety of social situations. Though each of these social situations might be classified differently according to the interests of the scholar, each responded similarly by yielding, at least in part, to the stratagems of the experimental analysis. The task of Part III is to consider some of the broader and more far-reaching implications which this mode of analysis may hold.

13

A Behavioral View of Some Sociological Concepts

Robert L. Burgess and Don Bushell, Jr.

> In science, we always argue that since the observed facts
> obey certain laws, therefore other facts in the same region
> will obey the same laws. We may verify this subsequently
> over a greater or smaller region, but its practical importance
> is always in regard to those regions where it has not yet
> been verified.   Bertrand Russell, 1931

Throughout the preceding chapters the central focus has been on
the ways in which the behavior of the individual is shaped, maintained, altered, or extinguished by the response-contingent changes
in his social environment. Since that environment consists largely
of social systems, reflecting a variety of structures, an important
test of this approach will come when it begins to deal directly
with the "causes" and consequences of structural variability. Grant-
ing that we have at our disposal some fundamental principles of
behavior, we have, simultaneously, a heightened awareness of what
we do not yet know about the operation of these principles in
social contexts.

The principles of behavior do not describe that behavior *in
vacuo*. Instead, they define the regularities which relate behavior,
discriminative stimuli, and response consequences. This complex
configuration must then be held up against the backdrop of behavioral history. That is, the function of a stimulus is determined
by previous experience with it plus current deprivations. Taken
together, the two factors of experience and deprivation are the
setting events or state variables discussed in Chapter 1. The behavior of a subject and the subsequent changes in his environment
may be observed directly, but the stimulus function of the environmental change must be determined empirically, for behavioral
history is usually beyond direct observation.

The relationship between individual behavior and social structure is balanced in the sense that neither is the "cause" of the other

—men create their social systems just as surely as they are shaped by them. Furthermore, the effective analysis of social process must explicate the relationships between individual behavior and patterned social interaction by developing equivalent purchase over each. At the moment, there is an imbalance in our analytical sophistication which favors individual behavior. The experimental psychologists who have developed the principles of behavior did so in a highly controlled environment. Within this setting they confined their observations to simple arbitrary responses which were chosen for reasons of experimental ease rather than social significance.

Only recently have attempts been made to investigate systematically the application of these principles to the analysis of social behavior. Some behavioral scientists attempt to address this problem by building deductive schemes, beginning with the general principles of behavior and ending with propositions at the level of patterned interaction. The emphasis is upon general forms of social behavior: networks of interaction, patterns of interaction such as cooperation, competition, exchange, power, and social change. The *exchange* approach to social behavior is one example (Homans, 1961; Blau, 1964; Emerson, Chapter 17 of this book).

Others are concerned with explaining specific forms of social behavior at a lower level of generality, for example, the particular form of reward distribution adopted by a particular group at a particular point in time. This requires a consideration of both the principles of behavior *and* social system variables, such as the existence of a specific set of norms. Thus, while the social system was the dependent variable in the preceding paragraph, it is an independent variable here.

Examples of both approaches are described in Part III, but a third tactic is also presented in this book which is inductive rather than deductive. Concern here is whether we can experimentally discover the conditions under which patterns of social behavior are generated, maintained, and altered. A point too often overlooked is that these three approaches supplement and complement each other and are united in pursuit of knowledge about social behavior.

Each of the preceding chapters, as well as those that follow, deals with *social behavior*. Some of the authors have been concerned with individual behavior within *social contexts*. Some have focused primarily on the social *interaction process*, that is, they are concerned with the conditions under which individuals mutually influence or control one another's actions. Others have emphasized the conditions under which certain *repeated* and *patterned* forms of interaction take place. Still others have been focusing on the development and maintenance of *normative patterns*. At least one article has measured the effects that certain interaction *networks* have on the effectiveness of individuals operating in concert. Depending on one's interests, training, and professional experience, the major problematic area of sociology may be social behavior, social interaction, social structure, or social systems. In view of this diversity, our selection of articles has exposed us to the charge of suggesting that the experimental analysis of behavior has something for everyone, regardless of his particular orientation. However untenable such a posture must appear, we will endeavor to hold it a few pages more so that we may give specific, if only preliminary, consideration to such topics as socialization, role behavior, social change, and, with the help of Skinner, the design of culture.

SOCIALIZATION

Socialization is one of the most ubiquitous of social processes. It is the means whereby behaviors are developed in the individual which allow him to function within an established and ongoing group. Let us define socialization as an interactional process whereby an individual's behavior is modified to conform to the rules or standards of the groups to which he belongs. Thus, for the sociologist, socialization is not a process which is restricted to infancy or childhood, even though its dominant dimensions are most readily observed during this period. All groups socialize new members (Brim and Wheeler, 1966).

Immigrants are socialized into their adopted societies, recruits into the army, junior executives into the company, freshmen into the campus community, and "new kids" into the play group on the block. In each and all of these situations three factors are generally assumed (Elkin, 1960). First, an ongoing group must exist into which the neophyte may be drawn. Second, the potential member must possess the fundamental, biological characteristics which will allow him to adapt to the normative requirements of the new group. That is, he must be free of such biological defects as describe the Mongoloid or the microcephalic idiot—we assume a "healthy" organism. The third factor described by Elkin derives from Cooley's notion of "human nature." However unsatisfactory such a phrase may be by contemporary standards, Cooley's intention is unmistakably clear. His purpose was to emphasize, above all else, those behaviors which are not inherited but are instead the product of the primary group. His preoccupation was with *learned* behavior which, even though it varied from group to group, was universally the result of intense face-to-face social interaction.

But no matter how great the differences in content due to cultural differences, persons in all cultures have ideas of right and wrong, worship heroes and feel self-conscious. Similarly men always seek honor and dread ridicule, defer to public opinion, cherish their goods and their children, and admire courage, generosity, and success (Cooley, Angell, and Carr, 1933).

With the techniques available to him, Cooley was best able to support his assertion by pointing to the cross-cultural similarities of primary groups in a descriptive way. He was less able to specify universal principles of behavior. It is a high compliment to Cooley's sensitive observing that we are now able to define "human nature" with greater precision without altering the significance of its role in the socialization process. More important than complimenting Cooley, however, is the fact that our growing precision offers the promise of improving the dependability and reliability of the socialization process.

The distinctions between the "hows" and "whys" of social behavior which have arisen in other portions of this collection confront us again in the context of socialization. The three prerequisites to socialization suggested by Elkin fall into the former category in that they describe *how* certain factors need to be arranged before socialization can occur. If this is accurate as a descriptive statement, then it is necessary to ask *why* this constellation of factors and not some other is critical to the process. The answers to such a question must be determined empirically, but the ease with which we may move from the conceptual to the empirical level is strongly influenced by the elements of the descriptive analysis. Take the case of the "ongoing group" prerequisite, for example. Is a group necessary just for linguistic reasons because we speak of individuals being socialized into a group, or is there something more specific about the nature of groups which needs to be specified in the analysis of socialization? According to the operant principles previously considered, a first approximation to the "why" question might take the following form.

Most definitions of "groups" contain references to the degree of stability which they demonstrate through time, the fact that they operate according to rules or norms which apply in varying degrees to all group members, and the fact that they distinguish their members from the members of other groups. In order to persist through any substantial period of time, all groups must work out procedures for dealing with changes in membership. Individuals must be recruited and trained to function with the group. Once trained, they must be provided with the opportunity to function in concert with other group members. Finally, the group must devise mechanisms for eliminating members when their behavior is no longer synchronized with current practice, and then their passage from the group must be accommodated to by their survivors. From the perspective of socialization such a group is necessary because it constitutes a programmed environment designed to support the acquisition, maintenance, and finally the extinction of specific behavior patterns.

The norms which contribute to the definition of a group consist of rules according to which certain classes of behavior will be reinforced, while, in the same situation, other behaviors will be punished, and still others will be ignored. Though the fact is less frequently discussed, these same norms may also stipulate a variety of schedules governing their application. The normative requirement for telling the truth, for example, carries different sanctions in the breach according to the status of the violator. A new or unsocialized group member may escape harsh sanctions for violating a norm on the grounds that he doesn't yet "understand," whereas a seasoned veteran may be dealt with quite harshly as a consequence of the same behavior. Similarly, a norm violation by a high-status person is less likely to be punished than the same violation by a low-status member. This aspect of group norms is convergent with what we have previously discussed in Chapter 1 under the general heading of *schedules of reinforcement*, the rules stipulating the conditions under which a response will be followed by a given consequence. In order to administer reinforcement schedules, however, a group must be organized in such a way as to permit a monitoring of behavior and the administration of consequences in a variety of ways.

It has been noted that the development of a particular response class requires that successive approximations to the desired terminal state be differentially reinforced. Successful shaping results from the very close supervision of responding so that approximations are not inadvertently extinguished simply because they are not noticed. Furthermore, the response capabilities of the subject must be well known by the agent doing the shaping, or reinforcement may be held contingent upon actions which fall outside the current behavioral repertoire of the subject. Indeed, it is apt to observe that successful shaping requires that the agent and the subject have a very intimate relationship.

Here then is another convergence between behavioral principles and the already familiar properties of primary groups. The most effective socialization takes place in the context of primary relations precisely because it is in this environment that large numbers of responses emitted by the new group member may be differentially reinforced. This is the environment most capable of developing new response patterns because it is most capable of maintaining a schedule approximating continuous reinforcement (CRF). As suggested in Chapter 4, initial shaping occurs most readily when the new group member is individually trained through the arrangement of consequences which are specific to his individual responses. Families provide highly individualized reinforcement programs for infants; the school system has indicated a preference for an initial kindergarten period which provides more individual training in the normative requirements of that social environment; industry and the military utilize on-the-job training for new members which allows for intensive supervision in a particular situation. The shaping requirement for intense one-to-one interaction is met more effectively by the primary group arrangement than by any other frequently encountered social device.

A CRF schedule is usually employed during the acquisition of a response or response class. During the postacquisition period, however, the relative inefficiency of CRF recommends the use of some type of intermittent schedule such as a large-ratio or long-interval schedule. With an intermittent schedule in force it is no longer necessary to monitor each response as it occurs. For example, a reinforcing consequence immediately following a response may be necessary only at periodic intervals. And as Schmitt's study (Chapter 2) indicated, it is better if these intervals are variable. In any case, the socializing agent so absolutely necessary during the acquisition period is no longer required; and, if the original shaping was effective, a rather loose environment arrangement will ensure the maintenance of the desired behavior.

All of this speculation is based, of course, on the premise that the group has the capacity to administer effective reinforcement. To ensure responding, the subject must be deprived along some dimension, but beyond that the agent must be able to assuage the deprivation contingent upon an appropriate response. In dealing with the individual vis-à-vis the group we have the option of attributing a gregarious nature to the subject, or we may set about the empirical task of identifying the resources of the group which are potential reinforcers. These can be identified by the effect that their manipulation has upon the responding of the subject, as was accomplished by Hawkins in the home, by Wolf and by Bushell in classrooms, and by Burchard in an institutional setting.

Certainly no group could operate effectively if it relied exclusively on the manipulation of primary reinforcers derived from biological states. Consequently, much of the original socialization process is devoted to the development of conditioned reinforcers. Observing the repeated occurrence of this phenomenon, many theorists have commented at length on the way in which primary relationships are responsible for determining an individual's hierarchy of values. That is, it is in such relationships that individuals decide which things are important to them—they acquire a set of values which are shared by the other members of the group. It does no violence to the notion of personal values to equate them to conditioned reinforcers, and it offers considerable advantage when dealing with the empirical phenomenon. Some people place a high value on money, others seek the esteem of their fellows, some prefer applause, others place a premium on seeing their names in print, still others emphasize personal freedom. To say simply that such preferences describe a person's values is at best descriptive and at worst simply redundant. To identify a particular value as the product of an individual's reinforcement history, however, immediately alerts us to the fact that the maintenance of a particular value, or hierarchy of values, or the development of new values will be a function of that person's current and future reinforcement history. Thus, where necessary, established techniques may be applied to modify, supplement, or strengthen an individual's hierarchy of values.

Values, in fact, are constantly being developed by the interactions between an individual and a variety of social groups. Children are *taught* to value parental approval; students are taught to value high marks, gold stars, the virtues of punctuality, classroom decorum, and peer-group cooperation; academicians are taught to value publication; and politicians are taught to value political power. The socialization responsible for all of these combines the principles of shaping, the development of conditioned reinforcers, and the graduation from high-density reinforcement schedules to highly intermittent ones.

DISCRIMINATIVE STIMULI FOR SOCIAL BEHAVIOR

Operant analyses generally focus on the quality and scheduling of reinforcement, but considerable attention is also given to the discriminative stimuli (S^Ds) that operate upon behavior. From Chapter 1 it may be recalled that S^Ds set the occasion for either the reinforcement or the punishment of specific responses. The verbal statement, "Hand me that book, please," is discriminative for the reinforcement of compliance. Great quantities of social behavior, however, are under discriminative control which is much more subtle than direct verbal instruction. The social signals given out by emblems, dress, language, posture, and speech have already been mentioned. Now, further comment is in order regarding some central sociological concepts which can be analyzed more sensitively if particular attention is given to the discriminative properties of social phenomena.

Role Behavior

Bales and Slater (1955) have pointed out a common characteristic of groups in the following way:

One important aspect of the social organization of groups which endure over any considerable time is the fact that usually roles within the organization are differentiated from each other. . .overt acts of certain qualities are expected of certain persons at certain times, while overt acts of other qualities are expected of other persons at other times (p. 259).

As a descriptive statement the above is impeccable, but it does leave something to be desired at the level of explanation. Why? What variables account for the fact that people act differently toward one another even within a small primary group?

A study by Donald Cohen (1962) examined this question under carefully controlled conditions with some interesting results. The subject for the study was a 13-year-old boy named Justin, and the problem at hand was the analysis of his relationships to his older brother, older sister, mother, a close friend, and a stranger. Justin was paired with each of these other subjects one at a time, and the "natural" pattern of their relationship was examined. This was accomplished by having Justin and the other subject seated in adjacent rooms where they could see one another through a window but could not converse. A plunger was mounted on the wall in front of each of them. If they pulled their respective plungers within a 0.5-second period, this was defined as a cooperative response and resulted in reinforcement. Since one concern of the study was to determine the leadership patterns which Justin and the others brought to the experiment, automatic records were kept indicating who pulled first in these joint responses.

Under these conditions, it turned out that Justin, presumably because of extra-laboratory experience, assumed the leadership role (pulled first) when his partner was his older brother or his friend. On the other hand, Justin assumed a follower role when his partner was his sister, mother, or the stranger. After stable response patterns were obtained, Cohen introduced controlled leadership. For example, in the case of his best friend, reinforcement resulted only when Justin responded second. In another instance, involving his mother, reinforcement was contingent upon Justin's response coming first. In every case, leadership among Justin and his various partners eventually shifted as a function of the contingencies in effect.

In designing the experiment Cohen was in part interested in diagnosing the nature of the relationship between individuals who had histories of extensive prior interaction. It is probably no surprise to learn that different people were discriminative for different types of responding by Justin, that is, he deferred to some but led others. It is, however, provocative to find that these patterns were quite plastic and that they systematically yielded to altered contingencies. Although this study does not conclusively "prove" that the behavior patterns which Justin brought to the experiment were shaped by the same process which experimentally altered them, it is certainly a step in that direction. Nevertheless, Justin's behavior nicely illustrates the fact that the social roles of others are discriminative for our behavior toward them.

Roles are generally complementary affairs; leaders have followers, teachers have students, husbands have wives, etc. The socialization process develops the individual's ability to perform the appropriate role when he comes in contact with other individuals whose roles differ from his own. Students learn to act in distinctive ways toward teachers because, during their socialization into the student role, certain actions emitted in the presence of the teacher have been differentially reinforced whereas other acts in the same circumstances have been the occasion for punishment. As a result, for the well-socialized student, the teacher has become a powerful S^D for some behaviors and an S^Δ for others.

This type of role analysis can be further illustrated by expanding an earlier discussion of the mother-child relationship. In Chapter 1 it was noted that, as a mother feeds, fondles, cleans, and plays with her child, she emits a variety of responses which reinforce the infant. In addition to reinforcing the child, however, these activities are exactly the ones which define the mother role in our society. A great number of reinforcement contingencies are arranged by the social environment to ensure the proper performance of such role behavior. A female parent who failed to perform these behaviors would, at the very least, be confronted with the aversive crying and irritability of her deprived child. If these consequences were not sufficient to command more appropriate role behavior, the community, acting through the courts, might respond to her negligence by taking her child away from her and labeling her a "bad" mother. If, however, she faithfully performed her role, she would be rewarded both by the responsive behavior of the child and by the general social approval of the community, which might acclaim her as a "good" mother. Thus the development and maintenance of appropriate mother-role behavior is not a private affair based on the dyadic interaction of mother and child; it is also the product of reinforcement contingencies arranged by the larger community. The appropriate performance of a role is reinforcing *to others* and, in turn, is developed and maintained by reinforcement *from others*.

The point to be stressed is that the role behavior of one person becomes discriminative for the behavior of others. A person performing the mother role will control from other group members different responses from those controlled by someone performing the waitress role. As a person assumes first one role and then another, his behavior is modified as a result of the shifting reinforcement contingencies. And since, in interaction, each person's behavior is discriminative for the behavior of others, changes in one will produce changes in the other. Consequently, a social role may be viewed as a special kind of extremely powerful discriminative stimulus in the presence of which certain classes of responses from others are likely to be reinforced.

VERBAL BEHAVIOR

For all the discriminative importance of environmental elements such as people, roles, objects, time, and location, social behavior remains largely a function of the discriminative stimuli presented through language. There is nothing new about this assertion. Mead distinguished man from lower animals largely on the basis of his symbol-manipulating ability. The verbal or communication patterns developed by interacting individuals help define them as group members. The importance of the language community has been dramatized by the studies of isolated children whose overall retardation appears closely tied to the absence of normally discriminative verbal stimuli.

Certainly a principal focus of the socialization process is the acquisition of appropriate language behavior. The infant must learn to control the behavior of others by indicating when he is hungry or thirsty, and by explaining how he is hurt; but it is even more essential that the shared symbols of the language community come to have the same effects on the individual's behavior as the physical objects and events which they represent. When the word "HOT" effectively cues the response of withdrawing the hand, much costly and painful trial-and-error learning can be circumvented. A great deal of blundering can also be avoided because of man's uniquely developed ability to rehearse long chains of responses well in advance of the actual performance by "talking it through." A large body of important and exciting research is concerned with the discovery of how it is that verbal symbols come to control behavior.

Social norms comprise a very significant class of verbal statements. A norm may be defined as a statement prescribing or proscribing certain behaviors at certain times. As we noted earlier, a norm often functions to specify the prevailing contingency of reinforcement or punishment. Although we certainly have much to learn about the emergence of norms, it is probably safe to say that many norms emerge after certain interaction patterns have been found to be successful in maximizing group reinforcement. A norm, then, serves the function of increasing the probability that these interaction patterns will recur. As such, norms can be analyzed as a specific kind of social discriminative stimulus. An experiment conducted by the psychologists Ayllon and Azrin (1964) is particularly relevant to this conception of norms. Their intention was to evaluate the relative significance of verbal instructions or normative statements on the one hand, and reinforcement on the other, in the modification of some specific dining-room behaviors of institutionalized mental patients. Simply giving verbal instructions failed to maintain the behavior, and providing reinforcement (extra desserts) for the behavior without prior instruction was also unsuccessful. When these two factors were combined so that proper responding to instruction produced reinforcement, the desired behavior was developed quickly and maintained effectively. In other words, before the verbal instructions could appropriately influence the behavior of the patients, these instructions had to be followed at least occasionally by reinforcement. These, of course, are exactly the conditions necessary for the establishment of discriminative stimuli.

THE SELF

The "self" may be parsimoniously defined as the overt and covert verbal statements an individual uses to describe his own physical characteristics and behavior patterns. Perhaps this too can be dealt with as a class of behavior, in this case verbal, which functions according to the same behavioral principles applying to other discriminative stimuli.

Of great importance . . . is the fact that human beings can discriminate their own actions, appearance, feelings, and successfulness. In the course of growing up, the child comes to "know" about himself; he becomes at least partially "aware" of his capacities and weaknesses, his likelihood of winning or losing in given situations, his physical and social attractiveness, his characteristic reactions. This is sometimes spoken of as the development or emergence of the "self," a word that is meant to designate the ability to speak of (be "aware" of) one's own behavior, or the ability to use one's own behavior as the S^D for further behavior, verbal or otherwise. The sociologist Mead spoke of the "self" as a social product, that is, it arises out of social interaction; but more specifically, we can say today that the individual is *taught* by his fellows to respond discriminatively to himself and his behavior. He can observe himself and judge himself with words like "good" and "bad." He can estimate his own efficacy as a social agent in pleasing people and in striving for social success; and if he discriminates what in his behavior is causing failure, he may switch to new responses, that is "improve" or "snap out of it." The "self," in short, is the person, his body and behavior and characteristic interactions with the environment, taken as the discriminative objects of his own verbal behavior. . . (Keller and Schoenfeld, 1950, pp. 368-369).

It might be added that "self" statements may acquire discriminative properties which can be responded to by others as well as oneself (Staats and Staats, 1964). For example, a person who makes deprecatory statements about himself will be responded to quite differently by others from the person who exudes self-confidence. Thus, to a growing list of powerful discriminative stimuli which reside in the social environment, we would like to add certain components of the concept "self."

MODELS

One final illustration of the leverage provided by the concept "discriminative stimulus" is in order. It has long been recognized that during childhood the growing boy or girl learns a variety of new behaviors and quickly develops much of the vast behavioral repertoire of the adult. These new behaviors may range from simple mannerisms or vocalizations to the performance of extremely complex social roles comprising numerous chains of verbal and motor responses, such as playing, and later being, "daddy," "teacher," or "doctor." The concept of imitation has frequently been used to describe and explain a child's acquisition of such complex behaviors. Children have been observed to imitate a variety of responses in many different situations. Consequently, some behavioral scientists have concluded that imitation is a basic behavioral mechanism which may account for much of the remarkable similarity in human conduct.

The observation of a model is, of course, basic to the performance of an imitative response. Some observations, however, do not lead to imitation. On certain occasions, the observing individual may perform a response quite different from that of the model, with perhaps greater success. Thus imitation should be differentiated from more general observational learning, as Baer,

Peterson, and Sherman suggested in Chapter 3. Following their analysis, we can accomplish this differentiation by viewing similarity of behavior between subject and model as the central feature of imitation. More specifically, we will call a response imitative only when one individual behaves to match the response of a model.

Imitation, as well as other kinds of observational learning, may act as a teaching technique which reduces the time needed to acquire new behaviors. In this case, the model's behavior becomes equivalent to a set of instructions which programs the behavior of the observer. Getting out of a tight spot or into a desirable one may be greatly facilitated by engaging in this complex form of "follow the leader." Like verbal instruction, modeling of this form can circumvent the necessity for long-term shaping programs. In short, the presence of an imitative repertoire may enable a child to short-circuit the long process of trial-and-error learning and quickly acquire many new and complex responses (Peterson, 1968).

Just how a child comes to imitate has for some time been a matter of conjecture. Imitation has periodically been thought to be the result of certain instinctive factors, classically conditioned reflexes, neurological mechanisms, or complex cognitive processes. As we saw earlier, there is now every reason to believe that imitation is an operant response class. In a previous study, Baer and Sherman (1964) studied imitative behavior by reinforcing children's responses which matched those of an animated talking puppet. The puppet was used to minimize the possible contaminating effects of many subtle social S^Ds, such as the raised eyebrow and slight smile, and was designed so that it could socially reinforce a child's response by "looking at" or "talking to" him (the puppet had a movable jaw, and the voice was provided by the experimenter talking into a microphone from behind a one-way glass). The children were reinforced for imitating three specific activities, but records were kept also of a fourth response which could be imitated even though such imitation was never reinforced. The fourth imitative response did occur when the other three were reinforced, and when the other three were put on extinction, the fourth, never-reinforced response also decreased in strength. When reinforcement was resumed for three specific responses, imitation of the fourth response again increased in frequency, although this response still was never reinforced.

From these observations it was concluded that the children

generalized along a stimulus dimension of similarity between their behaviors and those of the model. In other words, there may be a variety of situations where the responses involved in matching one's behavior to that of another produce stimuli which are conditioned reinforcers. Baer's subsequent work with Sherman and Peterson which we encountered in Chapter 3 provides additional support for this thesis and strongly suggests that there may be very powerful alternative approaches to the study of role models or the development of "significant others." Such a tack might even shed some light on the question posed by Homans concerning a behavioral analysis of the process called "identification." Against the background of work like Baer's, serious consideration must be given to the possibility that identification with another person or with a group is generated by a history of reinforcement for acting in accord with or after the pattern of others. Does this not also pose some provocative suggestions for the experimental analysis of "conformity"? The general qualities of discriminative stimuli which allow them to function as cues to action and as conditioned reinforcers serving to sustain responding over considerable periods without any other reinforcement deserve serious study by sociologists.

SOCIAL SYSTEMS

For many sociologists, the concepts "social system" and "social structure" provide the major conceptual focus of sociology; hence some discussion of these concepts is in order. A *social system* may be defined as an organized or patterned set of social relationships. The term "patterned relationships" is used to refer to relatively stable interactions over time which may assume certain forms or patterns. The emphasis is upon interaction patterns rather than people as such. *Social structure* is used to refer to the specific form or pattern that these interactions take. Other concepts which sociologists typically employ in the analysis of social systems are interdependence, homeostasis, and equilibrium.

Interdependence may be viewed as equivalent to the contingency existing between patterned forms of interaction on the one hand, and reinforcing consequences on the other. Defined in this way, interdependence may be analyzed as an independent variable responsible for the development, maintenance, and alteration of social systems. Our contention is that individuals will come together and engage in recurrent and patterned forms of interaction to the extent that they are dependent upon one another for reinforcement. Some social systems may be composed of elements that are more interdependent than those of other systems. Likewise, within a single system the degree of interdependence among the system elements may vary, that is, some units of the system may be more dependent than others on the system as a whole or on any of its parts. As Emerson points out in Chapter 17, this state of affairs leads to differentials in social power.

In any event, interdependence can be seen to be a necessary condition for the development and maintenance of patterned interaction which endures over time. We would argue further that these contingencies or conditions of interdependence govern the specific patterns or structures that interactions take. We have seen support for these assertions in this book. For example, Mithaug and Burgess (Chapter 4) found that individuals would enter into patterned forms of interaction to the extent that reinforcement was contingent upon such activities, that is, to the extent that the experimental subjects were in a state of interdependence. Similarly, the study by Wiggins (Chapter 5) supports the assertion that the specific patterns taken by interactions are determined by the contingencies connecting such interaction patterns with environmental consequences. Specifically, his data indicated quite clearly that the type of reward distribution operating in a group, whether egalitarian or differential, is determined by the consequences which follow that distribution. The field studies by Hawkins, Bushell, Wolf, and Burchard all bear upon this analysis.

Social systems must continually adapt to changes in their environments if they are to survive. In the process of so adapting, a system may accelerate or decelerate the rates of certain interaction patterns which have the consequence of limiting change in other of its patterns. This process is usually termed *homeostasis* by sociologists. Again the study by Wiggins is instructive. Given changes in the experimenter-controlled environment which altered the previously existing condition of interdependence, the system members accelerated and decelerated certain patterns—those of reward distribution—which had the effect of limiting change in other interaction patterns, namely, those pertinent to the solution of the "problems" posed by the experimenter.

Environmental changes, then, may result in subsequent

changes in the division of labor, or in the pattern of reward distribution, in a social system, to take just two examples. In either case, some of the behavioral patterns comprising the system as a whole may be undergoing changes in rate. Whenever a social system undergoes change such as this, we may say that it is in a state of *disequilibrium*. Where such interaction patterns are constant, a system is in a state of *equilibrium*. The utility of taking response or rate of interaction as a dependent variable was discussed in Chapter 7. Bijou, Peterson, and Ault (Chapter 8) elaborated upon this point by noting that the integration of experimental and descriptive studies may be facilitated by making rate of response our basic dependent variable.

This chapter has suggested how an operant analysis of more complex sociological problems might proceed. The other chapters in Part III demonstrate that an entirely new field of analysis is opening up before us. From the successes of field studies such as those already presented, it is clear that the experimental analysis is not limited to the confines of the laboratory but has begun to extend its effective domain to the complexities of operating social systems.

Such procedures involve difficulties, but these are due in large part to the small amount of control which can presently be exerted over the relevant aspects of the societal environment. Since usually only a few aspects of the societal environment can be altered, present efforts to create behavioral prerequisites must begin on a small scale. This is no easy task, but it is a possible one (Kunkel, p. 365) .

The experimental analysis of behavior thus has a very special relevance to the design of cultures. Only through the active prosecution of such an analysis, and the courageous application of its results to daily life, will it be possible to design contingencies of reinforcement that will generate and maintain the most subtle and complex behavior of which men are capable (Skinner, p. 378) .

Some of the areas considered in Part III as possible targets for experimental analysis are already under study, but it will probably be some time before any considerable portion of the myriad speculations offered is transformed into empirical inquiry. On the other hand, if enough social scientists are reinforced by their initial achievements with an operant analysis, this material may be the first portion of the collection to become obsolete. Such is our hope.

REFERENCES

Ayllon, T., and N. H. Azrin, 1964. Reinforcement and instructions with mental patients. *Journal of the Experimental Analysis of Behavior*, 7, pp. 327-331.

Baer, D. M., and J. A. Sherman, 1964. Reinforcement control of generalized imitation in young children. *Journal of Experimental Child Psychology*, 1, pp. 37-49.

Bales, R. F., and P. E. Slater, 1955. Role differentiation in small decision-making groups. In T. Parsons and R. F. Bales (Eds.), *Family, Socialization and Interaction Process*. Glencoe, Ill.: Free Press, pp. 259-306.

Bijou, S. W., and D. M. Baer, 1961. *Child Development:* Vol. 1, *Systematic and Empirical Theory*. New York: Appleton-Century-Crofts.

Blau, P. M., 1964. *Exchange and Power in Social Life*, New York: John Wiley & Sons.

Brim, O. G., and S. Wheeler, 1966. *Socialization after Childhood*. New York: John Wiley & Sons.

Cohen, D. J., 1962. Justin and his peers: An experimental analysis of a child's social world. *Child Development*, 33, 697-717.

Cooley, C. H., R. C. Angell, and L. J. Carr, 1933. *Introductory Sociology*. New York: Charles Scribner's Sons.

Elkin, F., 1960. *The Child and Society: The Process of Socialization*. New York: Random House.

Homans, G. C., 1961. *Social Behavior: Its Elementary Forms*. New York: Harcourt, Brace & World.

Keller, F. S., and W. N. Schoenfeld, 1950. *Principles of Psychology*. New York: Appleton.

Peterson, R. F., 1968. Imitation: a basic behavioral mechanism. In H. N. Sloane, Jr. and B. D. MacAulay (eds.), *Operant Procedures in Remedial Speech and Language Training*. Boston: Houghton Mifflin Company, pp. 61-74.

Russell, Bertrand, 1962. *The Scientific Outlook*. New York: W. N. Norton & Company.

Staats, A. W., and C. K. Staats, 1964. *Complex Human Behavior: A Systematic Extension of Learning Principles*. New York: Holt, Rinehart & Winston.

14

A Differential Association-Reinforcement

Theory of Criminal Behavior

Robert L. Burgess and Ronald L. Akers

INTRODUCTION

In spite of the body of literature that has accumulated around the differential association theory of criminal behavior,[1] this theory has yet to receive crucial empirical test or thorough restatement

[1] By 1960, Cressey had collected a 70-item bibliography on the theory; see Edwin H. Sutherland and Donald R. Cressey, *Principles of Criminology*, 6th ed., Chicago: J. B. Lippincott Co., 1960, p. vi. He has presented an exhaustive review of the mistaken notions, criticisms, attempted reformulations, and empirical tests of the theory contained in a sizable body of literature—Donald R. Cressey, "Epidemiology and Individual Conduct: A Case from Criminology," *Pacific Sociological Review*, 3 (Fall, 1960), pp. 47-58. For more recent literature see the following: Donald R. Cressey, "The Theory of Differential Association: An Introduction," *Social Problems*, 8 (Summer, 1960), pp. 2-5; James F. Short, Jr., "Differential Association as a Hypothesis: Problems of Empirical Testing," *Social Problems*, 8 (Summer, 1960), pp. 14-25; Henry D. McKay, "Differential Association and Crime Prevention: Problems of Utilization," *Social Problems*, 8 (Summer, 1960), pp. 25-37; Albert J. Reiss, Jr., and A. Lewis Rhodes, "An Empirical Test of Differential Association Theory," *The Journal of Research in Crime and Delinquency*, 1 (January, 1964), pp. 5-18; Harwin L. Voss, "Differential Association and Reported Delinquent Behavior: A Replication," *Social Problems*, 12 (Summer, 1964), pp. 78-85; Siri Naess, "Comparing Theories of Criminogenesis," *The Journal of Research in Crime and Delinquency*, 1 (July, 1964), pp. 171-180; C. R. Jeffery, "Criminal Behavior and Learning Theory," *The Journal of Criminal Law, Criminology and Police Science*, 56 (September, 1965), pp. 294-300.

Reprinted from *Social Problems*, Vol. 14, No. 2 (Fall, 1966), pp. 128-147, with permission of the authors and The Society for the Study of Social Problems. Slightly edited.

beyond Sutherland's own revision in 1947. Recognizing that the theory is essentially a learning theory, Sutherland rephrased it to state explicitly that criminal behavior is learned as any behavior is learned. In Cressey's two revisions of the textbook, the theory has deliberately been left unchanged from Sutherland's revision. Thus, the theory as it stands now is postulated upon the knowledge of the learning process extant 20-25 years ago.[2]

Sutherland himself never was able to test directly or find specific empirical support for his theory, but he was convinced that the two-edged theory—(1) genetic, differential association and (2) structural, differential social organization—accounted for the known data on the full range of crimes, including conventional violations and white-collar crimes.[3] The theory has received some other empirical support,[4] but negative cases have also been found.[5]

[2] The original formal statement appeared in Edwin H. Sutherland, *Principles of Criminology*, 3rd ed., Philadelphia: J. B. Lippincott Co., 1939, pp. 4-8. The terms "systematic" and "consistency," along with some statements referring to social disorganization and culture conflict, were deleted in the revised theory. Two sentences stating that criminal behavior is learned were added, and the terms "learned" and "learning" were included in other sentences. The modalities of duration, priority, and intensity were added. The revised theory is in Sutherland and Cressey, *op. cit.*, pp. 77-79. For Cressey's discussion of why he left the theory in its 1947 form see *ibid.*, p. vi.

[3] *Ibid.*, pp. 77-80. Edwin H. Sutherland, *White Collar Crime*, New York: Holt, Rinehart & Winston, 1961, pp. 234-256 (originally published 1949). See also Cressey's "Foreword," *ibid.*, p. x.

[4] John C. Ball, "Delinquent and Non-delinquent Attitudes Toward the Prevalence of Stealing," *The Journal of Criminal Law, Criminology and Police Science*, 48 (September-October, 1957), pp. 259-274. James F. Short, "Differential Association and Delinquency," *Social Problems*, 4 (January, 1957), pp. 233-239. Short, "Differential Association with Delinquent Friends and Delinquent Behavior," *Pacific Sociological Review*, 1 (Spring, 1958), pp. 20-25. Short, "Differential Association as a Hypothesis," *op. cit.* Voss, *op. cit.* Donald R. Cressey, "Application and Verification of the Differential Association Theory," *The Journal of Criminal Law, Criminology and Police Science*, 43 (May-June, 1952), pp. 47-50. Cressey, *Other People's Money*, Glencoe, Ill.: The Free Press, 1953, pp. 147-149. Glaser, *op. cit.*, pp. 7-10.

[5] Marshall Clinard, *The Black Market*, New York: Rinehart Co., 1952, pp. 285-329. Marshall Clinard, "Rural Criminal Offenders," *American Journal of Sociology*, 50 (July, 1944), pp. 38-45. Edwin M. Lemert, "An Isolation and Closure Theory of Naive Check Forgery," *The Journal of Criminal Law, Criminology and Police Science*, 44 (September-October, 1953), pp. 293-307. Reiss and Rhodes, *op. cit.* Cressey, "Application and Verification of the Differential Association Theory," *op. cit.*, pp. 51-52. Cressey, *Other People's Money, op. cit.*, pp. 149-151. Glaser, *op. cit.*, pp. 12-13.

The attempts to subject the theory to empirical test are marked by inconsistent findings both within the same study and between studies, as well as by highly circumscribed and qualified findings and conclusions. Whether the particular researcher concludes that his findings do or do not seem to support the theory, nearly all have indicated difficulty in operationalizing the concepts and recommend that the theory be modified in such a way that it becomes more amenable to empirical testing.

Suggested theoretical modifications have not been lacking, but the difficulty with these restatements is that they are no more readily operationalized than Sutherland's.[6] One recent paper, however, by DeFleur and Quinney,[7] offers new promise that the theory can be adequately operationalized. These authors have presented a detailed strategy for making specific deductions for empirical testing. But while they have clarified the problems in the derivation and generation of testable hypotheses from differential association, they still see its empirical validation as a very difficult, though not impossible task.

Regardless of the particular criticisms, the exceptions taken, and the difficulties involved in testing and reformulating the theory that have been offered, few take exception to the central learning assumptions in differential association. If we accept the basic assumption that criminal behavior is learned by the same processes and involves the same mechanisms as conforming behavior, then we need to recognize and make use of the current knowledge about these processes and mechanisms. Neither the extant statement of the theory nor the reformulations of it makes explicit the nature of the underlying learning process involved in differential association. In short, no major revisions have been made utilizing established learning principles.

That this type of revision of the theory is needed has been recognized, and some criticism of differential association has revolved around the fact that it does not adequately portray the process by which criminal behavior is learned. But, as Cressey

[6] See Daniel Glaser, "Criminality Theories and Behavioral Images," *American Journal of Sociology*, 61 (March, 1956), pp. 433-444. Glaser, "Differential Association and Criminological Prediction," *op. cit.*, pp. 10-13. Naess, *op. cit.*, pp. 174-179.

[7] Melvin DeFleur and Richard Quinney, "A Reformulation of Sutherland's Differential Association Theory and a Strategy for Empirical Verification," *Journal of Research in Crime and Delinquency*, 3 (January, 1966), p. 13.

explains, "It is one thing to criticize the theory for failure to specify the learning process accurately and another to specify which aspects of the learning process should be included and in what way."[8]

Sutherland, of course, was as interested in explaining the "epidemiology" of crime as in explaining how the individual comes to engage in behavior in violation of the law and insisted that the two explanations must be consistent.[9] Differential social organization (normative conflict) has been successful in "making sense" of variations in crime rates. But differential association has been less successful in explicating the process by which this differential organization produces individual criminality. This seems to be due not to the lack of importance of associations for criminal behavior but ". . . rather to the fact that the theory outran the capacity of either psychology or social psychology to give adequate, scientific answers to the question of why there are such qualitative (selective) differences in human association."[10]

It now appears, however, that there is a body of verified theory which is adequate to the task of accurately specifying this process. Modern learning theory seems capable of providing insights into the problem of uniting structural and genetic formulations. Although sociologists know a great deal about the structure of the environment from which deviants come, we know very little about the determining variables operating within this environment. The burden of criminological theory today is to combine knowledge of structural pressures with explanations of "why only *some* of the persons on whom this pressure is exerted become non-conformists."[11]

It is for this reason that the recent effort by C. R. Jeffery to re-examine differential association in the light of modern learning theory marks a new departure in the abundance of thinking and writing that has characterized the intellectual history of this theory.[12] DeFleur and Quinney, for example, in spite of their in-

[8] Cressey, "Epidemiology and Individual Conduct," *op. cit.*, p. 54.

[9] Sutherland and Cressey, *op. cit.*, p. 80. Albert K. Cohen, Alfred R. Lindesmith, and Karl F. Schuessler (Eds.), *The Sutherland Papers*, Bloomington: Indiana University Publications, Social Science Series, No. 15, 1956, pp. 5-42. That Sutherland intended an explanation of the twofold problem of rates of crime and individual criminal behavior is, of course, the basic point of Cressey's paper, "Epidemiology and Individual Conduct," *op. cit.*

[10] George B. Vold, *Theoretical Criminology*, New York: Oxford University Press, 1958, p. 198.

[11] Cressey, "The Theory of Differential Association," *op. cit.*, p. 5.

[12] Jeffery, *op. cit.*

tricate axiomatization of the theory, recognize that even they have left the learning process in differential association unspecified. But, they note, "Modern reinforcement learning theory would handle this problem. . . ."[13] This is precisely what Jeffery proposed to do, and to the extent that this objective is served by discussing learning theory and criminal behavior together, he is at least partially successful. However, Jeffery does not in fact make it clear just how Sutherland's differential association theory may be revised. His explanation incorporates differential reinforcement: "[A] criminal act occurs in an environment in which in the past the actor has been reinforced for behaving in this manner, and the aversive consequences attached to the behavior have been of such a nature that they do not control or prevent the response."[14]

This statement, as it stands, bears no obvious or direct relation to Sutherland's differential association, and nowhere else does Jeffery make it clear how differential reinforcement is a reformulation of differential association. Jeffery does discuss modern learning principles, but he does not show how these principles may be incorporated within the framework of Sutherland's theory, or how they may lead to explanations of past empirical findings.

Jeffery's theory and his discussion of criminal behavior and learning theory remain not so much incorrect as unconvincing. His presentation of learning principles is supported wholly by reference to experiments with lower organisms, and his extension to criminal behavior is achieved mainly through anecdotal and illustrative material. The potential value and impact of Jeffery's article are diminished by not calling attention to the already large and growing body of literature in experimental behavioral science, especially evidence using human subjects, that has direct implications for differential association theory. We are basically in agreement with Jeffery that learning theory has progressed to the point where it seems likely that differential association can be restated in a more sophisticated and testable form in the language of modern learning theory. But that restatement must be attempted in a thorough fashion before we can expect others to accept it. Jeffery begins to do this and his thoughts are significant, but they do not take into account the theory as a whole.

The amount of empirical research in the social psychology of

---

13 DeFleur and Quinney, *op. cit.,* p. 3.
14 *Ibid,* p. 295.

learning clearly has shown that the concepts in learning theory are susceptible to operationalization. Therefore, applying an integrated set of learning principles to differential association theory should adequately provide the revision needed for empirical testing. These learning principles are based on literally thousands of experimental hours covering a wide range of the phylogenetic scale and more nearly constitute empirically derived *laws* of behavior than any other set of principles. They enable the handling of a great variety of observational as well as experimental evidence about human behavior.

It is the purpose of this paper to take the first step in the direction to which Jeffery points. A restatement of the theory, not an alternative theory, will be presented, although, of necessity, certain ideas not intrinsic to differential association will have to be introduced and additions will be made to the original propositions. It should be pointed out that DeFleur and Quinney have been able to demonstrate that Sutherland's propositions, when stated in the form of set theory, appear to be internally consistent. By arranging the propositions in axiomatic form, stating them in logical rather than verbal symbols, they have brought the theoretical grammar up to date.[15] Such is not our intention in this paper, at all. We recognize and appreciate the importance of stating the propositions in a formal, deductive fashion. We do feel, however, that this task is, at the present time, subsidiary to the more urgent task of (1) making explicit the learning process, as it is now understood by modern behavioral science, from which the propositions of differential association can be derived; (2) fully reformulating the theory, statement by statement, in light of the current knowledge of this learning process; and (3) helping criminologists become aware of the advances in learning theory and research that are directly relevant to an explanation of criminal behavior.[16] No claim is made that this constitutes a final statement. If it has any seminal value at all, that is, if it provokes a serious new look at the theory and encourages further effort in this direction, our objective will have been served.

15 DeFleur and Quinney, *op. cit.*

16 Our main concern here, of course, is with the nine statements of the theory as a genetic explanation of the process by which the individual comes to engage in illegal behavior. We do not lose sight of the fact, however, that this must be integrated with explanations of the variation and location of crime.

DIFFERENTIAL ASSOCIATION AND MODERN
BEHAVIOR THEORY

In this section the nine formal propositions in which Suther-land expressed his theory will be analyzed in terms of behavior theory and research and will be reformulated as seven new propo-sitions. (See Table 1.)

I. "Criminal behavior is learned."

VIII. "The process of learning criminal behavior by associa-tion with criminal and anti-criminal patterns involves all of the mechanisms that are involved in any other learning."

Since both the first and the eighth sentences in the theory obviously form a unitary idea, it seems best to state them together. Sutherland was aware that these statements did not sufficiently de-scribe the learning process,[17] but the two items leave no doubt that differential association theory was meant to fit into a general ex-planation of human behavior, and as such is unambiguously stated in the prefatory remarks of the theory: an "explanation of criminal behavior should be a specific part of a general theory of behavior."[18] Modern behavior theory as a general theory provides us with a good idea of what the mechanisms are that are involved in the process of acquiring behavior.[19]

According to this theory, there are two major categories of behavior. On the one hand, there is reflexive or *respondent* be-havior, which is behavior governed by the stimuli that elicit it. Such behaviors are largely associated with the autonomic system. The work of Pavlov is of special significance here. On the other

17 Cressey, 1960, *op cit.*, p. 54.

18 Sutherland and Cressey, *op. cit.*, p. 75.

19 It should be mentioned at the outset that there is more than one learn-ing theory. The one we will employ is called Behavior Theory. More spe-cifically, it is that variety of behavior theory largely associated with the name of B. F. Skinner (*Science and Human Behavior*, New York: Macmillan, 1953). It differs from other learning theories in that it restricts itself to the relations between observable, measurable behavior and observable, measurable conditions. There is nothing in this theory that denies the existence, the importance, or even the inherent interest of the nervous system or brain. However, most behavioral scientists in this area are extremely careful in hypothesizing inter-vening variables or constructs, whether they are egos, personalities, response sets, or some sort of internal computers. Generally they adopt the position that the only real value of a construct is its ability to improve one's predictions. If it does not, then it must be excluded in accordance with the rule of parsimony.

TABLE 1

A Differential Association-Reinforcement
Theory of Criminal Behavior

Sutherland's Statements	*Reformulated Statements*
I. "Criminal behavior is learned." VIII. "The process of learning criminal behavior by association with criminal and anti-criminal patterns involves all of the mechanisms that are involved in any other learning."	I. Criminal behavior is learned according to the principles of operant conditioning.
II. "Criminal behavior is learned in interaction with other persons in a process of communication."	II. Criminal behavior is learned both in nonsocial situations that are reinforcing or discriminative and through that social interaction in which the behavior of other persons is reinforcing or discriminative for criminal behavior.
III. "The principal part of the learning of criminal behavior occurs within intimate personal groups."	III. The principal part of the learning of criminal behavior occurs in those groups which comprise the individual's major source of reinforcements.
IV. "When criminal behavior is learned, the learning includes (*a*) techniques of committing the crime, which are sometimes very complicated, sometimes very simple; (*b*) the specific direction of motives, drives, rationalizations, and attitudes."	IV. The learning of criminal behavior, including specific techniques, attitudes, and avoidance procedures, is a function of the effective and available reinforcers, and the existing reinforcement contingencies.
V. "The specific direction of motives and drives is learned from definitions of the legal codes as favorable or unfavorable."	V. The specific class of behaviors which are learned and their frequency of occurrence are a function of the reinforcers which are effective and available, and the rules or norms by which these reinforcers are applied.
VI. "A person becomes delinquent because of an excess of definitions favorable to violation of law over definitions unfavorable to violation of law."	VI. Criminal behavior is a function of norms which are discriminative for criminal behavior, the learning of which take place when such behavior is more highly reinforced than noncriminal behavior.

TABLE 1 *(Continued)*

A Differential Association-Reinforcement
Theory of Criminal Behavior

Sutherland's Statements	*Reformulated Statements*
VII. "Differential associations may vary in frequency, duration, priority, and intensity."	VII. The strength of criminal behavior is a direct function of the amount, frequency, and probability of its reinforcement.
IX. "While criminal behavior is an expression of general needs and values, it is not explained by those general needs and values since noncriminal behavior is an expression of the same needs and values."	IX. (Omit from theory.)

hand, there is *operant* behavior: behavior which involves the central nervous system. Examples of operant behavior include verbal behavior, playing ball, driving a car, and buying a new suit. It has been found that this class of behavior is a function of its past and present environmental consequences. Thus, when a particular operant is followed by certain kinds of stimuli, that behavior's frequency of occurrence will increase in the future. These stimuli are called reinforcing stimuli or reinforcers[20] and include food, money, clothes, objects of various sorts, social attention, approval, affection, and social status. This entire process is called positive reinforcement. One distinguishing characteristic of operant behavior as op-

20 It has been said by some that a tautology is involved here. But there is nothing tautological about classifying events in terms of their effects. As Skinner (*op. cit.,* pp. 72-73) has noted, this criterion is both empirical and objective. There is only one sure way of telling whether or not a given stimulus event is reinforcing to a given individual under given conditions and that is to make a direct test: observe the frequency of a selected behavior, then make a stimulus event contingent upon it and observe any change in frequency. If there is a change in frequency, we may classify the stimulus as reinforcing to the individual under the stated conditions. Our reasoning would become circular, however, if we went on to assert that a given stimulus strengthens the behavior *because* it is reinforcing. Furthermore, not all stimuli, when presented, will increase the frequency of the behavior which *produced* them. Some stimuli will increase the frequency of the behavior which *removes* them, still others will neither strengthen nor weaken the behavior which produced them. See Robert L. Burgess and Ronald L. Akers, "Are Operant Principles Tautological?" *The Psychological Record,* 16 (July, 1966), pp. 305-312.

posed to respondent behavior, then, is that the latter is a function of its antecedent stimuli, whereas the former is a function of its antecedent environmental consequences.

Typically, operant and respondent behaviors occur together in an individual's everyday behavior, and they interact in extremely intricate ways. Consequently, to fully understand any set of patterned responses, the investigator should observe the effects of the operants on the respondents as well as the effects of the respondents on the operants. The connections between operant and respondent behaviors are especially crucial to an analysis of attitudes, and emotional and conflict behaviors.

In everyday life, different consequences are usually contingent upon different classes of behavior. This relationship between behavior and its consequences functions to alter the rate and form of behavior as well as its relationship to many features of the environment. The process of operant reinforcement is the most important process by which behavior is generated and maintained. There are, in fact, six possible environmental consequences relative to the law of operant behavior.

1. A behavior may produce certain stimulus events and thereby increase in frequency. As we have indicated above, such stimuli are called positive reinforcers and the process is called positive reinforcement.

2. A behavior may remove, avoid, or terminate certain stimulus events and thereby increase in frequency. Such stimuli are termed negative reinforcers, and the process is called negative reinforcement.

3. A behavior may produce certain stimulus events and thereby decrease in frequency. Such stimuli are called aversive stimuli or, more recently, punishers.[21] The entire behavioral process is called positive punishment.

4. A behavior may remove or terminate certain stimulus events and thereby decrease in frequency. Such stimuli are positive reinforcers, and the process is termed negative punishment.

5. A behavior may produce or remove certain stimulus events which do not change the behavior's frequency at all. Such stimuli are called neutral stimuli.

6. A behavior may no longer produce customary stimulus

[21] N. H. Azrin and D. F. Hake, "Conditioned Punishment," *Journal of the Experimental Analysis of Behavior,* 8 (September, 1965), pp. 279-293.

events and thereby decrease in frequency. The stimuli which are produced are neutral stimuli, and the process, extinction. When a reinforcing stimulus no longer functions to increase the future probability of the behavior which produced it, we say the individual is satiated. To restore the reinforcing property of the stimulus we need only deprive the individual of it for a time.[22]

The increase in the frequency of occurrence of a behavior that is reinforced is the very property of reinforcement that permits the fascinating variety and subtlety occurring in operant as opposed to respondent behavior. Another process producing the variety we see in behavior is *conditioning*. When a primary or unconditioned reinforcing stimulus such as food is repeatedly paired with a neutral stimulus, the latter will eventually function as a reinforcing stimulus as well. An illustration of this would be as follows. The milk a mother feeds to her infant is an unconditioned reinforcer. If the food is repeatedly paired with social attention, affection, and approval, these will eventually become reinforcing as will the mother herself as a stimulus object. Later these *conditioned reinforcers* can be used to strengthen other behaviors by making the reinforcers contingent upon the new behaviors.

Differential reinforcement may also alter the form of a response. This process is called *shaping* or *response differentiation*. It can be exemplified by a child learning to speak. At first, the parent will reinforce any vocalization, but as time wears on, and as the child grows older, the parent will differentially reinforce only those responses which successfully approximate certain criteria. The child will be seen to proceed from mere grunts to "baby talk" to articulate speech.[23]

Of course, organisms, whether pigeons, monkeys or people, do not usually go around behaving in all possible ways at all possible times. In short, behavior does not occur in a vacuum; a given behavior is appropriate to a given situation. By appropriate we mean that reinforcement has been forthcoming only under certain conditions, and it is under these conditions that the behavior will occur.

---

[22] See Jacob L. Gewirtz and Donald M. Baer, "Deprivation and Satiation of Social Reinforcers as Drive Conditions," *Journal of Abnormal and Social Psychology*, 57 (1958), pp. 165-172.

[23] This seems to be the process involved in learning to become a marijuana user. By successive approximations, the individual learns (from others) to close on the appropriate techniques and effects of using marijuana. See Howard S. Becker, *Outsiders*, Glencoe, Ill.: The Free Press, 1963, pp. 41-58.

In other words, differential reinforcement not only increases the probability of a response but also makes that response more probable upon the recurrence of conditions the same as or similar to those that were present during previous reinforcements. Such a process is called *stimulus control* or *stimulus discrimination*. For example, a child when he is first taught to say "DADDY" may repeat the word when any male is present, or even, in the very beginning, when any adult is present. But through differential reinforcement, the child will eventually speak the word "DADDY" only when his father is present or in other "appropriate" conditions. We may say that the father, as a stimulus object, functions as a discriminative stimulus (S^D) setting the occasion for the operant verbal response "DADDY" because in the past such behavior has been reinforced under such conditions.

It has also been discovered that the pattern or schedule of reinforcement is as important as the amount of reinforcement. For example, a *fixed-interval* schedule of reinforcement, where a response is reinforced only after a certain amount of time has passed, produces a lower rate of response than that obtained with reinforcement based on a *fixed-ratio* schedule, where a response is reinforced only after a certain number of responses have already been emitted. Similarly a response rate obtained with a fixed-ratio schedule is lower than that obtained with a *variable-ratio* schedule, where reinforcement occurs for a certain proportion of responses randomly varied about some central value. A schedule of reinforcement, then, refers to the response *contingencies* upon which reinforcement depends. All of the various schedules of reinforcement, besides producing lawful response characteristics, produce lawful extinction rates, once reinforcement is discontinued. Briefly, behavior reinforced on an intermittent schedule takes longer to extinguish than behavior reinforced on a continuous schedule.

This concept, schedules of reinforcement, is one the implications of which are little understood by many behavioral scientists, so a few additional words are in order. First of all, social reinforcements are for the most part intermittent. One obvious result of this fact is the resistance to extinction and satiation of much social behavior, desirable as well as undesirable. This is not peculiar to human social behavior, for even lower organisms seldom are faced with a continuous reinforcement schedule. Nevertheless, reinforcements mediated by another organism are probably much less reliable than those produced by the physical environment. This is the case because social reinforcement depends upon behavioral processes in the reinforcer which are not under good control by the reinforcee. A more subtle, though essentially methodological, implication is that, because most social behaviors are maintained by complex intermittent schedules which have been shaped over a long period of time, a social observer newly entering a situation may have extreme difficulty in immediately determining exactly what is maintaining a particular behavior or set of behaviors. Nor can the individual himself be expected to be able to identify his own contingencies of reinforcement.[24]

An important aspect of this theory is the presentation of the general ways in which stimuli and responses can be formed into complex constellations of stimulus-response events. Although the basic principles are simple and must be separated to distinguish and study them, in actual life the principles function in concert and consist of complex arrays and constellations.[25] Such complexity can be seen in the fact that single S-R events may be combined into sequences on the basis of conditioning principles. That is, responses can be thought to have stimulus properties. In addition, more than one response may come under the control of a particular stimulus. Thus, when the stimulus occurs, it will tend to set the occasion for the various responses that have been conditioned to it. These responses may be competitive, that is, only one or the other can occur. When this is so, the particular response which does occur may also depend upon other discriminative stimuli present in the situation that control only one or the other response. Finally, although some of the stimuli to which an individual responds emanate from the external environment, social and otherwise, others come from his own behavior. An individual is, then, not only a source of responses, but also a source of some stimuli—stimuli that can affect his own behavior.

The most general behavioral principle is the law of operant behavior, which says that behavior is a function of its past and current environmental consequences. There have been numerous

---

24 Cressey encountered this problem in trying to get trust violators to reconstruct past associations. Cressey, *Other People's Money, op. cit.,* p. 149.

25 Arthur Staats, "An Integrated-Functional Learning Approach to Complex Human Behavior," *Technical Report 28,* Contract ONR and Arizona State University, 1965.

studies with children[26] as well as adults[27] which indicate that individual behavior conforms to this law. Of much more interest to sociologists is an experiment designed by Azrin and Lindsley in 1956[28] to investigate cooperative social behavior. Their study demonstrated that cooperative behavior could be developed, maintained, eliminated and reinstated solely through the manipulation of the contingency between reinforcing stimuli and the cooperative response. This basic finding has received much subsequent support. It has also been demonstrated that not only cooperative behavior but also competitive behavior and leading and following behavior are a function of their past and present consequences.

Another of the behavorial principles we mentioned was that of stimulus discrimination. A discriminative stimulus is a stimulus in the presence of which a particular operant response is reinforced. Much of our behavior has come under the control of certain environmental, including social, stimuli because in the past it has been reinforced in the presence of those stimuli. In an experiment by Donald Cohen,[29] a normal 13-year-old boy named Justin, when placed under identical experimental conditions emitted different behaviors depending upon whether his partner was his mother, brother, sister, friend, or a stranger. The results of this investigation demonstrated that Justin's social behavior was differentially controlled by reinforcement; but it also demonstrated that his behavior was different depending upon the social stimuli present, thus reaffirming the principle of stimulus discrimination. In other words, the dynamic properties of his social behavior, whether cooperative, competitive, leading, or following, were controlled by his previous extra-experimental history with his teammates, although the experimenter could change those behaviors by experi-

[26] See, for example, S. W. Bijou and P. T. Sturges, "Positive Reinforcers for Experimental Studies with Children—Consumables and Manipulatables," *Child Development,* 30 (1959), pp. 151-170.

[27] J. G. Holland, "Human Vigilance," *Science,* 128 (1959), pp. 61-67; Harold Weiner, "Conditioning History and Human Fixed-Interval Performance," *Journal of the Experimental Analysis of Behavior,* 7 (September, 1964), pp. 383-385.

[28] N. H. Azrin and O. R. Lindsley, "The Reinforcement of Cooperation Between Children," *The Journal of Abnormal and Social Psychology,* 52 (January, 1956).

[29] Donald J. Cohen, "Justin and His Peers: an Experimental Analysis of a Child's Social World," *Child Development,* 33 (1962).

mentally altering the contingencies of reinforcement. It is, of course, almost a truism to say that an individual behaves differently in the presence of different people. The significance of this experiment, however, is that the investigator was able to isolate the determining variables and the principles by which they operated to produce this common phenomenon.

Although this is by no means a complete survey of the relevant experimental tests of the behavioral principles outlined above, it may serve to point out that many forms of "normal" social behavior function according to the law of operant behavior. But what about "deviant" behavior? Can we be sure that these same principles are operating here? Unfortunately no studies have attempted to test directly the relevance of these behavioral principles to criminal behavior. But there have been several experimental investigations of deviant behaviors emitted by mental patients. For example, in a study by Ayllon and Michael,[30] it was shown that the bizarre behaviors of psychotics functioned according to these learning principles. In this particular study various behavioral problems of psychotic patients were "cured" through the manipulation of reinforcement contingencies. Such principles as extinction, negative and positive reinforcement, and satiation were effectively utilized to eliminate the unwanted behaviors.[31] This study was one of the first experimental tests of the contention that not only conforming but also many unusual, inappropriate, or undesirable behaviors are shaped and maintained through social reinforcement. In another experiment Isaacs, Thomas, and Goldiamond[32] demonstrate that complex adjustive behaviors can be operantly conditioned in long-term psychotics by manipulating available reinforcers.

[30] T. Ayllon and J. Michael, "The Psychiatric Nurse as a Behavioral Engineer," *Journal of the Experimental Analysis of Behavior*, 2 (1959), pp. 323-334.

[31] There is, of course, no intention on our part to equate "mental" illness or similarly severe behavior problems with criminal behavior. The only connection that we are making is that both may be seen to function according to the same basic behavioral principles and both may be in opposition to established norms.

[32] W. Isaacs, J. Thomas, and I. Goldiamond, "Application of Operant Conditioning to Reinstate Verbal Behavior in Psychotics," *Journal of Speech and Disorders*, 25 (1960), pp. 8-12.

In yet another investigation,[33] the personnel of a mental hospital ward for schizophrenics recorded the behavior of the patients and provided consequences to it according to certain pre-established procedures. Without going into the many important details of this long investigation, we may note that, in each of the six experiments that were carried out, the results demonstrate that reinforcement was effective in maintaining desired performances, even though these were "back-ward" psychotics who had resisted all previous therapy, including psychoanalysis, electroshock therapy, and even lobotomies.

"In each experiment, the performance fell to a near zero level when the established response-reinforcement relation was discontinued. . . . The standard procedure for reinforcement had been to provide tokens . . . [exchanged] for a variety of reinforcers. Performance decreased when this response-reinforcement relation was disrupted (1) by delivering tokens independently of the response while still allowing exchange of tokens for the reinforcers (Exp. II and III), (2) by discontinuing the token system entirely but providing continuing access to the reinforcers (Exp. IV), or (3) by discontinuing the delivery of tokens for a previously reinforced response while simultaneously providing tokens for a different, alternative response (Exp. I and VI). Further, the effectiveness of the reinforcement procedure did not appear to be limited to an all-or-none basis. Patients selected and performed the assignment that provided the larger number of tokens when reinforcement was available for more than one assignment (Exp. V).[34]

Again, we cannot review all of the relevant literature, yet perhaps the three investigations cited will serve to emphasize that many forms of deviant behavior are shaped and maintained by various contingencies of reinforcement.[35] Given this experimental evidence, we would amend Sutherland's first and eighth propositions to read:

I. *Criminal behavior is learned according to the principles of operant conditioning.*

[33] T. Ayllon and N. Azrin, "The Measurement and Reinforcement of Behavior of Psychotics," *Journal of the Experimental Analysis of Behavior,* 8 (November, 1965), pp. 357-383.

[34] *Ibid.,* p. 381.

[35] See also the following: H. J. Eysenck (Ed.), *Experiments in Behaviour Therapy,* New York: Pergamon Press, The Macmillan Company, 1964; L. Krasner and L. Ullman, *Research in Behavior Modification,* New York: Holt, Rinehart & Winston, 1965; L. Ullman and L. Krasner, *Case Studies in Behavior Modification,* New York: Holt, Rinehart & Winston, 1964.

II. "Criminal behavior is learned in interaction with other persons in the process of communication."

As DeFleur and Quinney have noted, the major implication of this proposition is that symbolic interaction is a necessary condition for the learning of criminal behavior.[36] Of direct relevance is an experiment designed to test the relative significance of verbal instructions and reinforcement contingencies in generating and maintaining a certain class of behaviors.[37] In brief, the results indicated that behavior could not be maintained solely through verbal instructions. However, it was also discovered to be an extremely arduous task to shape a set of complex behaviors without using verbal instructions as discriminative stimuli. Behavior was quickly and effectively developed and maintained by a combination of verbal instructions *and* reinforcement consequences. Symbolic interaction is, then, not enough; contingencies of reinforcement must also be present.

From the perspective of modern behavior theory, two aspects of socialization are usually considered to distinguish it from other processes of behavioral change: (1) only these behavioral changes occurring through learning are considered relevant; (2) only the changes in behavior having their origins in interaction with other persons are considered products of socialization.[38] Sutherland's theory may, then, be seen to be a theory of differential socialization since he too restricted himself to learning having its origin in interaction with other persons. Although social learning is indeed important and even predominant, it certainly does not exhaust the learning process. In short, we may learn (and thus our behavior would be modified) without any direct contact with another person. Hence Sutherland's theory may be seen to suffer from a significant lacuna in that it neglected the possibility of deviant behavior being learned in nonsocial situations. Consequently, to be an adequate theory of deviant behavior, the theory must be amended further to include the forms of deviant behavior that are learned in the absence of social reinforcement. Other people are not the only source of reinforcement, although they are the most important.

36 DeFleur and Quinney, *op. cit.*, p. 3.

37 T. Ayllon and N. Azrin, "Reinforcement and Instructions with Mental Patients," *Journal of the Experimental Analysis of .Behavior,* 7 (1964), pp. 327-331.

38 Paul E. Secord and Carl W. Backman, *Social Psychology,* New York: McGraw-Hill Book Company, 1964.

As Jeffery[39] has aptly noted, stealing is reinforcing in and by itself whether other people know about it and reinforce it socially or not. The same may be said to apply to many forms of aggressive behaviors.[40]

There are many studies which are relevant to social interaction and socialization on the one hand, and Sutherland's second proposition on the other. For example, in a study by Lott and Lott[41] it was found that, when child A was reinforced in the presence of child B, child A would later select child B as a companion. The behavior of selecting child B was not the behavior that was reinforced. The experimental conditions simply paired child B with positive reinforcement. In accordance with the principle of conditioning, child B had become a conditioned positive reinforcer. Hence any behavior which produced the presence of child B would be strengthened—such behaviors, for example, as verbal responses requesting child B's company. Thus, as Staats[42] has noted, the results of this study indicate that the concepts of reinforcing stimuli and group cohesion are related when analyzed in terms of an integrated set of learning principles.

Glaser[43] has attempted to reformulate Sutherland's differential association theory in terms of social identification. It should be recognized, however, that identification, as well as modeling and imitative behavior (which are usually associated with identification), comprises just one feature of the socialization process. Furthermore, such behavior may be analyzed quite parsimoniously with the principles of modern behavior theory. For example, in a study by Bandura and Ross,[44] a child experienced the pairing of one adult with positive reinforcers. Presumably this adult would

39 Jeffery, *op. cit.*

40 For some evidence that aggressive behavior may be of a respondent as well as an operant nature, see N. Azrin, R. Hutchinson, and R. McLaughlin, "The Opportunity for Aggression as an Operant Reinforcer during Aversive Stimulation," *Journal of the Experimental Analysis of Behavior*, 8 (May, 1965), pp. 171-180.

41 B. E. Lott and A. J. Lott, "The Formation of Positive Attitudes Toward Group Members," *The Journal of Abnormal and Social Psychology*, 61 (1960), pp. 297-300.

42 Arthur Staats, *Human Learning*, New York: Holt, Rinehart & Winston, 1964, p. 333.

43 Glaser, "Criminality Theories and Behavioral Images," *op. cit.*

44 A. Bandura, D. Ross, and S. Ross, "A Comparative Test of the Status Envy, Social Power and the Secondary Reinforcement Theories of Identification Learning," *Journal of Abnormal and Social Psychology*, 67 (1963), pp. 527-534.

become a conditioned reinforcer. Indeed, later it was found that the child imitated this adult more than he did an adult who was not paired with positive reinforcers. That is, the one adult, as he became a stronger reinforcer, had also become a stronger S^D for imitating or following behavior. Thus, Bandura's and Ross's results demonstrate that imitating or following behavior is at least in part a function of the reinforcing value of people as social stimuli.

On the basis of these results it is suggested that a change in the reinforcing value of an individual will change his power as a stimulus controlling other people's behavior in various ways. An increase in the reinforcing value of an individual will increase verbal and motor approach, or companionable responses, respectful responses, affectionate behavior, following behavior, smiling, pleasant conversation, sympathetic responses and the like.[45]

The relevance of these studies is that they have isolated some of the determining variables whereby the behavior of one person is influenced or changed by the behavior of another as well as the principles by which these variables operate. We have, of course, only scratched the surface. Many other variables are involved. For instance, not all people are equally effective in controlling or influencing the behavior of others. The person who can mediate the most reinforcers will exercise the most power. Thus the parent, who controls more of his child's reinforcers, will exercise more power than an older sibling or a temporary baby sitter. As the child becomes older and less dependent upon the parent for many of his reinforcers, other individuals or groups such as his peers may exercise more power. Carrying the analysis one step further, the person who has access to a large range of aversive stimuli will exert more power than one who has not. Thus a peer group may come to exercise more power over a child's behavior than the parent even though the parent may still control a large share of the child's positive reinforcers.

In addition to the reinforcing function of an individual or group, there is, as seen in the Cohen and the Bandura and Ross studies, the discriminative stimulus function of a group. For example, specific individuals as physical stimuli may acquire discriminative control over an individual's behavior. The child in our example is reinforced for certain kinds of behaviors in the presence of his parent; thus the parent's presence may come to control this

45 Staats, 1964, *op. cit.*, p. 333.

type of behavior. He is reinforced for different behaviors in the presence of his peers, who then come to set the occasion for this type of behavior. Consequently this proposition must be amended to read:

II. *Criminal behavior is learned both in nonsocial situations that are reinforcing or discriminative, and through that social interaction in which the behavior of other persons is reinforcing or discriminative for criminal behavior.*

III. "The principal part of the learning of criminal behavior occurs within intimate personal groups."

In terms of our analysis, the primary group would be seen to be the major source of an individual's social reinforcements. The bulk of behavorial training which the child receives occurs at a time when the trainers, usually the parents, possess a very powerful system of reinforcers. In fact, we might characterize a primary group as a generalized reinforcer (one associated with many reinforcers, conditioned as well as unconditioned). And, as we suggested above, as the child grows older, groups other than the family, for example, the adolescent peer group, may come to control a majority of his reinforcers.

To say that the primary group is the principal molder of an individual's behavioral repertoire is not to ignore social learning which may occur in other contexts. As we noted above, learning from social models can be adequately explained in terms of these behavioral principles. The analysis we employed there can also be extended to learning from the mass media and from "reference" groups. In any case, we may alter this proposition to read:

III. *The principal part of the learning of criminal behavior occurs in those groups which comprise the individual's major source of reinforcements.*

IV. "When criminal behavior is learned, the learning includes (a) techniques of committing the crime, which are sometimes very complicated, sometimes very simple; (b) the specific direction of motives, drives, rationalizations, and attitudes."

A study by Klaus and Glaser,[46] as well as many other studies,[47]

---

[46] D. J. Klaus and R. Glaser, "Increasing Team Proficiency Through Training," Pittsburgh. American Institute of Research, 1960.

[47] See Robert L. Burgess, "Communication Networks: An Experimental Reevaluation," Ch. 6, this book.

indicates that reinforcement contingencies are of prime importance in learning various behavioral techniques. And, of course, many techniques, both simple and complicated, are specific to a particular deviant act such as jimmying, picking locks of buildings and cars, picking pockets, short- and big-con techniques, counterfeiting, and safe-cracking. Other techniques in criminal behavior may be learned in conforming or neutral contexts, for example, driving a car, signing checks, or shooting a gun. In any event, we need not alter the first part of this proposition.

The second part of the proposition, however, does deserve some additional comments. Sutherland's major focus here seems to be motivation. Much of what we have already discussed in this paper often goes under the general heading of motivation. The topic of motivation is as important as it is complex. This complexity is related to the fact that the same stimulus may have two functions: it may be both a reinforcing stimulus and a discriminative stimulus controlling the behavior which is followed by reinforcement.[48] Thus, motivation may be seen to be a function of the processes by which stimuli acquire conditioned reinforcing value and become discriminative stimuli. Reinforcers and discriminative stimuli here would become the dependent variables; the independent variables would be the conditioning procedures previously mentioned and the level of deprivation. For example, when a prisoner is deprived of contact with members of the opposite sex, such sex reinforcers will become much more powerful. Thus those sexual reinforcers that are available, such as homosexual contact, come to exert a great deal of influence and shape behaviors that would be unlikely to occur without such deprivation. And, without going any further

[48] A central principle underlying this analysis is that reinforcing stimuli, both positive and negative, elicit certain respondents. Unconditioned reinforcers elicit these responses without training; conditioned reinforcers elicit such responses through respondent conditioning. Staats and Staats (*Complex Human Behavior*, New York: Holt, Rinehart & Winston, 1964) have characterized such respondents as "attitude" responses. Thus, a positive reinforcer elicits a positive attitude. Furthermore, these respondents have stimulus characteristics which may become discriminative stimuli setting the occasion for a certain class of operants called "striving" responses for positive reinforcers and escape and/or avoidance behaviors for negative reinforcers. These respondents and their attendant stimuli may be generalized to other reinforcing stimuli. Thus, striving responses can be seen to generalize to new positive reinforcers since these also will elicit the respondent responses and their characteristic stimuli, which have become S^Ds for such behavior.

into this topic, some stimuli may be more reinforcing, under similar conditions of deprivation, for certain individuals or groups than for others. Furthermore, the satiation of one or more of these reinforcers would allow for an increase in the relative strength of others.

Much, therefore, can be learned about the distinctive characteristics of a group by knowing what the available and effective reinforcers are and the behaviors upon which they are contingent. Basically, we are contending that the nature of the reinforcer system and the reinforcement contingencies are crucial determinants of individual and group behavior. Consequently, a description of an individual's or group's reinforcers, and an understanding of the principles by which reinforcers affect behavior, would be expected to yield a great deal of knowledge about individual and group deviant behavior.

Finally, the rationalizations which Cressey identifies with regard to trust violators and the peculiar extensions of "defenses to crimes" or "techniques of neutralization" by which deviant behavior is justified, as identified by Sykes and Matza,[49] may be analyzed as operant behaviors of the escape or avoidance type which are maintained because they have the effect of avoiding or reducing the punishment that comes from social disapproval by oneself as well as by others. We may, therefore, rewrite this proposition to read:

IV. *The learning of criminal behavior, including specific techniques, attitudes, and avoidance procedures, is a function of the effective and available reinforcers, and the existing reinforcement contingencies.*

V. :"The specific direction of motives and drives is learned from definitions of the legal codes as favorable or unfavorable."

In this proposition, Sutherland appears to be referring, at least in part, to the concept "norm," which may be defined as a statement made by a number of the members of a group, not necessarily all of them, prescribing or proscribing certain behaviors at certain times.[50] We often infer what the norms of a group are by observing

[49] Cressey, *Other People's Money, op. cit.,* pp. 93-138. G. M. Sykes and David Matza, "Techniques of Neutralization: A Theory of Delinquency," *American Sociological Review,* 22 (December, 1957), pp. 664-670.

[50] George C. Homans, *Social Behavior: Its Elementary Forms,* New York: Harcourt, Brace & World, 1961.

reaction to behavior, that is, the sanctions applied to, or the reinforcement and punishment consequences of, such behavior. We may also learn what a group's norms are through verbal or written statements. The individual group member also learns what is and is not acceptable behavior on the basis of verbal statements made by others, as well as through the sanctions (i.e., the reinforcing or aversive stimuli) applied to his behavior (and other norm violators) by others.

Behavior theory specifies the place of normative statements and sanctions in the dynamics of acquiring "conforming" or "normative" behavior. Just as the behavior and even the physical characteristics of the individual may serve discriminative functions, verbal behavior, including normative statements, can be analyzed as S^Ds. A normative statement can be analyzed as an S^D indicating that the members of a group ought to behave in a certain way in certain circumstances. Such "normative" behavior would be developed and maintained by social reinforcement. As we observed in the Ayllon-Azrin study[51] of instructions and reinforcement contingencies, such verbal behavior would not maintain any particular class of behaviors if it were not at least occasionally backed by reinforcement consequences. In an extension of their analysis, an individual would not "conform" to a norm if he did not have a past history of reinforcement for such conforming behavior. This is important, for earlier we stated that we can learn a great deal about a group by knowing what the effective reinforcers are and the behaviors upon which they are contingent. We may now say that we can learn a great deal about an individual's or a group's behavior when we are able to specify, not only what the effective reinforcers are, but also what the rules or norms are by which these reinforcers are applied.[52] For these two types of knowledge will tell us much about the types of behavior that the individual will develop or the types of behaviors that are dominant in a group.

For example, it has often been noted that most official criminal acts are committed by members of minority groups who live in slums. One distinguishing characteristic of a slum is the high level of deprivation of many important social reinforcers. Exacerbating this situation is the fact that these people, in contrast to other groups, lack the behavioral repertoires necessary to produce reinforcement in the prescribed ways. They have not been and are not

[51] Ayllon and Azrin, 1964, *op. cit.*
[52] Staats and Staats, *op. cit.*

now adequately reinforced for lawful or normative behavior. And, as we know from the law of operant reinforcement, a reinforcer will increase the rate of occurrence of any operant which produces it. Furthermore, given a large number of individuals under similar conditions, we would predict that they are likely to behave in similar ways. Within such groups, many forms of social reinforcement may become contingent upon classes of behaviors which are outside the larger society's normative requirements. Norms and legal codes, as discriminative stimuli, will only control the behavior of those who have experienced the appropriate learning history. If an individual has been, and is, reinforced for such "normative" behavior, that behavior will be maintained in strength. If he has not been, and is not now, reinforced for such behaviors, they will be weak, if they exist in his repertoire at all. And, importantly, the reinforcement system may shape and maintain another class of behaviors which do result in reinforcement, and such behaviors may be considered deviant or criminal by other members of the group. Thus we may formulate this proposition to read:

V. *The specific class of behaviors which are learned and their frequency of occurrence are a function of the reinforcers which are effective and available, and the rules or norms by which these reinforcers are applied.*

VI. "A person becomes delinquent because of an excess of definitions favorable to violation of law over definitions unfavorable to violation of law."

This proposition is generally considered the heart of Sutherland's theory; it is the principle of differential association. It follows directly from Proposition V, to which we must now refer. In Proposition V, the use of the preposition "from" in the phrase "learned from definitions of the legal codes as favorable or unfavorable," is somewhat misleading. The meaning here is not so much that learning results *from* these definitions as it is that they form part of the *content* of one's learning, determining which direction one's behavior will go in relation to the law, that is, lawabiding or lawbreaking.

These definitions of the law make lawbreaking seem either appropriate or inappropriate. The definitions which face lawbreaking in a favorable light in a sense can be seen as essentially norms of evasion and/or norms directly conflicting with conventional norms. They are, as Sykes and Matza and Cressey note, "techniques of neutralization," "rationalizations," or "verbalizations" which make criminal behavior seem "all right" or justified, or which provide defenses against self-reproach and disapproval from others.[53] The principle of negative reinforcement would be of major significance in the acquisition and maintenance of such behaviors.

This analysis suggests that it may not be an "excess" of one kind of definition over another in the sense of a cumulative ratio, but rather in the sense of the relative amount of discriminative stimulus value of one set of verbalizations or normative statements over another. As we suggested in the last section, normative statements are, themselves, behaviors that are a function of reinforcement consequences. They, in turn, may serve as discriminative stimuli for other operant behaviors (verbal and nonverbal). But recall that reinforcement must be forthcoming, at least occasionally, before a verbal statement can continue as a discriminative stimulus. Bear in mind, also, that behavior may produce reinforcing consequences even in the absence of any accompanying verbal statements.

In other terms, a person will become delinquent if the official norms or laws do not perform a discriminative function and thereby control "normative" or conforming behavior. We know from the law of differential reinforcement that the operant which produces the most reinforcement will become dominant. Thus, if lawful behavior did not result in reinforcement, the strength of the behavior would be weakened, and a state of deprivation would result. This, in turn, would increase the probability that other behaviors would be emitted which are reinforced and hence would be strengthened. And, of course, these behaviors, though common to one or more groups, may be labeled deviant by the larger society. Also such behavior patterns themselves may acquire conditioned reinforcing value and subsequently be enforced by the members of a group by making various forms of social reinforcement, such as social approval, esteem, and status, contingent upon that behavior.

The concept "excess" in the statement "excess of definitions favorable to violation of law" has been particularly resistant to

[53] Sykes and Matza, *op. cit.* Cressey, *Other People's Money, op. cit.,* pp. 93-138. Donald R. Cressey, "The Differential Association Theory and Compulsive Crimes," *Journal of Criminal Law, Criminology and Police Science,* 45 (May-June, 1954), pp. 29-40. Donald R. Cressey, "Social Psychological Foundations for Using Criminals in the Rehabilitation of Criminals," *Journal of Research in Crime and Delinquency,* 2 (July, 1965), pp. 45-59. See revised Proposition IV.

operationalization. A translation of this concept in terms of modern behavior theory would involve the "balance" of reinforcement consequences, positive and negative. The law of differential reinforcement is crucial here. That is, a person would engage in the behaviors for which he had been reinforced most highly in the past. (The reader may recall that in the Ayllon-Azrin study with schizophrenics it was found that the patients selected and performed the behaviors which provided the most reinforcers when reinforcement was available for more than one response.) Criminal behavior would, then, occur under the conditions in which an individual has been most highly reinforced for such behavior, and the aversive consequences contingent upon the behavior have been of such a nature that they do not perform a "punishment function."[54] This leads us to a discussion of Proposition VII. But, first, let us reformulate the sixth proposition to read:

VI. *Criminal behavior is a function of norms which are discriminative for criminal behavior, the learning of which takes place when such behavior is more highly reinforced than noncriminal behavior.*

VII. "Differential associations may vary in frequency, duration, priority, and intensity."

In terms of our analysis, the concepts "frequency," "duration," and "priority" are straightforward enough. The concept "intensity" could be operationalized to designate the number of the individual's positive and negative reinforcers that another individual or group controls, as well as the reinforcement value of that individual or group. As previously suggested, the group which can mediate the most positive reinforcers and which has the most reinforcement value, as well as access to a larger range of aversive stimuli, will exert the most control over an individual's behavior.

There is a good reason to suspect, however, that Sutherland

---

[54] This, then, is essentially differential reinforcement as Jeffery presents it. We have attempted to show how this is congruent with differential association. Further, while Jeffery ignores the key concepts of "definitions" and "excess," we have incorporated them into the reformulation. These definitions, viewed as verbalizations, become discriminative stimuli; and "excess" operates to produce criminal behavior in two related ways: (1) verbalizations conducive to law violation have greater discriminative stimulus value than other verbalizations, and (2) criminal behavior has been more highly reinforced and has produced fewer aversive outcomes than has law-abiding behavior in the conditioning history of the individual.

was referring, not so much to differential associations with other persons, as differential associations with criminal *patterns*. If this supposition is correct, this proposition can be clarified by relating it to differential contingencies of reinforcement rather than differential social associations. From this perspective, the experimental evidence with regard to the various schedules of reinforcement is of major significance. There are three aspects of the schedules of reinforcement which are of particular importance here: (1) the *amount* of reinforcement: the greater the amount of reinforcement, the higher the response rate; (2) the *frequency* of reinforcement, which refers to the number of reinforcements per given time period: the shorter the time period between reinforcements, the higher the response rate; and (3) the *probability* of reinforcement, which is the reciprocal of responses per reinforcement: the lower the ratio of responses per reinforcement, the higher the rate of response.[55]

Priority, frequency, duration, and intensity of association with criminal persons and groups are important to the extent that they ensure that deviant behavior will receive greater amounts of reinforcement at more frequent intervals or with a higher probability than conforming behavior. But the frequency, probability, and amount of reinforcement are the crucial elements. Hence it is the coming under the control of contingencies of reinforcement that selectively produces the criminal definitions and behavior. Consequently, let us rewrite this proposition to read:

VII. *The strength of criminal behavior is a direct function of the amount, frequency, and probability of its reinforcement.*

IX. "While criminal behavior is an expression of general needs and values, it is not explained by those general needs and values since noncriminal behavior is an expression of the same needs and values."

In this proposition, Sutherland may have been reacting, at least in part, to the controversy regarding the concept "need." This controversy is now essentially resolved. For we have finally come to the realization that "needs" are unobservable, hypothetical, fictional inner-causal agents which were usually invented on the spot

---

55 R. T. Kelleher and L. R. Gollub, "A Review of Positive Conditioned Reinforcement," *Journal of the Experimental Analysis of Behavior* (October, 1962), pp. 543-597. Because the emission of a fixed ratio or variable ratio of responses requires a period of time, the rate of responding will indirectly determine the frequency of reinforcement.

to provide spurious explanations of some observable behavior. Furthermore, they were inferred from precisely the same behavior they were supposed to explain.

Although we can ignore the reference to needs, we must discuss values. Values may be seen as reinforcers which have salience for a number of the members of a group or society. We agree with Sutherland in so far as he means that the nature of these general reinforcers does not necessarily determine which behavior they will strengthen. Money or something else of general value in society will reinforce any behavior that produces it. This reinforcement may depend upon noncriminal behavior, but it also may become contingent upon a set of behaviors that are labeled as criminal. Thus, if Sutherland can be interpreted as meaning that criminal and noncriminal behavior cannot be maintained by the same set of reinforcers, we must disagree. However, it may be that there are certain reinforcing consequences which only criminal behavior will produce, for the behavior finally shaped will depend upon the reinforcer that is effective for the individual. Nevertheless, it is the reinforcement, not the specific nature of the reinforcer, which explains the rate and form of behavior. But since this issue revolves around contingencies of reinforcement which are handled elsewhere, we will eliminate this last proposition.

CONCLUDING REMARKS

The purpose of this chapter has been the application of the principles of modern behavior theory to Sutherland's differential association theory. Although Sutherland's theory has had an enduring effect upon the thinking of students of criminal behavior, it has, till now, undergone no major theoretical revision despite the fact that there has been a steady and cumulative growth in the experimental findings of the processes of learning.

There are three aspects of deviant behavior which we have attempted to deal with simultaneously, but which should be separated. First, how does an individual *become* delinquent, or how does he learn delinquent behavior? Second, what *sustains* this delinquent behavior? We have attempted to describe the ways in which the principles of modern behavior theory are relevant to the development and maintenance of criminal behavior. In the process, we have seen that the principle of differential reinforcement is of crucial importance. But we must also attend to a third question, namely, what sustains the pattern or *contingency* of reinforcement? We only have hinted at some of the possibly important variables. We have mentioned briefly, for example, structural factors such as the level of deprivation of a particular group with regard to important social reinforcers, and the lack of effective reinforcement of "lawful" behavior[56] and the concomitant failure to develop the appropriate behavioral repertoires to produce reinforcement legally.[57] We have also suggested that the behaviors which do result in reinforcement may, themselves, gain reinforcement value and be enforced by the members of the group through the manipulation of various forms of social reinforcement, such as social approval and status, contingent upon such behaviors.[58] In short, new norms may develop, and these may be termed delinquent by the larger society.

There are many other topics that are of direct relevance to the problem of deviant behavior which we have not been able to discuss for lack of space. For instance, no mention has been made of some outstanding research in the area of punishment. This topic is, of course, of prime importance in the area of crime prevention. To illustrate some of this research and its relevance, it has been found experimentally that the amount of behavior suppression produced by response-contingent aversive stimuli is a direct function of the intensity of the aversive stimulus, but that a mild average stimulus may produce a dramatic behavior suppression if it is paired with reinforcement for an alternative and incompatible behavior. Furthermore, it has been discovered that, if an aversive stimulus is repeatedly paired with positive reinforcement, and reinforcement is not available otherwise, the aversive stimulus may become a discriminative stimulus (S^D) for reinforcement and consequently not decrease the behavior's frequency of occurrence. There are, in conclusion, numerous criteria that have been used to evaluate theories. One such set is as follows:

1. The amount of empirical support for the theory's basic propositions.

[56] Robert K. Merton, *Social Theory and Social Structure*, Glencoe, Ill.: The Free Press, pp. 161-195. For a more complete discussion of social structure in terms relevant to this chapter, see Ch. 13, of this book.

[57] *Ibid.*, and Richard A. Cloward, "Illegitimate Means, Anomie, and Deviant Behavior," *American Sociological Review*, 24 (April, 1959), pp. 164-177.

[58] Albert K. Cohen, *Delinquent Boys: The Culture of the Gang*, Glencoe, Ill.: The Free Press, 1955.

2. The "power" of the theory, that is, the number of data that can be derived from its higher-order propositions.
3. The controlling possibilities of the theory, including (*a*) whether its propositions are, in fact, *causal* principles, and (*b*) whether its propositions are stated in such a way that they suggest possible *practical* applications.

What dissatisfaction there has been with differential association can be attributed to its scoring low on these criteria, especially the first and the third. We submit that the reformulated theory presented here answers some of these problems and better meets each of these criteria. It is our contention, moreover, that the reformulated theory specifies not only the conditions under which criminal behavior is learned, but also some of the conditions under which deviant behavior in general is acquired. Finally, although we have not stated our propositions in strictly axiomatic form, a close examination will reveal that each of the later propositions follow from, modify, or clarify earlier propositions.

15

Some Behavioral Aspects of Social Change and Economic Development

John H. Kunkel

Homans' belief that it is necessary to "bring men back" into socio-logical analysis[1] has been vividly expressed in several recently pro-posed theories of social change; individuals have been considered as originators and carriers of social change, and especially as entre-preneurs, innovators, innovating personalities, achievement-ori-ented businessmen, intellectuals, etc.[2] The "return of men" im-mediately creates problems, however, concerning the nature of these men and their effects on sociological analysis. Emphasis on individuals and their activities in social change, for example, raises questions concerning the determinants of behavior, the rela-tionship between individuals and social structure, and the role of social structures in social change.[3]

[1] George C. Homans, "Bringing Men Back In," *American Sociological Review*, 29 (December, 1964), pp. 809-818.

[2] The most conspicuous examples are the following: H. G. Barnett, *Inno-vation*, New York: McGraw-Hill Book Company, 1953; Everett E. Hagen, *On the Theory of Social Change*, Homewood: Dorsey Press, 1962; Richard T. La Piere, *Social Change*, New York: McGraw-Hill Book Company, 1965; Don Martindale, *Social Life and Cultural Change*, Princeton: D. Van Nostrand Co., 1962; and David C. McClelland, *The Achieving Society*, Princeton: D. Van Nos-trand Co., 1961. Not all of these theories will be discussed in detail.

[3] Moore points out, for example, that controversies presently revolve "around questions of psychological or institutional primacy in the determina-

Reprinted in part from *Pacific Sociological Review*, Vol. 9 (1966), pp. 48-56, and *Economic Development and Cultural Change*, Vol. 13 (1965), pp. 257-277, with permission of the author and editors. Slightly edited.

Several recent theories of change emphasizing individuals answer these questions in terms of various characteristics and processes of man's internal state, such as his needs, personality, and mind.[4] These elements are combined into one or another psychodynamic model of man, and behavior is postulated to be a function of the various components and processes of man's internal state. Social structures are assumed to play a minor, limiting role and are usually treated as residual elements.[5]

This conception of man and the role of social structure in social change has been criticized on several grounds. Questions have been raised concerning, for example, the validity and adequacy of psychodynamic models of man,[6] the neglect of the social

---

tion of behavior, and the minimal significance attached to the possibility of adult personality transformation or attitudinal change." Bert F. Hoselitz and Wilbert E. Moore (eds.), *Industrialization and Society*, Paris: Unesco, 1963, p. 361.

[4] For example, the theories by Hagen, *op. cit.* and McClelland, *op. cit.*

[5] The problem of the role of social structure in social change is well illustrated by Hagen and Martindale, who assign a limiting role to social structure, holding that innovators are successful in altering their surroundings only when the social structure permits change.

[6] For examples and an analysis of the shortcomings of studies employing various elements of man's internal state, see Reinhard Bendix, "Compliant and Individual Personality," *American Journal of Sociology*, 58 (November, 1952), pp. 292-303, and William A. Hunt and Nelson F. Jones, "The Experimental Investigation of Clinical Judgment," in Arthur J. Bachrach (Ed.), *Experimental Foundations of Clinical Psychology*, New York: Basic Books, 1962. Wilbert E. Moore has criticized Hagen and other theorists emphasizing man's internal state as maintaining their positions "out of a desire for . . . purity of doctrine . . . and not out of an objective appraisal of real phenomena" (Wilbert E. Moore, "The Strategy of Fostering Performance and Responsibility," in Egbert De Vries and José Medina Echavarria (Eds.), *Social Aspects of Economic Development in Latin America*, New York: UNESCO, 1963, p. 236). The difficulties involved are well illustrated in Eliezer B. Ayal, "Value Systems and Economic Development in Japan and Thailand," *Journal of Social Issues*, 19 (January, 1963), pp. 35-51. He attempts to "find some causal relationship between the value system and modes of behavior associated with economic development. The transmission of the general orientation of the value system into action is conceived here as being materialized through the intermediary of 'propensities.' This shorthand term stands for internalized behavioristic and instrumental values, or predispositions to action, which have their origin in the value system" (pp. 38-39). In the course of his work Ayal describes the value system of Japan and Thailand and the behavior patterns of individuals in these countries. The link between these phenomena is not extensively treated, however, and remains essentially unclear.

environment as a determinant of man's activities,[7] and the difficulties encountered in explaining rapid social change.[8] It may be advisable, therefore, to consider alternative answers to the questions posed by the individualistic approach to social change.

Several writers have recently suggested that men's actions can be explained, and the relationship between individuals' behavior and the social context may be fruitfully analyzed, in terms of observable actions and their often repeated, specific relations to preceding and simultaneous events. Such a "learning" or "behavioral" approach has been advocated by Adler and Bolton, has been extensively employed by Homans, and has also been used, although somewhat obliquely, by Blau and Yinger.[9] LaPiere, who holds that "what is significant in the study of social change is not the motives of men, but their actions,"[10] exemplifies this position in the area of social change.

Despite the proposals set forth by these writers, much recent research and theorizing in social change still relies heavily on one or another psychodynamic model of man.[11] A major reason for the continued emphasis on various aspects of man's internal state is the fact that no systematic and reasonably complete alternative has been proposed so far. The behavioral approach in its extant form, including mainly the work of Adler, Blau, and Homans in

[7] As discussed, for example, by Alex Inkeles, "Personality and Social Structure," in *Sociology Today*, New York: Basic Books, 1959, pp. 249-276, and in Leonard Krasner and Leonard P. Ullman (Eds.), *Research in Behavior Modification*, New York: Holt, Rinehart & Winston, 1965.

[8] As described, for example, by Allan B. Holmberg, "Changing Community Attitudes and Values in Peru," in Richard N. Adams et al., *Social Change In Latin America Today*, New York: Harper, 1960, and by Gustav F. Papanek, "The Development of Entrepreneurship," *American Economic Review*, 62 (May, 1962), pp. 46-58.

[9] Franz Adler, "A Unit Concept for Sociology," *American Journal of Sociology*, 65 (January, 1960), pp. 356-364, and "The Value Concept in Sociology," *American Journal of Sociology*, 62 (November, 1956), pp. 272-279; Charles D. Bolton, "Is Sociology a Behavioral Science?" *Pacific Sociological Review*, 6 (Spring, 1963), pp. 3-9; George C. Homans, *Social Behavior, Its Elementary Forms*, New York: Harcourt, Brace, 1961; Peter M. Blau, *Exchange and Power in Social Life*, New York: John Wiley & Sons, 1964; and Milton Yinger, "Research Implications of a Field View of Personality," *American Journal of Sociology*, 68 (March, 1963), pp. 580-592.

[10] LaPiere, *op. cit.*, p. 147.

[11] The most conspicuous recent example, besides Hagen's work, is George K. Zollschan and Walter Hirsch (Eds.), *Explorations in Social Change*, Boston: Houghton Mifflin, 1964.

the field of sociology, contains so many gaps and raises so many questions, especially concerning larger social phenomena, that it cannot yet be considered as a useful alternative.

The following sections constitute an attempt to relate certain learning principles derived from one branch of experimental psychology to the analysis of social change. The behavioral model of man which forms the basis of the analysis is as yet somewhat crude and may have to be revised as the principles upon which it is based are refined. Even in its present tentative form, however, it contributes to the solution of the problems which are encountered when individuals are considered to be the causes and carriers of social change and economic development.[12]

A BEHAVIORAL MODEL OF MAN

The basic postulate of the proposed model of man is that most behavior patterns are learned through differential reinforcement. The specific principles involved in the shaping, maintenance, alteration, and extinction of behavior has been discussed in some detail in Chapter 1, and thus it is only necessary to point out that in the work of experimental psychologists the environment is usually regarded as "given," while emphasis centers on the individual's behavior. Learning principles are concerned with behavior *in general*; they cannot, by themselves, account for specific activities of individuals or particular types of social relations, because men live in a social context. In order to account for *specific* behavior patterns and social relations observed in a particular society or group, sociological elements must be added to the operation of learning principles.

SOCIOLOGICAL COMPONENTS OF THE MODEL

As long as behavior is considered to be largely a function of various components of man's internal state, the social phenomena surrounding the individual are of relatively minor importance. Ac-

---

[12] It should be remembered that the proposed model is only one of several which can be constructed on the basis of psychological principles, since every psychological "school" gives rise to a model of man appropriate to its underlying principles and point of view. Whether or not sociologists will benefit from a model, and which of several models should be used, depends on its validity and on whether or not the model can explain and predict the phenomena of interest in a particular analysis.

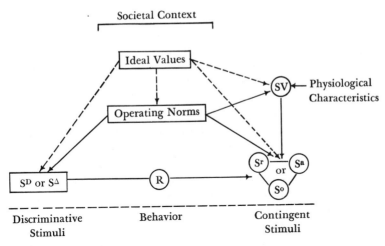

Fig. 1. Glossary of Terms. R: any activity. S^r: reinforcing stimulus (loosely speaking, rewards). S^a: aversive stimulus (loosely speaking, punishment). S^0: absence of any consequences. S^D: stimulus in whose presence R has been reinforced. S$^\triangle$: stimulus in whose presence R has not been reinforced. SV: state variables (i.e., conditions of deprivation and satiation).

cording to the proposed behavioral model, the social context of the individual, including his immediate family, the various groups to which he belongs, his community, and the society of which he is a part, plays an important role in the shaping, maintenance, and alteration of behavior. The immediate and wider social context, especially the value system and the norms arising from it, determine, as illustrated in Fig. 1, three things.[13]

1. *The Contingent Stimuli*
The contingencies of an individual's action, that is, the rewards and punishment, are largely determined by the values and norms

[13] The diagram centers on individuals and their activities, and assumes the values and norms as given. Values and norms could not be conceived in this fashion if the analysis were centered on larger units, such as institutions and social systems, for values and norms would in that case refer to the systematic behavior of others in the role of S^D and contingencies. A similar point is made by Judith Blake and Kingsley Davis in their "Norms, Values, and Sanctions," in Robert E. L. Faris (Ed.), *Handbook of Modern Sociology*, Chicago: Rand McNally, 1964. It should be remembered that the investigation of these principles is of relatively recent origin. As more information becomes available, especially on group phenomena, the simple model of man proposed here will doubtlessly become more complex.

of a society (or group), which may be said to perform functions analogous to those performed by the experimenter in the laboratory. A distinction should be made between "ideal values," which indicate the behavior that *should* be reinforced, and the "operating norms," which determine what behavior is *actually* reinforced.

2. The State Variables

The efficacy of any reward or punishment is dependent upon the set of deprivation characteristics of members of a society or particular group, and this set is a function of the social context, that is, the values and norms. Values, and especially norms, directly affect the creation of secondary (or learned) deprivations, for example, social isolation in a society emphasizing togetherness, but they also play a role in the definition of primary (or physiological) state variables, as in the cultural determination of the kinds of food permissible for the reduction of hunger. The set of effective deprivations, then, and the appropriate and acceptable procedures for their reduction may be expected to vary from group to group, thus giving rise to a variety of actions even within the same society.

3. The Discriminative Stimuli

By reinforcing particular behavior patterns when they appear in a specific context, the normative system of a society determines which aspects of an individual's context will eventually take on controlling properties. Honesty in social relations, for example, will usually be rewarded except in special circumstances when customs of politeness indicate the necessity of white lies. If there are ambiguities and conflicts in the normative structure regarding appropriate behavior and circumstances, the result will be incompletely established (S^D) and individuals will be uncertain as to how they should act.

From the point of view of this behavioral model of man, the analysis of social structure is centered on the norms and values of a society and the behavior of others which is usually involved in the actual rewarding and punishing of an individual's actions. Since behavior is learned in the past and maintained in the present, the social context of both the past and the present is an integral part of any analysis of men's activities; human behavior, in fact, cannot be understood except in terms of the operation of the social context. The sociologist's role in the explanation and prediction of men's actions may thus be taken to consist of two main parts.

1. The analysis of the social context through whose operation behavior elements, patterns, and chains are shaped, maintained, altered, or extinguished. For example, the expression of values and norms through the actions of others who thereby affect the behavior of the individual is an essential component of any explanation (and prediction) of behavior.

2. The analysis of interlocking behavior patterns and chains, especially as they are found in aggregates of individuals. This would include the description of the system of mutual differential reinforcement, the conditions for maintaining behavior, and the conditions which produce alterations in actions.

Questions concerning man's internal state are not at issue, for the existence of an internal state is not denied. What is important is the recognition that many behavior patterns of interest to the sociologist can be explained in terms of learning principles which involve a minimum of inference and supposition concerning man's internal state. These principles, in effect, form the important link between individual behavior and sociocultural phenomena, and thus contribute to the explanation of activities through the analysis of sociological characteristics and processes.

IMPLICATIONS OF THE BEHAVIORAL MODEL

The utilization of certain learning principles in sociological investigation does not necessarily lead to psychological reductionism, as has sometimes been charged,[14] since human activities, according to these principles, cannot be understood without reference to the role played by the social context in the shaping, maintenance, and alteration of action. The psychologist is interested in the processes involved in the establishment of behavior patterns and chains in individuals, but he usually takes the social context as given. No psychologist can answer the questions of the sociologist concerning how particular behavior patterns in a society originated and

---

14 For example, by Otis Dudley Duncan and Leo Schnore, "Cultural, Behavioral, and Ecological Perspectives in the Study of Social Organization," *American Journal of Sociology*, 65 (September, 1959), pp. 132-153, and by Rodney Needham, *Structure and Sentiment*, Chicago: University of Chicago Press, 1962.

what their functions are, how and why certain patterns of the thousands available to an individual or group are selected for reinforcement, how the societal context affects behavior, and how the social system operates to maintain itself through the inter-relations of millions of complex behavior chains.

A sociologist's concern with overt activities which can be observed and objectively measured should not lead to the conclusion, however, that all sociological concepts can be expressed simply in terms of behavior. Since behavior patterns not only are associated with present stimuli but are also a function of previous experiences—for example, reinforcement under similar circumstances—both the individual's learning capacity and his history must be included in the study of present behavior.

Adler's equating of values with behavior, for example, or Yinger's definition of personality in terms of behavior minimizes the temporal and dynamic aspects inherent in any behavioral situation. What is important in sociological analysis is not only behavior, but also the probability of men acting in specified ways. This probability is a function of men's perceptions of the probability of reinforcement in specific circumstances, and the degree of similarity between the previously established discriminative stimuli and the present context. A problem faced by sociologists is that the situation in which any man finds himself at any time is far more complex than are ordinary experimental situations in which the relevant variables are known or can be controlled. In ordinary life there usually are several unknown factors and uncertainties which affect behavior and its maintenance, and these must be taken into account. For example, conflicting or ambiguous standards of reinforcement (such as inconsistent societal norms), poorly established deprivation characteristics, changing or uncertain discriminative stimuli, inadequately learned behavior chains, and unknown or shifting reinforcement probabilities are present in any social situation. Thus it is impossible to speak of anything but actual and perceived probabilities, such as the probability that rewards will be given, that an action will occur, or that a person has learned—and can perceive the proper discriminative stimuli.

APPLICATIONS TO THE ANALYSIS OF SOCIAL STRUCTURE

According to this behavioral model of man, a society's or community's ideal values and operating norms influence behavior by determining the discriminative and contingent stimuli associated with an action. Actually, however, it is the activities of persons in the individual's social environment which affect his action. Behavior patterns labeled "hard work," for example, are reinforced by others through the payment of wages, the display of approbation, or the conferral of prestige (itself a complicated set of activities). The "connection" between one person's hard work and the consequent approval of other people is established by values and norms, as is the "connection" between one person or his action and the discriminative stimulus for the behavior of another. Such inferred connections or actually observed regularities among men's activities are described by the construct "norm," while theoretically existing connections or regularities are described by the construct "value." The social context which determines the actions of an individual may be considered to consist, therefore, of both the behavior patterns of other people and the "connections" which link some of them to the individual's actions. By itself, the behavior of other persons is of no significance for the individual, and by itself the normative or value system of a community is ineffective. It is only in the combination of these elements that an effective social context for the shaping, maintenance, and alterations of behavior patterns is established.

Figure 2 illustrates, in very simplified form, the operation of the social context in the maintenance of two behavior chains. A

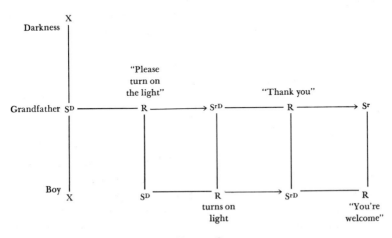

FIGURE 2

grandfather requests that a boy turn on the light in the evening. Darkness and the presence of the youngster are the S^D for the grandfather's saying, "Please turn on the light." These words and the associated gestures are the S^D for the boy's switching on the light. This action, in turn, is a reinforcer for making the request, and at the same time it is an S^D for thanking the youngster—hence S^{rD}. The grandfather's thanks reinforce the boy's turning on the light and are the S^D for the conventional final response of the interaction. In this example the horizontal lines in Fig. 2 indicate the sequence of action for one individual, while the vertical lines relate one person's actions to another's behavior and indicate the role which one individual's behavior plays in the learning and maintenance of someone else's activities. Generally speaking, the horizontal lines reflect the operation of learning principles and thus constitute the realm of psychologists' inquiries. The vertical lines reflect a society's values or norms (in this case both) and are the sociologists' focus of interest. In order to account for the uniformity of action which characterizes much of daily life, it is necessary to have a knowledge of *both* horizontal and vertical "lines" or relationships, that is, of *both* learning principles and sociological factors such as norms. Since one cannot be reduced to the other, psychological reductionism is impossible.

The oversimplified relations diagrammed in Fig. 2 show how a number of activities are chained together to form one rather coherent unit of action occurring within a short span of time. Peripheral elements, such as gestures, smiles, and the movements associated with turning on the lights, have been disregarded for the sake of clarity. Preceding chains—for example, those which established the various S^D, state variables (SV), and reinforcers—have not been included, although even this small sample of behavior cannot be completely understood without knowledge of the preceding events which established the presently operating discriminative and contingent stimuli.

The behavior patterns of interest to sociologists are usually much more complicated, of course, but even complex social phenomena consist essentially of chains like those illustrated in Fig. 2. Social structure, then, may be visualized as consisting of complex lattices, involving the behavior chains of large numbers of individuals in a variety of circumstances, affected by a number of (at times conflicting) values and norms. For some purposes it may be useful to combine individuals subject to the same S^D and contingencies into one unit and to speak of housewives as a group, for example, or to combine S^D with the associated behavior patterns and to speak of roles. If institutions are viewed as sets of roles, it is apparent that even large-scale social phenomena can be analyzed in terms of behavior and learning principles. It may be concluded, then, that any social unit, no matter what its size, can be dissected into small behavioral units and individual chains, and that an understanding of the form and operation of large systems depends on knowledge of how the constituent elements operate and are related to one another.

This conception of the nature and operation of the social context of individuals is in keeping with commonly accepted views of social structure. According to Levy, for example, social structure refers to "a pattern, i.e. an observable uniformity, of action or operation."[15] Parsons [16] speaks of social structure as a system of integrated roles (which are, basically, sets of activities), and Gerth and Mills,[17] to give a final example, view social structure as a set of interrelated institutions—which they define in terms of roles (whose basic referent is, again, behavior). The behavioral model's contribution to the analysis of social structure, then, is its explanation of how the activities of an individual are chained together, how behavior is shaped and maintained, and how the activities of a number of persons are related to form larger behavioral and social units.

The behavioral approach to the analysis of social phenomena concentrates *initially* on the actions of individuals and the principles governing their activities. Since, however, learning principles can explain behavior only in very *general* terms, sociological factors such as norms become necessary components of the analysis of *specific* behavior patterns. *How* men drink, *what* men drink, and *when* they drink, for example, can be explained only in terms of sociological factors—for learning principles it is important only *that* men drink. The behavioral analysis of social phenomena, therefore, *eventually* leads to the basic sociological position that social phenomena must be explained socially. By indicating the role of psychological (learning) principles, the behavioral approach

15 Marion J. Levy, Jr., *The Structure of Society*, Princeton: Princeton University Press, 1952, p. 57.

16 Talcott Parsons, *The Social System*, Glencoe: Free Press, 1951, pp. 114 ff.

17 Hans Gerth and C. Wright Mills, *Character and Social Structure*, New York: Harcourt, Brace, 1953, pp. 22 ff.

neither denies nor emphasizes the psychological characteristics of man.

APPLICATIONS TO THE ANALYSIS OF SOCIAL CHANGE

Since the behavioral model of man consists of principles which are postulated to govern behavior in general, it has neither a static nor a dynamic bias, and thus it cannot affect the remainder of a theory in either direction. Many of the problems encountered in the individualistic approach to social change can be profitably investigated by means of this neutral model of man. For example, questions concerning the determinants of behavior, the role of the individual and social structure in social change, and factors determining rates of change can be at least partially answered in terms of the behavioral approach. In addition, hypotheses concerning various aspects of social change unrelated to individuals arise in the behavioral analysis of social structure.

The Determinants of Behavior

Man's internal state as a determinant of action plays an important role in several recently proposed theories of social change. Hagen,[18] for example, explains individuals' activities in terms of needs and personality. According to him, social change occurs because, over several generations, changes in personality and need structures come into being, triggered by changes in the ways sons are treated by their fathers, who create various degrees of anxiety, frustration, guilt, and hate in their children. He postulates that the determinants of behavior are various components of man's internal state, largely created in childhood, and difficult if not impossible to change in later years. McClelland, in turn, hypothesizes that economic development is largely a function of the level of need achievement in both individuals and nations;[19] high need achievement motivates individuals to become economic entrepreneurs and nations to industrialize. He postulates that the determinants of behavior are to be found in man's internal state, specifically in a complex set of motives, which is largely the result of youthful experiences when particular need structures are built into a man's personality. Spengler, finally, in a less thoroughly worked-out hy-

[18] Hagen, *op. cit.*
[19] McClelland, *op. cit.*

pothesis, holds that social change is a function of what is in the minds of the people, and especially in the minds of the governing elite. Social change, thus, "above all entails (the) transformation of the content of the minds of individuals who are interacting in ways significant for politico-economic development."[20]

Although man's internal state is given great importance, the present lack of objective investigating procedures and accurate knowledge concerning it make its utility doubtful. Hypotheses which include the internal state as an important variable are difficult to test (and refute) since validated measuring devices are yet to be constructed—observers' interpretations and subjective inferences are the major sources of information concerning the internal state. The consequent danger, as Hagen himself notes, is that the

. . . analysis of sequences of personality change must be speculative, or to use the term loosely, intuitive. Sequences of action and of reaction within individuals are difficult to analyze, at least with the tools yet devised by social scientists. In the main, the analysis must be by introspective examination and rearrangement of elements of behavior within oneself until one feels that one has arrived at a sequence that accounts for certain outer manifestations in other individuals.[21]

McClelland's analysis of TAT tests, child-raising procedures, and observations of various behavior patterns (such as painting) makes his methodology less subject to criticism, but it may still be asked whether he is actually dealing with need achievement or only with its behavioral manifestations, that is, various activities. Actually, his work is based mainly on the behavior of individuals, the factors which give rise to certain actions, and the results of behavior (i.e., various products), and thus it may be asked why an internal characteristic such as need achievement must be postulated at all. Since, finally, it is postulated by these and other writers that the internal state, once formed, is difficult if not impossible to change (any change must occur over generations), successful planning for change and the existence of rapid social change do not fit into the theory. Examples of such phenomena cannot be satisfactorily explained.

20 Joseph J. Spengler, "Theory, Ideology, Non-economic Values, and Politico-Economic Development," in Ralph Braibanti and Joseph J. Spengler (Eds.), *Tradition, Values, and Socio-Economic Development*, Durham: Duke University Press, 1961, p. 5.

21 Hagen, *op. cit.*, p. 201.

When these theories are analyzed in detail—as examples of psychodynamically oriented theories—it becomes apparent that characteristics of the internal state are merely postulated, often on the basis of psychological theories which are yet to be tested and validated. Certain behavior patterns are assumed to reflect an internal state, and it is then assumed that in discussing these behavior patterns one is actually saying something about the internal state.[22] If an investigator is unwilling to rely on such postulates and assumptions, he is forced to restrict his discourse to observable actions or to make other assumptions—hopefully those which have some empirical foundations.

According to the behavioral model described above, the determinants of human action are to be found in learning principles and their operation within the social context. It should be possible, then, to explain the phenomena discussed by Hagen and McClelland on the basis of these principles. Such an illustration will now be provided. It must be remembered, however, that this quick recasting does not do justice to either the two theorists or the behavioral approach; it is merely an indication of how a behaviorist might proceed in the analysis of existing data and thereby derive further hypotheses from them.

According to Hagen, for example, the economic innovators who give rise to social change are usually members of the fallen elite who have acquired innovating personalities over a number of generations. According to the behavioral model, activities, once learned, persist until rewards cease, discriminative stimuli disappear, or incompatible patterns are reinforced. Members of a society's elite, along with peasants, continue to act in their accustomed ways since the relevant elements of their conditioning context have not changed. Members of the displaced elite, however, find that "old" patterns are no longer reinforced (e.g., by deferential behavior on the part of others), the discriminative stimuli have disappeared (e.g., their exalted position), and new patterns such as working with one's hands are no longer followed by punishment (e.g., derision). Under such circumstances new behavior patterns are likely to arise, since some old ones are being extinguished,

---

[22] This is a doubtful procedure since the inferences on which it is based cannot be validated with presently available analytical tools and since no independent measures of the internal state exist. For more extensive discussions of these procedural difficulties, see Melvin H. Marx, *Theories in Contemporary Psychology*, New York: The Macmillan Company, 1963.

others are no longer followed by aversive stimuli, and new patterns, such as entrepreneurial activity, are being increasingly rewarded. From these considerations it may be hypothesized that the appearance of entrepreneurial activity will be delayed by the perceived probability of a return to the "good old days" and the consequent verbal reinforcement of "old" activities, and by the perceived probability that new patterns, such as business activities, will not lead to success.

Hagen also points out that between the displacement of the elite and the rise of entrepreneurs there intervenes a period of "retreatism" or apathy. A similar phenomenon is observed when conflicting and incompatible behavior patterns are reinforced. Apathy as a function of incompatibility does not disappear until one pattern has been greatly weakened and the other has become clearly dominant. Anxiety, hate, aggression, guilt, and other phenomena of man's internal state, used by Hagen to account for changes in behavior and the long period of intervening apathy, need not be postulated in this behavioral explanation, for the activities of both youths and adults can be explained in terms of learning principles and their operation within a social context.[23]

McClelland's theory of need achievement and the data upon which it rests can be similarly reinterpreted in order to avoid heavy reliance on inferences concerning man's internal state and on the use of explanatory fictions. Since his work has been concerned with economic development rather than with social change as such, it will be discussed later in connection with that topic.

The Role of Individuals and Social Structure

The general approach of individualistic theories of change is exemplified by that of Martindale, who maintains, "The individual and only the individual is the source of all innovation. The fact that all patterned behavior is learned carries with it the possibility that at any time any individual can potentially transform the social patterns in which he participates.[24] Although it is ad-

---

[23] Support for this view is accumulating quite rapidly, especially in the area of behavioral therapy (as opposed to psychotherapy). For evidence and references, see Leonard Krasner and Leonard P. Ullman (Eds.), *op. cit.*, and Leonard P. Ullman and Leonard Krasner (Eds.), *Case Studies in Behavior Modification*, New York: Holt, Rinehart, & Winston, 1965.

[24] This quotation and the following ones are from Martindale, *op. cit.*, pp. 38-39, and 502.

missible that the analysis of social change begins with the action of individuals, the determinants of such action must also be considered. If social change is postulated to be the result of alterations in individuals' behavior patterns, the causes of such behavioral changes must be investigated, and the role of social structure must be specified. In most theories, social structure is a passive, limiting phenomenon whose role in social change remains quite unclear. Martindale's position, for example, that "innovation bubbles up wherever there is social space for it" is inadequate, but other long-time students of social change, such as LaPiere and Moore, have also been unable to resolve the central problem of individualistic theories of social change, namely, the relationship between individuals (and their actions) and the social context, that is, social structure.

The behavioral model of man presents one possible solution, as was indicated previously. At the same time, however, the model effectively reduces the role of individuals in social change. If a person's activities are in large part a function of the structure and operation of the social context, it is inadequate to speak of individuals as the "causes" of social change. Concern with the activities of individuals is merely one step in the analysis of social change (or of any social phenomenon, for that matter); individuals comprise no more than a methodologically convenient starting point, for the behavioral model of man leads from the activity of the individual directly to the operation of social and ecological factors.

An example of the effects of the social context on individuals is presented by Banfield in his study of Montegrano.[25] The major value system of the community—amoral familism—indicates that individuals are interested only in a kind of short-run hedonism centering on the nuclear family. People in this village are suspicious of each other and "lazy," no one tries to get ahead, gossip and scandal-mongering are rampant, cooperation is completely lacking, and there are no community or service organizations.

Such behavior patterns are shaped and maintained by the contingencies which are attached to them, in terms of other people's reactions. Men do not work hard, for example, because they have great difficulties in collecting their wages—only after several remonstrances do workers receive their pay. Those who try to get

[25] Edward C. Banfield, *The Moral Basis of a Backward Society*, Glencoe: Free Press, 1958.

ahead, perhaps by attempting to earn extra money or by producing more, are automatically assumed to be taking more than their share, and malicious gossip results. Local officials will not attempt to start services or projects because of the aversive consequences which are immediately forthcoming (e.g., rumors concerning bribes or embezzlement).

The absence of saving and capital formation in peasant communities of Latin America, to present another example, appears to be due to the aversive consequences of saving rather than to personality characteristics.[26] When villagers are expected to foot the bill for religious festivals, and when the number of such mayordomias for which one is responsible depends on the amount of money one is reputed to have, such obligations present effective aversive consequences not only of saving but to some extent of hard work also. The apathetic "character" of the people of Montegrano, then, and the absence of saving in the lives of many peasants can be explained in terms of behavioral principles operating in a social context. To test this hypothesis, it should be possible to show that the alteration of the social context, and especially of the contingencies of certain activities, should alter these activities. Such a test will be described below.

Two major sources of changes in individuals' activities may be derived from the behavioral model of man. Since one person's actions usually are part of the social context of other individuals, changes in one person's behavior patterns constitute alterations in someone else's social context, and thus the activities of the second person may be expected to change. If it is postulated that behavior patterns are not perfectly learned (i.e., the probability of their occurrence is not 1.0), and that individuals in the course of their lives interact with a variety of persons—each presenting slightly different contingencies—variations and changes may be expected to occur in any individual's actions and reactions, leading to changes in others' activities. Moore's postulate of incomplete socialization[27] is amplified and made more specific by the behavioral model.

[26] See, for example, Manning Nash, "Capital, Saving, and Credit in a Guatemalan and a Mexican Indian Peasant Society," in Raymond Firth and B. S. Yamey (Eds.), *Capital, Saving and Credit in Peasant Societies*, Chicago: Aldine, 1964.

[27] As discussed, for example, in Wilbert E. Moore, "A Reconsideration of Theories of Social Change," *American Sociological Review*, 35 (December, 1960), pp. 810-818.

Another source of change is the gross alteration of the social and physical environment (e.g., increased contact with strangers, soil exhaustion, or planning). This usually means that previously existing S^Ds disappear and that reinforcement probabilities attached to various behavior patterns are altered, leading to the extinction of some actions and the shaping of new patterns. Changes in secondary state variables—for example, the creation of new deprivations—similarly affect behavior through the establishment of new reinforcers such as money, and the reduction of formerly effective rewards (e.g., status in a village). It may be hypothesized, then, that social change can be planned and accelerated by the systematic alteration of the factors which affect the shaping and extinction of behavior, regardless of the "character" or "personality" of the people concerned.[28]

From the preceding discussion it is apparent that a strictly individualistic theory of social change cannot be rigorously maintained, for the determinants and effects of individuals' activities cannot be understood without the analysis of the social context. Psychological principles may explain *how* behavior patterns are established in individuals, but *which* activities are shaped, and *why* they are changed, are topics which cannot be discussed in terms of these principles.

Whether the social context inhibits or accelerates change, then, is basically a question of what types of action the operation of the social context shapes in individuals. One type of normative system, for example that of Montegrano, shapes behavior patterns which are not likely to bring about indigenous social change of the type usually termed "community development." Another type of context, such as that of Vicos, helps shape different activities, with far-reaching results, as will be shown below.

The Rate of Social Change

According to Hagen's theory, the rate of social change is always low. The slow pace of economic development, for example, is in

---

[28] When, conversely, contingencies cannot be altered, the probability of change is low. For cases, see William R. Bascom and Melville J. Herskovits, *Continuity and Change in African Cultures*, Chicago: University of Chicago Press, 1959, and Edward H. Spicer (Ed.), *Human Problems in Technological Change*, New York: Russell Sage Foundation, 1952. A slightly different point of view is presented in Charles J. Erasmus, *Man Takes Control*, Minneapolis: University of Minnesota Press, 1961.

part a consequence of the assumption that personality is created largely in childhood, changing only slightly, if at all, in later life, and that intergenerational changes in personality structure are quite gradual. Hagen postulates, for example, that several generations are necessary before the sequence "displacement of the elite → innovation" is completed. The exact amount of time varies from about 150 years (Japan) to around 700 years (England), but there is no way of predicting the time or explaining the variations so far encountered. Thus Hagen's theory condemns presently underdeveloped nations to poverty and stagnation for at least the next few generations.[29] Confronted by examples of rapid change, such as the great increase of entrepreneurs in Pakistan within a few years, Hagen can only hypothesize that "new personality may not cause a conspicuous change in behavior until it has burst through external barriers. Where institutional change suddenly eliminates former barriers and creates new economic opportunities, a slow budding process may suddenly burst into bloom."[30] The nature and operation of such barriers are not indicated, however, and the process of blooming personalities is not clear.

In McClelland's theory, too, change is assumed to be slow, for need achievement is created largely in childhood and is not expressed in behavior (e.g., innovation) until roughly two decades later. Since, however, need achievement can be created in schools, presently underdeveloped countries can engage in programs to increase the number of entrepreneurs twenty years hence. Although some historical experiences support the view that social change occurs slowly, there is increasing evidence that the rate of change may also be high, that it can be increased by human intervention, and that the usual low rate of change is the result of certain factors while a high rate is the function of other elements. A theory of change, then, should be able to account for varying rates of change by analyzing the types of factors which promote and retard change.

The behavioral model indicates what some of these factors are. Activities will remain unchanged as long as state variables, discriminative and contingent stimuli, remain the same. Thus, if the physical environment does not change and if no new tools are

---

[29] As has been pointed out by, for example, McClelland, "A Psychological Approach to Economic Development," in *Economic Development and Cultural Change*, 12 (April, 1964), pp. 320-324.

[30] Everett E. Hagen, "Comment" on Papanek, *op. cit.*, p. 60.

introduced, the probability of social change is quite low. Techno-logical improvements, or deliberate alterations of contingencies or state variables introduced from outside the society, will result in alterations of behavior patterns and relationships, that is, in social change. It may be concluded, then, that the rate of change depends on the effectiveness with which the factors affecting behavior are changed. Since many of these factors can be altered by social poli-cies, the rate of change is to some extent controllable. The high rate of industrialization in Pakistan, for example, has been due to the sharp increase in the number of entrepreneurs, which in turn was the consequence of governmental taxation and incentive pro-grams. In addition, deliberate efforts to raise the status of business-men reinforced the activities associated with that occupation.[31] A low rate of change, then, may be hypothesized to be due to a lack of systematic programs to alter behavior, or to inadequate power and knowledge on the part of officials to alter sufficiently the rele-vant factors of the social context of individuals.[32]

The slow rate of social change, especially in connection with programs designed to accelerate economic development, is an acute problem in many underdeveloped countries today. It is desirable, therefore, to briefly indicate the role of the behavioral approach in the analysis of economic development.

APPLICATIONS TO THE ANALYSIS OF ECONOMIC DEVELOPMENT
In the literature on economic development which has grown up within the last decade, the explanations and determinants of human behavior have usually been assumed to be one or another characteristic—or set of elements—of an individual's internal state.[33] From this assumption it follows that, if behavior is to be altered, the characteristics of the internal state must be changed first. A list of psychological prerequisites of economic development, such as the propensity to save, rising expectations, and the motivation to work in factories, has been proposed, and the conclusion is drawn that only if the content of men's minds, their values and attitudes, are changed, can behavior patterns conducive to eco-

---

[31] Papanek, *op. cit.*

[32] This is not to imply that *any* type of change can be produced by de-liberate efforts. The limits of the behavioral approach in fostering social change have not yet been investigated.

[33] See, for example, Ayal, *op. cit.*; Braibanti and Spengler, *op. cit.*; Hagen, *op. cit.*; and McClelland, *op. cit.*

nomic development—for example, risk taking—come into being. This point of view is illustrated in Spengler's thesis that "the state of a people's politico-economic development, together with its rate and direction, depends largely upon what is in the minds of its members, and above all upon the content of the minds of its elites, which reflects in part, as do all civilizations, the conceptions men form of the universe."[34] In addition to psychological prerequisites there are assumed to be social prerequisites, characteristics of groups or nations which must exist if economic development is to occur, or which must come into being along with industrialization. On the national level social prerequisites are usually considered in terms of political climate, social circumstances, or economic atmosphere.[35] Unfortunately, however, the social and psychological prerequisites of economic development are usually not well defined and are difficult to put into measurable terms. A more important problem is that no methods of changing values, attitudes, and personality are known at present, and thus the analysis of economic development in terms of social and psychological prerequisites never develops beyond the level of description and enumeration.

From the previous discussion it is apparent that concern with values, attitudes, and most other psychological prerequisites as causes of behavior rests on a fundamental misconception of human behavior and the disregard of basic psychological principles discovered in the experimental analysis of behavior. To change man's activities one need not be concerned with altering values; one needs to change only certain elements of the operant conditioning context of which all men at all times are an integral part. According to the behavioral model, the psychological prerequisites of economic development are certain behavior patterns, whereas the social prerequisites are the determinants of the reinforcing and discriminative stimuli by means of which desired behavior patterns are shaped and maintained.

Although individual and group values, attitudes, and personalities have been frequently employed in the study of social change and economic development, comparatively little attention

34 Spengler, *op. cit.*, p. 4.

35 For example, Clark Kerr et al., *Industrialism and Industrial Man* (Cambridge: Harvard University Press, 1960); Gerald M. Meier and Robert E. Baldwin, *Economic Development, Theory, History and Policy* (New York: John Wiley & Sons, 1957); Walt W. Rostow, *The Stages of Economic Growth* (Cambridge: Cambridge University Press, 1960).

has been paid to the meaning of these concepts and their implications for theoretical analysis and practical policies. In order to evaluate the adequacy and utility of these concepts, a few hopefully representative samples of the large number of extant definitions will be discussed. The questions and problems to which these definitions give rise will be outlined, and alternative conceptions, based on the behavioral model of man, will be presented. The utility of these alternatives will be evaluated in terms of four cases of economic development, and their implications for action will conclude the chapter.

Values

Values have been variously defined as "goals which are objects of inclusive attitudes";[36] "a conception, explicit or implicit, distinctive of an individual or characteristic of a group, of the desirable which influences the selection from available modes, means, and ends of action" (p. 395);[37] and "that aspect of motivation which is referable to standards, personal or cultural, that do not arise solely out of immediate tensions or immediate situations" (p. 425). The term value "implies a code or standard . . . which organizes a system of action" (p. 430) which the individual has internalized, and which has thus become part of a person's internal state. A complex set of values forms a value orientation, which has been defined as "a generalized and organized conception, influencing behavior, of nature, of man's place in it, of man's relation to man, and of the desirable and undesirable as they may relate to man-environment and interhuman relations " (p. 411). In studies not explicitly concerned with the elucidation of concepts, the definitions of value are usually more vague, such as the conception of a value system as "the syndrome of general rules, sanctions, and goals underlying the activities of a society."[38]

In everyday life the confusion of meanings may be overlooked, but in any serious attempt to explain and predict behavior a concept such as value presents severe limitations, since it must be inferred from behavior. The inferences made, however, cannot be

[36] Theodore M. Newcomb, *Social Psychology*, New York: Dryden Press, 1950, p. 130.

[37] This quotation and the following ones are from Clyde Kluckhohn, "Values and Value-Orientations in the Theory of Action," in Talcott Parsons and Edward A. Shils (Eds.), *Toward A General Theory of Action*, Cambridge: Harvard University Press, 1951.

[38] Ayal, *op. cit.*, p. 35.

validated with presently available means, since there are no ways of defining or measuring values independently of inferences based on behavior. This makes possible the capricious use of reaction-formation, a procedure which may be used to support any theory by either taking phenomena at face value or considering them in terms of their opposites; as a consequence any theory can be supported by any data. Whether such inferred characteristics can be considered as causes of behavior, useful in the prediction of human activities, is quite doubtful.

A way of eliminating the difficulties encountered with the definition and measurement of values is based on the simple question of how one knows what a man's values are. Knowledge of a man's values is based either on observations of his activities or on his verbal statements that he values, for example, honesty. But what are the dimensions of the value of honesty? One may say that a man values honesty highly, and that this value he has internalized determines his behavior. But what are the referents for this statement? In reality one is saying something about certain activities and nothing else. In speaking of a man's values, or in inferring his value orientation, one is in actuality only summarizing certain features of many of his activities in shorthand form. One is abstracting, from a great variety of behavior patterns, certain manifestations or elements called "honest" or "honesty" in a society. One is able to predict to some extent a man's behavior on the basis of his past activities in a particular situation, but one is not thereby saying anything about the causes of human behavior.

According to the behavioral model, a man acts honestly if honesty leads to success, for example, in terms of reducing deprivations or avoiding noxious consequences. The causes of the behavior called honest, then, are to be found in the conditioning history of the individual, in the course of which he has learned that particular behavior patterns, namely, those defined by his society as honest, are usually rewarded, whereas their opposites usually are not. Along this line of reasoning Homans has defined value as "the degree of reinforcement and punishment [a person] gets from [behavior]."[39] Other conceptions of value, emphasizing the indi-

39 George C. Homans, *Social Behavior, Its Elementary Forms, op. cit.*, p. 40. Adler defines values in an even more strictly behavioral fashion; according to him, "For the purposes of sociological scientific discourse, values and actions may safely be treated as identical" (Franz Adler, "The Value Concept in Sociology" *op. cit.*).

vidual's experiences of the past and expectations of the future within the dynamic social context, are the following.

1. From the point of view of the *observer*. An individual's value refers to the probability that a particular behavior pattern will occur under specific conditions. When it is said, for example, that honesty is a strongly held value, a well-internalized value, or that it is deeply ingrained in an individual or group, the speaker means simply that the probability of the occurrence of particular activities is high; conversely, if a value is lightly held, the probability of the occurrence is low. "Value" usually refers to specific elements in a set of behavior patterns, as, for example, "integrity." The value "integrity" indicates that certain activities—defined by a society as indicating integrity—are prevalent in a group or are commonly observed in an individual.

2. From the point of view of the *individual*. Probably the most common conception equates "value" with reinforcer. A person who values money, for example, may be expected to act so as to be rewarded with money. Value may also refer to the perceived set of probabilities that certain events will occur—rewards will be obtained—if particular activities are performed. When a person is said to value honesty, for example, it means that he believes that activities defined as honest by his society will be rewarded—and thus he will be honest quite often. These rewards may exist on earth or they may be conceived as being found only in heaven; if the latter is the case, a man may be honest even without material rewards and hence may be regarded as "irrational" by those who do not share the same definition of reward or who are not aware of the schedule of reinforcement.

3. From the point of view of the *sociologist*. Values are constructs which refer to the regularities of behavior patterns over time or, more specifically, to the relationships which exist (theoretically) between the actions of one man and the behavior of another. These regularities and relationships are often summarized in terms of "standards" which ideally determine state variables and discriminative and contingent stimuli. This conception, which was discussed in greater detail in a previous section, is quite compatible with the conceptions of value from the point of view of observers and individuals, for it differs from them mainly in terms of the inferences and ascriptions which the sociologist may be unwilling to make.

No matter how values are defined, and no matter what their

role is in an analysis, their foundation is always the observed behavior and/or its consequences. Thus it is necessary to investigate
the previous experiences of individuals and to study the history of
groups in order to properly understand the foundation and role
of values. In other words, "values" may be considered as summary
expressions of an individual's or group's conditioning history.

In terms of the behavioral model of man, the concept "value"
as used in daily life and in much scientific discussion has at least
five different meanings:

1. The probability that a behavior pattern will occur.
2. The reinforcer itself (with implications for the nature of
the state variables).
3. The probability that a behavior pattern will be reinforced.
4. The theoretically existing relationships among activities.
5. The ideal standards of behavior.

Since it is usually not clear which meaning is employed in a
discourse, it is best to disregard all meanings except the fourth
and fifth. That is, instead of using "individuals' values" one might
speak of the "probabilities of an action's occurrence." The term
"value orientation," for example, actually refers to nothing more
than the often complicated set of probabilities that a system of
behavior patterns and chains has occurred or will occur with great
frequency, implying thereby a complex set of discriminative and
contingent stimuli.

Attitudes

Allport has defined attitude as "a mental and neural state of readiness, organized through experience, exerting a directive or dynamic
influence upon the individual's response to all objects and situations with which it is related."[40] Newcomb admits that the concept
of attitude is nothing more than a theoretical device referring to
"the state of readiness for motive arousal. It is the individual's susceptibility to stimulation capable of arousing the motive in him.
. . . Attitudes thus represent persistent, general orientations of the
individual toward his environment."[41]

Such conceptions of attitude present great difficulties to the
student of economic development since "states of readiness" cannot be inferred with certainty and depend ultimately on actual

[40] Quoted by Kluckhohn, *op. cit.,* p. 423.
[41] Newcomb, *op. cit.,* pp. 118-19.

activities for validation. It is, furthermore, doubtful whether the determination of human behavior can be assigned to "theoretical devices."

The problem of what an attitude really is can again be approached best by asking what the referents of the term are. How do we know what a person's attitudes are? We learn by observing his behavior or by asking him directly, and we usually will not be content with his word but will try to observe his actions. We say that a person has a particular attitude toward an object, person, event, or someone's actions, if he behaves in specified ways, toward the object and if his behavior is consistent and persists over time. A "negative attitude" toward saving, for example, refers to certain elements of behavior which are common in his actions toward money, banks, and goods. "Attitude" thus is simply a shorthand term for certain abstracted characteristics common to a number of behavior patterns which are frequently repeated whenever certain conditions prevail.[42] Attitudes are to be considered as summary measures of behavior, a convenient labeling of actions, and not as causes of any activity. Once we know what the common elements of a large group of activities are, we can better predict the behavior of a person when his behavior pattern falls into the same group, or when he is exposed to the appropriate discriminative stimulus, but we can say nothing about the causes of his actions.

Personality

Another important term which appears in discussions of economic development is "personality," conceived by Hagen as the "complex of qualities other than purely bodily ones which determine how an individual will behave in any given situation."[43] Newcomb defines this elusive term as "the individual's organization of predispositions to behavior . . . that which 'holds together' all his motive patterns—that which determines that all his behavior, both attitudinal and expressive, shall be just what it is."[44] Thus personality is considered to be the totality of values, attitudes, needs, and motivations of an individual and is equivalent to the individual's internal state itself. The difficulty with the concept of personality lies in the fact that "personality is something that must be in-

[42] This conception is based in part on personal communications with I. Goldiamond.

[43] Hagen, *op. cit.,* p. 99.

[44] Newcomb, *op. cit.,* p. 344.

ferred from facts. Hence, in actual practice, the personality is an abstract formulation composed by the psychologist."[45]

The definition of this concept can be made more specific by considering the referents of personality: how do we know what the personality of a man is? Again the answer is his behavior—only by looking at his activities can we know his personality. A "pleasant personality," for example, on close examination turns out to be no more than a set of behavior patterns which is similar to our own or which we judge to be pleasant on the basis of some standard. The problem of the referent of personality has been implicitly recognized by some writers, for example, Parsons and Shils, who define personality as "the organized system of the orientation and motivation of action of an individual actor"[46] and then again as simply the "relatively ordered system of resultant actions in one actor."

According to the behavioral model, personality is defined as the set of behavior patterns which an individual has acquired under the special circumstances of his development and as a member of his society and the several groups to which he belongs. Personality, then, is not inferred from behavior or considered to be a cause of it, but rather *is* the sum of a man's activities which show some durability. Just as in the psychodynamic model the term "personality" includes all of a person's values and attitudes, so in the behavioral model it includes the behavior of individuals and the probabilities that various patterns of behavior will occur under specific circumstances. Changes in personality, then, refer not to changes in the internal components of this entity, but rather to the altered behavior patterns themselves and the changed probabilities of their expression based on the altered reinforcement contingencies and circumstances of the social environment. The determinants of change, then, are to be sought not in alterations of a man's values or attitudes, but in the changes of the social context which determines the perceived and actual probabilities of reinforcement in terms of which the individual acts—that is, the reinforcing stimuli, their schedules, and the associated discriminative stimuli provided by a society and the various groups to which the individual at all times belongs.

45 Clyde Kluckhohn and Henry A. Murray, *Personality in Nature, Society, and Culture*, New York: Knopf, 1953, p. 6.

46 This quotation and the following ones are from Parsons and Shils, *op. cit.*, pp. 7, 38.

An important component of personality formation is the process of internalization. The importance assigned to the process, however, has not resulted in a general understanding of it; as Kluckhohn says, "Most acquired or derived drives are dependent upon group values which the individual has somehow interiorized as part of himself."[47] According to the behavioral model, the internalization or interiorization of values refers to the learning of various sets of probabilities that certain behavior under specific circumstances will be rewarded or punished. This is not to imply that the individual is necessarily able to explicitly state these probabilities or their determinants. Internalization, or the learning of probabilities and discriminative stimuli, is the result of communication and experience and depends upon the consistency of reinforcement, the number of occasions on which particular behavior patterns have been rewarded under specific circumstances, and the reinforcement schedule in effect during the learning process.

Summary View of These Concepts
"Values," "attitudes," "personality," and "the process of internalization" are terms whose major function in everyday life is to communicate probabilities and descriptions of behavior. The statement that someone has a pleasant personality, that his values of honesty have been well internalized, and that he never lets his attitude toward success interfere with these values serves the major purpose of increasing the chance that an observer's predictions of his behavior will be accurate. Certainly we have a better idea of how a person will act than if we had no access to the statement. But although we can predict with some confidence how the person will act under certain circumstances, we cannot say *why* the person behaves in the particular way that he does.

Concepts such as "values" are useful in the language of everyday life but cannot be considered as explanations of behavior, since these terms have, as their ultimate referents, the present behavior of individuals and nothing else. In behavioral terms, any differences among these concepts are essentially differences in the abstractions made, in the point of view of the observer, and in the temporal context of the individual's activities. If one is interested in the description of behavior, these concepts may be used;

47 Kluckhohn, *op. cit.*, p. 429.

but it is not necessary that they be part of any causal analyses or that they be considered as part of any causal nexus.

The contribution of the sociologist to the analysis of economic development involves the investigation of the interrelation and reciprocal influence of human behavior and the social context, the study of the structure of the social context, and the analysis of the changes in the social context which are necessary to create behavior patterns conducive to industrialization. Any sociological analysis will be inadequate as long as poorly defined concepts are given great weight as integral parts of causal chains when, in fact, these concepts refer to the "end products" of such chains. The essential characteristics of attitude, value, and personality may best be summarized in terms of the probability that a particular behavior pattern will occur under certain conditions of deprivation and discrimination, based on the conditioning history of the individual. From the point of view of the individual, these concepts all include the perceived probability that a particular action, under certain conditions, will be reinforced by the social and physical environment. The specific task of the sociologist, then, includes the analysis of such sets of probabilities, their origin and determinants, and the study of ways to maintain or alter them.

The psychological and social prerequisites of economic development cannot be established by changing the values, attitudes, or personalities of people in underdeveloped countries, as has so often and so eloquently been argued in recent years. In fact, to say that values, attitudes, and personalities must be changed is to say nothing more than that changes in behavior patterns must occur. There is no disagreement on this point, but the question is: how can these changes be brought about? The belief that values, attitudes, and personality determine behavior, that behavior will change once attitudes or values are altered, and that one must consequently concentrate on the alteration of these, besides being meaningless, leads into blind alleys of theory and action. This is so because there are no generally recognized definitions of these terms which include elements other than behavior or inferences based upon it, since the components of these terms are often unclear (e.g., state of readiness), and since there are no generally recognized procedures for altering what are said to be a person's values or personality.

The behavioral approach, emphasizing the shaping of behavior by means of differential reinforcement and punishment, opens a way not only to the testable explanation and prediction of behavior but also to its alteration. The behavioral model of man leads to the conclusion that, if behavior is to be altered, changes must first occur in the reinforcing stimuli, in their presentation and schedule, and in the discriminative stimuli. Such modifications can be accomplished only through the alteration of the aspects of the social context which influence these components of the conditioning process. Changes in character, rather than being the prerequisite of economic development, are to be considered as concomitants and consequences, in so far as economic development means, for the average individual, changed reinforcers, altered schedules, and new behavior patterns, newly reinforced, under new circumstances. The problem of economic development, then, is not the alteration of character or certain elements of it, but the change of the selected aspects of a man's social environment which are relevant to the learning of new behavior. Analytical emphasis on the role of economic and industrial elites in underdeveloped countries rests on the fact that the necessary changes in the social environment would be difficult to produce for the population as a whole but are, in effect, produced by the social structure itself for a small number of persons.

The recent emphasis placed on the role of individuals in economic development has raised the question of the role of social structures in the process. The efficacy of the "structural approach" to economic development is explicitly recognized by the behavioral model of man, in that a person's activities at any moment not only are the consequences of a long conditioning history, but also are influenced by the immediately surrounding social context, which maintains or alters the probabilities of behavior patterns established in the past and is largely responsible for the shaping of new patterns. The behavioral model of man, then, reconciles the "individualistic" and the "structural" approaches to economic development by recognizing the effects on behavior of both the past and the present societal context. The difficulties encountered when values, attitudes, and personalities are considered as causal factors, and the advantages of considering these concepts from the behavioral point of view, will now be presented.

EXAMPLES OF BEHAVIORAL ANALYSIS

INDIAN VALUES AND ECONOMIC DEVELOPMENT

The uncertainties which surround the meaning and measurement of value as a causal factor are well illustrated in the recent discussion concerning the role of Indian values in the process of industrialization. The question which faces the social scientist is: Are Hindu values detrimental or conducive to India's economic development?

India's spiritualism, philosophy of renunciation, and asceticism, which especially in the eyes of Western observers present almost insurmountable obstacles to economic development, turn out to be quite different in reality from any deductions based on scriptures. As Singer points out, Indians in their everyday activities are as materialistically oriented as Western men; "this-worldly asceticism" is quite widespread; and the philosophy of renunciation is just that: a philosophy to which most men pay lip service, perhaps an ideal, but an ideal which attracts few practitioners in everyday life. In Singer's words, "The Indian world view encompasses both material and spiritual values, and these can be found in the behavior of the ordinary Indian existing side by side and in functional interdependence. . . . Overspecialization on the spiritual, the sacred, and the life-denying [is] to be found [mainly] in the interpretations of some Western scholars."[48]

The backwardness and stagnation of India's economic system thus cannot be explained in terms of other-worldly religious values. As Singer and Srinivas point out, Indian peasants are eminently practical in their approach to the physical and social world. Why then the backwardness? Because of social and political institutions, such as the caste system, say Srinivas and Lambert. In fact, "it is possible that popular interpretations or misinterpretations of *maya, samsara,* and *karma* were the aftermath of defeat—rather than its cause."[49] Carve, too, mentions that it is "not

---

[48] Milton Singer, "Cultural Values in India's Economic Development," *The Annals,* CCCV (May, 1956), p. 83. See also Richard D. Lambert, "Social and Psychological Determinants of Savings and Investments in Developing Societies," in Bert F. Hoselitz and Wilbert E. Moore (Eds.), *Industrialization and Society* (Den Haag: UNESCO, 1963).

[49] M. N. Srinivas, "A Note on Mr. Goheen's Note," *Economic Development and Cultural Change,* VII, No. 1 (October, 1958), p. 6.

necessary to go into the early economic and social history of industrially developed nations to show that the tempo of work is more often the reflection of opportunities of progress than a prime cause."[50] After all, Christianity, too, is quite other-worldly and glorifies poverty and humility, but this does not mean that men's lives revolve around these poles. As Singer points out:

> . . . a society dominated by a philosophy of renunciation need not be a society of ascetics. In India, ascetics and holy men have never constituted more than a tiny fraction of the population. There have always been a sufficient number of householders willing and able to do the world's work. And while the ideals of asceticism may indirectly influence the general population, not all of these influences oppose social reform and economic development.[51]

The reasoning of many Western observers of India seems to be as follows: The sacred literature of India contains certain values which are internalized by the people, who then act in accordance with these values; thus India is economically stagnant, and there is little hope of economic growth. This reasoning is based on a number of inferences and assumptions which have not yet been supported by evidence obtained by replicable procedures based on objective criteria of measurement. The major assumptions are that the sacred literature contains a particular set of values and no other, that this set is internalized by a majority of the population, that the values internalized by the Indians are precisely those which the Westerner "sees" in the sacred literature, that men's actions are a function of internalized values, and that the immediate circumstances in which the individual finds himself play a rather insignificant role in the determination of his behavior.

It is apparent from Singer's work, however, that the values "contained" in the Bhagavad-Gita, for example, are merely interpretations of words which men choose to make; Westerners interpret the work as "teaching" certain values, whereas Gandhi thought that quite different values were being "taught." The interesting questions which remain are: what values *are* contained in the Bhagavad-Gita; and have we any means of discovering which values *are* taught?

[50] D. G. Carve, "Comments," *Economic Development and Cultural Change,* VII, No. 1 (October, 1958), p. 7.

[51] Milton Singer, "Postscript," *Economic Development and Cultural Change,* VII, No. 1 (October, 1958), p. 11.

The controversy centering on the suitability of Indian values for economic development leads to the conclusion that, as long as definitions of values are vague, as long as proof of their existence and criteria for their measurement are absent, and as long as it is impossible to determine with any certainty the role of individuals' values in the determination of behavior, it is better to disregard the concept of "individuals' values" in the analysis of behavior. This conclusion is justified not only by the difficulties encountered in the use of the concept but also by the fact that the concept, as ordinarily conceived, is not necessary in the explanation and prediction of behavior. This point will be elaborated in the following sections.

THE ARGENTINE VALUE ORIENTATION AND ECONOMIC DEVELOPMENT

Fillol has hypothesized that "the basically passive, apathetic value-orientation profile of the Argentine society must be regarded as the *critical* factor limiting the possibilities of steady, long-run economic development" (p. 3).[52] Hence it follows that "only a transformation of Argentina's value-orientation profile towards higher degrees of activity can insure that economic gains achieved during one period will not be wiped out in a following one by social and political dislocations" (p. 110).

The starting point of Fillol's analysis is that actions are determined by personality and the environment. Personality, in turn, is considered as consisting of value orientations and a need structure. These elements are interrelated, for "in the process of personality formation, needs which have been acquired help to determine value orientations, and acquired value orientations help to determine needs" (p. 7). A society's basic personality type, which helps to determine the behavior of groups, is ascertained "by defining those dominant value orientations shared by the bulk of the society's members as a result of the early experiences which they have had in common" (p. 6).

Fillol's description of the Argentine value orientation is nothing more than a description of behavior and a listing of particular abstractions which are useful in tying-together various disparate elements of action. These abstracted elements of descrip-

[52] This quotation and the following ones are from Thomas R. Fillol, *Social Factors in Economic Development, The Argentine Case*, Cambridge: The M.I.T. Press, 1961.

tions of behavior (e.g., suspiciousness) are assumed to be causal factors, but there is no indication that they are anything more than abstractions of current behavior. One of the basic conclusions of the study, that the Argentine "value-orientation profile is inimical to the emergence of social relationships which would enable individuals to act concertedly in the pursuit of common goals" (p. 22), means nothing more than that the abstracted elements of a number of behavior patterns are incompatible with cooperation. Nothing has been said regarding causes, and to the extent to which causal qualities are assigned to simply descriptive abstractions, there is no way to break the vicious circle—or the circular argument—of cause and effect.

The insecure foundation of Fillol's argument is especially apparent in his discussion of needs. Need aggression, for example, is defined as "a characteristic of the individual's personality which makes [him] feel satisfaction from the act of being aggressive in thought or action, from attacking others and overcoming real or imaginary opposition forcefully" (p. 23). Such a need shows itself in various actions—that is, is inferred from behavior— and receives theoretical underpinning from psychodynamic theories which have yet to be validated. If the theories are not supported by behavioral data, reaction formation is assumed to have taken place, for no other reason than that the data do not fit the theory. An Argentinian's "apathy is actually a means of suppressing his need aggression, a cover for the anxiety and intense rage which must arise in a society built on authoritarian values" (p. 24). What objectively validated proof is there for the existence of a great variety of needs, the repression of some and the expression of others, and the statement that anxiety and rage *must* be created in certain societies? If such necessity follows from a theory, and if such a theory must be supported by the capriciously applied concept of reactionformation, it is perhaps better to investigate alternative means of analysis.

The behavioral model of man permits a much simpler explanation of the Argentine data, based on principles validated by often repeated experiments under controlled conditions. There is no necessity to refer to explanatory fictions such as need structures and value orientations or basic personality types. Fillol himself acknowledges repeatedly that an individual's previous experiences are of great importance. Early experiences result in value orientations, some needs are culturally transmitted, and thus personality (a combination of the two) is also the result of the socialization process.

Value orientations and needs are unnecessary and cumbersome abstractions which may be made but play no role in explaining behavior since they *are* aspects of behavior. Men learn to be suspicious, to be fatalistic (that is, to behave in ways defined as fatalistic), or to concern themselves only with the present, just as they learn to behave in opposite fashion. It all depends on what behavior patterns are reinforced and on what chains are slowly established over the years. There is, then, no need to postulate an intervening variable (such as value orientation) which explains nothing and only clutters up the analysis. Fillol's and especially Hagen's elaborate analysis of why people do not engage in manual labor rests, for example, on status and self-conceptions, feelings of superiority, and justification of individual worth.[53] According to the behavioral model, manual labor is not engaged in because it is followed by aversive reinforcers, such as derision, and because in the past the peasant who worked hard often lost the fruits of his labor. It would follow that, if the circumstances of work were altered, manual labor would occur more frequently; as we shall see, this is precisely what happens.

The fact that the concepts used by Fillol in his analysis of the Argentine problem are useless not only in the explanation of behavior but also in the manipulation of it—as in deliberately altering work habits—is illustrated in the discussion of how to change the behavior of individuals. Fillol's suggestions for the solution of Argentina's problem are essentially concerned with changes in the presently operating reinforcers and controlling stimuli.[54] New incentives for both workers and managers, worker participation in management, explanations of decisions to those affected by them, the encouragement of cooperation, and the hands-off attitude of government are all aspects of attempts to shape new behavior patterns through a new system of differential reinforcement. Fillol's theoretical foundation for proposing these changes—that parental rage will no longer be directed against children, and that therefore children will be less authoritarian and will thus bring about, in two or three generations, value orientations in harmony with economic development—is irrelevant and is based, in any case, on in-

[53] Fillol, *op. cit.,* pp. 16-17; Hagen, *op. cit.,* pp. 76-81.
[54] Fillol, *op. cit.,* Ch. 6.

correct conceptions of man and the determinants of his activities. At the very least, the relationship between managerial policy changes and alterations in needs and value orientations is not spelled out, and the process of the formation of values is not clear at all. It seems, indeed, that Fillol, in the last section of his work, pays verbal tribute to his earlier concepts but disregards them in his concrete descriptions of possible solutions. Behavioral analysis of the Argentine situation would have arrived at the same specific recommendations for the amelioration of the problem—the changing of behavior patterns—as did Fillol; the behavioral alternative would have been simpler, based on validated principles and relying on a minimum of inferences.

VALUES AND CHANGE IN THE PERUVIAN ANDES

In 1952 the Indian community of Vicos was in a highly disorganized state: "positions of responsibility in public affairs were lacking, . . . adequate leadership did not develop, and almost no public services were maintained" (p. 80).[55] In addition, "cooperation within the community was the exception rather than the rule, and resistance to the outside world was high. Attitudes toward life were static and pessimistic" (p. 81). In short, the tenor of life had not changed much since the arrival of the Spaniards three hundred years earlier. Agriculture was based on the motto "plant and pray," and Indian peasants usually worked slowly and produced little more than the barest minimum of basic necessities.

In order to change this situation, the determinants of behavior would have to be ascertained and alterations in them would be the first step in any project of change. Instead of altering the personality and attitudes of the Indians, however, Holmberg and his associates (there never were more than two advisors on the hacienda) began a broad and intergrated approach to the problem of development, involving economics and technology, nutrition and health, education, and social organization.

Holmberg did not asume that behavior is determined by childhood experiences converted into a largely unchangeable personality and value orientation which can be altered only over the generations. Rather than involve himself in the manipulation of the internal state of the Indians—for example, their values—he

[55] This quotation and the following ones are from Allan R. Holmberg, *op. cit.*

analyzed the contemporary circumstances of Vicos life and proceeded to change these. Up to 1952 the fate of the Indian had depended almost completely on the whims of the patron, who made all decisions and left Indian officials with only religious tasks to perform. If the context of the Indian's existence could be changed—if the reinforcement contingencies could be altered—behavior would be altered too. Holmberg and his associates assumed that "in the area of economic activity positive steps could be and were taken, for the desire to improve the community's livelihood existed, at least in a dormant state" (p. 84). The reason for this desire being dormant was to be found in the labor setup of the hacienda, for the Indian "is not willing to labor long and well under all conditions. In most instances he will do so only when he is working for himself or within his own culture. When working outside this framework, under conditions in which he is held in disrespect and generally receives little in the way of reward, he usually tries to get by with as little effort as he can" (p. 85). Furthermore, it was assumed that help given by outsiders should not involve unilateral activities—the villagers themselves should be involved in all projects; a "welfare approach [would not] lead to a solid type of environment, rooted in the desires and responsibilities of the community itself" (p. 85).

In terms of concrete action, the worst abuses of the hacienda system, such as unpaid maid service to the patron, were eliminated easily. Work for the patron began to be paid for. New agricultural methods and fertilizer were introduced through a system of loans to Indians, and peasants were allowed to keep what they produced. Power was gradually transferred to the Indian leaders of the community; weekly meetings were held, decisions were discussed, and gradually more and more important responsibilities were given to Indians—to make decisions, carry them out, and be responsible for the success or failure of their own activities. Education, which had not before been a goal, became one when the quality of teachers improved, when children were no longer used for maid and gardening service, and when a school lunch program was instituted. Later on, the ability to read and the knowledge of the outside world gained through education became sufficient reinforcers in themselves to make the school program a success.

The results of the Vicos project are indicated by the transfer of the hacienda to the Indian community in 1957, when the Indians gained complete control over the workings of the hacienda.

Holmberg's conclusions are significant in their optimism based on experience: The process of modernization within this long-isolated population can take place without the loss of certain fundamental and positive values that are deeply ingrained in Indian society: respect for work, frugality, and cooperation. . . . If granted respect, the Indian will give respect. If allowed to share in the making of decisions, he will take responsibility and pride in making and carrying them out. The fundamental problem of the sierra is largely a problem in human relations (p. 97).

The success of the Cornell-Peru project was due not to the alteration of Indian behavior (e.g., working hard) by means of a prior change in attitudes or values, but rather to changes in the reinforcing stimuli (e.g., the ending of exploitation and the instituting of wage labor), which altered the behavior preceding them. Holmberg's model of human behavior was, implicitly, the behavioral and not the psychodynamic one, for he set about changing the environment of Indian life. Although he used such terms as "dormant desires for improving one's livelihood," "ingrained values of work," and "values regarding education," he operated on the basis of an essentially behavioral frame of reference. This is especially notable in his discussion of education, which is almost a model of planned change based on the behavioral approach. As soon as educational experiences were no longer aversive (e.g., poor teachers who used students as servants), more students came and learned more, and when reinforcing stimuli were added (e.g., the school lunch program), the educational process became a fully accepted "value" within the community, based partly, of course, on the success of students in the intellectual and vocational subjects taught. "Values," then, seem to be easily created in the right circumstances—which follows logically from the behavioral model of man. The "problem of human relations" in the sierra consists, essentially, of the aversive stimuli reinforcers provided by the mestizo and white social environment. As long as Indian initiative and labor are not rewarded, and as long as the Indian's attempts to better his position are followed by punishment (confiscation and derision), the problem of the sierra as described by Holmberg and others will remain.

The experience of Vicos does not fit readily into the internalist model of behavior. Were men's actions determined by personalities and values, largely created during youth, any changes in a community would be slow in coming about, since changes in values and personality, especially in adults, are considered to take a long time if they can be produced at all. The fact that fundamental changes in the activities of the people of Vicos occurred in a five-year period—changes so radical that the Indians within five years were able to efficiently operate the hacienda by themselves, creating a surplus where for decades little more than basic necessities had been produced—shows either that internal states are unimportant in determining the behavior of man, or that these internal states can be easily and swiftly manipulated by alterations in the social environment. The behavioral approach, which holds that human activities are largely the result of operant conditioning procedures which are intimately tied to the social environment, finds support in the success of the Vicos project, whereas this project confronts the psychodynamic position with important questions which can be answered only by proposing fundamental changes in the conception of internal states and their relation to behavior.

ACHIEVEMENT MOTIVATION AND ECONOMIC DEVELOPMENT

McClelland and his associates have investigated the hypothesis that one aspect of man's internal state, the need for achievement, is largely responsible for economic development. "A society with a generally high level of n-Achievement will produce more energetic entrepreneurs who, in turn, produce more rapid economic development" (p. 205).[56] Need for achievement is one of a constellation of needs which characterizes man, determines much of human behavior, and is created largely during childhood. The sources of high need achievement are "early mastery training . . . provided it does not reflect generalized restrictiveness, authoritarianism, or rejection by parents" (p. 345), and the "'amplitude of affective change' associated with the achievement situation" (p. 352). Mothers who are actively involved in what their sons are doing are also likely to create high n-Achievement in them. The best environment for high n-Achievement consists of "reasonably high standards of excellence imposed at a time when the son can attain them, a willingness to let him attain them without interference, and real emotional pleasure in his achievements short of overprotection and indulgence" (p. 356). Conversely, "one of the ways in which the child can develop low n-Achievement is through having careless or indulgent parents who do not expect great things from him"

[56] This quotation and the following ones are from McClelland, *op. cit.*

(p. 351). The same effect is produced if achievement is expected too early, so that the child is not physiologically able to be successful.

The evidence for the existence of the achievement motive is the verbal, artistic, or active behavior of children and adults and the literature of nations. Children who build high towers, students whose stories based on TAT pictures show much "achievement imagery," and the "achievement imagery" found in plays, novels, and grammar school readers of ancient and modern nations are all considered to reflect the need for achievement. McClelland's data support the hypothesis, for economic development (variously defined, depending on the information available) usually follows periods of history in which the need achievement of a nation is found to be high.

Two questions regarding need achievement must be asked How valid are the inferences made, and what evidence—not based on inferences—exists for such an aspect of man's internal state? From McClelland's work it appears that there is no way to check on the validity of inferences except through other inferences; the high reliability of the scorers of stories, and the great consistency which various observers show in determining the degree of n-Achievement in various phenomena, simply indicate that observers, once trained, make the same inferences or, more accurately, are able to categorize stories, pieces of art, etc., with high consistency. This, however, does not validate the instrument and does not prove that n-Achievement exists. Need for achievement, it is apparent, is a theoretical construct, a characteristic common in the verbal and actual behavior of many individuals and groups. It is a hypothetical causal factor which is, in reality, nothing more than an abstraction of concrete behavior.

The behavioral analysis of McClelland's data leads to the following conclusions. They are based on the behavioral model of man and involve no characteristics of a postulated internal state.

Need for achievement is an abstracted characteristic common to various types of behavior, indicating achievement direction or striving for success. Like other activities, striving behavior, as the common element may be called, is shaped by means of differential reinforcement. The characteristics of child-rearing methods which create sons having high need achievement are equivalent to the positive reinforcement of striving behavior. High parental standards and the "amplitude of affective change" indicate that only certain behavior patterns—those which come up to the parental standards—are rewarded, through hugging and kissing, for example, whereas others are not. Conversely, careless parents who expect little of their children do not reward their offspring consistently for being successful, in part because there is no parental standard or definition of success. Indulgent parents, who reward a child often, even when he does not do well or come up to their expectations, do not by their actions shape striving behavior. Finally, if too much is expected of children too early, the continual failure of their efforts results in aversive stimuli, such as failure, being associated with attempts at achievement, so that striving behavior is effectively punished or at least not followed by rewards, to such an extent that it is either never shaped or soon extinguished.

If striving is consistently rewarded, the conditions under which it was rewarded, if present again, will in all probability be followed by the previously rewarded striving behavior. If a large variety of such behavior patterns is reinforced, a large response class is created, which will result in striving behavior being exhibited whenever the appropriate stimuli can be created by parents and other aspects of the social environment, resulting in a large stimulus class, including such initially neutral stimuli as TAT tests. It should be noted here that "striving behavior" is an abstracted element of many different behavior patterns and does not refer to a complete chain, for example, the writing of a story as such. It refers, rather, to those elements of behavior which, if present, make it highly probable that the end result of the chain will be a particular state of the environment (in relation to the individual) defined by the society as success or achievement. The shaping of striving behavior is difficult and complicated since only certain specific aspects and not all elements of a pattern or chain are reinforced. To the extent to which striving behavior is rewarded, discriminative stimuli are established which control future striving. These discriminative stimuli, again simply certain aspects of particular circumstances and characteristics of the environment, are not to be considered as being inherent in any situation. They are, rather, elements which the individual considers to be associated with a high probability of reinforcement of certain behavior patterns, on the basis of his previous experiences in similar situations.[57]

57 Eisenstadt's criticism that McClelland disregards many important sociological factors can be met by the identification of discriminative and reinforcing

If striving behavior is not reinforced, especially by one's parents, no corresponding discriminative stimuli are created, and thus no "signals" are established in the environment to indicate high probability of reinforcement if particular behavior patterns are exhibited. Thus, when striving potential exists for some people in a particular characteristic of the social and physical environment, this situation need not exist for all. The striving potential of a situation is a product of the conditioning history of the individuals who come into contact with the situation and are aware of it. In the case of Vicos, for example, one would hypothesize, in McClelland's terms, low *n*-Achievement before Holmberg arrived on the scene, and high *n*-Achievement afterwards, the change being due to the rewarding of success in agriculture, education, and other areas.

McClelland's data, then, can be easily explained in behavioral terms without the use of assumptions concerning man's internal state, such as the existence and creation of needs. If it is true that striving behavior, like any other, is shaped through differential reinforcement, there is no reason why an internal state, characterized in part by a constellation of needs, should have to be postulated as an essential element in the analysis of economic development.

CONCLUSION

According to the behavioral model of man, the characteristics of a person's internal state have no place in the study of psychological prerequisites of economic development. Instead, concern with the behavioral prerequisites themselves and their shaping and maintenance is required, and this includes, as an integral part of any analysis, the study of the structure of the social system, which plays a major role in the shaping process.

Among the behavioral prerequisites of economic development are the saving of money, the investment of savings, risk taking, economic innovation, the ability to wait for returns on investments, abandoning the land, selling one's labor, working in factories, buying food products, and hiring people on the basis of competence rather than affinity. All of these are requirements involving individuals, whose counterparts on the societal level are

stimuli in the social context. See S. N. Eisenstadt, "The Need for Achievement," *Economic Development And Cultural Change*, 11 (July, 1963), pp. 420-431.

rationality, functional specificity, a stable government, etc. [58] According to the behavioral model, such societal characteristics are to be considered as the context within which the shaping process occurs and in terms of which behavior patterns are created and maintained. The behavioral model, then, while it reduces the importance of some psychological (i.e., internal) characteristics as determinants of behavior, emphasizes the role of societal characteristics; it places the analysis of societal prerequisites of economic development within the framework of psychological processes and principles which operate in the creation and maintenance of behavior. In the interest of clarity, therefore, it would be best to either consider the "psychological prerequisites" of economic development in terms of behavior, or to speak simply of "behavioral prerequisites," since the analysis of industrialization centers not around man's internal state but rather around his behavior and its determinants.

As long as man's activities are considered to be a function of values or personality, little attention need be directed to the immediately surrounding social environment, since it is not so much the social structure of the present as that of the past which is most involved in the formation of values and personality. The delineation of societal prerequisites of economic development, according to this view, can accomplish no more than to prepare the ground for industrialization years, if not decades, in the future. However, as soon as behavior is considered to be a function largely of the surrounding social structure, both past *and* present, which affects behavior through the continuously operating determination of reinforcing and discriminative stimuli, the present social system takes on great importance. The behavioral prerequisites of economic development can be created only through alterations in the social structure, or certain elements of it, viewed broadly and including the economic system of a society.

The behavioral model of man also contributes to the clarification of so-called obstacles to development. As Hirschman[59] has

---

58 For a discussion of societal prerequisites of economic development, see Bert F. Hoselitz, *Sociological Aspects of Economic Growth*, Glencoe: Free Press, 1960, esp. Ch. 3; and Marion J. Levy, Jr., *The Structure of Society, op. cit.* esp. Ch. 4.

59 Albert O. Hirschman, "Obstacles to Development: A Classification and a Quasi-Vanishing Act," *Economic Development And Cultural Change*, 13 (July, 1965), pp. 385-393.

pointed out, many phenomena which in the past have been considered to be obstacles upon reexamination turn out to be neutral elements, assets, or characteristics whose elimination can be postponed. Hirschman mentions especially attitudes, beliefs, and personality as elements which need not be considered obstacles. He states, "Attitudinal change can be a consequence of behavior change, rather than its precondition,"[60] and concludes that attitudes inimical to development need not be insurmountable obstacles. Behavior patterns which are detrimental to economic development can be extinguished, and if obstacles are defined in terms of the *absence* of specific behavior patterns, such activities can be shaped. It is only necessary to define as exhaustively as possible the actions which are to be shaped or extinguished and to delineate, in as great detail as necessary, the associated discriminative and contingent stimuli. From this analysis the necessary alterations of the social context become apparent, and steps may be outlined to implement the program of change.

Because of the interrelation of behavior chains, stimulus generalization, and the existence of generalized reinforcers such as money, it is unlikely that one behavior pattern can be shaped or changed without affecting other components of an individual's repertoire. In general, it may be expected that a considerable number of interrelated chains must be taken into consideration when the shaping of even a small number of new behavior patterns is contemplated. In order to establish the behavioral prerequisites of economic development, therefore, much of a man's life is subjected to alterations. An illustration of this point is seen in Holmberg's attempt to change the conditions of the Vicos Indians; only a "total approach" had a chance of bringing about the desired changes.

A scheme of steps and procedures which might be drawn up on the basis of operant principles cannot be considered as a guaranteed method of instituting change, however, since much of the context of a community, or the structure of a society, is usually beyond the control of social scientists. The more limited the planner's control over the relevant aspects of the social environment (e.g., various reinforcers), the greater will be the difficulty of shaping new behavior patterns, the longer this process will take, and the greater will be the chance of failure. The behavioral model of man, then, may be considered not only as a tool for the alteration

60 *Ibid.,* p. 391.

of behavior, but also as part of the explanation of communities' resistance to change.[61]

The analysis of economic development, within the framework of the behavioral and societal prerequisites outlined above, does not lead to the pessimistic conclusions which are apparent in many studies concerned with the psychological requirements of the process of industrialization. There is no need to wait for a number of generations for the creation of new values and personalities. Alterations in the societal environment, sometimes even in minute elements of it, constitute the first step in planned action; behavioral changes will follow, and both will be reflected in changes in man's internal state as conceived and measured by today's clinical psychologists.

There is no foundation, on theoretical grounds, for the pessimistic outlook concerning the capacity of underdeveloped countries to industrialize in a short period of time. Pessimistic conclusions regarding the time necessary for the preparation of the right psychological conditions for economic development are based essentially on an incorrect conception of man and on the disregard of principles of behavior formation and maintenance derived from experimental psychology. This is not to imply that the tasks ahead will be easy. But whereas the alteration of man's internal state presents insuperable obstacles and is essentially beyond the reach of his present knowledge and power, various selected elements of the societal environment are amenable to change today, thereby making possible the shaping of behavior patterns necessary for economic development. Such procedures involve difficulties, but these are due in large part to the small amount of control which can presently be exerted over the relevant aspects of the societal environment. Since usually only a few aspects of the societal environment can be altered, present efforts to create behavioral prerequisites must begin on a small scale. This is no easy task, but it is a possible one.

[61] A good example of many which have appeared in anthropological literature is found in William R. Bascom and Melville J. Herskovits, *Continuity and Change in African Cultures* (Chicago: University of Chicago Press, 1959). The British were unsuccessful in their attempts to introduce economic and social changes into the Pakot tribe, for example, because they had no effective control over any of the important existing reinforcers. The problems discussed in Edward H. Spicer, (Ed.), *op. cit.*, also provide illustrations of the necessity of having control over reinforcers in order to bring about lasting change.

16

Contingencies of Reinforcement in the Design of a Culture

B. F. Skinner

The world in which man lives has been changing much faster than man himself. In a few hundred generations, characteristics of the human body once highly beneficial have become troublesome. One of these is the extent to which human behavior is strengthened by certain kinds of reinforcing consequences.

It was once important, for example, that men should learn to identify nutritious food and remember where they found it, that they should learn and remember how to catch fish and kill game and cultivate plants, and that they should eat as much as possible whenever food was available. Those who were most powerfully reinforced by certain kinds of oral stimulation were most likely to do all this and to survive—hence man's extraordinary susceptibility to reinforcement by sugar and other foodstuffs, a sensitivity which, under modern conditions of agriculture and food storage, leads to dangerous overeating.

A similar process of selection presumably explains the reinforcing power of sexual contact. At a time when the human race was periodically decimated by pestilence, famine, and war and

Reprinted from *Behavioral Science*, Vol. 11 (1966), pp. 159-166, with permission of the author and the editors. Slightly edited.

Lecture given at the Walter Reed Army Medical Center under the auspices of the Washington School of Psychiatry, March 26, 1965. Preparation of the manuscript has been supported by Grant K6-MII-21,775 of the National Institute of Mental Health of the U. S. Public Health Service and by the Human Ecology Fund.

steadily attenuated by endemic ills and an unsanitary and dangerous environment, it was important that procreative behavior
should be maximized. Those for whom sexual reinforcement was
most powerful should have most quickly achieved copulation and
should have continued to copulate most frequently. The breeders
selected by sexual competition must have been not only the most
powerful and skillful members of the species but those for whom
sexual contact was most reinforcing. In a safer environment the
same susceptibility leads to serious overpopulation with its attendant ills.

The principle also holds for aggressive behavior. At a time
when men were often plundered and killed by animals and other
men, it was important that any behavior which harmed or
frightened predators should be quickly learned and long sustained.
Those who were most strongly reinforced by evidences of damage
to others should have been most likely to survive. Now, under
better forms of government, supported by ethical and moral practices which protect person and property, the reinforcing power of
successful aggression leads to personal illness, neurotic and otherwise, and to war—if not total destruction.

Such discrepancies between man's sensitivity to reinforcement
and the contribution which the reinforced behaviors make to his
current welfare raise an important problem in the design of a
culture. How are we to keep from overeating, from overpopulating
the world, and from destroying each other? How can we make
sure that these properties of the human organism, once necessary
for survival, shall not now prove lethal?

THREE TRADITIONAL SOLUTIONS
One solution to the problem might be called the voluptuary or
sybaritic. Reinforcement is maximized while the unfortunate consequences are either disregarded—on the principle of eat, drink,
and be merry for tomorrow we die—or prevented. Romans avoided
some of the consequences of overeating, as an occasional neurotic
may do today, by using the vomitorium. A modern solution is
nonnutritious food. Artificial sweeteners have an effect on the
tongue similar to that of ripe fruit, and we can now be reinforced
for eating things which have fewer harmful effects. The sybaritic
solution to the problem of sexual reinforcement is either irresponsible intercourse or the prevention of consequences through contra-

ception or nonprocreative forms of sex. Aggressive behavior is enjoyed without respect to the consequences in the donnybrook. Some consequences are avoided by being aggressive toward animals, as in bearbaiting and other blood sports, or vicariously aggressive toward both men and animals, as in the Roman circus or in modern body sports and games. (Broadcasters of professional football and prize fights often use special microphones to pick up the thud of body against body.)

It is not difficult to promote the sybaritic solution. Men readily subscribe to a way of life in which primary reinforcers are abundant, for the simple reason that subscribing is a form of behavior susceptible to reinforcement. In such a world one may most effectively pursue happiness (or, to use a less frivolous expression, fulfill one's nature), and the pursuit is easily rationalized: "Nothing but the best, the richest, and the fullest experience possible is good enough for man." In these forms, however, the pursuit of happiness is either dangerously irresponsible or deliberately nonproductive and wasteful. Satiation may release a man for productive behavior, but in a relatively unproductive condition.

A second solution might be called with strict attention to etymology, the puritanical. Reinforcement is offset by punishment. Gluttony, lust, and violence are classified as bad or wrong (and punished by the ethical group), as illegal (and punished by the government), as sinful (and punished by religious authorities), or as maladjusted (and punished by those therapists who use punishment). The puritanical solution is never easy to "sell", and it is not always successful. Punishment does not merely cancel reinforcement; it leads to a struggle for self-control which is often violent and time consuming. Whether one is wrestling with the devil or a cruel superego, there are neurotic by-products. It is possible that punishment sometimes successfully "represses" behavior and the human energies can then be redirected into science, art, and literature, but the metaphor of redirection of energy raises a question to which we must return. In any event the puritanical solution has many unwanted by-products, and we may well explore other ways of generating the acceptable behaviors attributed to it.

A third solution is to bring the body up to date. Reinforcing effects could conceivably be made commensurate with current requirements for survival. Genetic changes could be accelerated through selective breeding or possibly through direct action on the germ plasm, but certain chemical or surgical measures are at the

moment more feasible. The appetite-suppressing drugs now available often have undesirable side effects, but a drug which would make food less reinforcing and therefore weaken food-reinforced behavior would be widely used. This possibility is not being overlooked by drug manufacturers. Drugs to reduce the effects of sexual reinforcement—such as those said to be used, whether effectively or not, by penal institutions and the armed services—may not be in great demand, but they would have their uses and might prove surprisingly popular. The semistarvation recommended in some religious regimens as a means of weakening behavior presumably acts through chemical changes. The chemical control of aggressive behavior (by tranquilizers) is already well advanced.

A physiological reduction in sensitivity to reinforcement is not likely to be acceptable to the sybarite. Curiously enough, the puritan would also find it objectionable because certain admirable forms of self-control would not be exhibited. Paraphrasing La Rochefoucauld, we might say that we should not give a man credit for being tranquil if his aggressive inclinations have been suppressed by a tranquilizer. A practical difficulty at the moment is that measures of this sort are not specific and probably undercut desirable reinforcing effects.

A FOURTH SOLUTION

A more direct solution is suggested by the experimental analysis of behavior. One may deal with problems generated by a powerful reinforcer simply by changing the contingencies of reinforcement. An environment may be designed in which reinforcers that ordinarily generate unwanted behavior simply do not do so. The solution seems reasonable enough when the reinforcers are of no special significance. A student once defended the use of punishment with the following story. A young mother had come to call on his family, bringing her five-year-old son. The boy immediately climbed onto the piano bench and began to pound the keys. Conversation was almost impossible and the visit a failure. The student argued for the puritanical solution: he would have punished the child— rather violently, he implied. He was overlooking the nature of pianos. For more than two hundred years talented and skillful men have worked to create a device which will powerfully reinforce the behavior of pressing keys. (The piano is, indeed, an "eighty-eight lever box." It exists solely to reinforce the pressing of levers

—or the encouraging of others to press them.) The child's behavior simply testified to the success of the piano industry. It is bad design to bring child and piano together and then punish the behavior which naturally follows.

A comparable solution is not so obvious when the reinforcers have strong biological significance because the problem is misunderstood. We do not say that a child possesses a basic need to play the piano. It is obvious that the behavior has arisen from a history of reinforcement. In the case of food, sex, and violence, however, traditional formulations have emphasized supposed internal needs or drives. A man who cannot keep from overeating suffers from strong internal stimulation which he easily mistakes for the cause (rather than a collateral effect) of his uncontrollable behavior, and which he tries to reduce in order to solve his problem. He cannot go directly to the inner stimulation, but only to some of the conditions responsible for it—conditions which, as he puts it, "make him feel hungry." These happen also to be conditions which "make him eat." The easiest way to reduce both the internal stimulation and the strength of the behavior is simply to eat, but that does not solve the problem. In concentrating on other ways of changing needs or drives, we overlook a solution to the behavioral problem.

What a man must control in order to avoid the troublesome consequences of oral reinforcement is the behavior reinforced. He must stop buying and eating candy bars, ordering and eating extra pieces of cake, snacking at odd times of the day, and so on. It is not some inner state called hunger but overeating which presents a problem. The behavior can be weakened by making sure that it is not reinforced. In an environment in which only simple foods have been available a man eats sensibly—not because he must, but because no other behavior has ever been strengthened. The normal environment is of a very different sort. In an affluent society most people are prodigiously reinforced with food. Susceptibility to reinforcement leads men to specialize in raising particularly delicious foods and to process and cook them in ways which make them as reinforcing as possible. Overanxious parents offer especially delicious food to encourage children to eat. Powerful reinforcers (called "candy") are used to obtain favors, to allay emotional disturbances, and to strengthen personal relations. It is as if the environment had been designed to build the very behaviors which later prove troublesome. The child it produces has no greater "need for food" than one for whom food has never been particularly reinforcing.

Similarly, it is not some "sexuality" or "sex drive" which has troublesome consequences but sexual behavior itself, much of which can be traced to contingencies of reinforcement. The conditions under which a young person is first sexually reinforced determine the extent as well as the form of later sexual activity. Nor is the problem of aggression raised by a "death instinct" or "a fundamental drive in human beings to hurt one another" (Menninger, 1964), but rather by an environment in which human beings are reinforced when they hurt one another. To say that there is "something suicidal in man that makes him enjoy war" is to reverse the causal order; man's capacity to enjoy war leads to a form of suicide. In an environment in which a child seldom if ever successfully attacks others, aggressive behavior is not strong. But the world is usually quite different. Either through simple neglect or in the belief that innate needs must be expressed, children are allowed and even encouraged to attack each other in various ways. Aggressive behavior is condoned in activities proposed as "a moral equivalent of war." It may be that wars have been won on the playing fields of Eton, but they have also been started there, for a playing field is an arena for the reinforcement of aggressive action, and the behaviors there reinforced will sooner or later cause trouble.

The distinction between need and reinforcement is clarified by a current problem. Many of those who are trying to stop smoking cigarettes will testify to a basic drive or need as powerful as those of hunger, sex, and aggression. (For those who have a genuine drug addiction, smoking is reinforced in part by the alleviation of withdrawal symptoms, but most smokers can shift to nicotine-free cigarettes without too much trouble. They are still unable to control the powerful repertoire of responses which compose smoking.) It is clear that the troublesome pattern of behavior—"the cigarette habit"—can be traced, not to a need, but to a history of reinforcement because there was no problem before the discovery of tobacco or before the invention of the cigarette as an especially reinforcing form in which tobacco may be smoked. Whatever their other needs may have been, our ancestors had no need to smoke cigarettes, and no one has the need today if, like them, he has never been reinforced for smoking.

The problem of cigarette smoking has been approached in the other ways we have examined. Some advertising appeals to the irresponsible sybarite: buy the cigarette that tastes good and inhale like a man. Other sybaritic smokers try to avoid the consequences; the filter is the contraceptive of the tobacco industry. The puritanical solution has also been tried. Cigarettes may be treated so that the smoker is automatically punished by nausea. Natural aversive consequences—a rough throat, a hoarse voice, a cigarette cough, or serious illness—may be made more punishing. The American Cancer Society has tried to condition aversive consequences with a film, in color, showing the removal of a cancerous lung. As is often the case with the puritanical solution, aversive stimuli are indeed conditioned—they are felt as "guilt"—but smoking is not greatly reduced. A true nicotine addiction might be controlled by taking nicotine or a similar drug in other ways, but a drug which would be closer to the chemical solution promised by anti-appetite, anti-sex, and anti-aggression drugs would specifically reduce the effect of other reinforcers in smoking. All these measures are much more difficult than controlling the contingencies of reinforcement.

(That there is no need to smoke cigarettes may be denied by those who argue that this need is actually composed of several other kinds of needs, all of them present in nonsmokers. But this is simply to say that cigarette smoking is reinforced by several distinguishable effects—by odor, taste, oral stimulation, vasoconstriction in the lungs, "something to do with the hands," appearing to resemble admired figures, and so on. A nonsmoker has not come under the control of a particular combination of these reinforcers. If any one should cause trouble on its own or in some other combination, it could be analyzed in the same way.)

MAKING CONTINGENCIES LESS EFFECTIVE

The problems raised by man's extraordinary sensitivity to reinforcement by food, sexual contact, and aggressive damage cannot be solved, as the example of cigarette smoking might suggest, simply by removing these things from the environment. It would be impossible to change the world that much, and in any case the reinforcers serve useful functions. (One important function is simply to encourage support for a culture. A way of life in which food, sex, and aggression were kept to a bare minimum would not strongly reinforce those who adopted it or discourage defections from it.) The problem is not to eliminate reinforcers but to moderate their effects. Several possible methods are suggested by recent work in the experimental analysis of behavior. The mere frequency with which a reinforcer occurs is much less important than the contingencies of which it is a part.

We can minimize some unwanted consequences by preventing the discovery of reinforcing effects. The first step in "hooking" a potential heroin addict is to give him heroin. The reinforcer is not at first contingent on any particular form of behavior; but when its effect has been felt (and particularly when withdrawal symptoms have developed), it can be made contingent on paying for the drug. Addiction is prevented simply by making sure that the effect is never felt. The reinforcing effects of alcohol, caffeine, and nicotine must be discovered in a similar way, and methods of preventing addiction take the same form. The process underlies the practice of giving free samples in food markets; customers are induced to eat small quantities of a new food so that larger quantities may be made contingent on surrendering money. Similar practices are to be found in sexual seduction and in teaching the pleasures of violence.

Reinforcers are made effective in other ways. Stimuli are conditioned so that they become reinforcing; aversive properties are weakened through adaptation so that reinforcing properties emerge with greater power (a "taste" is thus acquired); and so on. Processes of this sort have played their part in man's slow discovery of reinforcing things. It has been, perhaps, a history of the discovery of human potentialities, but among these we must recognize the potentiality for getting into trouble. In any case, the processes which make things reinforcing need to be closely scrutinized.

The excessive consummation which leads to overweight, overpopulation, and war is only one result of man's sensitivity to reinforcement. Another, often equally troublesome, is an exhausting preoccupation with behavior which is only infrequently consummated. A single reinforcement may generate and maintain a great deal of behavior when it comes at the end of a sequence or chain of responses. Chains of indefinite length are constructed in the laboratory by conditioning intermediate reinforcers. Teachers and others use the same method for many practical purposes. We may assume that something of the sort has occurred whenever we observe long chains. The dedicated horticulturalist is ultimately reinforced, say, by a final perfect bloom, but all the behavior leading up to it is not thereby explained; intermediate stages in progressing toward a final bloom must in some way have become reinforcing. In order for early man to have discovered agriculture, certain early stages of cultivation must first have been reinforced by accident or at least under conditions irrelevant to the eventual achievement.

The reinforcers we are considering generate many sequences of this sort with troublesome results. Ultimate reinforcement is often ridiculously out of proportion to the activity it sustains. Many hours of careful labor on the part of a cook lead at last to brief stimulation from a delicious meal. A good wine reinforces months or years of dedicated care. Brief sexual reinforcement follows a protracted campaign of seduction (see, for example, Choderlos de Laclos's *Les liaisons dangereuses* or Kierkegaard's *The Seducer.*) The campaign of the dedicated aggressor, domestic or international, is often similarly protracted and suggests a long history in which a chain has been built up. Problems of this sort can be solved simply by breaking up the conditions under which long chains are formed.

Another kind of exhausting preoccupation is due to intermittent reinforcement. A single form of response is repeated again and again, often at a very high rate, even though only infrequently reinforced. Activities such as reading magazines and books, going to the theatre, and watching television are reinforced on so-called interval schedules. So-called ratio schedules are exemplified by piece-rate pay in industry and by gambling systems and devices. (Ratio schedules are so powerful that their use is often restricted or controlled by law.) Large quantities of behavior are generated by such schedules only when they have been carefully programmed. Reinforcement is at first relatively frequent, but the behavior remains strong as the frequency is reduced. Thus a television program grows less and less reinforcing as the writer runs out of themes or as the viewer no longer finds the same themes interesting, but one who has followed a program from the beginning may continue to watch it long after reinforcements have become quite rare. The dishonest gambler prepares his victim by steadily "stretching" the mean ratio in a variable-ratio schedule. Eventually the victim continues to play during a very long period without reinforcement.

There are many natural systems which "stretch" ratios. As addiction develops, the addict must take more and more of a drug (and presumably work harder and harder to get it) to achieve a given effect. To the extent that novelty is important, all reinforcers grow less effective with time. The gourmet is less often reinforced as familiar foods begin to cloy. The ratio schedule of sexual reinforcement is automatically stretched by satiation. The enormities suffered by the unfortunate Justine in de Sade's story suggest that her many persecutors were being reinforced on ratio schedules severely strained by both aging and sexual exhaustion. Frank Harris suggested, in his biography of Oscar Wilde (1916), that the word "lead" in "lead us not into temptation" is an unconscious recognition of the progression through which more and more troublesome forms of behaviour are approached. Unwanted consequences are averted in all such cases by breaking up the programs through which infrequent reinforcement comes to sustain large quantities of behavior.

ARRANGING USEFUL CONTINGENCIES

We are usually interested—for example, in education—in getting the greatest possible effect from weak reinforcers in short supply. The problem here is just the reverse—we seek to minimize the effect of reinforcers which are all too abundant and powerful. Hence, instead of systematically building up long chains of responses, we prevent their formation, and instead of constructing programs which make strained schedules effective we break them up. We can use the same procedures in the more familiar direction, however, in another solution to our problem. Reinforcers can be made contingent on productive behavior to which they were not originally related. Soldiers have often been induced to fight skillfully and fiercely by arranging that victory will be followed by the opportunity to plunder, rape, and slaughter. It has always been particularly easy for the barbarian to mount an attack on a more advanced civilization which emphasizes the delectations of food and sex. It has been said, for example, that the wines of Italy (and presumably her well-groomed and beautiful women) made Rome particularly vulnerable. All governments make aggressive damage to an enemy especially reinforcing to their soldiers by stories of atrocities. Religious visions of another world have been made reinforcing in the same modes. Many of the offerings to the gods portrayed in Egyptian temples are edible, and Greek and Roman gods were distinguished by their taste for ambrosia and nectar, although less advanced civilizations have looked forward only to a happy hunting ground. Sex has its place in the Muslim heaven, where men may expect to enjoy the attention of beautiful virgin Huris, and some theologians have argued that one of the attractions of the Christian heaven is the spectacle of sinners being tormented in hell—a spectacle which, as portrayed, for example, in the *Inferno*, competes successfully with the Roman circus at its most violent.

Marriage is often described as a system in which unlimited sexual contact with a selected partner is contingent on nonsexual behavior useful to the culture, such as supporting and managing a household and family and, following St. Paul's famous principle, forsaking sexual activity elsewhere. Women have often raised moral standards with practices which were merely carried to an extreme by Lysistrata. Educators use the basic reinforcers rather timidly. Erasmus (1529) advocated cherries and cakes in place of the cane in teaching children Greek and Latin, but he was the exception rather than the rule. Homosexual reinforcement was explicit in Greek education, however, and a sadistic or masochistic violence has supported corporal punishment and competitive arrangements among students down to modern times. Economic transactions characteristically involve food, sex, and aggression since money as a generalized reinforcer derives much of its power when exchanged for them. In the nineteenth century it was expected that wages would be exchanged primarily for food, and charity was opposed on the grounds that the industrial system needed a hungry labor force. Better working conditions have made other reinforcers effective, but many of them are still related to sex and aggression.

Our reinforcers have, of course, a special place in art, music, and literature. Their place in science is not always obvious. Max Weber has argued, indeed, that the scientist is a product of the puritanical solution—profiting, for example, from the scrupulous or meticulous concern for exact detail generated by aversive consequences (the etymologies of "scrupulous" and "meticulous" show punitive origins). Feuer (1963) has shown, however, that almost all outstanding men in science have followed a "hedonist ethic."

A solution to our problem in which food, sex, and aggression are made contingent on useful forms of behavior to which they are not naturally related has much to recommend it. It should be acceptable to the sybarite because he will not lack reinforcement. It should also assuage the puritan, not only because objectionable consequences which seem to call for punishment have been attenuated but also because a man must work for the reinforcers he receives. It should not require any change in human behavior through chemical, surgical, or even genetic means, since a natural sensitivity to reinforcement is now useful rather than troublesome.

The solution has not yet been satisfactorily worked out, however. The contingencies of positive reinforcement arranged by governmental and religious agencies are primitive, and these agencies continue to lean heavily on the puritanical solution. Economic reinforcement is badly programmed. Wage systems only rarely make effective use of positive reinforcement. In practice, wages simply establish a standard from which the worker can be cut off by being discharged. The control is aversive and the results are unsatisfactory for both the employer (since not much is done) and the employee (since work is still work). Education is still largely aversive; most students study mainly in order to avoid the consequences of not studying. In short, some of the most powerful forces in human behavior are not being effectively used.

And for good reason. We are only beginning to understand how reinforcement works. The important things in life seem to be food, sex, and many other pleasant, enjoyable, and satisfying stimuli. These are things which define happiness. They are the "good" things which contribute to the greatest good of the greatest number. They characterize human purpose, for they are among the things men live *for*. When we design a better world, either utopian or theological, we make sure that there will be an abundant supply of them. We thus go directly to the reinforcers and are no doubt reinforced for doing so. We overlook a much more important consideration—the ways in which these wonderful things are contingent on behavior.

The concept of drive or need is particularly at fault here. We neglect contingencies of reinforcement because we seek solutions to all our problems in the satisfaction of needs. "To each according to his need" is the avowed goal of both an affluent society and a welfare state. (The principle is scriptural. St. Augustine discussed it long before St. Karl.) If those who seem to have everything are still not happy, we are forced to conclude that there must be less obvious needs which are unsatisfied. Men must have spiritual as well as material needs—they must need someone or something beyond themselves to believe in, and so on—and it is because these needs are unfulfilled that life seems so often empty and man so often rootless. This desperate move to preserve the concept of need is unnecessary because a much more interesting and fruitful design is possible.

Men are happy in an environment in which active, productive, and creative behavior is reinforced in effective ways. The trouble with both affluent and welfare societies is that reinforcers are not contingent on particular forms of behavior. Men are not reinforced for doing anything, and hence they do nothing. This is the "contentment" of the Arcadian idyll and of the retired businessman. It may represent a satisfaction of needs, but it raises other problems. Those who have nothing important to do fall prey to trivial reinforcers. When effectively scheduled, even weak reinforcers generate strong, compulsive, repetitive behavior which ultimately proves aversive. Only when we stop using reinforcers to allay needs can we begin to use them to "fulfill man's nature" in a much more important sense.

Contingencies of reinforcement are far more important than the reinforcers they incorporate, but they are much less obvious. Only very recently, and then only under rigorous experimental conditions, have the extraordinary effects of contingencies been observed. Perhaps this explains why it has not been possible to design effective contingencies simply with the help of common sense or of practical skill in handling people or even with the help of principles derived from scientific field observations of behavior. The experimental analysis of behavior thus has a very special relevance to the design of cultures. Only through the active prosecution of such an analysis, and the courageous application of its results to daily life, will it be possible to design contingencies of reinforcement that will generate and maintain the most subtle and complex behavior of which men are capable.

REFERENCES

Erasmus. 1529. *The Liberal Education of Children.* Cited by S. J. Curtis and M. E. A. Boultwood, in *A Short History of Educational Ideas.* London: University Tutorial Press, 1953, p. 129.
Feuer, Lewis S. 1963. *The Scientific Intellectual.* New York: Basic Books.
Harris, Frank. 1916. *Oscar Wilde, His Life and Confessions.* New York.
Menninger, Karl. 1964. Quoted in *Boston Globe,* December 13.

17

Operant Psychology and Exchange Theory

Richard M. Emerson

This book begins with a prologue by Professor Homans devoted to the relevance of behavioral psychology for sociological theory. The book now closes with a discussion of exchange theory—a form of sociological theory which is sometimes founded explicitly upon operant psychology. As a result, this chapter is properly viewed as an extension of the prologue. It is in no way an attempt to synthesize the intervening material, nor does it presume to offer a full-grown exchange theory.[1] Rather, this chapter will examine some questions of strategy in theory construction and explore some directions which exchange theory might fruitfully take.

A STRATEGY FOR THEORY CONSTRUCTION

To say that sociological exchange theory can be "founded upon"

1 Among the major works in exchange theory are the following: John Thibaut and Harold H. Kelley, *The Social Psychology of Groups*, New York: John Wiley & Sons, 1959; George Homans, *Social Behavior: Its Elementary Forms*, New York: Harcourt, Brace, 1961; Alfred Kuhn, *The Study of Society: A Unified Approach*, Homewood, Ill.: Irwin-Dorsey, 1963; and Peter Blau, *Exchange and Power in Social Life*, New York: John Wiley & Sons, 1964. For a more systematic treatment of exchange theory than what is presented below see the following: Richard M. Emerson, "Exchange Theory, Part I: A Psychological Basis for Social Exchange," and "Exchange Theory Part II: Exchange Relations and Exchange Networks," in Joseph Berger, Bo Anderson, and Morris Zelditch (Eds.), *Sociological Theories in Progress*, Vol. II, Boston: Houghton-Mifflin, forthcoming.

operant psychology implies two things. First, exchange theory can incorporate and use propositions from operant psychology; and, second, exchange theory is different from or adds something to operant psychology. *How* it might incorporate and use, and *what* it must add, are questions that I want to examine here. In doing so, we will get a glimpse into what social exchange theory is or might become.

As a point of departure, let me try to summarize Homans' main thesis in the prologue: a "theory" is a *small* set of propositions which, together with "given conditions," provides a large number of explanations (and predictions). To "explain" an event or a proposition is to deduce that proposition from a set of propositions (the theory) at least one of which is more general than the thing explained. A major aim of any science is the construction of such theory; measured against this aim, Homans does not think that sociology has done very well.

Most of what passes for theory in sociology is peculiarly lacking in explanatory propositions while being richly endowed with concepts. Furthermore, when we press the search for a deductive chain in what are offered as explanations, we arrive at (or Homans arrives at) a "vulgarized form . . . of behavioral psychology" such as "men are likely to take actions that they perceive are . . . likely to achieve rewarding results." Such an assertion may sound trite, but Homans argues that "these trivial truisms are nevertheless true, and . . . they stand in fact as the most general propositions of social science. This is the ultimate importance of the propositions of behavioral psychology."[2]

Just how important are these propositions for sociology? If they *are* implicit in sociological explanations, what is gained by stating them? Are they simply trite but true, or are they true by definition and therefore trite?[3] If we state them with explicitness and in proper, nonvulgarized form, will our theories then blossom forth?

Let us assume that these behavioral principles have extreme generality and explore their possible use as explanatory tools. For example, "in status hierarchies certain communicative acts tend to be addressed upward from lower- to higher-status."[4] Why?

---

[2] George Homans, Prologue to this book.

[3] For a discussion of this question see Robert Burgess and Ronald Akers, "Are Operant Principles Tautological?" *The Psychological Record*, 16 (1966), pp. 205-212.

[4] Harold H. Kelley, "Communication in Experimentally Created Hierarchies," *Human Relations* 4 (1951), pp. 39-56.

1. People perform operant behavior in such a way as to maximize reward (a vulgarized operant truism).
2. Certain communicative acts are operant.
3. Control over rewarding stimuli varies directly with status.
4. Therefore, people address certain communicative acts upward in status hierarchies.

Operant principles provide only Proposition 1, the truism; 2 is an empirical question not contained in operant theory, and 3 is a sociological proposition not provided by operant theory. Thus an operant "explanation" takes sociological knowledge (Statement 3) as a "given condition," and this is precisely what a sociologist has no business doing. Meanwhile the sociologist is likely to take both 1 and 2 as given and understood. Although they must be enunciated to make the explanation complete and explicit, their statement does not excite him. Rather, he is excited by 3 and 4 and it is his professional job to be so excited. In short, for a sociologist, Proposition 3 is the most crucial one in the explanatory chain above.

Propositions 3 and 4 illustrate social-structural arrangements among people. *The sociologist's main task is to explain such arrangements*, not simply to describe them as "given conditions" which bridge operant principles and individual behavior within these arrangements. As Homans has suggested, the organized arrangements among men called "social structures" should be taken as the *dependent* variables in sociology. The central task of the discipline is to understand the formation and change of such structures in terms of general principles. Although psychology may be of aid in pursuing this task, the task is not subsumable within psychology, as we will see in a moment. Nor is this the task of social history. Consider the following questions:

Why and under what conditions do status hierarchies emerge in the relations among men?

"Why in England in the eighteenth century [were] the first steps . . . taken to introduce power-driven machinery . . . ?"[5]

One of these is a sociological question. It contains an abstract concept concerning social structure, a concept abstracted from the particulars of time and place. The other refers to a unique historical event. It has possible sociological relevance only as data pertaining to some unstated concept such as "industrialization." I need not belabor the point.

Having defined the sociological task, can operant principles

---

[5] George Homans, Prologue to this book.

help us to handle it? Exchange theory offers a tentative "yes," provided we utilize and build upon operant principles in a judicious manner. This building process must start by recognizing a truth about the nature of science: *as propositions become more general, they tell us less and less about more and more.* Principles of gravitation tell us something about falling apples and something (the same thing) about moons which don't "fall." But they tell us very little about apples per se. Similarly, operant principles tell us something about men, . . ., all men plus pigeons, etc. But as they stand, they tell us very little about organized society among men *because* they are so general. How might we proceed to include them yet supplement them in the course of building social exchange theory? Consider the following propositions:

1. If, in situation S_1, action of type R_1 by an organism is more likely to produce S_2, and if S_2 is a "reinforcer," then the probability of R_1 in S_1 will become greater than the probability of R_2 in S_1 across repeated performances of R_1 and R_2 (differential reinforcement).

2. Group members tend to conform to group norms as a function of the probability of social sanctions.

Proposition 2 is less general than, and is contained within, Proposition 1. That one contains the other can be shown by translating terms.

The generality of a proposition is the level of abstraction of the concepts it combines. In Proposition 1, the situation S_1 is a "discriminative stimulus" and this concept is more abstract than "group norm." Why? Because a group norm has all of the attributes of an S^D (it *is* an S^D) *plus other attributes.* All norms are S^Ds, but not all S^Ds are norms. The concept "norm" refers to empirical attributes over and above those defining an S^D, and in this sense it is less abstract. The same is true of group member as compared with organism, sanction as compared with reinforcer. In short, Statement 2 can be translated, *with loss*, into Statement 1. Operant "explanations" of social phenomena often amount to little more than such translation, with the explainer overlooking the loss. In this process, the sociological task is left untouched. Meanwhile, moving in the other direction, Statement 1 cannot be translated into 2. Sociological research into the nature of group norms is needed in going from 1 to 2. Operant principles might provide a sound footing for such research, but they are no substitute for it.

The preceding discussion of norms and S^Ds is meant to illustrate the first point in strategy for theory construction: if exchange theory is to be built upon operant principles, we should (*a*) reduce the generality of operant principles through the introduction of new concepts containing social structural attributes; and (*b*) focus our attention upon these added attributes, now embedded in the initial (operant) principle. If we start with a general proposition and then reduce the level of abstraction of its concepts, the proposition will (1) become less general, that is, gain more specific or restricted empirical focus (toward the subject matter of sociology), and (2) remain "true" if it was true at the outset. But this "truth" is purely analytic, and it might not show up empirically. Having introduced additional empirical attributes, these might in turn introduce confounding variables. Or conversely, if the less general statement is empirically true, its truth might depend upon these additional attributes rather than upon the more general proposition alone.

This point is of immense importance in any discussion of "reductionism," and it can be seen more clearly in the case of S^Ds and norms. An S^D is a stimulus which signals the occasion on which a specified action is more likely to result in reinforcement (positive or negative). By "sanction" I mean a reinforcing stimulus (positive or negative) administered or withheld by the members of a group *acting in concert*. By "norm" let us mean a class of communicative behavior by the members of a group *acting in concert* which signals the occasion on which a sanction is more likely to occur. Notice that a sanction differs from a reinforcer, and a norm from an S^D, by virtue of an additional attribute called "action in concert," that is, the behavior of a social coalition or a person representing a coalition. Now, I submit that the second proposition above, relating conformity to sanctions, has reliable empirical truth *only* if this attribute is included in the definition of norm and sanction. In other words, Proposition 1, concerning S^Ds, behavior, and reinforcers, is not empirically reliable in social situations containing three or more persons, despite its "general truth." Thus a parent's sanctions can go for nought if the child finds rewards from third parties who are not in coalition with the parent in the norm-stating, sanction-administering process. Hence, the problem becomes inherently sociological. Conformity can be understood only in small part through the direct application of operant principles. Of equal or greater importance is the social organization (e.g., coalitions reflected in normative organization) surrounding the potential conformist.

As illustrated above, structural concepts like norm can be built within an operant framework, if "additional attributes" are judiciously introduced. These additional attributes bring us to the second crucial point in our strategy: having started with a small set of general operant propositions, *need we reach outside of this set for principles governing the behavior of these additional attributes?* This is an empirical question, but in the interests of parsimony we must explore the relevance of the original operant propositions. In addition to being an S^D, a group norm entails behavior by people in a "coalition" (e.g., action in concert). In the interest of parsimony and explanatory power we must ask, Do operant principles tell us anything about the formation and behavior of coalitions? Operant principles clearly tell us a lot about how individuals react to certain stimulus arrangements in their environment. Do operant principles also tell us something about how the environment comes to be so organized? Concepts like coalition do not exist in operant language. But we are free to introduce them, and when we do we may find that operant principles will carry us part way into the complex fabric of social structure treated as a dependent variable.

In a general way, I have attempted to point out what I mean by making *use* of operant principles in the formation of exchange theory. I have in mind a far more powerful use of these principles than is found in their straightforward application to the behavior of individuals in society, with society taken as a "given condition."

A final point in this strategy for theory construction must be made clear. If we are to use basic operant propositions as a starting point, we should state them with technical care, not in vulgarized (i.e., misleading) form. Communication across traditional boundaries of disciplines requires greater, not less, semantic precision. Allow me to cite Thom Verhave as a technical authority. He states, "The term 'positive reinforcer' is a label for those behavioral consequences that increase or maintain the frequency of a behavior when presented, that is, when they are made contingent upon a certain bit of behavior."[6] He then defines "negative reinforcer" in similar terms. We can define an "operant" (as distinct from a respondent)

---

[6] Thom Verhave, *The Experimental Analysis of Behavior,* New York: Appleton-Century-Crofts, (1966), p. 25.

as behavior whose frequency is controlled by reinforcers, that is, by stimulus consequences. Note that respondents also have "consequences" of some kind (everything has) but their occurrence is not controlled by them. Thus it is clear that operant and reinforcer as concepts are defined in terms of each other. They hang together as a single package sometimes called a feedback system (singular).

A person who has read the earlier chapters of this book may wonder why I repeat these basic points. The reason is that a technical use of terms makes it clear why sociologists might view some vulgarized forms of operant psychology as "trivial truisms." They are true by *definition* and for *that* reason seem trite. Rather than being the most general propositions available for social science explanations, some can be read simply as *names* for described events For example, the assertion that "if an action has been rewarded [reinforced], the probability that the action will be repeated is increased" is remarkably close to Verhave's *definition*.

But the utility of Homan's position does rest upon a proposition, and it goes something like this: "If a stimulus is a reinforcer in relation to one behavior of a given organism, it will reinforce any other operant in the repertoire of that organism." This proposition is seldom stated[7] but it *is* a proposition, and there is a vast body of evidence supporting it.

This proposition may be a truism in the sense that most of us are likely to take its truth for granted, but it is nonetheless of considerable importance. Consider, for example, the fact that, if a person's eating behavior is reinforced by food (thereby placing food in the category of reinforcers), and if I control food for that person, then by this proposition I can control any operant behavior on that person's part which I may choose to control. There are only three restrictions upon this control. One is my limited ability to control food. The second is my limited ability to control other reinforcers whose strength is equal to or greater than that of food for this person. The third is the extent to which *I am similarly controlled* by this person or others in the way I use food. In short, the relevance of operant psychology for sociology is, first and foremost, *social power*. Indeed, a glance into the work of authors contributing to exchange theory (for example, those listed in foot-

---

[7] The proposition is stated by Robert Burgess and Ronald Akers ("A Differential Association-Reinforcement Theory of Criminal Behavior," *Social Problems* (Fall, 1966), p. 142) as follows: " . . . a reinforcer will increase the rate of occurrence of any operant which produces it."

note 1) will reveal that social power and influence emerge as topics of major concern. This fact is most explicitly acknowledged in the work of Kuhn and Blau, as indicated in the title of Blau's volume, *Exchange and Power*. My own interest in operant psychology and exchange theory grew out of prior interest in social power. But, as the title of Blau's volume suggests, exchange is more fundamental than power and the latter should be organized within the broader structure of exchange theory. Meanwhile, the most casual glance across the work of operant psychologists reveals a focus placed on the *control* of behavior. Although its principles apply to "behavior aquisition" or "shaping," it is not specifically a theory of learning.

But simply acknowledging that operant psychology might tell us a lot about social power hardly solves the problem, for two of the three restrictions listed above are inherently social structural. For example, parents do in fact have control over a child's access to food and a large variety of other reinforcing stimuli. They do, knowingly or unwittingly, place these reinforcers in contingent relationship to various kinds of behavior and they do in fact exert considerable influence. However, the exertion of influence by a parent, in most cases, stops far short of where it could go. This may be due in part to the parent's ineptitude in effectively managing schedules of reinforcement. But it is also due to additional social facts: (*a*) the child in turn has control over certain reinforcers for the parent, and this places restrictions upon the parent's behavior, including that behavior through which he exercises his own power (social relations involve effective reciprocity which few operant studies deal with, but which a sociologist cannot ignore); and (b) the parent is, in addition, subject to control from agencies outside the parent-child relationship. It is clear that the operation of social power, while involving operant principles, is also embedded in an exceedingly complex structure of exchange relations among people. The conceptual framework for organizing such social-structural aspects is not found within operant psychology as it stands. It is in this sense that exchange theory must add to operant psychology as well as incorporate it.

SOCIAL EXCHANGE THEORY
In this section I wish only to sketch some broad outlines of where exchange theory might go. The suggestions are aimed at social structure and structural change with a focus upon social power, and

they are guided by the strategy considerations[8] previously discussed. The first section outlines some features of *exchange relations*, taken as the smallest meaningful unit in terms of which more complex exchange systems are analyzed in the subsequent sections.

SOCIAL EXCHANGE RELATIONS

At the core of operant psychology are three concepts: operant, discriminative stimulus, and reinforcing stimulus. These three concepts are defined in terms of each other, and as a result they form a single, inseparable conceptual unit. If, in a given *situation*, the likelihood that a given organism will perform a given *behavior* is increased or maintained by a *stimulus* which is contingent upon both that act and that situation, the situation is said to be or to contain a discriminative stimulus, the behavior is called an operant, and the stimulus is named a reinforcer, all for that specific organism. Let us represent this unit as $Ax;Sy$, where x is a class of actions by organism A, S is an environmental situation, and y is a reinforcing stimulus. We understand that y is contingent upon S and x, and the *recurrence* of x is contingent upon y (and therefore upon S).

This three-cornered conceptual unit is entirely empirical-descriptive, and it describes a longitudinal organism-environment interactive relation. Furthermore, anything which does in fact behave in a manner contingent upon the results of behavior qualifies as an "organism" in this very general formulation, be it a guided missile interacting with a planet or a government interacting with farmers. A might be a federal administration, x actions within a farm policy, S American farmers, and y votes. Or A might be a parent, x providing dessert, S a son, and y good study habits. The defining features of $Ax;Sy$ are the contingencies listed above, one of which, the contingency of x upon y, must entail "feedback." Such feedback can be described only through longitudinal data, and this three-cornered conceptual unit therefore entails a longitudinally conceived set of relationships. No other restrictions are imposed. However, whether or not additional operant principles such as satiation will apply to specific instances of $Ax;Sy$ is an empirical question. Presumably a guided missile is not subject to satiation for radar signals, whereas an administration probably is "satiable" for votes. Once it has enough votes, additional votes are of less value (less reinforcing).

8 For a more systematic effort along these lines see Emerson, "Exchange Theory," Parts I and II.

With $Ax;Sy$ clearly in mind, we can now define an *exchange relation* as the special case $Ax;By$, in which B is also an "organism" in the above sense, with x as a reinforcer for B. Notice that both the contingency of x upon y and that of y upon x are now feedback processes, and each organism is a discriminated situation to the other organism.

With this definition some "additional attributes" have been added to basically operant concepts. The behavior x by A (and y by B), in addition to being an operant, is also a reinforcer for the other party. Any operant in ego's repertoire which is also a reinforcer for some alter will henceforth be called a *resource* of ego in an actual or potential ego-alter exchange relation. This concept allows for the possibility that in any ongoing exchange relation a party may have additional resources not currently employed in the exchange. Furthermore, in any instance of exchange in $Ax;By$, if A performs x we will say that B is thereby *rewarded*; and A is said to absorb some *cost* in the use of his resources. With the term "cost" we introduce the psychology (or economics) of action alternatives. A's cost in performing x with B is conceived as the "reward foregone" by A in other lines of action not taken ("opportunity costs" in economics and similar to CL_{alt} in the Thibaut-Kelley scheme). Cost in the form of negative reinforcers encountered can be taken as a special case.

The main additional attribute introduced by the concept of an exchange relation is reciprocal reinforcement. What follows is largely an analysis of this attribute based upon operant principles. Meanwhile, with this definition we have specified the domain of discourse for a theory of exchange. The social relation rather than the person is the unit. In adopting this unit, statements such as, "If A rewards B for his action the probability of B's action is increased or sustained," are explicitly recognized as true by definition. This observation follows from the fact that the three basic operant concepts span the relationship and are defined in terms of one another. Clearly, if a sociological theory starts with operant psychology, social relations rather than persons must be taken as the unit of analysis. But this choice of unit has substantive implications. For example, Gouldner has written about the "norm" of reciprocity.[9] Whether it be a norm or not, exchange relations are

[9] Alvin Gouldner, "The Norm of Reciprocity," *American Sociological Review*, 25 (1960), pp. 161-178.

by definition reciprocal, and if this reciprocity is broken the relation will extinguish over time.[10] As Gouldner suggests, to accept a "gift" is to incur an obligation in any lasting relation, whether or not the giver views it as a gift. Otherwise gift-giving activity must entail no cost to the giver; it must be a nonrecurring activity. Either way, it lies outside the domain of exchange theory.

Balance and Dependence

We are now in a position to specify some of the main variables on which exchange relations can be compared. We have seen that reciprocity is not a *variable* attribute of exchange relations. However, reciprocity does not mean that x and y are "equally" reinforcing to (valued by) B and A. As a result, Homans can speak of distributive justice-injustice, and Thibaut and Kelley can analyze differential outcomes in presumably viable dyads. In their terms, if CL for one party is greater than CL_{alt}, that party will stay in the relation regardless of what the others' rewards may be. Thus, within the "additional attribute" of reciprocal reinforcement, the concept of an exchange relation contains an "exchange ratio" which we will treat through a variable property called *balance-imbalance*. This variable sets the stage for introducing three other concepts: dependence, power, and cohesion.

The pigeon in the Skinner box takes on sociological relevance if the observer includes Skinner in his observations, and if these observations suggest that Skinner is reinforced by the orderly pigeon behavior he controls. But given such reciprocal control, who controls whom the most? In approaching such questions in any exchange relation it will be useful to speak of the *dependence* of A upon B (D_{AB}) for y to summarize the current state of two variables: (1) the strength of y as a reinforcer for A (the *value* of y for A); and (2) the strength of the contingency of y upon B. If y can be obtained only through or from B, this contingency is complete. If y is attainable through *alternatives*, C, D, etc., this contingency is partial and A's dependence upon the relation is reduced.

Without knowing the relative values of orderly subject behavior and food for Skinner and the pigeon, respectively, there is still reason to assert that Skinner is less dependent upon the pigeon than the pigeon is upon Skinner, for Skinner has *alternative* orderly

[10] Viable exchange relations are reciprocal *by definition*.

subjects available (rats, people, etc.). Skinner, however, is the sole source of food for the captive pigeon. Thus the relative dependence of the two parties to an exchange relation can be assessed in part from the objective structure of their alternatives. With dependence defined, we can define a *balanced* exchange relation as one in which $D_{AB} = D_{BA}$. The degree of imbalance then equals $|D_{AB} - D_{BA}|$. Notice that, with the relation as our unit, both dependencies must be included in any meaningful analysis.[11]

Dependence and Power

Since the pigeon is more dependent upon Skinner, Skinner is "in a position to" exercise more control over the interaction in that relation.[12] Furthermore, with cost defined as value foregone in a path of action, the *power* of A over B (P_{AB}) can be defined as the amount of cost which A can induce for B. It then follows that $D_{AB} = P_{BA}$, and the *power advantage* of A equals $D_{BA} - D_{AB}$.

The "Use" of Power

In the case of Skinner and the pigeon, Skinner not only can but also does exert more control (impose more cost) upon the pigeon than the pigeon does upon Skinner. But how can the costs of two parties be compared? When we say that one party exerts more control than the other party, we mean only the following: across continuing interaction the "exchange ratio" changes in a direction favorable to one party. B is said to *use* power if, consequent to his actions, A's rewards decrease or his costs increase, while B's rewards do not decrease and his costs do not increase. We make no assertion about whose rewards or costs are "greater" in any absolute sense, for this is a metaphysical question.[13] Now, it follows by definition that, if A has power over B, it *will be used* across continuing transactions with B if (a) additional rewards are achievable

[11] For an early formulation of these variables see R. Emerson, "Power-Dependence Relations," *American Sociological Review* (February, 1962), pp. 31-41; and "Power-Dependence Relations: Two Experiments," *Sociometry*, (September, 1964), pp. 282-298.

[12] The phrase "in a position to" is pointedly taken from Max Weber's widely used definition of "social power," in *The Theory of Social and Economic Organization*, New York: Oxford University Press, 1947, p. 152.

[13] Economists have wrestled with this problem in the form of "interpersonal utility comparisons." See the dissertation of that title by Ilmar Waldner, Stanford University, 1966.

through B (if B had additional resources) and (b) *if* these rewards are not offset by costs incurred by A in the use of power.

The previous statement is true by definition. It says, in effect, that people tend to maximize rewards and minimize costs, and in strict operant terms a "rewarding" condition is anything which a a person tends to maximize. As a result, "costs incurred in the use of power" is a useful conception concerning restraints upon power use only if the sources and conditions of incurred cost are specified further.

Power and Balance

The costs one might incur through use of his power can be thought of in Durkheimian terms as "external restraints" on the use of power.[14] Again in Durkheimian terms, such "internal restraints" as conscience or moral concern for another's welfare will be passed over here as socialized restraints of external origin, and we will restrict our discussion to the basics. These basic external restraints appear to fall into two categories. When A uses power over B, countercost may be imposed upon A by B from within the $A;B$ relation, or costs may be imposed by third parties C, D, *etc.*, acting directly or indirectly in B's behalf.

Let us first examine restraints stemming from within the $A;B$ relation. It is clear that B's capacity to impose countercost is equivalent to B's own power (or A's dependence). Thus the main restraint upon the use of power by A is A's own dependence upon B. Therefore *imbalance promotes power use* (thereby altering the exchange ratio within the relation), and *balance is a stable state* discouraging its further use. Since power used by A stimulates adaptive behavior by B (e.g., exploration of alternatives), and since a change in the exchange ratio also changes dependence, *unbalanced exchange relations tend to change toward balance* across continued transactions in the relation. To have a power advantage is to use it, and to use it is to lose it.

These latter assertions form the core of a theory of balancing tendencies in social exchange. However, to avoid misinterpretation we must emphasize again that these are longitudinal assertions. Nor does this theory imply in any way that people are motivated to produce balanced relations as a desired end. A wide variety of

14 See Emile Durkheim, *The Rules of Sociological Method,* Chicago: University of Chicago Press, 1938, pp. 1-13.

conditions can operate to slow or accelerate the process or to determine the specific path which balancing processes take. As we will see, such seemingly disparate events as coalition formation on the one hand, and progressive "alienation" combined with "cultivated incompetence" on the other, constitute paths of change toward balance. Some of the conditions affecting the speed of or the path taken by power use and balancing processes involve cognitive states or knowledge on the part of the participants. It might be argued that Skinner dominates the pigeon not because the pigeon is more dependent but because Skinner is smarter. The exchange approach argues that power is based upon the other's dependence; a power advantage is used; and "intelligence," information, or other cognitive states simply implement its use. Skinner uses his power advantage over the pigeon quickly and effectively because he is aware of the contingencies defining the relation and he "knows" when to stop (e.g., what level of food deprivation to impose) lest he lose a valuable bird.

Another important condition qualifying the speed and form of balancing changes consists of the situationally determined paths of action open to the disadvantaged party. Operant psychology can assert that, under imposed cost or reduced reward, these paths will be explored, but the paths are situationally determined. For example, suppose that a child finds "love and respect" rewarding and his father provides it. Suppose, in addition, that the father becomes increasingly demanding, making love and respect contingent upon increased scholarly performance, while such performance has a variety of high costs for the child (exclusion of recreation, fatigue). If the child can find others who give respect and love, he will be responsive to these persons, partly because of the father's demands, and the father-son relation will move toward balance as these alternative relations form for the child. If there are no available others, the child's recreation and other nonscholarly values may be achieved if he convinces his father (and possibly himself) that he is scholastically incompetent. If the father continues to require total effort, even for minimal grades, the child's nonscholarly values are achievable only at the expense of father's love and respect, in which case the *value* of such love will diminish (a conditioned reinforcer can extinguish). As this value declines, the father-son relation changes toward balance through the child's alienation from the father.

Balancing Operations and Cohesion

As discussed elsewhere,[15] the variables governing dependence specify four generic types of balancing process. If $D_{AB} > D_{BA}$, any one or more of four changes will move the relation toward balance: (1) an increase in the value of x for B; (2) a decrease in the value of y for A (alienation); (3) an increase in social alternatives for A; or (4) a decrease in the social alternatives for B. The last commonly takes the sociologically important form of *coalition formation*. Note that this balancing process brings in the other category of external restraints upon the use of power. This theory also argues that coalition formation lies at the heart of norm formation, to be discussed below.

Situational factors, notably the objective opportunity structure, govern which operations will take place. For example, if A's power advantage over B is based upon relations with alternative persons C, D, etc., his advantage is structurally based. A structural change through Balancing Operation 4 is then likely to take place, if there is communication and possible exchange open among B, C, D, etc. However, if A uses his location in the structure and the power that it provides to restrict such communication, the process will be moved into another avenue such as alienation.

When such situational factors are held constant, certain balancing operations have more likelihood than others. Notice first that a balanced relation can be balanced at different levels of reciprocal dependence. Let us provisionally define the *cohesion* of an exchange relation as $D_{AB} + D_{BA}/2$. Cohesion, then, is the level of reciprocal power in the relation, the level of cost which the relation can absorb and survive. Now, if $D_{AB} > D_{BA}$, mobilizing change toward balance, Operations 2 and 3 will decrease relational cohesion, whereas Operations 1 and 4 increase cohesion and are therefore more viable over time. The rise of organized labor can be taken as an historical instance of Balancing Operation 4. Therefore, organized labor has increased the cohesion of employer-employee relations. As a result, both the viability and the productivity of modern capitalism (as well as the failure of Marxist predictions to date) can be plausibly traced to the rise of organized labor as a power-balancing process. The relation of cohesion (reciprocal power) to "productivity" is obvious. Productivity can take economic form in cohesive employer-employee relations. It might

[15] Emerson, "Exchange Theory, Part I."

take the form of homosexuality in cohesive relations based on the exchange of affection. Notice that a highly cohesive relation can involve high levels of cost and conflict.

Values and Alternatives

Virtually all of the foregoing points concerning exchange relations stem from the concept of dependence and the application of the principle of differential reinforcement. This concept is used to summarize the current state of two variables: the *value* of y for A, and the contingency of y upon B. The latter varies inversely with A's social *alternatives* to B as a source of y. As a result, power is governed by the value of resources and the position of the person in the objective structure of alternatives commonly called the opportunity structure.

However, of profound sociological significance is the fact that, although value and alternatives govern power dependence at any point in time, there is reason to believe that *value varies inversely with alternatives* over time. The economic concept of "diminishing utility" suggests that, if y is plentiful or easily obtained, its value will diminish. Behind this principle, operant psychology suggests that the value of y for A increases if y is on a variable-ratio schedule, if acquisition of y on a given occasion is *problematic* or uncertain, difficult for A to predict. Conversely, in operant terms, we suspect that the value of y will decrease relative to other classes of reinforcers if A has a history of satiation for y.

These points can be summarized by saying that the value of any reinforcer is diminished if that reinforcement is easily obtained and its value increases if its acquisition is problematic. Since these conditions are largely governed by the objective structure of alternatives, power and dependence are then largely governed by that structure. Thus, if the two variables governing power, social alternatives rather than value of resources is the more fundamental, and it is a social-structural variable.

GROUP AND NETWORKS AS EXCHANGE STRUCTURES

While focusing upon the unit exchange relation defined in terms of two actors, the preceding discussion has drifted into exchange situations involving two or more parties through the variable of alternative exchange relations. This transition into complex systems should be made with more analytic care.

Networks and Groups

In approaching social structure this exchange point of view suggests that we make and adopt a major distinction between groups and networks as structural forms. The distinction derives from two fundamentally different types of contingency within exchange relations. Among the writers using exchange notions, Alfred Kuhn, an economist, has gone farther than most in recognizing and building upon this distinction.[16] Interaction among a number of persons can either *produce* utility or reinforcements, or it can *distribute* these products through ordinary exchange. A producing unit may be considered as an "actor." If the actor is an individual organism, the productive process entails the psychological conversion of energy into valued action. If the productive actor is a set of interacting individuals, we have a "collective actor" (a group or organization) which can be treated as one party in unit exchange relations with second parties. In this more sociologically interesting case, the productive process entails the internal structure of exchange contingencies within the group (e.g., the division of labor) with valued consequences as output from that structure.

The basic distinction involved here can be seen in two types of exchange relations. The first one is the type we have been discussing so far. In $Ax;By$ we have assumed that the behavior of y by Person B is reinforcing for person A *regardless of what the action x might be*. In short, x and y are independently reinforcing for B and A, respectively, and since A and B are persons, "production" of utility is a psychological process in this case. Let us call this type of exchange a *simple* exchange relation. The relationship between two friends who exchange favors and help when these are needed is an illustration of such simple exchange.

By contrast, consider two persons playing checkers, chess, or tennis, both of whom find the joint activity rewarding. In this second type of exchange relation reward contingencies for each party are fundamentally different. For A, y is not in itself rewarding, nor is x or B. Rather, x and y interact to produce z, a rewarding outcome for A and for B alike. In this instance, the productive process is an interpersonal one. Let us call this type a *productive* exchange relation. In the two-person case, it defines a two-person group, but this type can accommodate any number of persons. Furthermore, the product z need not be directly rewarding to A

---

16 Kuhn, *op. cit.*, pp. 413-416.

and *B* if it is in turn employed in external exchange, yielding *w*, an outcome which *is* rewarding for *A* and *B*. Thus, we have a relation something like $(Ax;By)z;Cw$, where *A* and *B* form a group as an actor in an exchange relation with *C*. For example, let *A* and *B* be professional tennis players and let *C* be a spectator who pays *w* to watch the match *z*.

The analytic basis for locating the boundaries of groups within exchange structures is the distinction between productive and simple exchange. Imagine a population of persons joined to one another through various patterns of social interaction. Groups of persons can be treated as single actors if they are joined through a careful analysis of productive exchange. Actors, whether individual or collective, are then joined through simple exchange in structures called exchange networks.

Networks

An exchange network can be defined as a set of two or more connected exchange relations. Any two relations *A;B* and *B;C* are said to be *connected* at *B* if the frequency or magnitude of exchange in one relation is a function of exchange in the other relation. Since the function referred to in this definition can take many forms, a typology of network connections can be constructed.

Elsewhere I have suggested a two-by-two typology as a basis for the study of network structures.[17] If exchange in each relation is an inverse function of exchange in the other relation, the connection will be called *bilateral negative*. While the members of each relation are engaged in cooperative exchange, when two relations are negatively connected, in this case *A* and *C* indirectly through *B*, *A* and *C* are engaged in indirect competition for the resources of *B* and have common resources to provide *B*. In this form of connection, *B*, located at the point of connection, has a structurally based power advantage in both relations, for *A* and *C* constitute alternatives. Therefore, we can generalize that in a negatively connected network power is a function of the centrality of position in the network. Furthermore, if a single resource dimension (e.g., "friendship") is common throughout the network, the *A-C* relationship can form, introducing a cycle (*A-B-C-A*) with equal centrality at all points in this "closed" network. It follows that such closed networks are structurally balanced, and therefore

---

[17] Emerson, "Exchange Theory, Part II."

single resource networks tend to change toward closure. Once the network is closed, new parties entering it will encounter high cost in the process of entry. One is reminded of initiation rites.

If exchange in each of two relations is a direct function of exchange in the other relation, the connection will be called *bilateral positive* (in which case A and C stand in an indirectly cooperative relation). Similarly, if the function is asymmetrical, we may speak of unilateral positive or negative connections, completing a two-by-two typology of network connections. Some of these will be illustrated below.

Although this typology presents an oversimplified conception of real network connection processes, it provides the basis for analyzing a very wide variety of complex network structures. But most important, as suggested previously for the case of negative connections, power implications can be unambiguously specified within such structures and structural change can be predicted from balancing processes. A more complete analysis of networks is presented elsewhere,[18] including the formation of stratified networks,[19] coalition and norm formation, and the formation of cliques and "social circles" as closed networks. Rather than discuss networks as such, let us comment upon the division of labor in network terms as a prelude to an analysis of groups as productive exchange systems.

The division of labor in networks or communities can be analyzed in terms of a variety of positive network connections stemming from ecological and other factors. For example, if a company (A) employs men (B_i), men in turn can support women (C_i), forming a structure based upon a *unilateral positive* connection $A \to B_i \to C_i$, where $\to$ indicates directional resource flow. In the two relations $Aa;B_ib$ and $Ba;C_ic$ let the resources a, b, c, be money, work, and affection, respectively. Notice that B at the point of connection receives two forms of reward: money and affection. The connection is unilateral positive in that a to C is contingent upon b to A, while b to A is not contingent upon a to C. Given this connection, it follows that both a and c and c to B are contingent upon b from B to A. As a result, when an employee marries, the employer gains increased power over the employee, for he indirectly controls the wife's resources as well as his own.

---

18 *Ibid.*

19 Robert Leik, Richard Emerson, and Robert Burgess, "The Emergence of Stratification in Exchange Networks," Institute for Sociological Research, University of Washington, 1968 (mimeographed).

We can further deduce that the wife has less power over B than does the employer, without consulting the relative value of money and affection for B.

Since A gains added control through B's marriage, suppose that he adopts a policy of hiring only married men. The A-B-C connection is now bilaterally positive (and C gains added power during courtship). But, more to the point, B has two "needs" satisfied in such positive networks based upon a division of labor or resources in the network. Furthermore, unbalanced relations and the use of power therein can stimulate the formation of new divisions as a balancing process. In this example, A has a power advantage over B_i for two reasons: B is dependent upon A for c from C, while A has b from alternative Bs. That *is*, the system also contains negative connections, B_i-A-B_j, in which A is central. B_j's power disadvantage can be removed *to everyone's benefit* if this negative connection is either discontinued or converted to a positive connection. This in turn is achieved if $Aa;B_ib$ changes to $As;B_id$, while B_j continues to use b as a resource. Now A has two "needs" satisfied through divided labor, his power advantage is reduced, both B_i and B_j have increased power (through one form of Balancing Operation 4), and the cohesion of the entire system is increased. Note that A's use of his initial power advantage can stimulate B_i's search for new resources for exchange with A. Notice also that the same power dynamics imply that B_i should resist the entry of added persons into his resource area, and this resistance should be a direct function of the number of persons already in that division of labor. Furthermore, as this number increases, the pressure to leave that category (further subdivide) increases.

GROUPS AND ORGANIZATIONS

Continuing the same example, we now consider two forms of divided labor. In one form the different resources, b and d, satisfy different "needs" of A. That is, b and d are independently reinforcing for A, both relations are *simple* exchange relations, and the actors, A, B_i, and B_j, are therefore separate participants located within the network. In the other form, the positive connection is based upon the fact that the resource d amplifies the value of resource b and vice versa, forming productive exchange. Thus we move directly to a form of divided labor in which different behavioral inputs interact to produce value contingent upon all inputs. In this case the divisions of labor are properly called *roles* in a system which functions as one productive unit.

These two forms of divided labor involve one very important difference. In the positively connected network B_i-A-B_j, founded upon separate needs of A, it is imperative to both B_i and B_j that they not duplicate one another (encroachment will be resisted). But exchange in either relation can profitably take place in the (at least temporary) absence of exchange in the other relation. As a result, there is relatively little incentive for B_i to induce B_j to provide A with b. That is, B_i is unlikely to coalesce with A in demanding b from B_j. By contrast, in productive exchange, B_i's resources are valued only in combination with those of B_j and vice versa. As a result, role encroachment will be resisted, but in addition all members save one will tend to coalesce in demanding role behavior from that one. A *coalition* is a set of persons who, acting under a single policy (a norm), confront another party as a single unit. When that other party is a participant in productive exchange, the norm which emerges in the synchronized actions of a coalition is, as a special case, properly called a *role prescription*. *Norm formation* is the result of, and a contributor to, *coalition formation*. The actions of a coalition are properly called social *sanctions*.

Given the contingencies defining productive exchange, an emergent normative-coalition structure will form, providing a group of N members with social unity. As a result, the simplest exchange structure, internal to a group of N members, can be analyzed as a set of N member-group exchange relations of the form $Gx:M_iy$, in which the "group" G is a coalition of $N - 1$ member in relation with member M_i. When this coalition acts through a specified spokesman, that spokesman is said to have "authority." This conception of authority leads directly to an hypothesis: If one of the N members has authority, this person will be the spokesman for and have access to the resources of the coalesced group in exactly $N - 1$ of the N group-member exchange relations which constitute the group. In the other relation, wherein he stands as the object of the coalition of other members, the coalition will often have no instituted spokesman, and as a coalition it will frequently be far less effective for that reason. Many implications concerning the use of legitimate power in positions of authority and control over the use of such power might flow from this simple fact.

Role and Status

Any group operates within an environment. Therefore let us return to the relation $(Ax;By)z;Sw$, in which x and y are now role behaviors interactively producing z; z takes place in an environment S resulting in w, which must then be distributed as rewards between A and B. To accommodate larger groups, let us simplify this notation to $(G)z;Sw$, understanding that (G) is the set of N relations $Gw;M_1a$, $Gw;M_2b$, . . . , $Gw;M_Nn$, *with roles a, b, . . . , n.*

We may now define the *status* of member M_i (or role x) as the magnitude of w in $Gw;M_ix$, currently received by M_i, relative to w for other members, where w is one reward or any combination of them obtained within the group (e.g., salary, prestige, or affection). Now, returning to power and dependence, it is clear that current status among members reflects their *previous* relative power in the group-member relations, and current power differences represent potential changes in status. *A member's power is based upon the group's dependence upon him.* Therefore, in $(G)z;Sw$, with M_i performing x in (G), the dependence of the group upon M_i is a function of the *value* the group places upon role behavior x and the contingency of x upon that member. If many members can or do perform x, this contingency is low and the group has *alternatives* to that member. If, like the tribal shaman who alone has learned the curative rites, M_i is the only member capable of producing x, his power and his subsequent status will be high, assuming that x is valued by the group.

Thus the two variables which govern dependence when placed in group context also govern status. However, as indicated above, the relation is the unit, and both the dependence of the group upon a member and that member's dependence upon a group must be simultaneously treated in any fully meaningful analysis. Hence balance, balancing operations, and group cohesion are again involved. In other words, status is a "negotiated" state in the group-member relation. The variables governing this negotiation are the same four which define our four balancing operations: the value of x for G, G's alternatives to M_i as a source of x, the value of w for M_i, and M_i's alternatives to G as a source of w. Holding value constant, if the member has no alternative groups while many other members possess his resources, his status will be low or falling. Conversely, if by virtue of his rare talents other groups offer him similar rewards, his status will be high or rising. But we can deduce another less commonly recognized principle: Holding

D_{GM_i} constant across all members, *status will vary inversely with the value M_i places upon it.* For example, if role performance by members is contingent upon "recognition" (a status dimension), and if one member values recognition a little bit less than other members, the group will have to give him more recognition than it does other members, or elevate him on some other status dimension which he values more highly.

The two variables governing status on the group side of the relation turn out to be essentially the same variables specified in the Davis-Moore theory of stratification, though with one important difference.[20] First, scarcity of people to perform a role in their theory is identical to our absence of *alternatives*. Second, their very slippery variable called the "functional importance" of a role is related to but different from the *value* of the role behavior *x* for the group. In untangling this important topic we must first clearly note that in this exchange theory (*a*) status is relative rewards received by members in exchange for *x*, (*b*) status is "negotiated" in the interactive exchange process, and (*c*) the value of *x* for the group, although very important, is only one factor operating in the negotiation. By contrast, in some nonexchange approaches, the value placed upon a role *is* the "status" accorded that role, and "functional importance" is said to fix that value, at least partially.

It is now possible to speak more directly about the idea of "functional importance." In a system of roles *a, b, c, . . ., n* which interact to produce *z*, the functional importance of role *x* is the strength of the contingency of *z* upon *x*. I know of no better analytic statement of the idea. Furthermore, once it is stated in such contingency terms, the idea, if not the empirical reality becomes quite manageable. By definition, in this system *z* is or mediates valued rewards. Hence, by the the principles of stimulus discrimination and continued reinforcement, *x* becomes valued as a function of the strength of the contingency of *z* upon *x*. This operant analysis supports Davis-Moore, and the analysis is straightforward. However, conditioned reinforcement requires that the contingency of *z* upon *x* be experientially encountered. The group must, so to speak, (*a*) go without *x*, (*b*) experience a resulting diminution in *z*, and (*c*) repeat this pattern enough times to sense the contingent or causal relation. I submit that such group experi-

20 Kingsley Davis and Wilbert E. Moore, "Some Principles of Stratification," *American Sociological Review*, 10 (1945), pp. 242-249.

ence, as distinct from intellectual analysis of contingencies, governs the social value of *x*. But I further submit that such experience for a given role is a function of two variables: (1) a scarcity of members to perform the role (e.g., few alternatives) and (2) the degree to which performance of the role by any member is problematic and therefore variable in quality. Neither of these factors touches upon "functional importance" as such. Recall that the second factor, the *problematic* aspect of reinforcement, was mentioned previously in relating value to a history of intermittent reinforcement. This principle states, in effect, that *the status enjoyed by role occupants varies inversely with their ability to perform the role*, provided that no other members can perform it better. If doctors enjoy high status, it is partly because they know so little about medicine, and the general public knows even less.

The principle also says that groups as collective actors behave much like individuals in one abstract sense: they come to value (i.e., they direct their resources into) areas of activity which address currently unsolved problems. This is a highly functional or adaptive pattern for any organism to follow, be it a person or a group. When a class of problems is solved, energy is then directed to the solution of new or currently unsolved problems and away from the now routinely solved tasks. Solved problems then provide a secure base from which new problems are approached. Thus the system "grows." However, this implies that the valued and problematic (high-status) areas of activity are likely to be located at the periphery of the system, where the contingency of *z* upon *x* is low, while the system as such is functionally predicated upon solved problems now routinely carried out. We close with one last hypothesis based on this developmental premise: In complex social systems *status varies inversely with functional importance*. "Dirt farmers" enjoy far less status than nuclear physicists under current cultural values, yet in terms of "functional importance" our society seems clearly to be more contingent upon the farmer. Perhaps professionals are less likely to go on strike than are many categories of working men, not because such action is "unprofessional," but because for them it would be less effective.

SUMMARY

One of the main tasks of sociology is the formulation of principles governing the formation and change of social structures. This chapter began with a discussion of strategy for the construction of sociological exchange theory explicitly addressed to this task.

The strategy advanced here argues that our knowledge of social structure can be furthered if established bodies of psychological knowledge are used, not for ad hoc "explanations" of known social events (reductionism), but as a *base* upon which new principles of social structure and structural change are built. I submit that (1) the task requires *construction* rather than *reduction*; and (2) psychological principles provide valuable building blocks, along with sociological concepts. An exchange theory which follows this strategy will be, at its very core, explicitly tied to psychological concepts and principles. As Homans has reminded us, society *does* involve the behavior of men, and psychological principles are, therefore, relevant to our task. Beyond that core, however, the theory will branch out, through conceptual distinctions and additions, in directions governed by sociological (i.e., structural) questions. The section entitled "Social Exchange Theory" (pp. 386–402) is an attempt to illustrate this strategy.

The sketch of a theory in progress presented here branches out from operant psychology along pathways consciously chosen or engineered to lead into sociological subject matter. In this sense, the end points were at least vaguely predetermined, and it was a question of building a few bridges in this armchair undertaking. Clearly, this process is preliminary and cannot long endure in continued theory construction. The game will become much more exciting when the end points are unknown, when the boundaries of current sociological knowledge have been reached. The game will then entail research as well as "theory construction."

Meanwhile, most of the conceptual pathways broadly examined in this essay flow out of specific points of departure in operant psychology. The first one is the observation that *operant, discriminative stimulus,* and *reinforcer* constitute a single conceptual-empirical unit. Applied to social interaction, this unit spans both sides of the interactive relation, making the social relation a single conceptual unit. With the adoption of this unit, the pitfalls of tautology, so troublesome in exchange theory, are effectively by-passed.

As a second point of departure, we focus on the contingency of a reinforcer upon a discriminative stimulus. This strictly environmental contingency provides the basis for the all-important variable called *alternatives,* as one variable governing *dependence.*

A third point of departure is the strength of a reinforcer, relative to other reinforcers, and the possible relationship of "variable reinforcement schedules" to this strength. These points lead us to *value* as the second variable governing dependence and to the hypothesis that value is an inverse function of alternatives over time. But, most important, *alternatives* is a social-structural variable, leading to the analysis of networks.

The fourth point of departure is one of the main axes of operant psychology: the contingency of reinforcement upon behavior. This contingency provides a bridge into *social power*. In addition, when this contingency is reciprocal in a social relation, it provides the basis for a major distinction. In one case, each person's behavior is reinforcing for the other (*simple* exchange). In the other case, reinforcement is jointly contingent upon the behavior of both (or all) parties (*productive* exchange). This distinction provides an analytic basis for the study of networks versus groups and organizations as fundamentally different forms of social structure. However, *as a result of the strategy followed here*, both forms are anchored to a single theoretical framework. This theory in turn contains principles of power-balancing processes from which we can make predictions about structural change.

In branching out from operant psychology, this theory has been highly selective and, in large part, arbitrarily so. For example, negative reinforcement (and "aversive control" in exchange relations) has been virtually ignored, despite its obvious importance in social affairs. There is much more available in operant psychology to be drawn upon. But, even more to the point, *this theory* (so far) *has been narrowly selective in choosing operant psychology as its sole psychological base.* Not all psychological knowledge is contained within the operant framework, and the strategy put forth here is free to draw upon reliable and relevant principles wherever they can be found. Furthermore, in support of those who are bothered by "psychological reductionism," it is safe to say that much of the psychological knowledge which a sociologist needs is not yet available. Nor is it safe to assume that psychologists will ask the questions which sociologists want answered. I submit that sociologists, in the pursuit of exchange theory explicitly tied to psychology, will inevitably raise *and answer* new psychological questions.

Is operant psychology, as an *initial* choice in this work, an arbitrary choice? I think not. One reason for the choice, however, is the *method* which characterizes operant research. The method to which I refer could be called "longitudinal experimentation" or "experimental case study," in which cause-effect relations are identifiable within developmental processes. If the main sociological task, as I have suggested, is the study of social structures as dependent variables, the "historical case method" and *longitudinal* experimentation must be among its main tools, for social structures are developmental entities.

Name Index

Subject Index